ROAD RUNNER

ADVENTURES OF A TRIKE HOBO

by STEVE GREENE

The views expressed in this book are those of an experienced overland trike traveler, and may differ widely from those of the reader. What may present little mental or physical stress to one person may lead to severe emotional unrest and bodily injury in another. If you do not feel comfortable embarking upon journeys as discussed herein, do not do so. This book is not meant as a substitute for one's own common sense and perceived abilities, and thus should be viewed only as an entertaining and motivational discourse by one enthusiastic wilderness adventurer. No guarantees of personal safety are offered to anyone by either the author or publisher of this written material. The reader accepts full responsibility for all subsequent decisions, actions, and resultant risks associated with tricycle travel as presented in this book.

1

EVOCATION

~

Only a Mile

Speed and distance on a tricycle are profoundly different than speed and distance in the traditional transportation modes of affluent first-world countries, namely petroleum powered automobiles. On a trike, miles are not aspects of the trip that blow by as indifferent blurred visions outside of glass windows, not simply progress markers mentally dulled by the extreme speed of climate controlled convenience. Only a mile? Sixty miles every hour? Five hundred miles each day? Only a mile!

Well, on a human powered recumbent tadpole tricycle, a mile is a thing of beauty, a long and intimate mingling with the natural world not even remotely possible for the steel box dwellers from the land of modern expectations. Indeed, a mile is a memorable place in time for the overland triker, often experienced on challenging ascents as personal struggles upon the landscape, where blades of grass, fields of flowers, and whispering pines gently swaying in the wind remind the three wheeled hobo of the connections of all life on our tiny outpost of Earth. Sixty miles in one day? Quite an achievement!

There is the sound of the triker's breath, the noise of the chain sliding through the tube, and the sights of nature in every plane and angle of vision. A journey through overland territories teaches the tired triangular traveler what a mile truly is. Trike phantoms are humbled by every mile that passes beneath their trio of tires. Each mile, only a mile, is a small victory of sorts as the journey, the adventure, the odyssey unfolds slowly in a manner totally unknowable to the human swarms powered by petroleum.

Only a mile, you ask? Any seasoned trike hobo knows very well what a mile is, and knows to never take one for granted. Each and every mile tells a story, holds an entire epic adventure within its 5,280 feet. Yes, it may be only another dull blurred highway marker for those in the boxes, but for us on the tricycles, it is what life is all about.

Your triking friend,
steve greene, trike hobo
sixty-fourth year of life

<u>Trike</u> <u>Hobo</u>: One whose passion is human powered travel, and love of the journey. One who is free on three, no longer caught in the web of capitalism and time. One who lives simply, embracing the adventure.

INTRODUCTION

Once Upon A Time, there lived a wee lad, in a corduroy jacket, who pedaled a tiny tricycle. He did not go far, nor did he go fast, yet each day would find him on a quest of adventure. The lad's father told him that nothing was impossible, and encouraged him to pursue his interests and dreams. The tiny triker's feral realm of discovery became the local neighborhood. As the years rolled on, these innocent modest beginnings coalesced into a solid, but for a time forgotten, life foundation.

He also grew up in yet another world of fast automobiles and motorcycles. Everyone had at least one of them, and all the kids on the block dreamed of the day they could have their own set of petroleum-powered wheels to impress their friends. Kids had bicycles and tricycles to ride around the neighborhood, but they were only temporary two-wheeled steel toys to hold them over until the day a coveted driver's license made its way into their pockets and purses.

Human powered pedal transport became only a memory in the minds of most, destined to remain but a brief and transient part of a life with other dreams of grandeur. Now, with the newly obtained power to operate fast and lethal cars bestowed upon them by their regional kings, the immature adults rocketed gleefully into the world of gasoline, insurance, and repair bills – heady with notions of true adulthood, and intoxicated with their newfound authority.

The once small and innocent lad outgrew his brown corduroy jacket, left his humble and pure beginnings, and followed the ways that were persistently taught to him as essential markers of human success and prestige. Somewhere along the way, his little red and white tricycle found a new home, perhaps a place where yet another new person could pretend until the time when youth forever evaporated.

Within this book are three of his tales about returning to the three-wheeled realm from whence he came. These are his journals of coming full circle, how he acquired his second tricycle, and how he set off on his most intrepid life adventures yet – once again pedaling.

Three journeys are chronicled here: one to Badwater Basin in Death Valley National Park, one along and through the eastern Sierra Nevada Range, and one following North America's Pacific Coast on Highways 101 & 1 through the giant Redwoods and Big Sur territory:

~

ADVENTURE ONE:
DEATH VALLEY

**Florence, Oregon to Badwater Basin, California,
into the lowest, driest, & hottest land of North America
594 miles, 37 days (age 58)**

"I felt like the cowardly lion from the Wizard of Oz as I began my adventure on the yellow brick road. Oh, I had a brain, a heart, and I even had courage ... yet the unknowns on my way to the emerald city still lurked in the dark forest surrounding the talking trees. Perhaps scarecrow's viewpoint would have served me better. Brains get in the way sometimes." - trike hobo

Once I obtained my "learner's permit" at 15.5 years of age, I fell head over heels into the motorized model of human transport. My old man published and edited automotive and motorcycle magazines for a living, so my story followed his ambitions. I would always have a car, usually something custom and very cool. There was no doubt about it.

Well, as things go for humans, the mind changes over time. It took me 43 years of driving two and three-ton steel boxes with internal combustion engines at their core before I took drastic measures. Unlike my father, who unfortunately chose to initiate a deadly nicotine dependence during the second world war, I traveled the path of health and fitness crusader. If I couldn't live forever, I was surely going to do my best and give it the old college try! Automobile exhaust and the air I breathe continually could not harmoniously coexist for one who is intent on maximum functional longevity. It took a while for me to come to grips with this realization though. I was addicted to cars, just like you.

As a result of this ever-increasing psychological battle in my brain, I realized I had to do something if I wanted to escape being labeled as hypocritical. More importantly, I wanted to do my part for my air, and although I am only one guy in an exceptionally small minority, it was one more step by one more person in the name of fresh air. The time had finally come for me to step up to the plate!

December 22, 2008, a date I shall never forget, I sold my final vehicle that was powered by the ubiquitous infernal combustion engine. In my late fifties, it was like teaching an old dog new tricks. My motivation powered me through the sale, and as I watched a like-new, ultra low mileage Nissan Xterra drive away from the house at half the price I paid for it, I wondered if I had lost my mind. After all, every human needs a car! How else would we go fast, make appointments on time, and travel in the rain? The automobile model of life was so utterly entrenched in my society that no one could really believe my actions.

I walked everywhere for the next five months. My fitness level increased noticeably, and I was wearing out shoe soles instead of tires. I paid no more expensive insurance premiums, oil change fees, or costly automotive repair bills. I no longer spewed deadly toxins into my air as 4500 pounds of steel, rubber, plastic, and glass moved my diminutive 160 pound body around the small town in which I lived. Although I still retain a driver's license to occasionally drive for family members now and again, my personal ownership is a thing of the past.

Then, as providence prevailed, in May 2009, I was invited to be a guest speaker about one of my Death Valley National Park books. My author's presentation was scheduled to be approximately 900 miles distant. It was to occur in November 2009. I had no car. This was a test. Could I remain true to my ideals and dreams, or would I fold? Clearly, I needed a car, or so I was being told by those who knew me. As a budding author, I shouldn't pass up a speaking engagement that could potentially boost book sales as part of my retirement package, so I faced a dilemma. My brain weighed the evidence and needs.

Still buried deep within my distant awareness, were images of a simpler time, thoughts of a brown corduroy jacket, and a small human powered vehicle I once rode in my driveway. As I was growing up, my father had always asserted that nothing was impossible. He left this world when I was only 26, and could not advise me now on the best course of action, so, based on memories, emotions, and an inner need to craft what I perceived as the most advantageous choices, an old personal paradigm of transportation again surfaced in my mind. Fifty-four years ago, I had the right idea. I was now one year older than my dad had ever been.

My dear old mom, an 82-year veteran of human survival, offered to front the money necessary to rent a car to make the trip south from my Oregon coastal town. This would allow me to be present for her November birthday commemoration, and also celebrate the Thanksgiving holiday with her and my sister. Surprisingly, when she told me this on the telephone in May 2009, I had no trouble saying that an automobile was not a solution I wished to embrace for this trip. And when I informed her of my tentative plans, she truly thought I was joking. I wanted to ride a tricycle to Death Valley!

For about a year prior to our conversation, I had had my eye on the acquisition of a human-powered quadcycle or tricycle. I studied them intently online, attempting to figure out which would best serve my needs. Now, with a standing invitation to speak at a well-attended national park event only 16 weeks away, I had to make a decision.

With little thought about whether I could even successfully make such a trip, I committed to it fully, and purchased a recumbent tricycle. I moved so fast in my preparations that fear of failure or change of heart factors had virtually no room to shackle my progress. This I was going to do, or die trying, as the saying goes. I was finally going to take a meaningful stand for something I believed in, something that others thought foolish, and thereby transport myself into a world full of unknowns and questions. My reality was soon to change.

My resolve surprised even me. Often I dream. Yet to abandon something so near and dear to millions of humans on this planet, was almost unthinkable. Sure, I had stopped watching television many years prior, but that is different. You can live without TV. You can't live without a car, so they say. Well, I was going to give it my best shot.

October first was my scheduled launch date. It had been October 12th, but I got to thinking the better of leaving so late when I had to be in Stovepipe Wells, California by November 6th at 8:00 AM at the Author's Breakfast. I moved it up to October 7th, yet still my mind questioned how long it would take. Everyone said that 50 mile days were doable. Perhaps even more daily mileage if the terrain cooperated. I wasn't taking any chances. I moved departure to the first day of October at 7 in the morning.

That was only 16 weeks away, but I cloaked the urgency of it by stating it as four months, which fooled my mind into thinking I had all the time in the world to acquire all the needed expedition gear, gather all the knowledge necessary to actually pull off a trip of this magnitude, and train my body to ride a recumbent 8-10 hours per day everyday for weeks. Tall order. Good thing that ignorance is bliss!

I needed to quickly acquire my trike expedition gear, things like panniers, tent, rain clothes, shoes, food, and a seemingly endless list of incidental items related to cross-country cycling journeys according to those in the know. Truly, it was becoming mind boggling trying to decide what I really needed and what I didn't, based only on what others were telling me, and my perceived notions of what this would be like to live on a trike and on the ground in a tent for many days and weeks.

Things began to come together, and I was accumulating a bunch of weird looking bags and containers for my new ethereal odyssey, because I had to have a few storage solutions on the new trike. My friend Matt sold me a pair of Canadian Arkel touring panniers that were practically brand new, and these formed the basis for my cargo load. The rest I figured out through independent study:

Trike Cargo Containers:
Arkel GT-54 dual rear rack panniers – 54 liter cargo capacity
Radical Lowracer dual seat panniers – 25 liter cargo capacity
Otivia rear rack plastic cargo trunk – 11 liter cargo capacity
Rubbermaid ActionPacker trailer trunk – 132 liter cargo capacity
Total cargo carrying capacity: **222 liters**

Never had I ridden a human-powered cycle any distance greater than around a few blocks when I was a kid. That was it. Now, I hoped to ride one through three states, give a talk, and ride it back home again, a total distance in excess of 2,000 miles. And since the presentation date was set in stone, my plan included returning over high mountain ranges at the end of November, which could mean snow, ice, and bitter cold if an early storm hit. I was told I was not thinking clearly. I responded that I would just hunker down in the tent if snow stopped my passage.

There's nothing quite like a good monumental challenge every now and then to really make a person feel alive. The gravity of what I was about to attempt was so well hidden beneath my groundwork that fortunately I was able to watch the weeks go by with little thought of bailing out. Besides equipment purchases from Hostel Shoppe, my training rides kept me so busy physically that I felt fine. As my body adapted to the strange world of recumbent pedaling, so my confidence soared, and I found myself eager to get on the road.

Aches and pains associated with first time triking came and went. Bizarre numbness in my posterior, humorously referred to as "recumbent butt" by seasoned riders, passed quickly. Hot spots in my feet, areas of uncomfortable aching from many miles of pushing on the pedals, also came and went, but I was confident that they too would not stop me. A few hip and knee twinges along the way got my attention, but as they faded, so did my concern. My cardiovascular fitness was top notch. I never got winded or felt like I couldn't go on. Each week I became stronger, and more familiar with my new trike. We were becoming a fine-tuned machine that would function as one for this journey to North America's lowest walkable land, at 282 feet below the level of Earth's ocean – 282 feet below my coastal home. Weird.

Badwater Basin in Death Valley was my prize, an otherworldly and feared locale that I had visited many times during the past 55 years, but always in a car. Practically anybody can do it in a car. Where's the challenge in that? I was going to ride a tricycle there, a Herculean task perhaps equivalent, in my mind at least, to cleaning the Aegean Stables or defeating the Cretan Bull. Boy, do I ever love a challenge!

A fanatical preacher of the early twentieth century once

adamantly proclaimed that he could literally hear the wails of the damned emanating from beneath the barren and arid salt playa, a place he called the literal roof of religious hell. With summer temperatures sometimes reaching 136 degrees Fahrenheit, it was clear why folks might believe his tirade. The Bailey Geological Survey party of 1900 placed a sign in front of their camp while studying this apparent wasteland, which stated: "20 miles from wood. 20 miles from water. 40 feet from hell." Interesting place. Think I'll take my chances on a trike.

I had grown up in and around Death Valley. My parents first brought me here when I was only four years old. They first came eight years before that, on my dad's 1947 Harley-Davidson motorcycle. As a kid, visiting this remote and lonely landscape on a regular basis was normal fare, so what the public imagined as an inhospitable and deadly badland, was to me a wonderful expanse of exciting natural world to explore. I thought nothing of spending days out there in the desert and surrounding mountains in my 4wd Jeep, camping primitively as I bonded with nature. It was in my blood.

When I told people I was going to pedal a human powered tricycle to Death Valley, they thought I was crazy on two noteworthy psychological levels. First, they questioned my sanity for even wanting to visit Death Valley at all, having heard all the sensationalized horror stories from 1849 to the present. Second, they questioned my sanity for wanting to pedal myself only 8 inches from the asphalt to get there. What?!? No car? Are you nuts? You won't make it out alive!

Maybe, but life's more interesting that way! My credo is: If you're not living on the edge, you're taking up too much space. I'm a minimalist and naturalist. I don't believe in taking up more room or resources to exist than I have to. I would rather be an integral part of my natural surroundings than one who is isolated deep within the confines of a consumptive metropolis. I refuse to be a prisoner in the middle of normalcy. I like the edge … there are less people here!

Still, it took all I could muster to forge ahead and pull this off. Two local friends kept me primed with enthusiasm whenever they noticed me in second-guess mode. Matt Jensen, trike guru of the Oregon coast, taught me all I needed to know to keep the three-wheeled steed viable over the miles. Without his help, my learning curve would have been seemingly insurmountable. He also embraces a unique ideology of life that helped calm my inner spirit when thoughts of speeding cars or wayward thugs crept into my gray matter. Terry Butler, a retired university professor, worked with me in defining success, so I would realize when and if I attained my goals. We identified the objectives –benchmarks that were necessary in my mind– never mind what the minds of other people thought. I wasn't out to prove anything to anyone. I had real goals and plans to accomplish them.

My ICE Qnt from England, now my new vehicle, was geared for one thing: going fast. It was a rig with real quick potential, thus the nomenclature of Q for quick. Quick is nice, but I had several high and steep mountain ranges that must be crossed on this journey, and just getting over them was going to be an ordeal. The primary reason for this challenge was because I was convinced I had to pull a trailer with a serious food supply inside so that I could be self-sufficient for at least two weeks no matter what developed during the ride. Well, this adds weight. Weight slows a cyclist down. A lot of weight slows a cyclist down a lot. I had a lot of weight! Unknown to me, I would be slow.

The trailer weighed in at 16 pounds of aluminum, plastic, and rubber. The cargo trunk atop the trailer weighed in at 20 pounds of plastic. That's 36 pounds of weight just to pull even more weight of my food and water. In the trunk I placed a gear bag with 50 pounds of food that would last two weeks, and five extra liters of water (in case the four liters I had aboard the trike ran out). Also in the trunk were my tent, sleeping bag, and any other incidentals that didn't fit elsewhere. I was prepared for anything all right, but all that preparation also led to considerably less daily mileage as I was to find out (and a more massive daily caloric expenditure).

I knew the total weight of my entire ten-foot long rig, including my bodyweight, far exceeded 350 pounds. I learned this both through pre-trip calculations, and also by weighing a few times at truck scales. Keep in mind that the trike by itself is only a 35 pound vehicle! My legs and feet were required to turn pedals that moved all this weight forward, no matter how long or steep the mountains. A lesson was in the making, one that was to be hard learned. Rolling weights of 370 are crazy!

On the rear of the trike, the gearing was changed to a mountain bike cassette, with an 11 to 34 range, which would allow me to gear way down for the steep long grades that would be many. The chain rings on the front were changed from a road setup (30-42-52) to numbers more friendly on endless uphills (24-36-50). Between these two power transmission alterations, my new trike could nearly climb trees. The difference was very obvious. I still had a decent top-end speed at 50 teeth on the large ring, but that 24 tooth small ring would save me from coming to a grinding halt on daunting mountain passes. To perform a transmission upgrade like this in a car would have cost a month's salary, but on the trike, it was just the price of the materials, as work was done at home in the garage. Can't beat that! A real "do it yourself" project.

I had a welder fabricate a light bar that originates vertically from my left seat tube, where I placed my headlight and taillight for easy access while I was underway. Turns out this was a great idea, as I did end up riding for more than 20 hours in darkness over the course of the entire trip. When no cars were coming, I did enjoy shutting off my headlight to ride by the light of the moon. I had wanted to fabricate a shade cover also, which would keep the sun off my head in the desert, but with a tight budget, something had to give, and so it never materialized. I put a long home-made bill on my helmet instead, and I also wore a towel over my head (looked weird, but it worked).

One significant pre-trip assessment led to major modifications to my tire setup, which proved to be one of the best decisions that I made. I removed Norm's thin light-duty road tires and standard inner tubes, and replaced all three with expensive extra thick tires designed to eliminate punctures (Schwalbe Marathon-Plus). Lining each tire, I placed tube protectors, yet another layer of thick plastic with the sole purpose of stopping intruding sharp things from reaching the tube (EarthGuards). And for the tubes, I used a special extra heavy duty rubber that was more like a hose than a tube. It was thick and highly puncture resistant (Kenda thorn-resistant Q-Tubes).

Everyone, including seasoned cyclists, said it was overkill, but that was okay. The last thing I wanted to be doing was constantly changing flat tires like so many cyclists are always having to do! What if a tire had gone flat during one portion of the trip where my life was actually in genuine danger from hypothermia? Changing tires is no picnic anyway, let alone doing it when the hands are going numb from deep cold, and the body is shaking every time I stopped for a food infusion or bathroom break. My intuition paid off, as no tire on the trike ever went flat, even after riding through hundreds of goatheads, huge hideous thorns that are the cyclist's curse. By way of comparison, the tires on the trailer were not so equipped, and both did finally succumb.

This trike tire system was heavy and expensive, with each tire/liner/tube combo lessening my financial load by approximately $75. It was the best money I could have spent. Even now, long after the end of this trip, the tires are still holding air. Spend money up front and do it right, or spend it later to rectify things out on the road. The choice was an easy one for me. I wanted to ride, not repair!

One choice was not so easy. In fact, right up to the final week before departure, I was still pondering and testing solutions for my feet and connecting to the pedals. I would be doing quite a bit of hiking on this overland trek, so I preferred to wear my Merrill Moab Ventilator hiking boots, strapped to the pedals with a device called a Power Grip. This, as it came to pass, was a very poor decision, and it led to foot issues that radically altered the journey.

I did not engage in sufficient pre-trip study of footwear and recumbent trike foot considerations because so many other things had my attention during those 16 weeks. After the trip, and much online gathering of known cycling knowledge, I now realize that a hard sole cycling shoe that uses a cleat binding system of attachment would have been necessary to avoid the foot gremlins that plagued me, and shortened my total riding time considerably. My choices led to severely inflamed Achilles tendons on both legs from over arching the foot around the pedal on millions of rotations, and two numb toes on each foot from extensive over compression of central mid-foot nerves and arteries (called hot-spots commonly, or Nerve Compression Syndrome).

The Power Grip straps work well for traditional bicyclists, where their feet are on top of the pedals, and the straps prevent them from sliding forward off the pedal. However, on a recumbent trike, the rider's feet are behind the pedals instead, so I had to adjust the straps to keep my feet from falling backwards on to the ground. To accomplish this, the straps had to be opened up to allow my foot to insert past the ball, which was a primary mistake that led to the problems. Further, these straps keep the feet secure by restrictive tension on a recumbent trike. You put your foot in at an angle, and then rotate it straight to bring the tension into play, further reducing blood flow. The flexible soles of my Merrill boots were the final ingredient that brought this odd dynamic to a head. It was a failure waiting to happen, but I didn't know.

On my 50 mile training rides through the coastal mountains, I had hints that these issues were afoot, but my inexperience did not recognize them for what they were. I developed "hot spots" mid forefoot on some rides where I wore really lightweight walking shoes, areas that became painful, but would disappear simply by twisting my foot towards the outside for a few minutes, or getting off the trike. The toe numbness also crept into the mix, but I incorrectly figured that it was just my body getting used to the new riding position. Now, I know better, and have since been implementing a new system that I will use in all future travels (discussed later in the book, and on my trike website).

One mistake that I was able to avoid by testing options during the 16 weeks prior to departure was that of headgear. Initially, I tried wearing a full-face motorcycle helmet, thinking that it would offer the most protection if I inadvertently pedaled off the side of the road on a high mountain pass, or if a car struck me. Well, let me ask you this: What do you think it would be like to take an aerobics class for 8 hours straight with something like this on your head? Yes! The immense heat buildup has no place to go, and muscular functions in the body eventually begin to fail due to extreme overheating, leading to debilitating cramping and acute exhaustion. Once I switched to a traditional bicycling helmet with 17 vents, all was well. Matt told me that I would be leaving that helmet on the side of the road eventually. He was partially correct. I left it behind before I ever started. Nothing like actual experience to answer one's questions! It would have killed me.

By the end of September 2009, I felt ready. I had been pulling my trailer around on some of my rides, filled with dumbbell plates to simulate an extra heavy load, and I still made it ... tough, but doable. The training rides with Matt, Terry, and Dave Beck had paid huge dividends. I finally reached the point that I was eager to leave. Have you ever trained for something to the point that you were just dying to get started on the actual experience? I felt I was as ready as I'd ever be. Just in time too ... the first of October was now only hours away!

DAY 1 - *Death Valley*
Thursday, October 01, 2009
Central Oregon coast to Bunch Bar river landing – 51 miles
(running total: 51 miles)

At 6:30 AM on Thursday, October 1st, a reporter from central Oregon's largest newspaper parked his car in front of my abode. I had eaten a granola breakfast, rechecked all my gear that I had packed the night before, and was now nervously chatting with my friend Matt in the garage. Departure was looming its head as a dragon would stare down a knight. There was no turning back on this journey I had crafted for myself, my first cross country trek on a tricycle ... alone, except for the first 20 miles with Matt on his trike.

The reporter had already taken a few notes, and was now snapping some photos with his large digital camera. First light had fallen upon the landscape outside the garage, air was cool, the time was 7:00 AM to the minute, and there was no further reason not to start pedaling. As I strapped my feet onto the pedals, and pushed the right one forward to begin the journey, a powerful surge of momentary fear coursed through my consciousness as reality truly made itself visible. There was no more talking of this trip in the future ... it was now! I was leaving for a long solo ride laced with countless unknowns.

I've heard it said that courage is not the absence of fear, but rather moving forward in spite of it. I kept moving towards that emerald city. Matt served the role of tin man, scarecrow, and Dorothy, creating an immediate sense of safety in numbers. I wasn't in Kansas anymore.

It all seemed so surreal to me. I was aware of pedaling out of the driveway, yet it was almost as though it really wasn't happening. My senses barely captured anything around me, so intent was I on reconciling the impact of what I was in fact beginning to do. The reporter ceased to exist in my mind. Even though I had planned this to the nth degree, and wanted to do it, a voice within yelled that I should stop, albeit only for the briefest of seconds. I was now pedaling a tricycle to Death Valley's Badwater Basin, a destination only thought possible via automobile by nearly all rational people.

A well-wisher sent her final verbal thoughts of safe travel to my ears as Matt and I crested the hill to begin the slight descent to the coast highway. I did not look back. Not only is it difficult to do on a low-slung recumbent trike, but to have done so would only extend the emotion-laden transition. I had committed my head to the journey!

In an instant, the comforts of home were gone. In an instant, my world was now the open road and nature. Just like that! Everything changed in a few heartbeats! My survival now depended on me and what I had brought along. The sting of this conversion was lessened within a few blocks through chatting with Matt as we pedaled our tricycles south. He is a seasoned cross-country solo cyclist, so his reassurance and calm voice played heavily on soothing my spirit ... a spirit that had just been traumatically torn from its daily routines.

Mental survival automatically kicked in. My mind focused intently on bringing to reality what had heretofore been only thought as the city blocks rolled by. With each passing street corner, I slipped into the "now" of my actions, seeing the brightening eastern sky, hearing the birds, feeling the cool air against my face, and deciding how to route my trike out of town. I was happy to have Matt riding along to the next coastal town with me. While the first miles are the easiest physically, they are by far the most demanding mentally, so his presence kept me together throughout the morning.

Within minutes after leaving, we crossed the first river on an old bridge built in the 1930s. It had deteriorated with the years, so a state work crew had recently begun a year-long refurbishing project. Traffic was nearly nonexistent this early, so Matt and I rode leisurely across in the center of our lane. As we passed two Oregon Department Of Transportation (ODOT) workmen, I happily waved and spoke a cordial greeting to them with a smile. The second man, overweight with a cigarette in his mouth, replied: "You guys are fuckin' idiots!"

Well, that was not exactly the type of reception I had expected, and certainly not the best way of starting off my trip. Hopefully, this was not a harbinger of things to come. It was an odd feeling to think that a fellow human being could be so blunt and nasty, especially considering that he was a state worker and had been greeted appropriately by me. It was even more intimidating because he was walking on an elevated sidewalk, and I was sitting in a recumbent trike cockpit only eight inches from the pavement. He was an insulting man, his face looming several feet above mine. He was also not worth spending an instant of my life power worrying about, because I refuse to let toxic people erode my spirit. The problem was his, so I left it on the bridge!

Miles of forested coastal landscape rolled by while Matt and I talked about trikes and touring. His rig was unfettered by the weight of touring gear, so it required conscious effort on his part to adjust his speed closer to my slower pace, especially when the uphills came along. Downhills were a different story however!

As we neared our separation point, a long and steep downhill portion of coast highway presented itself, perhaps a mile at least. Our speeds quickly passed the 40 MPH mark, a well deserved break of exhilarating and adrenaline-pumping excitement. Matt closed in behind my trailer, saying that he could feel my draft of air causing his trike to accelerate. He shot out beside me, and then pulled away at a speed far too fast to pedal. Yet, as he was now back in the full force of air resistance, it was only about five seconds before my trike again took the lead, due to the extra weight of my rig. The fascinating thing about this little fun exchange was that it was only dependent on the laws of physics for how it played out, and had nothing to do with either of us pedaling our trikes. It was the first big thrill of the journey!

We rolled into Matt's turn-back point with huge grins on our faces. The sun was now fully upon us, as the Coastal Range forests were cleared by the little harbor town. Matt treated me to an early lunch of a vegetarian burrito and chips. The waitresses were curious about our odd modes of transport, and even came outside to see them close-up since the lunch crowd had not poured into their Mexican restaurant yet.

After lunch, I faced my second little traumatic test. Matt pointed his Catrike 700 north, and rode back home. I continued east towards the summit of the coastal mountains, along the beautiful Umpqua River. I had enjoyed his company, but now was truly on my own. He had delayed this final feeling of oneness at least for the majority of the morning, perhaps easing me into this journey in a kinder and gentler way – two steps instead of one. We had fun riding together. Now, the authenticity of the trip came to the forefront of my mind.

Where would I sleep tonight? No bed awaited me. Would it rain? No house would shelter me. Would I be safe? No locked door would protect me. Could I find a place to camp legally? Governments do not design roadways for cyclists' convenience. Questions filled my mind, and answers, in one form or another, were only hours away.

A flock of geese flew along the surface of the Umpqua for a period, and my road was just alongside. What a treat to see and hear the magnificent birds so close. Up ahead, a flagman stopped me. The highway was being refinished. Soon, a long line of automobiles was stacked up behind my diminutive tricycle. Amazingly, my nervousness had diminished enough that I realized the road also belonged to me, and happily, the State of Oregon agrees with their "share the road" law. Not only that, but motorists had been very respectful thus far on the trip, so fear of cars was, as Matt had predicted, lessening in my mind.

After some chatter on the walkie-talkies, the flagman motioned me on ahead to give me a long lead on the metal monsters that would follow. He told me to ride on the newly refinished pavement because my rig was so light. I did not have to wait for the oncoming traffic to clear like everyone else did. About half way through the construction zone, some workmen said I had better get out on the old pavement, as the newly surfaced asphalt was about to get too hot for my tires. I had to pass the oncoming line of motorists in only one lane, but because I was so small, my rig easily fit by. There were no negative incidents.

Finally I came out the other side of the construction zone, and still no cars behind me! How refreshing. It was as though I had the forest road to myself. A lady driving a Toyota Prius the other way slowed as she passed and said "Hello fellow cyclist", which put a smile on my face. Perhaps I was not truly alone after all.

I stopped wearing a timepiece about twenty years ago. I didn't need one because are clocks everywhere I went. So, my only clue about when it was getting near to the time I needed to stop and set my camp was that which the natural world provided me, most notably, the sun. This road was very much in deep forests however, so I could not be precise in the sun's location, but I had been pedaling now for about 51 miles and felt like calling it a day.

Living on wilderness time is my preferred way. Go to sleep when the world gets dark. Awaken when it gets light. Simple. Less stress. This journey was to be experienced wholly on wilderness time. I was now in an alternative realm far from those folks speeding by in automobiles, which suited me just fine! I prefer not to be normal.

Up ahead a huge turnout right on the river became visible, called Bunch Bar. It had a portion that was hidden from the highway, which would provide an excellent place to pitch my small tent. A nice concrete block toilet facility was there, but, as motorists and myself would learn, had locked doors. Go figure! The sky was cloudy now. I erected my tent on an area of cedar chips, ate my first meal from the

15

trailer, brushed my teeth, used the bushes, and then climbed into my sleeping bag, content with a solid 51 mile day behind me. After a short journal entry to record the day in words, off to sleep I went.

DAY 2 - *Death Valley*
Friday, October 02, 2009
Bunch Bar river landing to Wilbur, Oregon – 35 miles
(running total: 86 miles)

Last night it rained lightly on and off. I did not completely stake out the tent's fly, so it contacted the tent material in places, allowing moisture through. Where my sleeping bag touched the tent at my feet, it became damp. The tent was an REI Arête ASL (all season light), a two-person tent that provided ample space to keep my panniers inside at night, on one side, while I slept on the other. It is not a big tent, and if two people really used it, quarters would be very cramped. I would more realistically classify it as a one-person structure, where you can actually sit up, dress, write in a journal, and stow gear (with absolutely no room left over).

The morning was mostly cloudy and damp, but the temperature was comfortable with a jacket. From my trailer's 50 pound supply of food, I pulled out some Crunchy Nuggets, a cheap generic brand of Grape-Nuts. Into the bowl with the nuggets went a handful of raisins, some high fiber cereal, and water (since to carry soy milk would make the load even heavier). It was a tasty mix, not my favorite, but the easiest for me to bring in bulk. This was to be my breakfast for nearly every day of the trip, along with a couple of dried plums as a treat.

After the panniers were placed back on the trike, and the tent and sleeping bag stashed in the trailer, I hit the road at about 8:40 AM. Around an hour later, as the sky was clearing, I passed through the tiny mountain town of Elkton. After a quick use of the restroom at the local library, I eagerly resumed my pedaling through the coastal range.

South of this town, there are some steep and long uphill grades, which have no effect on people being propelled along the asphalt by gasoline engines, but really slow down cyclists … especially those laden with over a hundred pounds of additional cargo. It was a low gear affair to the top of each hill, with a top speed of about 3-4 miles per hour. Fortunately, the scenery is top notch, passing rolling hills with farms, pastures, and quaint old barns mixed amidst the evergreen forests.

On an Oregon bicycle map, Highway 138 is shown as lightly traveled and bicycle-friendly. For the most part, this is true. The apprehension came occasionally at curves in the steep road that had

16

absolutely no shoulder, thereby forcing me into the automobile lane. Normally, this is not an issue when the road is open, as cars can see a cyclist ahead of time. However, when a cyclist enters into what I term a "blind right" curve on a shoulderless road, he is in danger if a car does not see him enter the curve.

A blind right hand curve is anxiety producing when one is cycling at 3 miles per hour on a steep hill because a car can come speeding around without knowledge of the cyclist's presence. Well, on this stretch of road, precisely this happened to me with a huge motorhome, and was to be the only incident on this entire trip where anger was clearly demonstrated towards me. Due to my slow speed, I was necessarily in the curve for what seemed like eternity, and I heard the behemoth vehicle's engine heavily straining to maintain speed as it labored up the long curvy mountain hill, soon to overtake my diminutive trike and trailer. In fact, I knew this noisy box was coming long before I could see it, hearing its engine get louder and louder, becoming an ever swelling blight on the serenity of my silent passage.

This road is one lane in each direction, and it is narrow. This particular blind-right was in a section that was cut out of the mountain on both sides, meaning no leeway beyond the lane whatsoever. As soon as I saw the motorhome in my rearview mirror, the driver saw me, with only feet to spare. Obviously, he was not expecting a ten-foot long trike and trailer to be here. The driver adeptly slowed and moved over the center line, and there was no honking of horn or anything to indicate he was upset. His wife, on the other hand, offered an emotional response.

It all happened so fast that I did not understand a word she said, but my experience as a human told me that she was clearly not a happy passenger. For the briefest of split second, her hateful and obnoxious voice showered down upon me like poison-tipped arrows from the sky (good thing I had a helmet), but since hubby didn't want to slow his trip, they were gone in mere seconds around the next left-hand curve. My trike was so close to the rock cliff face on my right that I was darn near scraping it at this point. I guess she was unaware of Oregon's "Share the Road" law. The law does little good however, when governments demonstrate little regard for the life of people who use human-powered vehicles by not widening the roadway.

My ride returned to the silence of a primitive forested world once again. A notable upside of tricycle travel is passing through the natural countryside in silence, as no engine or tire whine spoils the sounds of nature. It is indeed a silent passage. At eight inches from the roadway and slow speed the norm, a trike pilot's realm allows for true appreciation of all that unfolds in this mystical forested world. Happily, automobile traffic is indeed light and scattered today, so nine out of every ten minutes are enjoyable.

Another aspect that is readily appreciated when triking in mountainous terrain is this: For every long and taxing uphill, there is often an equally long downhill. What may have taken well over half an hour to climb, can easily require only a few short minutes to descend, and the descent is clearly an all-out adrenaline pumping delight.

Tadpole tricycles (the two wheels in front and one in the rear) inherently make for a very stable and safe platform for quick curvy downgrades. Serious speed can quickly be attained on steep grades, speeds easily passing the 40 miles per hour mark. If the hill lasts long enough and is steep enough, another ten can be realized. There have been enough downhills so far on this trip, and in my training rides, for me to know that I find them a thing to be coveted. Of course, from a health and longevity standpoint, it is the slow pedaling up the hill that delivers the goods, and strengthens my physical body, whereas the downhills essentially strengthen only my happy and playful spirit.

Once over the crest of the Coast Range, there is one ultra-long downgrade into the town of Sutherlin, which straddles Interstate 5. By the time I reached the town, I was well rested, but weary of sitting so long. The town's visitor center lawn made a nice place to spread out my tent fly so it could dry in the sun. I met Bernie Sigmond, the happy elder volunteer, who was surprised to see my mode of transport, and amazed by where I was headed. Outside at picnic table, I ate my second night's dinner, a convenient one-pound pouch of rice and veggies, happy to be relaxing in the pleasant afternoon light. A fair amount of traffic motored by on the road behind me, but I paid little heed to it, tired as I was. Recumbent trikes are very comfortable, but like car, it feels good to stop and stretch. Time indeed to mellow out a while.

After this half-hour interlude, I figured I best get packing on south and east, for the sun was sinking lower towards the mountains, which were now to my west. I had no desire to locate a camp area here in a town environment, because to do so would mean a fee-based campground, which I prefer to minimize whenever possible. My way is most often what is termed "wild stealth camping", where I find a nice piece of public, but concealed, earth where I can be at one with the natural world. So, off I pedal on a side road to the interstate for five miles until I reach the tiny village of Wilbur.

The sun is still up when I arrive. I locate Road 200, locally known as the North Bank Road, in mid-Wilbur that cuts east, and I make the turn. This road skirts the northern bank of the Umpqua River, and will take me up and over many miles of rolling hills dotted with stately oak trees, on the way to Glide, Oregon, at the western base of the mighty Cascade Range, a volcanic wonderland of tall trees and cascading waterfalls.

From past experience on this road with a car, I know the hills are steep, and if tomorrow is sunny, it will be a very warm experience, as there are no large forests to shade me like I had been riding through so far. I also know that the property alongside this country road consists of huge privately-owned ranches, and there is only one large turnout midway where I could probably pitch a tent, but even then, I would be readily visible to any passing motorists. My mind seeks solutions, and seeing the Wilbur United Methodist Church up ahead, I pull into the paved lot, park under some shade trees, and decide to get some sleep.

I chose not to set my tent here, so as not to draw attention and possibly be asked to leave, so after a short walk, I decided to sleep on the trike. This is relatively easy to do, with the low and reclined seat. I just straightened my legs out in front of me. The night was working up to be a nippy one, so I donned some warm coats and a polar fleece hat to settle in. It had been a 35 mile day, not as many as yesterday, but considering the numerous steep grades, it was all right with me.

Sleep is intermittent and interrupted due to the close proximity of train tracks and the interstate, not to mention the barking dog 15 feet behind me in a neighbor's yard, which led to him wondering if I were some unsavory transient. Once he felt secure that I was an educated traveler with a legitimate agenda, I was left to myself. Of course, here in a town, there are bright street lights to keep the evil spirits away, so it never really got dark enough to sleep soundly. Plus, it was getting chilly.

Finally, around what must have been about midnight, it dawns upon my restless mind that the sky is perfectly clear and the moon is perfectly full, and very bright! Street lights are unnecessary.

DAY 3 - *Death Valley*
Saturday, October 03, 2009
Wilbur, Oregon to Susan Creek Campground, Cascade Mts. – 31 miles
(running total: 117 miles)

I am cold. Having been sitting on the trike seat for the past several hours attempting to sleep, the lack of movement has led to a chilling of my bones, even though not a wisp of wind was present. My down vest, polar fleece jacket, all-weather rain jacket, and polar fleece skull cap, have done an admirable job retaining my body heat considering the chilly night air, but they don't take the place of a toasty mummy bag in a tent. Trike sleeping is really a last-ditch choice.

Gazing towards the full moon, I started to debate the wisdom of just leaving this little berg of Wilbur right now, in the middle of the night. Even though I was under a large tree, the nearby streetlights kept it bright enough that sleeping was a challenge. And when a freight train would slowly rumble by, it made me wonder how long it took the neighbors to get used to it. I figured that remaining here would probably not get me much more in the way of restful sleep, so I might as well be pedaling, especially since it was so bright out that a headlight would not be necessary. This would be a unique experience.

All things considered, I decided to resume my journey. Since I was already dressed and not in the tent, it was a simple matter of putting my feet on the pedals and heading out, and since the trike is noiseless, no one would even be aware of my departure. The road out of town is straight and uphill, so warming up came quickly. It was cold enough though, that I wore my water and windproof motorcycle gloves instead of my lightweight cycling gloves.

Within a few minutes, I felt confident that traveling this stretch at night was a good idea. The moonlit sky was so bright that I kept my headlight turned off unless a rare car motored by. I did keep the flashing red tail light operating however, as well as my marine rescue strobe on the back of my trailer. With this setup, I was as visible at night as in the day. My tail and head lights were manufactured by a company called Cateye, and the products were doing a fine job thus far.

Road 200 climbs in elevation as it proceeds east towards the mighty Cascade Range, yet there are many downhill portions that make for rapid progress. Night travel required less water intake, but I still stopped atop one summit hill for a couple of energy bars. It was incredible! The full moon was so illuminating that I accessed my food supply in the trailer with no other lighting necessary.

I learned about an aspect of trike travel this early Saturday morning that I found interesting. Thermal regulation is something that must be constantly monitored and adjusted. When I was sitting idle on the trike at the church, I was barely able to keep warm with my clothing. After pedaling the weight of my heavily loaded rig up a few hills, my body temperature rose rapidly, and I had to remove a layer or two, even though it was the middle of the night. But then, on the downhills of the North Bank Road, with wind whipping me at 20 to 40 miles per hour due to my trike's speed, I quickly chilled once again. This led to the big question of whether to endure the cold on the downhill grades until the next uphill, or stop and put back on the warmer layers of clothing. I chose to endure the cool air, knowing that it wouldn't be long enough to become totally miserable.

Fortunately, being the first week of October, temperatures were still bearable at night. The still night air helped. Of course, the Cascades were yet ahead, where I figured it would be much colder. But then again, neither would I be riding at night up there – I'm not that crazy! I'd be all cozy in my tent by the time the sun left my sky. I prefer staying warm, and my mummy bag does a top notch job of seeing to it.

The plan for Saturday night is to camp at Susan Creek Campground, on the western slope of the Cascade mountains. It is a nice campground on the river, with amenities like warm showers. I have stayed there before, and the huge forested canopy makes it a pleasant temperature in the warmer summer months. It sits just off Highway 138, which I will again intersect once I reach the small town of Glide. I have a pass to camp one night at Susan Creek gratis, courtesy of the Bureau of Land Management, which opted to contribute this small memento towards my epic expedition to Death Valley. I am happy for their generosity. It can pay to be friendly to government folks sometimes!

Up ahead, I spy what looks like a large black cat in my lane, but this one has a wide white stripe spanning its length, telling my sleep-deprived brain to take the oncoming lane and give the skunk a wide berth. Along the 17 mile route from Wilbur to Glide, I encounter a number of animals, most of which I either hear or see a glimmer from pairs of eyes off to the side of the road. None chose to examine my trike or me up close. A small part of my mind wondered about mountain lions, so I did keep my knife in the jacket pocket, but I saw none.

Had I been traveling this road tonight in an automobile, I would have missed many sensory delights. I would not have heard the rushing Umpqua River down below the embankment, nor would I have noticed the moon's distorted reflection on its churning waters. I would not have listened to the crickets' melodic notes for mile after mile, nor would I have even been aware of animals at all. I would have missed the owl's hoot, and as I neared Glide, the rooster's early morning call would have deflected right over the top of the speeding car. Seated only eight inches from the roadbed, out in the open air, many new experiences awaited me, things that could only be possible from a trike.

First light had not yet appeared when I rolled into the outskirts of Glide, a landscape dotted with nice homes on acreage. I crossed the river and came to Highway 138, where cars were already active even this early. My appetite was again calling, so I sought somewhere to dine.

Mister moon was beginning to play hide and seek with me behind increasing cloud cover. I found a truck scale station with a street lamp above it, so chose to pull in to the unmanned area to get well off the highway, behind a three-foot high concrete wall, partially hidden

21

from the road. Down the thorny embankment to the north was a property littered with many junk cars. I ravenously chewed through two more high-calorie energy bars, and could have easily eaten a third, but realized the value of modest rationing.

Matt had told me a few weeks ago that during my trip, I would be expending between 5,000 to 7,000 calories per day. I was beginning to believe it. By my calculations, my planned daily allowance of food would supply about 2,000 calories at most, which indicated that I would be in at least a 3,000 calorie deficit each day at the current rate. Since the human body requires a shortfall of 3500 calories to lose a pound of bodyfat, I wondered what the future had in store. One thing I already knew was that the number of bars I was now consuming exceeded what I had planned, and my morning bowl of Nutty Nuggets was destined to overflow with those tasty barley crunchies. Well, I had a lot of nuggets in my trailer, and a lot of food bars, and a lot of rice and veggie packets, all of which were the big reason for my slow progress.

More than once, I started to wonder if the over stuffed 50-pound Cordura bag of caloric fuel I was pulling in my trailer was self defeating. In other words, would I require the extra calories due to my extra labor each day in pulling them along behind me? Or, put another way, if I had not brought along all that food, would I easily make it to the occasional country store or market quicker, thereby negating the need for the bag? When you're riding a trike up long hills, you have considerable time to ponder these truly important world questions.

Standing still, I had to put back on my down vest under my jackets. The bright orange-tinted street lamp above me lit my panniers so I could locate the vest. As the rotation of Earth continued towards first light, I just hung out for a while, as I didn't wish to start riding Highway 138 in the dark, due to the increasing number of cars flying by at ultra high speeds. I would wait until daybreak, taking a stroll down some side streets in the meantime. It felt good to walk.

Finally enough light painted my world to proceed. Back into the recessed cockpit of the trike I lowered myself and pedaled on eastward, towards the imposing mountains that stood between me and the dryer hinterlands of desert country, all the while slowly gaining altitude. This was looking like it might take a while!

As I rode out of Glide, one of those places where if you blink, you miss it (in a car – you miss nothing in a trike), I was glad to see the sun poking through the misty shroud at long last, but I was concerned about the large mass of blackened clouds that seemed poised to swallow the bright orb. How long would my heat source and lighting last at a comfortable level? Would it warm up as the morning progressed? Or would the specter of precipitate-laden moisture command the day? I was definitely heading right into an increasingly darkened world.

My answer soon grew clearer, as I was eventually under a sky with no visible star and no visible blue. It was only October third, I reminded myself, and was convinced that things would clear up for my summit push, making for a gorgeous ride over the top of this volcanic range of peaks. Wet and cold weather typically doesn't inundate the region this early in the season. Sure, I would expect such on my return trip five weeks from now, but not today.

This highway is a beautiful drive regardless of weather. Long straight stretches slowly prepare travelers for the mountains, as the trees become gargantuan sentinels on either side of the asphalt, making it clear that the forest of all forests is being entered. Highway 138 is called Oregon's waterfall road because there are numerous waterfalls along its Cascade length that draw thousands of tourists yearly to see rivers plummeting down through the air great distances. Some of the falls are visible from the road, while others require a hike to reach. I am hopeful to be able to pull in and see a couple on my way. Even though I have hiked to most of them, they still hold a magic grip about my memories.

Susan Creek Campground seemed ever elusive today, perhaps because I was comparing my arrival to the last time I drove here in a car. It was taking forever, yet the ride was magnificent, so I did not mind, especially knowing a hot shower, riverside campsites, and a pleasant rest awaited me. A few sprinkles kept appearing, not enough to really dampen my gear, but sufficient to make me wonder what was ahead on this portion of my still young journey.

When I at last saw a sign for the campground, I was tired. The mileage to the camp was not much since my short stay in Wilbur, but it involved considerable climbing the whole way. Of course, that was minuscule compared to the Cascade Range, the lower slopes of which I was now ascending. Thirty-one miles is a short day by any cyclist's standards. Gee, I rode 50 mile training rides in 5 hours, so I had a realistic idea of my snail's pace so far. Of course, those rides were often unencumbered by an additional 100 pounds or more of cargo.

It had been raining at Susan Creek. The campground road was full of puddles and all the campsites looked very waterlogged, a far cry from my summer visits that led to an immediate appreciation of the high dense forest, and a natural desire to go sit by the rushing river. Today, with water dripping from all the branches high above me, I just wanted to pitch a tent before the rain restarted, and get myself a hot shower before completely relaxing.

No sooner was the tent pitched and the rain fly on, then the rain commenced. I looked across the way at the campground hosts, all cozy in their huge motorhome, watching television while the wife began preparing a snack. I quickly placed my four panniers (saddlebags) in the tent, gathered the needed clean clothes and supplies, and walked to the shower facility. The showers are all private little rooms, with your own lockable door, so once inside, I was sheltered from the elements.

Into the slots I placed my quarters, and the warm water began to cover me in needed bliss. Before my departure on this trip, I buzzed my hair so that washing of it would take mere seconds. Turns out that was a good thing, because less that 60 seconds into my pleasurable cleansing, the unthinkable happened! Yes, my nice warm water was quickly loosing its warmth. I had figured that showering this early in the afternoon would get me plenty of hot water, but alas, there must have been a run on long hot showers today within the last half hour, and I was the chosen one to either take a cold shower or get out. I slapped water as quickly as I could to clean up, yet I wasn't fast enough. No soap, little water, minimally cleaner, and definitely cold once again.

Well, life doesn't always go as one would wish. After drying off and getting into a couple of jackets and rain gear, I warmed back up and headed out to the tent … in the drizzles.

While the rain fell, I just lounged atop my sleeping bag, waiting to hear it stop. When it finally did, I ventured out, opened my trailer's food supply, and had a pouch full of rice and veggies. To make up for all the abuse I had suffered today and at the campground so far, I even indulged in a Cliff Bar for dessert, along with a few dried plums. There has to be some justice in this world!

Soon, John and Brian Massey, from Salem and Coos Bay respectively, came back to their camp next to mine. They saw me eating cold food, and invited me over to their roaring fire to spend some time before hitting the sack. It felt good as the heat penetrated my clothing. I was offered a beer, but declined. John and Brian are father and son, who came here for a few days of camping. Once it got dark, I excused myself, climbed into the tent, and wrote about the day's events in my journal. The rain during the night kept me sleeping well!

DAY 4 - *Death Valley*
Sunday, October 04, 2009
Susan Creek Campground to high Cascades – 35 miles
(running total: 152 miles)

Sleepily, I open my eyes enough to determine whether it is still night. The mummy bag is so cozy and warm, that once I realize the day

24

is beginning its earliest stages of dawn, I hesitate to crawl out. Water drops continue to hit the tent's fly, but not from a constant rain, rather only from lingering drips falling off the evergreen branches and needles high above, for the rain has stopped at long last. After getting dressed, I peak out the tent door to discover everything is still very wet and soggy. Fortunately, the ground around the tent consists of bark chips, not dirt.

Having a complete bathroom only a 20 second walk from the tent is a nice convenience. On this trip, I am not shaving, for I have found that doing so can be uncomfortable in cold weather with only cold water. Besides, it takes time, and I prefer to concentrate on being out in the wild instead of maintaining a cultural expectation. Out here on wilderness time, the beard seems apropos. A warm shower would be nice to make up for last afternoon's failed attempt, but I know the Cascade traverse occurs today, so I best not linger any more than necessary. By now, pedaling all day is the new normal.

My mind ponders the diverse landscapes I will be crossing on this extended journey. My senses experience the towering evergreens, large leafy ferns, misty fog, churning river, and heavy dampness. It all seems a world away from my arid and warm destination 282 feet below sea level. Here, I struggle to keep dry and warm. There, in the maw of Death Valley, I will yearn to be wet and cool – small window of comfort.

The reality of the trip is still sinking in, as I am only three days and about 119 miles from home. Other than rain, the ride has been mostly uneventful from a commonly perceived negative standpoint. My perception of this grand spectacle of nature varies somewhat from the masses though, who traditionally call rain "bad weather" or some other downbeat label. In many ways, I enjoy witnessing and experiencing all that nature offers. It has been told that there is no such thing as bad weather, only bad preparation. This rings truer in my mind. Today I have donned raingear in response to the moisture-laden heavens. Fortunately, my body is waterproof anyway, so I don't have to worry one way or the other. Clothing always dries, so no need to miss adventure because of it.

The plan is to camp at Diamond Lake tonight, a picturesque body of water that is around 50 miles distant. This certainly seems doable, even with the steep grades ahead. The Cascade Mountains are large and wide. Getting over them will take slightly more than one day, I reckon, as Diamond Lake is still shy of the highest road summit by a few miles. Two months from now, this same road will be buried in snow.

The tent has to be packed wet this morning – no way around it. I'll dry it out later, or hopefully pitch it next in dryer weather and it will dry naturally. After attaching the fly, which is the wettest piece, to the top of my trailer so that it can get air flow as I ride, and pulling the rain covers over my Arkel panniers, I pedal eastward on the long straight section of highway. Sprinkles come and go the first several miles, and then, surprises of surprises ...

Once the road starts climbing more, the sun pokes through to greet me for the first time this Sunday. I am ravenously hungry because I did not partake of my normal bowl of cereal this morning, choosing instead a quick bar because the campground table was soaked and I had hoped the sun would come out for a later breakfast. Well, now was the time! A nice outcrop of rocks up ahead allowed for full sun exposure as I ate a couple more bars. Yeah, I guess I prefer sun like everyone else. It just feels so nice to get warm from the air.

When I park the trike on a hill like this, I engage the two parking brakes, one on each brake lever. They consist of two metal tabs that push in and keep the handles secure. They are not foolproof however, especially considering how heavy my overall rig is, so usually I face the trike sideways if I can, or, since that's not possible here on this narrow dirt parkway, a rock behind a tire works well. With the trailer extending the trike's length from 6 to 10 feet, parking choices are not always very many. It would be nice not to have this trailer, but then again, when it comes time to eat to my heart's delight, it sure is nice to know that I have a never-ending source of calories (or so it seems when I gaze down at the gear bag containing my 50 pounds of food).

Continuing on, my coats are mostly unzipped to allow the heat buildup to escape. It's amazing how much the sun can affect this so quickly. Just as quickly though, after a few more miles, away goes the sun, the clouds once again thicken, and the rain begins anew. The jackets get zipped. Good thing I kept my rain hood on under the helmet. I had left my rain pants on, kind of figuring this might happen.

It rained lightly all the way to a place called Steamboat, where a cozy lodge with rooms and restaurant awaited mountain tourists. By the time I rolled in, my world was wet and dark. After finding a parking place in the tight lot, I walked in, trying not to look too conspicuous, but knowing that dressed as I was, I stood out like a sore thumb to all the dry patrons and workers. The heated bathroom was a welcome relief, and I stood in the lobby for a while to warm up and see if the sun would return before my departure. I could not wait too long though.

A Steamboat worker strolled up to my pathetic dripping body and asked where I was going. I told her my story, and after her surprise and admiration for my intrepid plan (or crazy idea perhaps), she offered me a weather update, having just driven from the eastern side of these mountains in her car. She was very sincere when she said:

"You know, a heavy snowstorm rolled in last night at the higher elevations. The state snow plows are out in full force up there clearing the roadways right now. You might want to think twice before trying to go over the top with your trike. I had trouble in my car. They're calling it a winter storm warning, and it's only the first week of October!"

Okay, this was serious news here. Snow? Sure, I figured that it was a possibility on my return trip a month and a half from now, but not this early. Of all years for an freak storm to slam into these mountains, it had to be today! Just my luck, of course. Normally, ski resorts pray for snow in November, and often don't get it, but this year just had to be the exception. I wondered how one-wheel drive trikes pulling a heavy trailer do in snow, although I could imagine well enough the scenario. I keep trying to remember that there's no such thing as bad weather, only bad preparation. Then, I push it out of my mind so I can move on.

I thank the kind woman for providing a few moments of warm conversation, bid her farewell, and walk hesitantly back out to my trike. The sky is not clearing at all, and with this news, I decide to proceed with all due haste, hopefully to reach my destination before conditions make forward travel not possible. The open mesh seat of my trike is wet, but no big deal with my rain clothes. At least water does not collect.

Rested from my Steamboat interlude, I pedal with renewed determination up the increasingly steep grade. Then, wonder of all wonders, out comes Mr. Sun once again! Mentally transformed, I launch into a grand appreciation of all that surrounds me, speaking audibly to the trees, rocks, birds, and the marvels of nature, thanking them all for providing me this unsurpassed paradise through which I may pedal. I speak loudly and grandly in formal tones, in a manner that could be construed as consistent with the way the first primitive Americans may have beheld their surroundings during past centuries. Out here on an open tricycle, unprotected from the elements, I could only be closer to the natural world if I were backpacking on a dirt trail. Never in a car would I have felt like performing this unique spiritual ritual of communication. There is no traffic. Only the ears of animals hear me. I receive pleasure from this bonding.

There is no odometer on my trike. There used to be when I bought it, but I gave the $50 marvel away because I chose not to get boxed into a technical world of human electronics that keep me posted about everything I do, including average speed traveled. I am here for the sheer enjoyment of the ride ... mileage is not important. Thus, in this telling of my story, precise figures are not generally a part. The method I use to have a rough idea of my progress is by roadside mileage markers, which keeps my mind active always performing the math.

Around 15 miles from Susan Creek Campground, having just

climbed a very steep grade, the Dry Creek Store appears on the left, an old log building. It has a gas station, restroom, and small market. A number of pickup trucks are parked around, mostly from area hunters, judging by the clothing many of the men are wearing. I needed some bananas, and buy three for $1.80 (the first money spent on this trip so far), which I ate on the front log bench. A fellow sees me taking a picture of my trike, and offers to take my photo standing in front. I take him up on the offer, smiling and waving for the camera, even though the sky is again getting very dark, and the ladies inside the store have readily confirmed the hazardous weather into which I was currently heading.

The guy who took my picture, who had just come down from higher elevations, advised me to turn around now. I thanked him, and then proceed east. Who knows what those hunters all thought of me. Must have a screw loose somewhere! I ignored his warning.

One thing I did notice while walking around at the store was an issue developing with my feet. This morning, I had put on a second pair of shoes, all leather waterproof Hi-Tec low-top hiking boots. This is my first wearing of them for any lengthy time, having only broken them in slightly by walking pre-trip. The back of each Achilles tendon is getting rubbed by the stiff rear of the shoe, causing a tender area. I tried to adjust my foot angle enough to mitigate the situation after leaving the store, but it didn't help much. I would rather have on my Merrill Moab Ventilators, which I have worn up until today, as they are super comfortable, but they are not waterproof, so I endure the Hi-Tec shoes.

So preoccupied was I with the shoe and tendon thought that I failed to realize I rode the first three miles from the store with my left parking brake engaged. Well, I wondered why the trike seemed to be handling a little odd! At least I figured it out fairly soon.

At the Dry Creek Store, I was told that during the next 35 miles east, I would experience a 4,000-foot elevation gain, up past the 5100 foot mark. This continually rising road kept my progress very slow. There was already increasingly deeper snow appearing in the woods around me, and by mid afternoon, it was right up to the road, where the plows had pushed it off the asphalt. The road was wet, but not icy. Into a winter wonderland I proceeded, with the evergreen branches feeling the weight of accumulated white stuff. Like a man with a mission, I pushed the pedals as powerfully as I could, hoping to reach Diamond Lake by dinner. The thought of pitching my tent and crashing into a deep slumber was inviting.

Because the day had been heavily overcast so far, with occasional light snowfall, I could never get an accurate read on the sun's location, which is the means I use to tell time when I'm in the wild places. As the hours passed, it all looked the same, seeming like it was always some time in the mid afternoon. My slow speed led to an almost trance-like monotonous state, that pulled me into a dream world. At one point however, reality hit me full force.

My body was overly warm on the grades, and I was very hungry. I needed a couple of high calorie energy bars soon. At a place where the road actually took a slight dip downward for a short distance, I pulled over to remove a jacket layer and access my food. I always kept a few bars handy in a side pannier that hung on the seat so I could get to them without the agony of opening the trailer, which involved keying the lock, removing the hold-down straps, opening the lid, and getting to the food bag. And agony it would have been now, because it became abundantly clear to me that I had a situation rapidly developing.

Within seconds after stopping and unzipping my jacket to vent my body heat, the cold hit me in a most dramatic way! In mere seconds, I began to shiver and shake slightly. Having removed my bulky warm gloves so that I could eat, my fingers felt bitter cold all of a sudden. It was bad enough that I knew I could not take the time without gloves to even try to access my food in the trailer, but I had to so that I could replenish my handy food supply for quick eating along the way. It was not a choice. Now, I was truly starting to feel the cold sink deeply in, which brought my thoughts to the time of day. Was it late?

My mind had missed how dark it was getting. With clouds my companion for so long today, my thoughts subconsciously processed the darkness simply as heavier clouds, with little thought about the time. So deceived was I that just moments prior to this stop, I was still hoping to take a short hike to one of the many beautiful waterfalls along this Oregon waterfall scenic route. One was only a couple of miles ahead, the tallest of all, and I wanted to see it again. Yet, this was not going to happen. My mind focused clearly upon my state of affairs.

Thermal regulation, energy maintenance, approaching darkness, and more miles than I wished to contemplate filled my immediate thoughts. I had to put on my goose-down vest now, because later it would prove even more challenging, having to remove my rain jacket and polar fleece coat first before I could slip it on. Just the time it took to take off the jackets to get the vest underneath resulted in increased shivering. If I overheated while pedaling, I would have to manage the temperature by how high I kept it all zipped. On my head I placed a cotton balaclava under the polar fleece skull cap and the rain jacket hood, both of which were under my bicycle helmet.

By my best mental reasoning, it was probably after 8 PM, having been snapped back into a more lucid state and roughly calculating mileage, speed, vague shadows, and such. How could I have possibly missed this gradual, but dramatic, change of setting? Still, I was feeling strong and felt that sooner or later I would reach a crest and then coast downhill to the lake, thereby making up for lost time. However, at the time, I had also forgotten the critical fact that this particular Cascade crossing did not peak until after the lake, meaning that I had constant elevation rise ahead of me this evening. I was later to be reminded.

Once it started getting dark, it happened so fast that I was in disbelief. Seems like it was just afternoon! I stopped my tricycle again to actuate my marine emergency beacon strobe that I had attached to the rear of my trailer. Out here on this open mountain highway at night, I am the last thing a motorist would expect to see, especially under these adverse weather conditions. Cyclists just don't do this sort of thing. I also turned on my ten-LED flashing tail light, and the super bright headlight, which allowed me to see mileage markers. Progress was so slow that I had plenty of time to head the trike at an angle so the light would fall upon the mileage marker posts buried in the snow, and keeping track of them would give me something to keep my mind active. It got to the point that I would rejoice with each number that would confirm my progress. Seeing waterfalls and hiking faded into oblivion.

A couple of times, an Oregon Department Of Transportation gigantic orange snow plow would pass going the opposite direction. I have no doubt that the driver must have been shaking his head, once he figured out what exactly he was seeing. Traffic was very light, even though this was a major pass road, most likely due to the winter storm warnings that had apparently gone public. Now and then, a motorist would slow to see if I wanted to signal for help, but then would continue on in his comfortably-heated metal box. I existed in another universe.

Around midnight, or so I figured, the clouds would part every once and a while, allowing Mr. Moon's full bright light to illuminate my wintry white kingdom. When I would realize this was happening, I would switch off my headlight because the snow-laden world around me was so incredible to behold in its naturally lit state. I may have been ever entering deeper levels of distress, yet my mind marveled nonetheless in the beauty of this magical realm, seeing scenes in such a way that few would ever experience themselves. Here I was, pedaling a tricycle over Oregon's Cascade Range, in the middle of the night, while writing a chapter of my life that will always remain indelibly etched in my psyche.

Somewhere in the middle of this Cascade Range traverse, the day technically changed, having passed the midnight mark. This daily occurrence was not known to me on a conscious level as I pedaled upward towards my goal. Survival became my reality and objective.

DAY 5 - *Death Valley*
Monday, October 05, 2009
High Cascades to Diamond Lake Lodge – 15 miles
(running total: 167 miles)

Panic is not an option in my personal toolkit of life solutions. My logical mind searches for alternatives that provide me a reasonable chance at success. Although, as the hours progress into the early morning of Monday, and the temperature continues to fall, if a person were so inclined to enter such a mentally unstable state, this set of circumstances would quickly bring it on. I feel the fear, and realize that I have allowed myself to enter a potentially life-threatening condition.

I define a state of panic as fear out of control. We all experience fear, for it is an inborn trait that helps us define moments when action must be taken for self-preservation. It is akin to a red flag signaling our brain that something is amiss. The ironic aspect of this is that precisely when panic sets in for most folks is the time when rational and calm thinking is critical, for a panic response often does not contain a fair probability of a favorable outcome. Panic often leads to disaster.

Around 2 AM or thereabouts, based on the position of the moon from last night's ride, and the amount of time I perceive I've been pedaling since nightfall, it becomes clearly apparent to me that I am truly out here alone on the high slopes of the Cascades, and I am definitely in real danger. Virtually no cars are out any longer. The snow level up this high is about two feet just off the sides of the highway. It is getting much colder, and the rare sign indicating the mileage to Diamond Lake Lodge tells me I have at least a couple hours of pedaling ahead of me!

I wonder if I can sustain the climb. I am becoming weaker and colder – that much is certain. I consider the possibility of creating a crisis bivouac camp, one where I would simply park the trike right on the road's shoulder, unfurl my emergency bivouac bag, slide my sleeping bag inside, rough out a deep snow trench, and hunker down until daylight. My body heat is still sufficient enough that such a scenario would result in a controlled retention of warmth, or so I believe. Once settled in, I could probably survive until morning. Such action would have to be undertaken prior to any serious hypothermic condition to be successful. My challenge is to determine how close to that point I am, as the frigid extreme cold numbs my mind.

The decision against such an option is reached after roughly three very slow miles of solemn thought. Unbelievably, during the time I am attempting to decide, I find myself dozing off, just like a auto driver

31

might do having had insufficient sleep. This amazes me when I pull myself back to full awareness, because I am pedaling a tricycle! How can I be going to sleep during active movement like this? And, just like a motorist who weaves from his lane, my trike heads over the center line since I am riding in the middle of my lane and not on the icy shoulder.

An emergency bivouac is not totally out of contention, but for now I will go on. I believe I can make it. The road seems flat, but the fact that I am still in lower gears, and can't hold an upshift but for a fleeting moment, tells me that indeed I am still climbing. The coldest time of any 24-hour period is immediately before the sun actually shines on an area, so if I did bivouac, I would have to remain in it well into mid-morning, because to leave at first light would gain me little, unless I had really warmed up a lot, and had consumed quite a few calories in the process. My hands are very cold even in my heavy winter gloves, and to attempt to use them without gloves to set camp and get to my food supply would seem unwise. I would slip even deeper into a frozen state.

When the clouds cover the moon, I must switch on my headlight to see where I'm going. Since it sits just to the left of my head at eye level, the beam also illuminates the front of the trike. On my ride from Wilbur 24 hours ago, I found this allowed me to see my gear shift indicators on the hand grips, which was useful because after a long stretch in the same gear, one can forget where the chain is on the sprockets and rings with twist grip shifters. It also illuminates the front spokes, which in low gear, turn ever so slowly, a constant visual reminder that tonight's epic haul is going to be a long one.

I have rarely felt so alone, and yet, there is a certain indescribable peace in it all. Noise does not exist in these woods at this hour, and any infrequent vibrations that do hit my ears, do so after being muffled and absorbed by the thick blanket of white snow everywhere. This period of the trip is clearly an exceptionally silent passage. Only rhythmical mechanical sounds emanating from the trike keep me company. This trike is called an ICE Q, mockingly apropos for the conditions where even if I could speed up significantly, it would be unwise due to intermittent road ice. I am traveling to the hottest place on planet Earth, yet now exist in a frozen land of snow and ice!

A furnace requires fuel to remain hot, and so it is with the human body. As long as I am pedaling, I remain just warm enough for comfort, but what is my heat source? Why am I remaining warm? Calories! For my furnace to heat the structure, calories must be eaten, and lots of them in a situation like this. I did not have my regular high calorie breakfast at Susan Creek, a place that seems oddly distant now. I did not consume my standard dinner, for it would have required manual dexterity not comfortably available at these low temperatures. My fuel source on this Cascade traverse has been a few energy bars, which have fallen far short of replacing what I am expending in this frigid ascent.

This caloric deficit is made worse by the fact that I have been riding well past my normally planned day of eight hours. In fact, by my estimation, approximately 17 hours have elapsed since my campground departure this morning, or as would be technically correct, yesterday morning, since today is now Monday, and I left Susan Creek Campground on Sunday morning. The bars I have eaten would have maybe been enough for an eight hour day ... maybe, but not for this protracted duration. The lack of calories also is causing undesirable fatigue to set in, which further promotes the onset of exhaustion.

Yet, in spite of all this, I am happy! I am achieving a goal, the likes of which I have never come close to even considering, let alone doing. On a tricycle, pulling a heavy trailer, I am crossing Oregon's expansive Cascade Range by myself, and on a cold wintry night no less. Not too many folks could pull off something like this. Of course, not too many folks would even want to. I am enjoying the challenge, and the tougher it gets, with odds continuing to stack up against me, the better I like it. There is something primal in my being that seeks this extreme adventure, a phantom that drives me onward to find my limits, and then exceed them! These circumstances are the purest sense of my inner belief that only those who risk going too far will discover how far they can go. It is the only way to determine one's potential.

Inner peace fills me, and allows me to be fully in the now. I am not brooding over what happened in the past, as so many people always do. My past is what makes me who I am, but it does not control my present. Nor do I worry about the future, as most of what people worry about never comes to pass anyway, thus wasted life energy. I am perfectly in the present with all my spirit, realizing that I may be in way over my head, but taking pleasure in this matchless moment that will not again be duplicated during my life. The challenge makes me feel alive and full of purpose. This is existence in the raw elements, alone.

I am not a pessimist, one who habitually sees the bad in life's turn of events, nor am I an optimist, one who consistently sees only the good. I am a mild-mannered naturalist and a realist, one who dwells in the moment, assesses the situation, makes a decision, and sculpts my life into one that delivers inner peace and happiness. I see the bad and good, and I see how they coexist in my reality. Pessimists are typically anxious, frightened, and negative in their actions, which are responses that short circuit their tranquility and longevity. Optimists often are disheartened, having faith that good will always prevail, and when it does not, as is often the case unfortunately, they face an emotionally depressed state. My objective is to take it all as it comes, and turn it to my advantage realistically. With this mindset comes peace, and an end to suffering.

I may be getting tired and living in a state of lowered body temperature, but I am far from dead, and far from out of my mind. I muster the inner resolve necessary to keep on trikin' out here in nature's incomparable wonderland. Besides, I think to myself, this leg of the journey will make for some very captivating story telling when it's all over. I have found that the need for armchair adventure is alive and well in our society, and many seek a surrogate explorer in order to live out a secret self-image of their inner conqueror. After all, such is the successful foundation of Hollywood's action adventure movies.

Though I would not trade this experience for the world, truly, I am ready for warmth and relaxation after several more hours of cycling under Earth's full moon, thick clouds, and imposing evergreens. The last signpost indicates that the Diamond Lake Lodge is a mile distant, and I can feel my respite beginning already. The lodge sits on a side road that parallels Highway 138. The wheels of my trusty trike make a sharp right, as if the ICE Q knows where to go, and we begin a fast descent down to lake level and the lodge, where all is quiet and still this early in the morn.

It's only a paltry half mile downhill to my salvation, yet since I am not pedaling, I am no longer generating inner body heat. The speed of the Q dramatically increases, and damn, I'm really getting cold all of a sudden! I mean, in a heartbeat, I am shaking as the bitter chill sucks what seems like my final vestige of heat from my destabilized carcass. A slight pressure on the two brake levers eases the frigid pain, and reduces the likelihood of skidding out of control on the icy patches that are lurking beyond my knowledge. That's all I need – to end up crashing a quarter mile from the lodge.

I see lights through the stately snowbound trees. Looks like the maintenance plow has been working overtime here. I have been to this lodge before, but still am not sure which of the many buildings is the office, so as I enter the parking area, I coast slowly and look for signs. Everything appears different tonight than it did before in the daytime.

Cautiously, I coast to a flat area near the main lodge entrance, sliding a little in the process. I set my parking brakes and ever so slowly arise from the low recumbent seat. My first priority is warmth. The front door is locked. I see an inside stairway off to the right, and find the doors to it are unlocked for guests. Up I go, into a multi-purpose room with overstuffed couches and about 70 degrees of splendid hot air. I can grab a few winks on this couch until daybreak, as all doors off this room are locked, so I return back down to the trike to retrieve my wallet.

Well, it seems like someone has indeed been aware of my arrival, for as soon as I reach the trike, the lodge door opens and Mike O'Sullivan, the night security attendant asks if I need assistance. With any semblance of charm remaining within me, I graciously reply in the affirmative, and we walk into the building. Wonder what he's thinking! My beard is still covered in ice.

A few miles back, I had decided I would break my prime directive that keeps me wild on my overnights in a tent. I would ante-up the cash and get a room as a little treat for myself for surviving this epic crossing still in one piece, albeit a decidedly cold piece. While filling out a brief form, which asks for my car license plate (I write "none"), I relate to Mike a brief rendition of my trip. A room for one night is $59.59, not too bad for a resort destination like this. Must be past the tourist season. Since it is Monday morning (4 AM by the way!), the rental is for tonight, meaning Monday night. But, I'm dead tired now, so Mike says to sack out on the huge couch ten feet from a massive stone fireplace and mantel, where the inviting flames are dancing wildly.

For a few moments, I sit on another couch and watch ESPN that he has going on the TV. We chat for a bit, as I fully enjoy every warm and comfy moment (talk about savoring the now), and Mike asks how long I've been riding. Well, I tell him, I left Susan Creek Campground on the western slope of the Cascades on Sunday morning around 8 AM. He is in disbelief, of course, because what kind of a nut would ride a tricycle for 20 hours in rain, snow, ice, and subfreezing temperatures? Hmm, guess Mike is looking at him!

After ten minutes of relaxing visiting, I remove my jackets and headgear, and go over to lie down in front of the fire. It's still dark outside when I sign off to a subconscious state. When I awaken, I notice two things immediately. First, I am hotter than a poker, and I must get up and walk away from the fireplace. Second, the initial glow of day is beginning to paint the window with an increasing radiance. I ask Mike what time this little lodge restaurant opens. He says six o'clock, which is only about twenty minutes from now. I decide to forgo my Nutty Nuggets on this glorious Monday morning, and instead offer up a few more bills from my wallet to eat a breakfast like a king.

Marsha O'Shea, my waitress, asks about my circumstances, seeing as how my dress and appearance are a little different than the average lodge guest. She is entertained as I continue to order food after eating a large Spanish omelet breakfast, including hash browns, toast, and a cup of hot chocolate. After that, I ordered a large bowl of oatmeal with butter, brown sugar, and raisins. It is my time for one transgression after another it seems. First, I get a room for tonight. Now, I am eating a non-vegan breakfast. It's okay though. I need calories, lots of them, and I need them now! My body will appreciate these animal products I am sending down. Darn, it has been years since I've eaten a Spanish omelet, and wow, does it ever hit the spot, especially since I top it with loads of salsa. Matt was right again. I'll eat whatever I can find!

It was still early Monday morning when I wolfed down my final oat and guzzled the last drop of hot chocolate. No clouds were in the sky this morning, not even one tiny puff! The sun was now illuminating Diamond Lake, which was only a matter of yards from my picture-window view at the table. I must say that it was a striking scene, particularly after the past twenty hours of not seeing my world so brightly. Snow was already beginning to slowly melt under the rays.

As I stood finishing up a final conversation with Marsha, and holding my jackets and helmet, my peripheral vision noticed another person patiently standing off to my right, apparently intent on the words being spoken, which, of course, centered around my risky jaunt. Marsha walked off and another woman introduced herself to me. This was Alex Grove, who, I came to find out, had been hiking for many weeks with her backpack, while enjoying portions of an epic walk along the Pacific Crest Trail. She hails from Nelson, British Columbia! Her adventures certainly put mine in vivid perspective, seeing as how I only left from Oregon four days ago.

And I thought I had come a long way. Goes to show that there is always someone out there who is even crazier, more experienced, or both. Immediately, she had my total respect.

Well, Alex invites me to sit with her and talk while she orders up a hearty breakfast. Seems that she has been developing a notable lower leg problem during the past week and chose to get some R&R at the lodge for a couple of days. Alex has a hiking and biking website, located at http://hikerbiker.org/home.htm, which tells the stories of her cycle touring adventures, wilderness treks, and other ramblings of a hiking biking vagabond. In 2008, she did a North America solo bike tour. Okay, she obviously knows how to make a go of things in the wild.

She asks me to talk about what I am doing while she eats her steak, which, she assures me, is not her typical vegetarian fare, but she figures a massive protein infusion wouldn't hurt the healing process. So I tease her, but then let on that I just ate eggs, milk, and butter myself. The two of us have a good laugh. Yep, food is survival in the outback, so sometimes homebound regimens take a back seat.

I am amazed at how quickly and completely human bonding occurs when kindred spirits cross paths on journeys that push the limits of endurance and survival. Within minutes, we are chatting like old friends, sharing our trials and tribulations, the joys of human-powered travel, and the wonders of nature beheld while unprotected in the midst of all its wildness. This is my first such experience with a fellow adventurer, but it will not be my last on this overland journey.

Even though I am dead tired and sleepier than I have ever been, I remain relatively alert and continue our conversation while she finishes the feast. It's time for me to crash, so we bid each other a temporary adieu and I head out the door to the trike. With my room key in hand, I slowly walk over to the Q, which is still in the shade of the lobby on icy ground. The first thing I notice is that the trike's parking brakes, which I set at 4 AM this morning, are frozen in the locked position – last time I do that. After some fiddling, they loosen up and I begin pedaling the Q up the asphalt parking lot towards my room, until the rear wheel just starts spinning freely on the ice. Time to go another way.

My room is in full glorious sun, but the air hovers just below the freezing mark. I park the trike right next to the building in front of my window. The snow from the roof is now melting and dripping all over me as I take my gear inside. I spread out the tent and fly in the sun to begin drying, and later will take them inside for some heat. The first order of business is a short nap, followed by a shower, doing the laundry, and then another afternoon nap. Gads, I'm wiped out!

As I take off my shoes and socks for my second nap, I notice a problem. The Hi-Tec waterproof hiking boots I wore from Susan Creek Campground had caused tender spots on the back of my Achilles tendons, as the boots are much stiffer than my Merrills. I cannot wear them from here on out due to this issue, and since I am probably past all the rain and snow, I decide to mail them, and some other unused foul-weather gear, home after I awaken from the nap. I notice also that both Achilles tendons are considerably swollen, a manifestation that I simply attribute to the shoe irritation. Strangely though, the Achilles feel stiff, which I would not expect from an external rubbing by a shoe. In any event, I assume it's temporary, prop my feet on a folded pillow, and fall off into a blissful needed sleep.

Upon arising, I put on my flip-flop sandals to give my feet a break, and step outside. It's still perfectly sunny, now pleasantly warm (relatively speaking, of course), and much of the snow is gone, only remaining in deeply shaded areas. That was a quick melt. It costs $8.30 to ship 6 pounds, 10 ounces of gear home from this little post office substation that luckily exists right at the lodge. Not only was that gear weighing me down that much more, but now I have some extra packing room. I buy new batteries for the headlight and marine strobe, both of which were beginning to dim down after the high pass crossing. The

Cateye headlight advertises more than 90 hours of runtime, yet between the two night rides I have taken, the accumulated hours aren't even at 15 yet. So much for grandiose and exaggerated claims! Perhaps the subfreezing cold had something to do with killing the light so soon.

After chatting a bit with Brian Richardson, the front desk assistant who found my trip interesting because he had once worked in Death Valley National Park, a lady standing nearby says she heard me talking about the Achilles tendon problem. She then launches into a detailed story about how her athletic husband tore one of his, which resulted in it rolling up like a curtain into his calf muscle, something she relates as the most intense pain her husband had ever felt. After surgery and a long time of excruciating rehabilitation and healing, he finally returned to normal. Great! That's all I need to hear when my trip is still in its early stages. I wonder if my extra hard physical push to get to the lodge in the wee hours this morning may have led to my inflammation, especially considering the cold air.

Well, I don't want to hear anymore horror stories, so after buying some overly expensive V8 juices, eating an early dinner of rice and veggies in my room, and writing in my journal, I slide into bed for a long night's sleep at 4:30 PM, with no concern about departure time tomorrow morning. The heater is making an annoying fan noise as it keeps me warm, but I am out quickly, happy that Tuesday's ride will be on dry pavement, hopefully with more sun! Man, does it ever feel good to relax in warmth. Tricycle journeys change one's perspective on life!

DAY 6 - *Death Valley*
Tuesday, October 06, 2009
Diamond Lake Lodge to north of Klamath Falls – 50 miles
(running total: 217 miles)

Somewhere around four in the morning, nearly twelve hours after I went to sleep Monday night, I awaken to loud talking, the sound of a diesel pickup truck running next to my trike, and fumes infiltrating my room and lungs. I had left the window cracked ever so slightly last night for fresh air, but now had to quickly close it before the air grew any more toxic. With no back window to this room, I felt trapped like a rat. Diesel is 6 to 8 times more carcinogenic to human lung tissue than standard gasoline engine emissions, so I take inhalation seriously. The two road crew workers are also smoking cigarettes as they discuss the upcoming day's project with absolutely no regard for other lodge guests still trying to sleep. Amazing the consideration deficit in the heads of some people!

I dismiss the idea of speaking with them, knowing my trike is vulnerable outside, and wondering if such intolerably rude behavior may be indicative of people who could at least entertain ideas of malicious retribution should I upset them with a request to shut down the engine and their thunderous voices. I also consider calling the front desk, and just about the time I am sufficiently disturbed to pick up the phone, they get in the truck, drive off, and peace again returns to the otherwise tranquil lakeside setting.

After another hour of just lounging for the pure sake of it, I notice first light starting to fill the sky, so I decide to get an early start. It will take some time to repack everything that I have scattered all about the room to dry, so may as well get going on it. This morning, I just eat Nutty Nuggets in my room, while calculating that my elapsed mileage so far is roughly 169 miles, with 733 more between me and Badwater. I hope the last 50 miles were as challenging as it gets on this trip. Ah, the heat of Badwater Basin now sounds inviting!

The sky above is again pure blue, with nothing whatsoever to impeded the warming rays of the sun. It did not snow last night. I predict that today will be a grand ride, what with full sun, the Cascade summit now only a few miles distant, and then one very long downhill leading to Highway 97. Last night, I made a spur of the moment route modification. Original plans called for me to enter Crater Lake National Park this morning after leaving the lodge, and take one of the most scenic routes in the state down to Klamath Falls. Considering the snow I already encountered Sunday and Monday, and the fact that the national park is quite a bit higher in elevation, it seems prudent to avoid any further brushes with hypothermia and death, not to mention the fact that I just want to go downhill for a change.

It may not be any warmer down below, for central Oregon around Bend and points south become very cold late in the year, but elevations of 3,000 feet, and less, certainly increase my changes of fairer weather at least. I am amazed at how quickly the scene has changed here. When I arrived Monday morning at 4 AM, this was a snowbound winter wonderland, yet now, about 27 hours later, much of the snow has melted. The evergreen trees next to my room were white when I parked the trike, but now are green. It is still cold, but at least it's much dryer.

As I am finishing up packing the gear on the Q and in the trailer, Alex walks over from her room in the next wing. Seeing me prepping to shove off, she wants to say goodbye, as the chances of another meet in the future are mighty slim. Even though I am eager to start pedaling again, it is worth taking the time to talk with her, and share our common philosophies of natural world stewardship. In this world, relationships with others, even fleeting ones, are worthy of cultivation, for bringing an uplifting feeling to folks is one of my life priorities. Life isn't about money and power, at least not in my realm. It's all about being good to people and the planet. The other upside to spending a while chatting is that it is pleasantly warm in the room.

We finally hug and bid each other a final farewell and wishes of safe travel. Alex takes a digital photo of me by the trike, and then watches as I slowly coast down the hill towards the exit. The first several miles this morning are partially shaded on the north/south portion of highway, and the downhill portions are quite chilling while coasting. I dare not put on another coat or vest under my all-weather jacket, because I would really overheat on the uphills, so, I brave the cold bursts, which are still short-lived with the summit yet ahead.

My Achilles tendons were both stiff when I began pedaling today, yet they loosened up after a couple of miles of purposefully light stress due to the cold. I think I will baby these things each morning until the inflammation vanishes. Bathroom breaks are easy up here with such a thick forest only a few yards walk from the pavement. Traffic is light. Shoulders are wide. The ride is easy. I survived the Cascade crossing – well, I still have an hour to go – but I can see things will be just fine.

Not far past the entrance to Crater Lake National Park, where I was originally going to turn, is the Cascade Summit sign, which I stop to photograph. Maximum elevation on this highway is but a few feet under 6,000, and now my way down is clear. This pass, unlike the other Cascade passes, is straight as an arrow (literally) from the summit to Highway 97 below. There is not one turn or curve in it, and it's all downhill, steep enough for me to really pick up some serious speed and make up for lost time. Actually, since Sunday, I have put in more time than if the two days had been normal and unproblematic, but the total mileage for twenty hours of riding was only fifty, which would have translated into two 25 mile days. So, I will now make up for lost mileage, rather than time. Although, come to think about it, there is no way to make up the mileage. Oh heck, who cares! This is the journey of a lifetime, and I want to savor every moment of it, tough, easy, or in between. No need to make up for anything really. It is as it is.

After taking the photos, and cresting the summit, about ten miles below me I can see the speck of highway where I will turn south towards Klamath Falls. Ten miles will probably be my longest coasting distance of the entire trek. Other downgrades may last for several miles, but I don't think any are longer than this one. Realizing that I will not be generating much body heat while coasting on the trike, I go ahead and suit up for the cold and fast air that will be whirling by me for quite a while. Sure, the sun is out, but temperatures still remain below freezing, and I am totally exposed as I ride. Trikers have little protection.

At one point in my preparations for this trip, I installed a Mueller Wind Wrap fairing on the trike. This would have been perfect for such an extended downhill speed run, but the framing of the fairing was precisely at eye level, and I didn't want to look at a black metal bar for hundreds of miles. The instructions said that if this were the case to simply raise the angle of the recumbent seat so that you could see over the bar. Well, I happen to like the seat reclined to 37 degrees off the horizontal, so I had no intent to change it. This angle of reclination is super comfy, and it also allows for a lower center of gravity in turns, and for higher speeds due to less wind resistance. So, the fairing was shipped back to the manufacturer for a refund, and never made the trip. It would have surely cut the wind chill though!

Most of the pavement on the eastern side of the expansive Cascade Range is covered at around 40 miles per hour. Gee, if only I could maintain this speed everywhere, but then again, I would be falling into the same mindset as automobile drivers who are always in a hurry (I know because I used to be one for 43 years). Even this fast on a trike though is better than a car because I am still in nature as I go by, and not sequestered away inside a heated steel and glass box, excluded from nature but for what my eyes would see.

Out here on the trike, all my senses come into play. I feel the cold rushing air on my face. I smell the trees and bushes. I hear the sounds of wild life. I taste the occasional bug, and I see this world from only eight inches off the ground. People in cars probably look at me and feel sorry for my "deprived" condition. I look at them and pity that they will never know what travel could be. Yes, I'm on the edge, but I like it here, where I take up little space, but have all the space I need as I enjoy the natural world instead of contaminating it.

I'm not trying to sound self-righteous here, for I have indeed done my share of defiling this air with expended petroleum fuels over the years, but I feel a certain inner pride now that I am finally making a difference in ways that soothe my primal spirit. Seen from space, the atmosphere is so unbelievably thin, it is a wonder we can even exist at all, with billions of miles of airless vacuum on the other side. Our atmosphere is so very finite. Once we ruin it beyond repair, we are done! I'm only one guy in the current six billion inhabitants of Earth, but there are many others like me. Perhaps someday you'll join us?

Three miles down from the summit there are two backpackers heading up across the roadway. But they have their backpacks off on the ground, and their thumbs extended. They have been walking about seven miles up this crazy steep grade so far, and now they turn to watch me rocket past in the other direction. We exchange a friendly wave and smile, and then I watch their figures shrink incredibly fast in my rearview mirror. It's not often I've seen backpackers hitchhiking, seeking a car!

Never once do I use the brakes on this downgrade, until, that is, I reach the large stop sign at the intersection of Highways 138 and 97. In roughly ten miles, from 6,000 feet to about 3,000 feet, the temperature has warmed nicely. I remove some of my warmer clothing, turn right, and head south on 97, which is predominantly downhill all the way to Klamath Falls. The mileage to that town is more than I can do today, so I know I will be seeking a stealth camp location later this afternoon. My pace on Highway 97 is rapid, and much of this portion I now easily remain in my highest gears, clipping along at a respectable average of probably in the neighborhood of 12-15 miles per hour. It feels good to see the milepost markers coming and going so quickly!

I have come more than 25 miles from the lodge, and it is not quite midday yet. The shoulder is wide so far, wide enough for at least two trikes to ride side by side. If I had a companion triker, we could easily be talking up a storm right now. Along the way, I occasionally stop for more energy bars, a seemingly endless supply of which is horded inside my large cargo trunk on the trailer.

At one point, there is a three mile section of highway striping in progress, as many miles of this road have recently been repaved (makes for superb riding on a recumbent, by the way – no rough jitters). The flagman tells me that the huge striping truck is northbound, and when it gets to the northern end here, will turn around and probably pass me heading south. He says I'll have to pick up my vehicle and move it off into the dirt by the woods. I don't like that idea at all, as I am heavily weighted down with supplies, so I shift up to high gear again and really stoke the pedaling fires. Slightly downhill, it is no problem keeping the large front chainring spinning very quickly.

A half mile into the striping area, I see the gigantic truck pass me going the other direction, spraying a fine white mist onto the new asphalt. This means he is one mile behind me, so if I can keep up my current speed, and keep him from catching me in the next two and a half miles, I won't be breathing any paint fumes today, or have to lug all my gear off the roadway into the loose dirt. This provides extra motivation to keep knocking down the miles. As I pass out of the southern end of the striping zone, I cannot even see the truck in my mirrors. Oh yeah! I kept the monster at bay.

The day is pleasant. This trike freeway is the best cycling I've done so far, from a car/trike standpoint at least. I feel completely safe with so much room. The afternoon is finally wearing on, so I begin scanning for a suitable stealth camp area. The Cascades are to my west, so the sun will disappear long before dark this evening. I like pitching camp when it is still fairly warm because it is more pleasing not to have cold hands while performing typical camping chores.

There have been many miles of an old dirt road paralleling the highway, with short access roads to it every few miles. The highway bed is raised quite a bit, so when I find a spot, it will necessitate riding down the embankment. I have been keeping mental track of my progress with the mile marker posts, and after about 50 miles today, I finally pull down into a promising forested area that should provide me some privacy from speeding cars and eighteen wheelers. The embankment is composed of little pieces of red lava rock since this is a predominantly volcanic region. The Q and trailer have no problem traversing it. The dirt road is soft, but I can pull through the somewhat loose material with a little extra effort in low gear.

Happily, I have these fat Schwalbe Marathon-Plus tires on the trike, which provide extra traction. With only one-wheel drive propelling 370 pounds through soft dirt, I need all the help I can get. I am also glad to have overbuilt my tire setup, and give nary a thought to puncturing a tire or tube on the lava stones.

I find the perfect spot to pitch, with a thick stand of ponderosa pines separating me from the raised roadway 25 yards distant. I want to turn the trike around before I set camp, as I prefer to be heading the right direction when I get up in the morning, when it will be too cold to be fiddling with such a maneuver. This is only a very narrow two-track dirt road, very old and overgrown in the center. My vehicle is ten feet long, so to turn it, I have to stand next to it, and manually steer and maneuver it, first forward and then backward. This necessitates me having to pick up the rear of the trailer numerous times to finally get it facing south again. The soft and dusty ground make a mess of my rear dérailleur and chain, covering it in dust. There is no way around it though. Doing this takes about five minutes. It is no picnic.

The tent gets pitched right in one of the old road's tire tracks, but there is little concern about anyone driving over me tonight. This road hasn't seen use in many years. There are no tire marks of any age. The soft ground will make for a super soft sleep, especially with my inflatable air mattress under the sleeping bag.

This is a restful evening, taking dinner at my leisure, and enjoying the woods despite passing traffic out on the highway. No one will ever see me. They are all going way too fast even if they are looking into the woods. Besides, it's getting darker by the minute now, and I am becoming invisible. The air is beginning to get cold again. Might be colder here than up at the lodge. This central area of Oregon is known for frigid night air. I make a little doormat of pine needles for the tent. The panniers are all inside with me to keep little varmints from nibbling through the Cordura fabric. This happened to some trike friends I know, and the wife had to stitch the hole in the morning.

A few minutes in my down mummy bag and my body is toasty warm. I am at peace. What a difference from triking through the night!

DAY 7 - *Death Valley*
Wednesday, October 07, 2009
North of Klamath Falls to Altamont, Oregon - 45 miles
(running total: 262 miles)

It is very quiet outside. It must also be very cold, because if I extend an uncovered arm out of the sleeping bag to get my water bottle, I can feel the air quickly chilling my skin. I prefer to remain in the bag, so I do. No sense in rushing things. The water in my cycling bottle is mostly frozen anyway, so I won't be drinking that for a while. It should be an easy day. I'm only about 35 miles north of Klamath Falls, with no significant uphills. An eighteen wheeler chugs by. There is frost on the tent. Clearly, it had been a very cold night.

Certain physiological manifestations cannot be delayed very long once they reach a given point of urgency, and since my healthy living dictates that I consume a fair amount of water on a regular basis, the impending consequences require an action I would rather not tend to in this cold. What goes in must come out, so out of the tent I go to obviate any further distress. After leaving the offering on reddish volcanic soil underfoot, one glance at the tent fly verifies that things are a bit on the chilling side, for it is covered in a thin icy veneer.

No sense in crawling back in now, as first light makes camp operations doable, so I grab all my warm clothing and initiate the layering principle. I wore my polar fleece skullcap last night, and had the mummy bag pulled up to further cover my head. As much as possible, I shake and knock the icy frost off the fly so that in a while I can hopefully pack things up easier. Pine trees shade me from the sun's first rays, unfortunately, so while eating breakfast, I move a few yards away to find a sunny spot, although so far, it's marginally warm even there.

My only food right now is a semi-frozen Clif Bar, which I must laboriously work on with my molars to break into bites. To fix a bowl of cereal would require dexterity of ungloved hands, and so I decide to pack up and ride for an hour or so before eating my full course. There is a lumbering wayside and museum with picnic tables not far south, and that will be my chosen place to dine. Breaking camp is done in spurts, for my hands become so bitter cold with each folding of the tent that I must warm them for about a minute or more after about 30 seconds of messing with the tent. Finally, it is done, and I lower myself into the cockpit of the icy ICE Q.

This old side road is soft dirt, overgrown, with downed branches here and there. I left the trike in low gear coming in last evening because I knew it would necessitate easy pedaling to get moving on the yielding roadbed come morning. With effort, my trike and trailer slowly arrive at the clearing that leads up to the paved highway, but when I attempt to pedal up the short twelve-foot hill, the rear tire just digs into the volcanic pebbles. No way one-wheel drive is going to get 370 pounds up this grade. I'm stuck – so close and yet so far! There is only one solution for this trike hobo today.

I walk to the front of the trike, and grab hold of the dérailleur post. Hunched over and walking backward up the steep little slope, I pull my ten-foot long train onto the pavement. Fortunately, this early there is virtually no traffic, because I need to use the entire lane to get squarely onto firm ground. If I did not have a trailer behind me, it would have been a simple matter with a trike to lift the rear tire and pull it backwards while I walk forwards, which is a very stable method of moving a trike through deep sand. Pulling from the front, as I must do, is inherently unstable, as it unweights the front tires, which causes the trike to want to fall to one side or the other due to the single wheel pivot point in the rear. Recumbent trikes are extremely unstable when lifted.

Once pulled back onto the road's shoulder, I kick the red dirt off my boots and settle back in for some leisurely pedaling on this frigid, yet sunny, morning. Highway 97 remains primarily slightly downhill all the way today, as I keep falling in elevation on the route to the Oregon border. At one point, there is a long and fairly steep section, perhaps a mile and a half, which allows for some quick mileage with no effort. I love these over-too-quick intervals when they happily appear. As the miles roll by at a good clip, the sun is reaching me through the trees with increasing frequency. Life is good.

Up ahead is the Collier State Park Logging Museum. The gate is open, so I swing in and coast up to a huge log picnic table, now in the sun. There are full restrooms here, along with a small gift shop, which has wood smoke gently curling up from the stovepipe in the log cabin's roof. A retired husband/wife crew are staffing this tourist stop early today. It is about 9:00 AM, and I am roughly 7 miles south of last night's camp. The friendly couple in the tiny gift shop ask me how I'm traveling. Naturally, my reply arouses the same incredulity I've come to expect. Amongst other conversation, they also say it reached a low of 23 degrees Fahrenheit this morning – explains my nearly frozen Clif bars!

After a fine dining experience in the sun on the logs, a thorough teeth cleaning, and partaking of the exquisite rest facility, I'm off to Klamath Falls. My early morning winter clothing is also all packed away again. As the morning passes into afternoon, traffic increases, but with the nice shoulders most the way, it is of little concern. Ground snow is nonexistent now. At scattered places along this route, a mammoth mountain called Shasta comes into my view, and then again disappears behind the forest – hide and go seek, or peek-a-boo.

Seventeen miles north of Klamath Falls, I pull into an independent gasoline station that has an "Under New Management" banner stretched across the store front. I think a V8 juice would be nice, as I haven't had any vegetables yet today. Within seconds after arising from my trike, I realize that stopping here may have been a mistake.

As I am walking into the store, a man who towers above my six-foot frame walks up from my left and asks if I need help. He is wearing full black leather clothing, has long hair and a beard, and is smoking a cigarette. Inside, with him behind me, I ask the man seated behind the counter if they have V8 juice. This second man sports an even more intimidating appearance, again in full black leathers, with an ample beard, chains hanging about his outfit here and there, tattoos visible, and an earring. He too is puffing on the nicotine. He informs me that they don't carry juice.

I say "thanks anyway" and turn to leave. The huge guy behind me, reminiscent of Lurch from the Addams Family television comedy many years ago, says I don't want a V8 juice. Rather forcefully in his voice, he "suggests" that I need some of their whiskey. My inner sensations are telling me that a situation may be developing here, and it would be best to depart with all due haste. Even with years of police training in my background that has taught me the essentials of surviving altercations with bad guys, I still would rather not have to deal with such thoughts, so I happily say "No thanks, I'm driving" and slide past and out the door. He follows me and continues to insist that I come back in and buy some of their stuff.

Seated in my trike, only eight inches from the ground, the Goliath stands looming above. It's kind of a vulnerable feeling, so I waste no time clicking into my pedals and getting my cranks turning. At the highway, I make a fast hard right and put the coals to the fire for some rapid travel. The upshifts come quickly, as the road is level and my legs are powerful. Feels like I just left the twilight zone. Wonder what motorists buying fuel must think. Maybe those two had just knocked off the real owner and were in the midst of a robbery when I pulled in. Perhaps they were simply posing as proprietors. I'll never know because I never looked back. Okay, that's enough excitement for today.

Klamath Lake is coming up to the southwest on my right. It's a huge lake that runs for many miles, and the road skirts it on the eastern shore. The water will be my visual companion for a long time this afternoon. Railroad tracks run between me and the big blue. It's a sunny day, with a few billowy clouds sprinkled about. Unfortunately, the wide shoulder that has graced my tire tracks since entering 97 yesterday has now disappeared. What shoulder there is certainly does not contain my 27.5 inch wheel track, and there are many times where it is no wider than about eight inches, forcing me to ride mostly in the traffic lane. The shoulder is also filthy, full of all manner of junk parts and sharp debris that constantly requires my attention to avoid ripping open a tire. This close to Klamath Falls, auto traffic has become quite heavy, so it's one car after another whizzing closely by on the one lane. Yet, due to the continual drop in elevation, I can at least keep up a decent speed, even with the trailer in tow. My trailer offsets slightly to the traffic side.

When I get to a mass of debris such as the rusted steel cords from a trucker's blown-out tire, I must sometimes slow considerably if a car is imminent, so I can actually pull out and avoid the tire-eating metal. If I think I can beat the car, I'll pick up my speed momentarily to race out around the obstacle and get back onto the minuscule shoulder. It's kind of a cat and mouse game out here.

Entering Klamath Falls, the road gains elevation on a series of small hills. Up ahead there is a truck weigh station, and since I am hungry, I pull in. With hand signals, I ask the attendant weighmaster in the glass booth if my rig can be weighed. He motions "yes" with his head, so, just like a big rig driver with my tractor and trailer, I ease the ICE Q and Burley trailer forward onto the underground scales, and then stop. Looking up at the large digital monitor, the same number registers as did in Glide several days ago: 350 pounds.

An eighteen-wheeler pulls in behind me, so I park off to the side. I wonder what the driver is thinking as he looks down from his commanding cab to see me on a tiny weird conveyance. I chat with the weighmaster for a moment and learn about how the scales round off, and since this is for trucks weighing thousands of pounds, what would normally be a small margin for them is considerable for me. I may never know the precise weight, but surely it has decreased since I left the coast last week. My original figures at home came in around 370 to 375 pounds, so again this has been confirmed. I am just way too heavy!

Here, I eat a bag of my rice and veggies dinner and finish off with a bar for dessert. I have covered a fair amount of ground so far today, have more to go, and have worked up quite an appetite. I watch the truckers come over the scales and see the digital readout really soar. Fortunately, there is an outhouse right here. This is good news because I'm still on the outskirts of town, and the road is kind of like a miniature freeway now, with no handy brush concealment anywhere close.

Once underway again, an "off ramp" splits to the right, and I must remain on the highway that stays to the left. This necessitates me getting right out in the lane of traffic to make the maneuver, but it's really no big deal, as cars are very accommodating. Besides, the road is now two lanes, so it is not difficult for them to pass me. With my 8-foot flagpoles and orange and yellow flagging, my rig is highly visible.

As I ride deeper into town, and then cross the boundary into the adjacent city of Altamont, it dawns on my calorie-deprived brain that it must be rush hour. The sun is in the right spot for it (my method of timekeeping), and the traffic just keeps getting heavier. I'm now on a main thoroughfare that connects the two cities, and attempting to follow the signposts that will direct me to California on Highway 39. At one major intersection, with three lanes in each direction, I must turn left, so out in the middle left-turn lane I pedal, with cars thick around me. My eyes are at headlight level, which makes me feel pretty puny out here.

There are no negative incidents whatsoever. All cars are treating my presence with the utmost respect, even though they are probably all eager to get home from work. Sleek new luxury sedans, old beat-up farm trucks, and large delivery vehicles honor my right to turn left. Still, I take every precaution, making sure to signal when necessary to move over a lane. I usually try to make lane changes in open spots when possible. City driving keeps my brain active.

Now, I am riding eastbound on 39 through the Altamont business district, two lanes in each direction, tons of traffic, and a nice shoulder to keep me out of the flow. The downside is that the city saw fit to place large steel gratings and other industrial stuff in the shoulder, which means that several times per block I have to veer out left. I hope the motorists don't think I'm drunk.

Sun is getting lower, and my progress has been notably slowed having to stop at traffic lights. This is my first relatively big city complex on the trip so far. I must soon locate a place to pitch my tent, because I certainly do not wish to do it after nightfall. There is a church right in the middle of all this ruckus, but I am hopeful that I can find something just outside the city limits a few miles from here. An Albertson's market is coming up. I want a couple of fresh bananas and some V8 juice (still), so I pull into the congested parking lot.

Okay, now where can I park? Since this is a big city, must I lock up the trike? I can still be ripped off from my zippered panniers, but it's just mostly clothing, nothing valuable. The trailer cargo trunk is locked, but of course, it could simply be lifted from the trailer if someone were determined. There is a large paved walkway about 15 feet wide in front of the store, so I swing around from the side and park about 30 feet south of the main doors, next to the building. My decision is to just park right out in the sunny open, where people are everywhere, and not cable lock the trike to anything. After all, no one hardly knows what this contraption is anyway, so why would they want it? And who would have the nerve to steal my wheels with so many rush-hour folks coming in and out of the market?

I abandon all fears and walk boldly away from my unsecured transport. The market is packed. I get my food, and return to my trike to eat it, keeping one banana for later. Then, it's back into the traffic stream to find a stealth camp if possible.

Things are not looking good as the road becomes increasingly rural and narrow on the southeast side of town. It's one house after another. The sun is not far from setting. Traffic is still heavy enough that my visibility at dusk will be declining very soon. Up ahead is a community college with a large parking area, so I pull in for assessment. I could pitch at the edge of the lot, where a large dirt field exists, but after walking around for a minute or two pondering this, I see that powerful street lights laced in amidst the trees will be coming on later, making me easily spotted by any police officer wishing to enforce the letter of the law. I assume it's illegal to pitch a tent on this property, so all things considered, I pedal on with an increasing sense of urgency.

The last thing I want is to get all settled in and then be ejected in the middle of the night. Not only that, but it would be nice to have a somewhat private place to offload excess water later when the impulse beckons. I highly value my sleep, privacy, and autonomy.

All the agricultural and ranching fields I am passing are privately owned and fenced. The only way off this road is on someone's private driveway. Not good for a trike pilot and a tent. My thoughts return to something Matt Jensen told me prior to leaving on this trip: churches are always good bets. Apparently, he knew this from personal experience. Maybe I will pass a church?

On the left up ahead is the Harvest Outreach Christian Center, with a generous swatch of lawn to the south of the parking area. It backs up to a farmer's field and fence. As I pull into the lot, a very well-to-do lady gets out of her car and goes inside. There is only one other car in the lot. I don't approach her because I feel my appearance

49

would frighten her. We have eye contact, but I remain distant at the end of the lot, where I park the trike.

After removing my helmet and dishtowel from my head (the towel is used to keep me shaded from the sun), and sprucing up my social facade as much as possible, inside the double doors of this refined sanctuary I meekly stride, knowing not what I'll find. There is organ music coming from what appears a large and ornate chapel area. It is the same well-dressed lady playing. A large stately gentleman in a suit is standing near her and the stage, so down the isle I proceed to meet him, attempting to structure my thoughts and needs into a presentation that will bestow pity upon my poor and unsheltered self. My current appearance does not exude a feeling of confidence or safety in others, especially since I buzzed my head last week to keep the need for washing my hair minimal on the road, and my beard may make me appear even more publicly divergent. I could be an escaped convict!

Briefly, I tell Ben and Clara Wampler, the two pastors, of my journey, my former law enforcement background (to instill needed trust), and my need for a place to erect my night's shelter before darkness sets in. I ask if I could camp on the far south lawn. Happily, Ben, a gargantuan man, agrees with a smile and hearty handshake, and even offers the restroom should I need it. Turns out a large communal gathering is about to begin here in a little over an hour, so I take my leave and try to become invisible in the grass.

The tent pitches quickly on the padded lawn. Ben assured me that no automatic sprinklers would be coming on tonight. I can hear the horses whinnying at the farm next door. Traffic is still heavy on Highway 39, only 25 yards distant, but I am safe at last in my temporary haven, with full permission no less! It is a comforting thought. I barely have time to eat some more food before the sun is gloriously setting across the fields to the west. It feels like nirvana after my Cascade traverse!

The cellular telephone service is also excellent, which allows me to notify one of my three blog correspondents of my daily progress, something that does not happen every night due to lack of service. These folks are keeping a weblog updated during this journey to Death Valley, so anyone interested in my travels might follow along at home. The blog is aptly named Badwater or Bust, the Death Valley Tricycle Expedition. Link: http://badwater.wordpress.com/

The weather is warm here. No snow. No rain. No wind. No cold hands. I will sleep well tonight after pedaling 45 miles today. The super thick grass underneath the tent makes for the finest of cushion. It is even warm enough that I lie atop the bag for a while as I write in my journal before calling it a day. Tomorrow, I shall finally leave Oregon.

DAY 8 - *Death Valley*
Thursday, October 08, 2009
Altamont, Oregon to Modoc National Forest boundary, California – 37 miles (running total: 299 miles)

There is another upside to this thick deep grass on the field where I am camped, and as I am preparing for today's ride, it becomes apparent. It makes for an automatic cleaning solution!

My rear dérailleur on the trike, the mechanism that changes the rear gears for those who are unfamiliar, was totally covered in dirt and grime during my previous camp. On that old overgrown road next to Highway 97, I had to pedal through soft earth, and turn the trike around, which caused the low dérailleur to drag through the soil and bushes. Since the chain is lubricated, and the various sprockets therefore also have lubricant on them, the dirt immediately stuck to every exposed piece of metal. It was so heavy that I wondered if I would be able to shift properly. The sight was enough to bring any cyclist to tears!

I cleaned it off the best I could that night and next morning (because I had to ride to the pavement), but out here on the open road, I can't do the best job. Well, the grass at the Harvest Christian Outreach Center reached out and did what I could not. Thousands of green blades of the lawn, tall and thick as they were, essentially provided the ultimate cleaning with no added effort on my part. Just riding out to where I pitched the tent got the sprockets and chain fastidiously fresh once again. And this morning, I have to ride over to the parking lot, further cleaning the works. It must be providence, considering my location.

The full and warming sun is up early here, as this is flat and open agricultural countryside now. I am south of the massive skybound mountains, but more will be coming later today and tomorrow. There is minimal dew on the tent fly and footprint, yet it dries quickly in the full unobstructed sun. Eating my Nutty Nuggets breakfast is painless here, as I watch tons of commuter traffic and school buses whiz by on the Oregon/California connecting highway. The setting is so comforting that I almost hate to leave, but hey, trike hobos are always on the move!

Today's ride should prove relaxing, with few, if any, uphill grades. Later this morning, I will be entering California, leaving behind my home state. There is something about crossing borders, even if they are only arbitrary and imaginary human political lines on my planet. Today's crossing, which will probably only be marked by a sign, signifies that I am indeed a long way from whence I started. It may be considered short in the minds of fast paced petroleum powered humans, but in my

51

human-powered world, this is clearly significant. It makes me proud to know that all these miles are achieved by my own sweat and muscle. What is mundane to the multitudes is monumental to me.

Perhaps after a few more long distance tours on the trike, I will see this distance as less important an achievement than I do now, but for my first cross-country ride, I find pleasure in slowly but surely attaining this personal success. I am making a difference for the air of my world, a distinction that few people would even recognize. I am passing silently into a new paradigm of living for myself. Practically no one would choose to celebrate this quiet abandonment of my former transportation model, so I do it by myself, out here on the open road. It is a road with two meanings, the physical one of my actual travel, and the symbolic one that leads to new and harmonious horizons of my relationship to Earth. It's easier to philosophize when the weather is warm and sunny. I best get going! Things are looking up and yes, the Earth is flat.

No one is at the church this early, so I cannot thank them for the fine lodging. I must wait at the road entrance of the parking lot for traffic to thin a bit before I pull out onto the narrow country road called Highway 39. Fortunately, from here south, the automobile congestion lessens quickly in the rural regions through which I will be pedaling for a long time now. I stick out like a brilliant beacon with my flagging, so the cars that do overtake the ten feet of my trike and trailer are not surprised; they can see me far in advance in this flat and open terrain. As has been my experience so far, nearly all motorists are courteous and provide plenty of room as they pass. Former fears were unfounded.

What a way to see the countryside! Reclined a comfortable 37 degrees off the horizontal, the mesh seat of my ICE Q tricycle provides a show like I am sitting at home in the lounger. It's better than passively watching television, for this is real adventure unfolding, with no set script. It is a documentary directed by me, one where I actively participate and gain life extension benefits in the process. My spirits are up with the sun! Piloting a trike is hard, but highly satisfying, work.

About seven miles north of a tiny Oregon town called Merrill, the last one prior to the border, I pull into a little business called Mac's Store. It's out here in the middle of farm country, with nothing much else than an occasional farm house and lots of roadside fences. There are two reasons for stopping. First, I desire to use a sit-down solid waste station, and second, I think I need some non-steroidal anti-inflammatory drugs. Or, put into the typical initialed vernacular so prevalent in our society, I seek SDSWS and NSAID. Okay, you figure out the first one based on what you read in this paragraph.

The elder lone woman behind the counter directs me to the

nearby plastic outhouse for customers, telling me that there is no such indoor plumbing in the small building. The large clock on the wall shows 10 AM. She adds that even she must use it each day. Oh well, when nature calls, one cannot always be picky. My diet high in grains and vegetables makes the business quick and easy, as I listen to cars rocket by twenty feet to my right. Good thing the plastic walls are not clear.

Back in the store, I ask her if they carry any ibuprofen products, explaining about my increasingly inflamed Achilles tendons. Apparently, something is amiss with my foot situation, but I do not really have a handle on what it is. Each morning since my nighttime Cascade traverse, both tendons are stiff, and require increasingly more easy pedal time before they warm up for unhampered performance. It is an annoyance only, as once they warm up within the first mile or so, I have no negative sensations whatsoever, and only a visual inspection would reveal any swelling. I originally thought the rubbing of the Hi-Tec waterproof boots was causing the tenderness, but I must have been incorrect in that assessment. Something is not right.

Anyway, the lady says they don't carry Advil or any of the other types of these drugs. I started on self-prescribed aspirin therapy last night, but wondered if Advil would fix me up faster. Normally, I don't do drugs, but I can't let this little tendon issue obstruct my journey. Feeling sorry for me, she pulls a bottle from her purse. She uses it for her arthritis pain. In the spirit of helping a fellow human in distress, she pours out a supply that will last me several days, and tells me how many to take. I am grateful for her willingness to assist, especially since this stuff is rather pricey compared to aspirin. She accepts no payment.

I then buy a couple of bananas and a V8 juice, and sit down at their small table for a snack, which also includes a Clif bar. There is a daily newspaper here, but being a dropout from all the nastiness of habitually headlined human hatred, I opt to ignore it, and instead converse with the clerk. I am feeling no sense of urgency to get back on the road quickly. I am living in the here and now, reveling in the senses associated with this tiny entrepreneurial enterprise on the expanses of southern Oregon. I enjoy the hospitality, the rural atmosphere, the sounds of country travelers out on the road. I am very alive, and excited about my trek through life. I savor every sight, sound, taste, smell, and texture. I think a trike trip accentuates these sensory delights, at least for anyone open to accepting them with a happy spirit.

Once back out on 39, it's a laid-back jaunt to Merrill, where I choose to again stop and experience the people and atmosphere. A couple more bananas make their way into my stomach, and at the larger store here, I also purchase a small bottle of Motrin, figuring that it will knock-out the swelling prior to the last pill. It is pleasant speaking with the small town locals, who eagerly come up to see my unusual mode of transport. Everyone asks the same questions at each stop, but that's okay, because I endeavor to be an enthusiastic ambassador for human powered alternatives to spewing lethal toxins into our finite air supply.

This is travel at its best, not only because of its clean and green consequences, but also because of the nice people I meet when not in a hurry to cover hundreds of miles in one day. By its very nature, the trike inspires me to take life slower, both physically and mentally. At the same time, the trike is making me healthier in the process. It's a win/win situation in all respects, assuming the rider is willing to relinquish the need for speed. Slow down. Enjoy the details of my world.

Somewhere in the neighborhood of 1 PM, several miles south of Merrill, I see a rather large blue sign up ahead on the right, held aloft by two metal supports. There are illustrations of golden orange poppy flowers on the sign, and large letters that read: "Welcome to California"

Now, I know precisely where I am! On that thin black map line that separates two states, I park the Q right in front of the border sign for a couple of digital photographs. After all, I have to prove to any skeptical folks that I really have ridden my tricycle at least this far. There is no one around to get me in the picture, and I don't recall how to use the camera's self timer, so I just shoot the trike and trailer. I would have had to set the camera in the dirt anyway, as everything out here is flat as a pancake. I am now leaving the Beaver State, and entering the Golden.

Roughly seven miles into the Golden State, I roll into the small village of Tulelake, an agricultural town by what I can see, things like grain bins. I wonder if the "Tule" part of Tulelake has something to do with being out in the tules, for it most certainly is. Heck, I don't even know if tule is how the word for a remote place is spelled, but it sounds correct anyway. Certainly, I am far from everything I know.

I have to turn right and ride over some railroad tracks to reach the town's market, where I park the Q out front, to the curious stares and smiles of local resident shoppers. This is a very relaxing atmosphere.

My right shift cable, the one that changes the gears on the rear cassette of the trike, has been making a strange little squeak sound on my midrange shifts for a few miles now, so I check inside the store to see if they have anything that might mitigate the noise. Their hardware and auto section is very short on common supplies, so back out front I go, where I meet Fermi Sandoval, a sixty-something local handyman, who has an old pickup truck full of all kind of various and odd supplies.

After explaining my mystery noise, he hands me a can of WD-40, which I squirt into the upper cable landing. I don't know if I'm supposed to be doing this, but if it terminates the faint, but annoying, sound, and helps lubricate whatever is amiss, then I'll be happy. I can only hear the noise under the most quiet of conditions, but it wasn't there for the first six days of this trip. I wonder if all the dirt at my Highway 97 camp had anything to do with it.

Fermi and I bid each other a cordial farewell, and he wishes me all the best in my travels. Back over the tracks to the main highway I go, resuming my southeast path to Death Valley. With this flat road, I am able to clip along in high-range gears at a decent speed, which is a good thing because with all the time I've been spending chatting with the small town folks along the way, I'll be lucky to get much mileage in today. For me though, the human relationships in the small towns of my journey are more important than just seeing if I can crank out loads of miles each day. I am living in a bold new world, not known by others.

Not far out of Tulelake, a long pasture area is coming up on my left, and I see a black stallion heading my way, accompanied by perhaps a dozen other horses. He is definitely focused on me, as I am the only thing happening out here. As I get closer, he begins to run towards me, as if to greet my silent, but very visible, passage. I call out a cheery "Hello horse" as I pass, ever enjoying my conversations with other species of animals, and I give the horses a wave. I also speed up some, because it looks like the stallion is rather frisky and wanting some play.

Sure enough, he, followed by his group, charge along the fence line only one lane removed from me. This goes on for roughly a half mile, as the fenced area is truly a large acreage. The stallion is moving his head left and right, snorting, and doing all sorts of actions indicative of an animal fully engaged with attempting to comprehend my bizarre appearance. The experience is truly exhilarating for me, and I assume also for the horses, based on their behavior, which ends as I exceed the distance of their freedom. They seemed very happy. What a grand day!

Two miles later, a little red ladybug lands upon my left knee, moving up and down with the knee as I pedaled each revolution on the recumbent trike. On a regular bicycle, such an occurrence would not be so comfortably observable. This ladybug is right in front of my eyes the way I sit. A mile later, my lilliputian red friend takes off to who knows where. I say goodbye, and wonder what the ladybug hears.

Highway 139 would be more aptly named Potato Highway, so that is the new moniker I bestow upon it as I cycle through California's most northern reaches. Of all the farms and ranches in this vast Klamath Basin, potato farms seem the most prevalent for many miles here. The Wong Potato Farm must be the king of all such farms, as nearly every huge potato truck that passes me in both directions has the Wong name on the side. Potatoes are stacked up to overflowing on these monster vehicles, and some fall off, onto the highway margins.

The Potato Highway is littered with abandoned potatoes along the shoulder for miles. Sometimes I have to steer around them. If I were low on food, the free supply is ample, and I could easily snatch up scores of potatoes as I ride by. With my rear end only eight inches from the pavement, it is an easy matter to pick up anything lying on the roadway. Gee, I could even eat on the go! Some are pretty well dinged up from hitting the ground, but most are surprisingly intact. A simple washing would have provided me plenty of carbohydrates and natural sugars, but having spent so much time thus far today talking with everyone I meet, my focus now moves to reaching the distant mountains to pitch a tent later this afternoon.

Most of the potato truck drivers find my odd appearance amusingly curious, and wave or toot their air horns. We smile and wave. This plays out for many miles and a few hours. I've never seen so many potatoes in my life. I should spear one on my front dérailleur post for some light hearted fun, but my speed is up so I keep on chuggin' along.

The day is perfectly temperate for long distance trike touring. With the sun out, cold is a thing of the past. All I need on my torso is my long sleeve light cotton shirt. Too bad I don't have my Shimano SPD open-toed sandals now, for they would provide the perfect atmosphere for my toes. At least the Merrill Moab Ventilator boots are pleasantly cool. What a difference this is from several days ago in the Cascade Range! It's hard to imagine it's the same time of year. Autumn is usually very mild, but that uncommon snow storm sure surprised everyone.

The road ahead begins transforming from flat to hilly as the afternoon wears on. The elevation is now perceptibly increasing, and my speeds slow to midrange. Juniper and pinyon trees, at first scattered randomly about the countryside, thicken the farther I progress. Farms and ranches become less dense, until I see no more at all. The ground appears volcanic, with millions of the rocks everywhere. According to the map, I am not far from the northwestern Modoc National Forest boundary, and since it's getting close to camp time, my eyes start their standard daily search for the ideal wild trike hobo camping spot.

Well, as luck would have it, a camp area with a wonderful view crops up on the right, so I gear down to low range for extra traction, and pull in on the soft and silty dirt road. It's fairly deep in spots, and requires aggressive pedaling to reach the perfect tent setting under a large tree. There is a large turn-around area of dirt road circling the tree, but to pedal my trike into facing the other direction would be far too tedious considering the nearly total lack of traction. Okay, it's up to my old tricks of turning the trike and trailer around by hand as I stand alongside. The maneuvering raises a dusty powder and gets my boots, the rear dérailleur, and chain totally filthy again. So much for my grassy cleanup last night! Oh well, the life of a trike hobo is filled always new.

Perched high in the tree above me, out of my visual senses, comes the sweet sounds of a single singing bird. Is this little creature welcoming me to this remote realm? It seems so, and as I pitch my camp, I relax in the charming melody of primitive song. Life doesn't get any better than this! I'm the only human around.

Not more than 50 yards to my south is the large wooden sign for the Modoc National Forest, so I am easily able to pinpoint my precise location on the map, right where the highway enters the green shaded portion on the paper. The elevation is still relatively low, so no ponderosa pines exist here, only pinyon and juniper. Off in the distance to the southwest, I can clearly see a massive volcano called Mount Shasta. I have driven past this mountain many times in my life on Interstate-5, but have never seen it from this viewpoint until right now. In my mind, I can imagine the whole cartographic assemblage of features, and have an excellent sense of my current place in it.

I am just off the paved highway by a few yards, but there is little traffic this far out, so the sounds of nature keep me company with little interruption from whining rubber tires. My bird continues to serenade me, as I eat dinner and walk around my private camp, taking in all that the natural world provides my spirit. There is a stand of trees that hides me from the highway to a certain extent, but it doesn't matter. No one stops or bothers me. I feel totally safe and happy.

A half hour after the gorgeous sunset, I finally crawl into the REI Arête tent, write in my journal, and call it a day. That was an enjoyable 37 miles, well worth taking my time. Having left myself abundant time to make this trip, I feel no anxiety on lower mileage days. That is the best way. Other than whacking myself on the noggin with a thick low branch of my camp tree when I was pitching the tent, the day was without negative incident. A warm breeze lulls me into a restful and long sleep, out here in the great wide open.

DAY 9 - *Death Valley*
Friday, October 09, 2009
Modoc National Forest boundary to Canby, California – 44 miles
(running total: 343 miles)

Today, I plan to traverse part of the Modoc National Forest, drop out at the tiny town of Canby, and then head slightly northeast on

Highway 299 towards Alturas, California. The map mileage looks doable, but of course, that depends on how the terrain dictates my progress. I won't know until I go! I should be pretty close to Nevada by the time the sun again sets, at least by automobile standards.

As I am still in the process of awakening, my mind reviews the expedition progress thus far. I'm about 640 miles out from Badwater Basin in Death Valley at this point, having ridden a little more than 300 miles up to last evening. Other than my potential disaster up in the Oregon Cascades, everything is coming along quite smoothly, yet still, I wouldn't trade that mountain traverse for anything. I felt more alive and thoroughly engaged in the now than ever that night. Yep, living on the edge makes for an interesting life, and makes us stronger in mind and body. Trikers live on the edge as part of their normal existence.

Before I started on this journey, I did quite a bit of reading from other long distance trikers and bikers. One thing I found to be unfortunately common is the frequency that flat tires occur. My friend Dan Price took a 4500 mile trike trip on a TerraTrike a few years ago, and had so many flats between eastern Oregon and Portland that I wondered if there was a better way to do tires. The last thing I want to be doing is changing tires on the roadside!

This is why I opted to go overboard with my tire setup on the trike, as I mentioned earlier. If all the hype of manufacturers was right, I shouldn't have any flats, and so far, that has proven accurate. Three hundred miles and not one flat tire! All five are still holding air just fine. Of course, I didn't do the same tire setup on my Burley trailer because it already came fully tired, and I had no more money I could spend on tires at the point I acquired the Burley. It would have run another $150 to outfit the trailer like I did the trike. I am hoping the trailer's Kenda tires and stock tubes go the distance, but I am more concerned for the trailer than the trike when I ride through heavy shoulder debris now and then.

I have one spare Schwalbe Marathon-Plus tire bungee corded under the trailer, just in case I end up shredding a tire somewhere. These Marathon-Plus tires are like steel! Mounting them is one big pain in the neck (and thumbs), but having done so six times for pre-trip practice, I have full faith that they will get me to Badwater without incident. Those tires, along with the ultra-thick thorn resistant Q Tubes and EarthGuard tire liners ease my mind when the going gets sharp and tacky.

This morning, the air is dramatically warmer than it has been earlier in the trip. I am in the Modoc National Forest, but the trees are still sparse and small at this elevation, so my camp receives full morning sun. This allows me to have my normal Nutty Nuggets breakfast right here, after I break down camp and pull the trike by the front dérailleur post out into the sun on the dirt road. I like the price of these roadside camps, and I like the peace and quiet too. Why pay a campground fee to be mixed in with a lot of people and feisty kids, when I can do this for free? And this camp has a glorious morning view of Mount Shasta, with its early reddish glow. If my inexpensive digital camera had a telephoto option, I could get a nice shot of the volcano, but it's too far away for the camera to do it justice. My eyes work just fine however.

Somewhere around 20 miles into the day, I arrive at a California State Agricultural Inspection Station, for inbound trucks and vehicles. Locating a bathroom would be convenient right about now, and I figure they must have several up ahead. I brought along a folding toilet, which I have in my trailer cargo trunk, but have not used it yet. I considered doing so before I left camp this morning, but figured that sooner or later I'd come across a store or something. The toilet consists of a normal seat with four folding aluminum legs. It's very lightweight, and takes up virtually no room in the trunk because it folds nearly flat. Matt Jensen had a good laugh before I left, saying I wouldn't need such a thing. Well, I've carried it for years, back when I drove a 4x4 vehicle through the wilds of the planet, and it can come in real handy at times. Not only that, but the views while using it surpass even the best of bathrooms! Makes daily business a thing of pure pleasure.

Okay, so I pedal into the agricultural inspection station in lane one. Traffic is light to nonexistent. All the employees come out with their digital cameras and ask to snap a few shots of me. Guess they must not see too many trikers ride this road. Heck, maybe they've never even seen one, other than me, of course. Obligingly, I sit and smile and tell my story. Then, in return for my patience and sharing, I ask where their restroom is located. I am told it is out of order, and no facility exists currently. This seems highly unlikely and illogical to me, for this station is seriously out in the middle of proverbial nowhere, and the employees must drive for some great distances to get here I reckon, unless they live in a small handful of log cabins just across the highway.

Even when I tell them I'm a retired cop, hinting that I'm trustworthy and in need, the answer is still the same. No amount of cajoling, even my pleading that on a tricycle my travel is so slow that I could be many hours from a toilet, improves my situation one iota. People in cars can be down to Canby in short order, as the mountains don't slow them. But my situation is radically different. You know how it is when you think you are about to use a toilet? Seems like psychologically the urge increases about five-fold, right? The closer you get, the more you have to go! Well, seeing I'm at a dead end with these folks, I hightail it back out on the highway, hoping for a solution soon.

Thanks California. You got your photographs and amusement this morning when I pedaled in. What did I get? Seems like it could have been a fair trade to me. They must have figured that if they let one use the throne, they'd have to let everyone else who asks. Of course, I was the only one here to know about it. And, no one else rides a tricycle!

Oh well, within a half mile, my brain suppresses the need enough that I can carry on, especially after offloading the liquid portion. It's still a long way to Canby via trike. If things progress to that point, I can still use my portable facility in the woods, which are becoming increasingly thicker and more user friendly from a privacy standpoint.

Around 17 miles farther on, I reach a high pass later in the afternoon. Guess my body has burned up all the extra food inside me, as I'm doing fine now, likely in a calorie deficit condition anyway. From the AG station to here, the mountainous road has been slow going, with uphill grades and increasing elevation. Stretched out below me are miles of downhill. Steep downhill! Yahoo!

Rest time has arrived. This will be one big-time coast to the distant bottom, probably about seven miles worth! The map indicates that I am soon to leave the Modoc National Forest, probably somewhere during this rapid descent. Down I go, faster and faster, and when a rare car does pass me, it's not going that much faster than me! I am traveling just under 50 miles per hour on this stretch, and the speed limit is 55. Now isn't that a hoot! Talk about a great adrenaline rush of pure excitement – this makes all the uphills worth every effort needed to reach the top! Wonder what that last motorist thought when he saw me? Probably his first time! Surely, it left an impression!

The curves are mostly open and gradual, requiring only a little bit of body lean to maintain full tilt and not use the brakes. With my ultra-low center of gravity on this British ICE Q trike, along with the road-absorbing suspension system, there is nothing to slow me down. Even pulling this heavy trailer does not seem to affect my handling at all. Now, if the road curves were tight, then the trailer would be a hindrance, but here, and on most of these highway descents, the curves allow cars to maintain highway speeds, so the trike and trailer perform superbly. I like finishing off a day with a special treat like this.

The mountains are now casting longer shadows as I reach the 'T' intersection of Highway 299, having left the national forest a few miles back. I made it all the way through the forest lands in one day. This junction is where I now turn left, or east, towards Canby, Alturas, Cedarville, and ultimately the most remote and dangerous stretches of the northwestern Nevada desert, out where the alternative Burning Man city comes to life once each September. I lost an incredible amount of elevation in that descent, but realize that I will have to regain it somewhere along the route prior to reaching my objective in Death Valley. The journey started at sea level and is going to below sea level, but there are lands of many mountains on my gauntlet in between.

Having made the turn east on 299, I can see buildings up ahead, and in a half mile, I pass the Canby, California "city" limit sign, which reveals a population of 413 residents who prefer solitude in a serious way. This tiny village is a long way from anywhere, as has been my journey since leaving Tulelake. I like it this way though, much better than crowded city streets and hundreds of cars. Okay, they must have a restroom here someplace! Gotta' go find it – gotta' go!

As soon as I enter the town, I can see the other end. It is only a few blocks long, what there is of it anyway. An old defunct motel on my right sits decaying in the late afternoon sun. On the left is a motel and bar combo business, so I park the Q to go inside and inquire about camping. There are a couple of twenty-something guys next door at an old gasoline station, one with tattoos and an earring, but they seem benign enough, as I assess my trike's safety quickly in my mind. Even though I do my best to not prejudge folks, old teachings die hard, and the traditional markers of fear for well-to-do folk are all over.

I'm tired. I'll take my chances. After all, what would they do with my gear anyway? I could scour the town in minutes on foot. I tell myself what a fool I am for falling prey to such ridiculous thought in the first place. Gee, if they look at me, which they do, I look a whole lot more suspicious and misguided than they do! And I bet I smell a whole lot worse too. Trike hobos rarely, if ever, pedal through here!

The heavy-set gal running the dark and empty bar and motel puffs on a cigarette and watches a football game on the television above the bar as I walk in, taking off my cycling helmet. I inquire about camping or, in the alternative, a room here. She says all her rooms are booked for tonight (strange, as no other cars are anywhere around, and the town appears completely deserted but for the three people I've seen so far). She also has no idea of where I could pitch a camp, but tells me to talk to the two guys at the gas station. Maybe they'll know something. I ask if I could use the restroom. She says "sure" and points down the long narrow dark hall towards the back of the old building.

It's a tight squeeze to get in the little room, and there are signs about how long to hold down the handle, and not to leave the faucet water turned on. Better late than never, especially considering I have no idea where I'll be camping tonight. Relief at long last.

Business done, I walk next door to inquire of the guys about a camp. The Q is still exactly how I left it. They are amazed at what I am out here doing, and how far I've come. Actually, they are both really nice guys. They just look a little ragged around the edges. The main fellow who runs the aging station points across the street to the town's park and recreation facility, which is but a minuscule building. He says that I can camp in the back, completely out of sight. He also adds this proviso: "Just don't die back there, because you won't be found for a long time." Well, that's just what I want to hear. It means I'll have the whole place to myself!

I thank him and pedal on over, timing my ride to not get hit by the eighteen wheeler coming through. There are two chain link fence gates into the one-acre area. The one to my left heads through a paved basketball court, and the one to my right heads down a walkway and around the corner by a huge tree. Six to one, half a dozen to the other. I chose the larger of the two gates and head into the basketball area.

Being the fall, there are about seven inches of colored birch leaves all over the ground by this gate, which crunch as I ride through them. Once into the court, I can see it is completely fenced in, and entrance to the rear park area is not to be had this way, so I turn the trike around and head back through the huge pile of leaves. It's about twenty feet across, and I enjoy the sounds of pedaling through the crisp leaves. Through the other gate I go, but since there is a three inch rise in the paved walkway from the dirt right at the gate line, and it is barely wide enough for the trike and trailer, I get off and guide the trike through while standing.

This is when I notice I have a very unwelcomed problem that will have a dubious outcome. This is a cyclist's worst nightmare! Or if not the worst, right up there near the top of the list anyway.

Just inside the gate on the walkway that leads to the large grassy park area, my keen eyeballs, tired as they are, pick up on the fact that my left front tire no longer has a black tread. It appears to now be a whitish beige. Pulling off my dark polarized polycarbonate sunglasses and stooping over a bit to get a clearer look, I am in disbelief of what I am seeing. This is a major issue if I've ever seen one.

By the way, I got these polycarbonate sunglasses so that if a tire from a speeding motorist threw up a rock, I'd still have eyes with which to see. Polycarb doesn't shatter like ordinary glass, or break up like traditional plastic lenses. My $125 Serengeti sunglasses, with real glass, stayed at home this trip. When you're cycling at tire level, can't be too careful. I also have found that the polarization is a great feature! This is my first pair of sunglasses with this, and I am impressed with the difference between them and regular lenses. All the glare from the road, water, or darn near anything shiny simply disappears, making it much

62

easier to see where I'm going. This feature also keeps me from squinting so much, thereby prolonging my childlike facial skin texture (*Give me a break. Can we just get back to the story please?*).

Well, sometimes if I fail to mention something right when it crosses my aging mind, I might never mention it, so I take what comes as it comes. Okay, yeah, back to the big brewing crisis in my mind at the Canby "city" park – check this out:

The reason the tire's tread is no longer black (and that's no fooling either) is due to the fact that the entire tread surface all around the tire is covered in a certain nasty portion of the Tribulus terrestris plant – at the very minimum I'd say at least 100 of these dreaded tube slayers, commonly known as goatheads, have firmly embedded themselves in the tread like ticks on a deer. It's unnerving! I have heard about them, and the horror stories associated with being so unfortunate to ride through a community of the merciless spikes, but this is the first time I've actually seen one personally. And I'm not just seeing one either! I'm seeing hundreds at once. It's not a pretty sight.

I'm trying to ignore what my peripheral vision is sending my way, from over on the right side of the trike, but alas, I must glance over. Dang if the right tire isn't similarly affected! Being the astute triker genius that I am, I deduce that perhaps the tires that came after these front two might also have been the unhappy recipients of this little Canby welcome souvenir, and a quick check reveals that the remainder of my afternoon will be laden with pulling chores. Yep, sure enough, the treads of all five of my tires are literally covered completely with goatheads. No tread is visible, on any tire, period. It's my lucky day!

From Wikipedia, here is a wee bit of background information for those not yet initiated:

"It is a taprooted herbaceous perennial plant that grows as a summer annual in colder climates. The stems radiate from the crown to a diameter of about 10 cm to over 1 m, often branching. They are usually prostrate, forming flat patches, though they may grow more upwards in shade or among taller plants. The leaves are pinnately compound with leaflets less than a quarter-inch long. The flowers are 4–10 mm wide, with five lemon-yellow petals. A week after each flower blooms, it is followed by a fruit that easily falls apart into four or five single-seeded nutlets. The nutlets or 'seeds' are hard and bear two to three sharp spines, 10 mm long and 4–6 mm broad point-to-point. These nutlets strikingly resemble goats' or bulls' heads; the 'horns' are sharp enough to puncture bicycle tires and to cause painful injury to bare feet."

Okay, so here I am in a little remote village called Canby, days from the nearest bicycle shop, with five tires full of nutlets! I hate it when that happens. I was also considering riding on to Alturas this afternoon, 18 miles east, as the light is still in the sky, but this seals the deal. I'm not going anywhere. Good thing I have boots on at least. It's a bad seed day – forget about my hair.

Right on the walkway, I begin carefully extracting these ugly horns from my tires with my Swiss army knife, and as I do, I kick them into the grass so that when I come out of here tomorrow morning, I won't run over the same ones a second time. A simple flick with the blade dislodges all but the most stubborn. My back starts aching after quite a while of doing this, seeing as how there are literally hundreds of these nutlets in my tires, so I just kneel and continue on. I have to keep rolling the trike forward a bit at a time to move the next batch to the top. Most of them are gone now, so I go ahead and roll my rig to the rear of the building to begin setting camp.

What a beautiful little park this is. It's all fenced in, with fields just outside the fencing. There is running water too, so I can refill my dangerously low water supply. Things are looking up. There is even an electrical outlet so I can finally recharge the cell phone I borrowed for this journey. I have no idea if the sprinklers will automatically come on tonight, so I set the tent up on the concrete area, underneath a huge old oak tree. With my air mattress, it won't make any difference. A few feet away are recycling bins for cardboard, plastic, and glass. There is even a bar area, where the fire department auxiliary sells beer on hot summer days, or at least that's what the signs indicate. Five large picnic tables allow for plenty of room to spread out my stuff as I prep my camp.

The tent is set, the sun is getting low, and all feels comfy and under control, as much as it can be anyway, considering that I could have five flats sometime soon. Popping out the remaining goatheads, I see something that further gets my attention. A tiny little gray speck, about the size of a pinpoint, is on the tread of one tire. It looks no different than a minuscule speck of dirt, and I would normally never even pay it any mind. Using the point of my knife blade, I try to scrape it off. It doesn't move. Now, I try carefully prying at it, and after a few seconds, my worst fears are confirmed. A spike broken off from one of the goatheads I pulled out earlier finally comes out with my knife blade. It is several millimeters long. Further investigation reveals that these little specks are also all over the five tires, so when I thought the large head portion was all there was, I was wrong. Due to my inattentive and fast removal of the goatheads using a simple sideways scraping method, I had inadvertently broken off many of the spikes, which remain in the

64

tires. My laborious work was just beginning.

They are really hard to even find, but at least the soon-to-be-setting sun is brightly illuminating my treads. Every little speck I pry at is indeed another of these broken-off thorns, and when each one comes out, I am astounded at how long they are, certainly long enough to pierce a traditional bicycle tire and tube. Obviously, these things were under all those lovely leaves through which I pedaled at the basketball court. This entire mess is consuming a lot of my time because I have to keep rotating the tires to make sure I don't miss any that could continue to work their way into the rubber if I were to ride on them tomorrow. I'm getting hungry now, but I must finish this unpleasant chore before the sun sets, as it requires good light to see these nearly invisible gremlins. Ahh, the joys of being a trike hobo!

At long last it is done! My treads are once again black, spic and span clean. I wonder to myself what local kids must feel if they come to the park barefooted. Ouch! These hideous things are seriously harmful to anything they touch. Amazingly, I didn't prick myself at all.

Now, all I can do is wait and see if anything develops. The three trike tires all feel solid as ever, holding their maximum 70 pounds of air. The left trailer tire seems fine also, apparently holding its 65 pound maximum. The right trailer tire seems a little squishy, but not bad. I'll have to keep an eye on it. Just to make sure by tomorrow morning, I get out my Topeak Road Morph pump and make sure all five are at max air tonight. Then, I turn my attention to other things.

First order of business is dinner. As I eat, I can see the long road to Alturas stretching out east from here. The elevation declines in that direction, as Canby sits in the foothills of the northeastern most remnants of the Sierra Nevada Mountains. A fair amount of traffic, especially trucks, is traveling Highway 299 this evening. Tomorrow I will be on that road, which appears easy going considering the elevation drop. By tomorrow night, I should be somewhere past Cedarville, up in the forest near the Nevada border, and then by Sunday, my journey will doubtless be heading across the notorious Black Rock Desert in Nevada, the epitome of utter remoteness! It could also be hot there.

That northern section of Nevada desert presents my greatest food and water challenge, for one stretch is more than 80 miles of literal nothingness, meaning no re-supply areas such as stores, houses, or people. On a tricycle pulling a trailer, 80 miles can translate into two days easily, especially since there are several small mountain grades out there, one of which a pre-trip telephone call to the local Sheriff verified was quite long and steep from a cyclist's viewpoint. If I break down out there, the cell phone will be my needed salvation. Here, the day prior to this section of the trek, I ride through a goathead patch, Murphy's Law!

Jack Freer is the Chief Deputy with the Carson City, Nevada Sheriff's Department. Nearing retirement, he is a serious Death Valley enthusiast, and we met online a year or so ago when he began communicating with me about one of my Death Valley websites. He wanted to meet me out there on my next expedition, but little did he realize that I had sold my Xterra SUV. As things came to pass though, it all came together, and he agreed to be my failsafe squad in exchange for me showing him around the national park in his Jeep. Can't beat that offer, I thought, so I at least know that Jack is in my corner.

I haven't yet met him in person, but we have spoken extensively on the telephone regarding trip plans and preparation. We have a solid plan in place, which includes him meeting up with me in western Nevada just before I hit Death Valley National Park. We will camp together, and he will follow me in on a dirt road I have been planning to take from the northern boundary. Although, considering how poorly the trike performs in deep sand, I am now rethinking this dirt road idea, and instead considering using pavement, which will add about 45 miles to the trip. We shall see.

Anyway, Jack has instructed me to call him at any time if I hopelessly break down and am in need of assistance or rescue. He can be anywhere in the northern Nevada region in a matter of hours, and he assured me that he's got me covered. This eases my mind as I stare off into the vast expanse of tomorrow's ride. Jack is also one of three correspondents with whom I am sharing my trek as I progress. I call these folks on the cell phone, when and where there is service, tell them what the latest is, and then they post it on the Badwater or Bust blog set up for folks who have requested to follow along at home. I decided not to bring a laptop computer and do it myself, for I would never get anywhere once I started typing at a Wi-Fi hotspot. Not only that, but a tiny cell phone is a heck of a lot lighter than a laptop, and my rig is already way too heavy as it is. I can't afford to go any slower!

With all my camp chores complete, and dusk yet providing light, I retrieve my charging cell phone and try to call a couple of people. It has been a day since I have had service, so I must make up for lost details. Each time I call, I have my journal handy to remind me of the events, and the correspondent has pen and paper handy on their end (which is all cozy in their homes while I am out in the open wild lands).

First, I call Desert Dune, the lead correspondent. After relaying all the latest updates for a new blog post, Desert Dune informs me that extremely hazardous weather is predicted for my intended path, and there has been a lot of chatter on the blog as people are worried I don't know about it yet. True enough, this is the first I've heard of it. Everything seems fine looking at the sky here in Canby right now.

Desert Dune tells me that I must immediately call Jack, because he has all the details printed out from the National Weather Service website. Apparently, a typhoon called Melor has been wreaking havoc out in Pacific Ocean, and it has made landfall. NOAA says that the remnants from Melor are striking northern California hard, with extreme winds, heavy rains, snow in the Sierras, and flash floods possible in desert areas. One hundred mile per hour winds are expected on the higher mountain ridges. This sounds serious, still, it appears fine here.

Okay, my ear is tired from holding the cell so tightly to my head to drown out truck traffic, so after the call, I set it down for a few minutes before calling Jack. I am sitting on a picnic table top, with my feet on the bench. I have my flip flop sandals on, and since my pant legs have somewhat inched up due to my seated position, I notice my Achilles tendons for the first time during the last 24 hour period. I am still taking my Motrin tablets on schedule, but wonder if they are doing much good. The inflammation has increased for yet another day, so either the drugs are doing nothing, or they are keeping it from getting even worse. I have no idea. I feel like a drug addict.

Both Achilles, the tendons that attach the heels to our calves, are puffed out in all directions. Looking directly from the rear, they are about double their normal thickness, and looking down the rear of my leg from above, instead of the normal sweeping concave look, they arch outwards enough that I am concerned. The funny thing is that other than about a mile's worth of stiffness each morning when I begin riding, they seem asymptomatic. However, if I chose push on them, I can feel an uncomfortable sensation. They are not slowing me down or hurting, but then again, they are continuing to enlarge with each passing day.

Fortunately, Canby has excellent cell service. Must be a tower on a mountainside nearby. I call Jack. He and his wife just finished dinner, and he is happy to hear from me. He asks if I am aware of what I am about to ride into once in Nevada, and I tell him that Desert Dune just told me a little about the supposed dangers. Jack, a level-headed man whom I completely trust due to his professional law enforcement background and calm rational thinking, says things are not looking good for my intended route. He reads me multiple warnings from the NOAA website, all stating clearly that this storm can be life threatening depending on one's location. Jack and Desert Dune have apparently been posting the warnings on the Badwater or Bust blog in the hopes I might somehow see it, since I have been out of contact via cell lately. I haven't seen a computer this whole trip. I didn't have a clue!

Jack tells of flash flood dangers in the northwestern Nevada desert. He says, according to predictions, the remnants of Typhoon Melor are calculated to arrive there the very days I will be pedaling through, and that it would be one hell of a wild ride if I continue on. At the very least, I would be drenched for a couple of days with monsoonal rains and pummeled by extreme winds – and at the worst, I would be caught in a flash flood, washed away down some nondescript sandwash out in the middle of an endless Nevada desert where people are aliens. I'd never be found or heard from again. What a way to go!

I like adventure! In fact, I love it. Moving forward with the odds against me somehow excites the essence of my adventurous spirit. Let's assess what's going on in my mind as I talk to Jack. Here is what I tell him as the day is quickly darkening:

All five of my tires have been seriously afflicted by goatheads, and any or all could be flat and useless by tomorrow morning. My Achilles tendons are both looking like sinuous yams. I am about to enter the longest and most remote stretch of the entire trip that has no water or people. And, to top it all off, a colossal deadly storm is going to overtake my slow little trike right in the middle of a place where I might as well be on the moon. Guess that pretty much defines some adventure! Hmm, this has become quite a unique afternoon!

As Jack and I speak, I notice the sky is becoming increasingly smoky. One of those guys at the old gas station said they were having a prescribed burn to the west somewhere. Now I can finally see that they were right. Our conversation takes on a more serious tone at this point, for it's decision time. I am half a mile east of a road junction that allows for another route if necessary. Progressing farther east tomorrow morning on Highway 299 would finally remove this choice. We discuss options, and I ask his assessment. It's getting dark now.

Regarding my tire situation, I do have two spare Q Tubes, the extra heavy duty kind that are supposed to reduce the likelihood of punctures. I also have one spare Schwalbe Marathon-Plus tire, but that would only be necessary if I end up shredding or cutting a tire, which, as bad as these nutlets are, won't be a factor. If two tubes turn up bad tomorrow morning, having lost air during the night, I can replace the tubes, but then I would not have any backup tubes. If only one proves bad, I would still have one other backup tube. If three or more tubes are disabled by sunup, then I'm out of luck right here, unless the leaks are very slow, and I can still progress by the old "stop and reinflate" methodology from time to time.

After thinking for a moment, Jack advises me to modify my plans. He advises that I instead head southwest on Highway 299

68

tomorrow morning, which would put me on course to reach the northern California town of Susanville. He feels that to head east on 299 could prove a big mistake considering just the Typhoon Melor issue, let alone the tendon and tire problems. Seems like the three Ts are trying their best to bring me down: typhoon, tires, tendons.

My adventurous spirit is becoming dampened the more we talk. Jack is right. This is no time not to play it safe. This journey is not about proving anything to myself that could end up crippling me or, worse yet, killing me. There is probably not cell phone service anywhere out in that isolated northern Nevada desert on Road 447 to ultra-remote Gerlach, so calling Jack will probably not even be an option in those unforgiving hinterlands. There is too much at stake. After all, I have been asked to speak about my book, and I cannot lose sight of that objective for the sake of a thrill. I must get down to Death Valley in one piece.

I tell Jack that I will head southwest on Highway 299 tomorrow. He also advises that I probably need to let my Achilles tendons return to a normal state if I wish to continue on to Death Valley, still many miles distant in southern California, and offers to pick me up in his truck the day after tomorrow so that I can recuperate at his home for a couple of days. Glancing at my tendons in the dwindling light, I concede to his wisdom. Somewhere north of Susanville, we will meet on Sunday. He describes his truck. Obviously, he won't miss me, a lone triker on a long haul through the vast northern California forests.

We say our goodbyes, knowing that tomorrow I will probably not have cell phone service, and our next talk will, in all likelihood, be in person way up in those mountains to my southwest. The plan is set, we hang up, and I crawl into the tent after recharging the telephone for a few more minutes and filling all my water containers. I have total privacy here. No one bothers me the entire night.

DAY 10 - *Death Valley*
Saturday, October 10, 2009
Canby to 12 miles south of Adin, California – 34 miles
(running total: 377 miles)

Sunrise comes early to this in-town camp, as the eastern horizon is relatively flat with distant mountains. My original plan called for descending into the morning sun on Highway 299 and ultimately Nevada Road 447 to Gerlach, but that changed last night after a lengthy telephone meeting with Jack. The weather is clear, the temperature is pleasant, and it should prove to be an enjoyable ride, now ascending into the western mountains headed for the small town of Adin, California on my newly planned route. Up to Adin from here, the highway will be a combination of 299 and 139, and then at the Adin fork, I will continue on 139 south towards Susanville. It has been said that the best traveler is one with no set destination. Well, that's not my case, but it kind of adds to the adventure making an eleventh hour route modification like this.

As I climb out of my tent, to a day that gives no hint of wet weather brewing, a quick glance at my ruthlessly attacked tires and tubes of last evening reveals that none appear flat. So far, so good, but only by squeezing them with my fingers and thumb will I know the rest of the story this morning. Looks can be deceiving.

All three trike tires, the ones I spent a fortune on to make sure they don't go flat, are fine to the touch. The left trailer tire feels somewhat low, even though it looks fine, and the right tire feels okay. Out comes my Road Morph pump, which confirms no air loss in any trike tire (all still fully at 70 PSI), but tells me that the left trailer tire probably has a slow leak, because last night I aired it up to a full 65 PSI, and over the course of the night it has lost enough to feel. So far, the right trailer tire is holding at 65. I will keep an eye, fingers, and pump on the trailer tires for a while. I'm good to go!

My current location is roughly 80 miles north of Susanville, so somewhere up in these mountains I'll be pitching a Saturday night stealth camp. I am confident that it will be south of Adin however, a town only about 22 miles distant from Canby. I should make Adin this morning if I get moving soon.

On last night's telephone conversations, my correspondents told me that the third correspondent, David Wright, has been busy with his cartography work. Dave is a life-long explorer of the Great Basin and Death Valley regions, and maintains a complete website about all his travels. It proves useful for anyone wishing to know what particular dirt roads look like ahead of time. Dave leaves no stone unturned.

Anyway, Dave is a guy who has become quite adept at digital map rendering, and I asked him a few months ago if he would be interested in providing cartographic (map) updates periodically to show the progress of this trike journey. Well, he readily agreed, and has apparently posted a map or two on the Badwater or Bust blog. Guess I'll get to see his handiwork once I plop myself down in front of a computer, an electronic item with which I have had no contact since the inception of this trip. Actually, it's kind of nice to be away from it for a change! Thanks Dave, for all your assistance.

After a leisurely and sunny breakfast on one of the five picnic tables of this quaint little town park, I'm off to see the wizard, and push my trike and trailer back out to the highway from behind the town park building, being careful not to run over any goatheads from last night. Traffic is light as I begin the tenth day of pedaling, now heading west on 299 instead of my originally intended east. The mountains lie directly ahead of me, and the first four miles out of Canby prove a slight uphill grade, but easy enough that I maintain a fairly fast clip of perhaps ten miles per hour. If I had not given away my fancy speedometer, I would know for sure, but since the natural world of which I am part is more important than human technology, I'm not the least bit concerned. Estimating is good enough for me.

The next five miles are a different story though. Here is where I begin extending my life span dramatically today, as pedaling up to the summit of Adin Pass keeps the wheels turning much slower. The scenery is magnificent, so the creeper speeds at times allow me unparalleled opportunity to soak it all up in great detail. It's fun to watch little flowers slowly pass to my right, just inches from my hand, realizing that motorists will never have this experience, and even bicyclists aren't this close! Riding a trike even surpasses riding a bike if you love nature.

Trikes are great conveyances, for nothing else brings travelers closer to their world. There is no battle of balance on ultra-slow uphills due to the three wheels, so speed becomes less relevant. A trike pilot can simply stop at any time, take a digital photograph or get a drink of water, and then just take off again, all without swerving or reattaching to the pedals. I am definitely hooked. The comfort factor is awesome.

I am gaining around 1,000 feet in vertical elevation on my way to Adin Pass, which tops out at 5,173 feet according to the sign at its summit. This is grand forested countryside, with hardly a car to be found anywhere this Saturday morning. Thermal regulation is always a consideration while triking, and as I climb higher, it gets cooler, and the shady areas could call for another layer of clothing, but then when in the sun, I'm fine, so I just keep the jacket setup where it is. Pedaling up to mountain summits pretty much keeps me warm, as my body is generating plenty of heat as it burns up its calories. Good thing I had a full breakfast this morning!

On the summit, I get out my old Samsung 1.3 mega-pixel digital camera to capture the obligatory summit shots of conquest. A yellow diamond-shaped sign shows an eighteen wheeler icon on a steep downhill grade, a welcomed sight for nearly any cyclist who just made the grade. This means my work is over for a while as I get to rip down the other side, faster than a speeding bullet (or so it would seem – everything is relative). I was more powerful than a locomotive coming up, and I'm certainly up in the sky, but I'm not a bird or a plane, nor am I Superman – just an ordinary trike pilot on a mission of adventure!

It's thirteen miles from the summit to Adin, a place that looks like a small country village based on what the map shows me. I eat a bar, chug some water, nestle into the cockpit, and off I go, flying down the mountainside with the wind furiously embracing my face and body. It's a thrill every time I do this. I wish it could last longer than these five miles, but at least once I come off the mountain, the land just flattens out into agricultural countryside, and I don't have to think about chugging up another hill. Roughly eight miles of Adin Valley now separates me from the town.

Arrival in the quaint rural community comes at 12:30 PM, a fact I know because they have clocks here. The road curves around at the south end of the valley, goes over a small rise, curves left, and then straightens out in as picturesque a rural setting as one could want. Large trees line the main street of the small parish, with their leaves beginning to transform into fall's flaming colors and fall onto the ground. You just can't help but leave all your worries at the town limit, for this is truly a place of peace and serenity – a traditional old American settlement.

On my right is an old-time country store, so I park my trike and head inside for some food. The old wooden floors of yesteryear creak ever so slightly as I walk atop them, while gazing all about in every direction to take in all the marvelous antiques and lodge-like atmosphere that defines all that this business is. Here is a small market and a gift shop for all weary travelers who are fortunate enough to find themselves in Adin, California. You just gotta' love this place!

This morning's pleasant 22 mile ride is capped by a relaxing lunch of three bananas, two V8 juices, and one Grandma's chocolate chip cookie (the latter a rare treat for myself because they had them readily displayed at the old wooden checkout counter). As I sit at the small round table by the front window, I eat and write in my journal. In the restroom are photos of John Wayne and other country cowboy stuff. This whole place is done up with superb backcountry atmosphere. It is so pleasing to be here that I take a lot of time just hanging out. I also have one of the gals at the counter fill my water bottles. Everyone is polite and friendly, the weather is picture perfect, and life is most definitely good!

Having exhausted every legitimate reason for remaining in the store, I begin my journey yet again, but only get two blocks before I pass an ice cream parlor. I have no intention of stopping here, but a large team of high school basketball girls and their chaperons are sitting under the umbrellas eating their ice cream and clearly taking an interest in my unique means of locomotion. So, being the friendly ambassador for triking that I am, I turn my rig and pedal up to their tables to say hi and chat with their coach. I explain my trip, get the usual "wow" response, everyone smiles happily, and then back onto the main street I go.

Just outside of town, the road spits, and 299 continues on southwest. Highway 139 diverts here to the south, so I get into the left turn lane and commence my silent passage through a few miles of fairly flat crop land, fenced on both sides of the road, with ranch houses here and there in the distance, usually at the end of long driveways. My travel is so quiet on this trike that I can hear the air fluttering from the wings of grasshoppers – literally thousands of them during the next few miles! This should be called the Grasshopper Highway, so I ceremoniously rename it such, just as I assigned the Potato Highway moniker earlier in my grand triangular travels.

Being a trike pilot bestows high privileges upon the intrepid spirits who chose this path, including the desired capacity to rename roadways without political debate or social deliberations. I christen whatever I wish at my whim. What a life! Now if I can just keep a grasshopper from entering my revered facial area that is surrounded by my dishtowel sunshade, I'll be fine.

My journal reflects a list revealing a few of my favorite things on this trip so far. They include hearing the birds sing, wide open spaces, little towns with friendly people, lack of automobile traffic, and downhills. There are more, but since I'm writing from the journal notes, that's all there is right now.

The day is so fine I decide to make camp a little earlier than usual. I have been climbing back into the Modoc National Forest again after I left the Grasshopper Highway phenomenon, and the trees are transitioning from juniper and pinyon to ponderosa pines. The uphills are also with me as signs of people diminish by the mile. Although I prefer a stealth camp, one that is private from the eyes of others, nothing is cropping up that fits the bill, so when I reach a point where the road obviously begins a very steep ascent at one point, and there just happens to be a generously sized large dirt turnout at the bottom, I seize the opportunity, and pull my tricycle and trailer off the road.

To my right is a rancher's fence line, and down below are fields and grazing cattle. There is a line of pines along the fence. I am at the interface of high rolling hill ranch land and mountain forests. The views are outstanding, and I am able to situate my rig over by the fence, far enough away from the highway that I feel secure. A few small trees partially block motorists' views of me, enough to give me a wild feel. I wedge the tent in between the trike and fence. But it's of little concern anyway, as there just is not that much car traffic out here this afternoon. Every once in a while a car or truck motors by, but mostly I have a peaceful vista of fields, cattle, a creek, and forested hillsides.

The birds are singing to me here, the breeze whispers through the pine needles, and the stream below gurgles as it flows lazily down the secluded valley. There are few sounds I like better than the wind in the trees of inviting forests. I feel at home when I hear it. Cows moo.

At one time, prior to my final itinerary decisions, I had planned to take this road to Highway 395 at Susanville, and then take 395 south through the eastern Sierras so that I could enter Death Valley from the west. I eventually decided to take the far more remote route through northern Nevada instead so I'd have the road to myself more often. Yet, as it has turned out, I am now on this road anyway! Interesting.

A large highway sign grabs my attention after dinner, so I walk on down to it. The letter arrangement decodes in my brain, and the message tells me that tomorrow morning I will be entering a snow zone. Well, this is a big clue that the road really heads up to the high country again, so I best get a good night's rest tonight for some tough pedaling after sunup! I don't think I'll encounter any road snow up there, unless tonight brings a surprise from Typhoon Melor's remnants, but the mystery of it all increases the spirit of adventure. I am alive, living in and for the now, not worried about yesterday or tomorrow, and relishing every moment here in the wilds. This journey is the prize. The destination is just a little icing.

DAY 11 - *Death Valley*
Sunday, October 11, 2009
South of Adin to 37 miles north of Susanville - 17 miles
(running total: 394 miles)

The tent is still in the shade when I must arise to offload water. Mind you, I'm just a few yards off the paved road, and there is scant concealment available in the way of trees and shrubbery. Fortunately, I can see enough road in each direction, and any car is also easily detected by my ears in this quiet nearly-natural environment, that no sense of nervous urgency psychologically hinders the business at hand.

As I face the Highway 139, to my left, from whence I pedaled yesterday, is a foothill valley and gently meandering pavement that leads north to Adin, and to my right are steep mountains and curvy roadway that leads south into the Modoc National Forest. Straight ahead, across the road are transitional hills covered in pine trees, with the sun about to crest the eastern ridge, and behind me is a picturesque rancher's field and stream to the west, far below the rocky slope, with a roaming herd of cattle lazily dining on grasses. It doesn't get much better than this!

Today, Jack Freer is scheduled to meet me somewhere south of here on this road. He has gladly volunteered to give my Achilles tendons a deserved break by scooping my trike, trailer, and me off the asphalt for a petroleum-powered ride to his Gardnerville, Nevada ranch. Nice!

Although, I must admit a certain hesitancy about this whole thing. After all, my goal is to ride my human-powered ICE trike to give my talk, and I am attempting to steer way clear of gasoline in the process. Now, only on my 11th day out, it appears that I will at least temporarily concede an impromptu setback of my best laid plans. Sure, a little company for a while is welcomed, and sure, letting my tendons return to normal would be nice, and okay, lazing out in a truck for enough mileage to replace several trike days has a certain tempting ring to it after riding and living on the ground for so long, but still, I feel like I am about to cheat on a school test!

Not only all that, but who knows what would have happened to me helplessly in the path of Typhoon Melor's remnants in the vast Nevada desert. I have this vision of me pedaling for all I'm worth towards Gerlach, surrounded by the endless Black Rock Desert, and looking over my right shoulder to see the lethal clouds bearing down upon me, thundering their mighty roar of destruction as the rains pelt the dry sands, and the accumulating torrential waters cascade through a massive rocky sandwash. At ninety degrees off my starboard bow the water hurls towards me, and it is clearly evident that I cannot pedal fast enough to escape my entombment beneath several tons of earthen debris! So, I humbly opt to forfeit a few miles in the name of sanity.

I could lie. The conspiracy would involve only Jack and me. No one else need be any the wiser. As far as the rest of the world is concerned, I'm lost anyway, and wherever I show up, my story would be believable. Yeah, I rode the trike the whole way. Never mind those Achilles the size of bananas. I'm a warrior, an animal tough as nails, one who never says die. One problem with that. It's not my way.

Nope, I'll document the entire journey just the way it happens. No dramatics or fabrications necessary. The adventure is adventurous enough as it is. No need to stretch things for an effect. I'll take a break for a couple of days. It's okay. After all, this is my first tricycling trip. At least I have come eleven days and about 400 miles so far on my own power. Haven't stopped at a gasoline station yet! That's one heck of a lot farther than most folks could do, so I console myself with these thoughts as I begin turning the cranks of my Sugino XD-600, brushed aluminum, 152 millimeter triple chainset, with 24-36-50 chainrings.

I'm really starting to get used to this life out on the road. The fact that it will be cut short today promptly brings home the point that I am most definitely cut out to be a wild trike pilot. There's something about making your own way, living by your own wits, and moving efficiently over long stretches of ground that gets into your blood. I like the maverick essence of it all, coloring outside the lines of culture, living on the edge, never really sure of what the next bend brings my way. Yes, this is living! And no one knows it but me.

I tried calling Jack a few minutes ago before I packed the cell phone away into the side pocket of my left Arkel GT-54 pannier, but the surrounding high mountains have thoroughly obliterated the signal. I'll try again later, once I am higher in elevation. Just like John Denver's famous Colorado Rocky Mountain High song, I am in a mental high from the escapade unfolding right now in my life. These mountains aren't as high as those where I used to live in Colorado by a long shot, but out on my trike, anywhere is just as grand to me!

The air is crisp in the shade, yet as I round turns into the full rising sun, I warm up quickly. Then it's back into the morning shade, but since the road is steep and my body is stoking the internal furnace while I move about 370 pounds skyward, lack of thermal comfort is not an issue. Even though I have been eating for days now, my chow bag still seems pretty full to me, and pretty heavy. Water is constantly refilled at each little town, so that weight never goes away. Even when I drink it down from the Camelbak bladder hidden behind my seat, or my twin front-side bottles, the weight is still there; it's just inside my body now.

What a fantastic way to experience northeastern California! Roughly 17 miles from last night's camp, and only a few miles south of Earth's human delineation of the 41st parallel, I am on a very long, and seemingly endless uphill section, so I stop to upload some calories from a Clif Bar into my ever-hungry muscular machine. Gotta' keep feeding the boiler to make the train go! While I'm stopped in the warming sun, I whip out the tiny cellular device and attempt to converse with Jack. I wonder where on this road he is. No signal. Back to triking I go.

It's Sunday morning. The religious faithful are still in church. They haven't started their Sunday drives yet. And this far out, even if they had, it would be a while before I see them. I have the road to myself. Up ahead, the terrain seems to be telling me that I am not far from peaking before heading down the long grades past Eagle Lake and then down farther yet into Susanville. I work hard at these uphill gains, and I want to have the enjoyment of what's on the other side – downhills! But sometimes, things just don't work out the way you want:

I can see a good half mile ahead up the mountain, and a little white speck emerges from the farthest uphill curve in my sight. It's a car, heading north towards Adin. Once onto the straight section, and close enough for my eyes to identify the minuscule object as a pickup truck, the vehicle makes a quick u-turn and comes to rest amidst the pines in a large pullout on my side of the road. Well, my trained police mind resourcefully assesses what my brain just perceived, and offers me two potential explanations for the sudden deviation of the vehicle's path:

> **1)** This is a lowlife criminal predator, who, deducing my helplessly alone state out here in the midst of nothingness, will soon rob me of all my cash, rip off my trike, and toss my formerly alive body into the roadside thickets.
> **2)** It might just be Jack, who has also identified me at this distance, seeing as how no one else is out here, especially anyone riding a tricycle over these mountains on a Sunday morning. I continue to pedal towards the mystery.

Calling upon additional, and often untapped, cranial skills, I make a leap of faith by assuming option number two, and now get ready to chow down on my Nutty Nuggets. Oh yeah, I forgot to mention that I left camp with only a bar in my belly today, hoping to save time and get in more mileage before Jack would come along and spoil my game.

Well, a man now exits the white truck, still a quarter mile distant, and steps into the middle of the roadway. He raises his hands up to his face, and seems to be holding something black. I knew it! He's lighting the fuse of a bomb with his cigarette! Surely, he's going to roll it down the road towards me. Maybe the pavement will extinguish the fire. But wait – no, it's not a bomb after all. It's a cannon!

But it's spelled Canon with a capital C, because it is a 10 mega-pixel digital camera (which I will learn in just two minutes from now), and Jack is gleefully snapping photographs of this deluded trike hobo as he pedals up for their first face-to-face meeting. The time is 10:00 AM as these two guys meet 37 miles north of Susanville, California. I know this because Jack has a watch. Albert Einstein once said that a man with one watch always knows what time it is, but a man with two is never sure. Good thing I don't have a watch.

We shake hands and exchange some greetings, exactly what, I don't recall because all I can think about is putting down the tailgate so I can spread out my bowl, cereal container, raisins and all. I am hungry, so I ask Jack if he minds me taking a late breakfast break as we talk. He says not at all, and assures me to take all the time I want to relax and eat. After all, Jack has a fast gasoline burner, so we can make good time down this mountain. But on the trike, I could have made good time also. Okay, slower perhaps, but still good from my standpoint.

An hour and a half later, breakfast is over, my trike, trailer, and cargo box are all loaded into the rear of his truck under the camper shell, and we are off. It feels so bizarre to be sitting in a car! My body is so used to the daily travel by trike that this simply seems surreal now. Trees are speeding by at breakneck speed. I look over at Jack's speedometer. Gads, he's driving like a bat out of hell, a whopping 55 miles per hour! What a maniac. Funny how everything is relative. Even on my longest steepest downhill, I never reached this speed on the Q. Came close at times, but still, to attain that extra five would have been awesome.

All kidding aside, Jack is a cool guy, a few years younger than myself, but still about to retire from the cop shop after a full career. We get along great. It's like we already know each other fairly well from months of emails and telephone calls in preparation for this trip. But Jack is still a cop, and almost every normal cop has a serious drug addiction – to caffeine! He needs his fix, and I come to find out that our first stop will be at Susanville's Starbucks. After driving down the grand pappy of all hills into town, which would have been an absolute blast on my Q (might have been able to hit 55 here), we pull into the crowded lunchtime parking lot. It's weird seeing so many people again. I hate it.

But, it gives me the opportunity to stretch my legs as I walk around seeing males in business suits and females in business dresses chatting on their little electronic cellular devices while they down their midday lattes. A professional woman, smartly dressed with cell phone in hand, parades from the counter with her caffeine towards the comfy couch by the front window. She sits down, crosses her legs, and revs up her heart with the java, prepping for the afternoon's client meeting. Those nylon covered legs and high heels wouldn't get her too far on a tricycle. I've gone over the edge into another world. I don't belong here. I'm an alien on my own planet!

Not only do I not drink coffee, but I no longer live in a superficial world of high fashion clothing and impressing others. I opted out of that a while ago. I tried working for a living for about 30 years once. Wasn't my cup of tea (decaffeinated white, of course – higher in antioxidants). So now I follow my own hopelessly lost drummer.

A couple of hours later, we pull into the driveway of Jack's rural acre and cedar sided home. It sits on the southeastern outskirts of Gardnerville, with magnificent views of the Sierra Nevada Range to the west. I am envious of his abode. Mrs. Jack, aka Stephanie, comes out the front door to greet me. Oh, I'm the guy who – yeah, Jack told me all about what you are doing out there. She's really nice too, and makes me feel right at home. I try to apologize for interrupting their normally scheduled life, but she insists that it will be fun having me stay a bit.

These folks are gracious hosts, and open their cozy home for my recuperation and safe harbor from the ever impending mega-storm.

Things are a blur. I have just been ripped back into the customary world of America, right out of my little unimportant trike realm, and it takes me a while to readjust back to civilized living with all the pleasures of 2009, like big screen televisions, computers, real beds, and hot food. Turns out Jack is a gourmet chef, something he didn't tell me earlier, but for tonight, he and Stephanie just order in two massive pizzas to compliment their cupboard full of fine wines. It's like the twilight zone for me. You just don't make a transition this fast without some mental fallout! Pizza? Wine?

But, I'm not complaining. Having just stood on a scale at Stephanie's insistence that I look awfully thin (or is that awful and thin), the resultant number reveals a loss of ten pounds since I left the coast on October first. That would roughly coincide with Matt's prediction of 5,000 to 7,000 calories per day expenditure. Based on my intake of approximately 2,000 daily thus far, a ten pound loss indicates a ballpark deficit of 3,500 calories per day. My mind is too dulled to do the math properly, but it's good enough for me. Nearly a pound per day?

From the trike, I bring my panniers and food into the bedroom they made up for me. I take a much needed shower, throw on some lightweight sleeper type clothes, and then come out to join them for all the pizza and red wine I can handle. I'm certainly not a wine or beer drinker, but no sooner than my glass gets near the bottom, Jack makes sure it's topped right off again. And I don't even have to arise from my reclining chair to get my pizza! They delight in keeping my plate full, apparently feeling pity for my swollen Achilles tendons, which are now clearly visible to everyone, as I am only wearing flip flops, and my pants cover only to mid calf. Stephanie says they really look bad.

Tonight, my body gets an over supply of calories for a change, and a big over supply at that! When I finally arise from the chair, my new world seems somewhat unstable, as I attempt to maintain my balance over to the kitchen. In this condition, I would be unable to get up and off my trike! I'll be darned – I'm drunk.

We talk about the journey thus far. They show me the Badwater blog on the computer so I can see what people are saying about the trip. We watch some television. For a brief time, I have no cares. I can do as I please. The news says the remnants of Typhoon Melor will indeed be hitting the region hard in the next day or two. They say to expect heavy rains and high winds, and to stay away from the low ground of dry riverbeds. It's coming, as they had predicted, but I am now safe.

I do a little Achilles tendon research on the computer before hitting the sack. The consensus is that it will take longer for them to fully heal than I have here in Gardnerville. Tonight I do not worry. I just go to sleep in the rural silence. The trike is still in the back of Jack's truck. I'll get it out tomorrow and do some cleaning and maintenance.

DAY 12 - *Death Valley*
Monday, October 12, 2009
Gardnerville, Nevada - zero miles (running total: 394 miles)

My standard method of operation is to arise early each day. I go to bed early, and usually awaken naturally and refreshed. This morning, I purposely lie here just for the sake of pure luxury. Stephanie and Jack have been quiet as mice with whatever they are doing, so I take full advantage of their supreme hospitality. During this brief honeymoon period, I am like royalty. It's kind of fun, for a couple days anyway.

Once my Achilles deflate somewhat, I plan on leaving. Last night's online study indicated an over-use injury of this type might take weeks, or even months to fully return to normal. I didn't like reading that part! I've been on non-steroidal anti-inflammatory drugs since just before crossing the California border, yet no real improvement seems apparent. Maybe with a couple of days where the pedaling is not happening will help put them in the fast lane towards recovery.

After finally getting up and dressed, I go out into the living room and make my greetings. Jack has planned on some time off for this Death Valley trip, so he is off today. He says he'll be going into the office on and off the next few days. Today, I eat my Nutty Nuggets sitting in a chair at a table. What a switch!

Jack and I drive in his Jeep Wrangler, which he is prepping for Death Valley, to Scolari's Market in Gardnerville for some groceries so that he can fix the three of us some fancy meals for dinner. I take the opportunity to stock up on healthy foods for my own breakfasts, lunches, and snacks. Things like a big V8 juice, two bags of dried plums, two bags of granola, two bags of nut trail mix, one packet of MetRX super protein, four 20-gram protein Clif bars, a bunch of bananas, three quarts of Soy Dream soymilk, and one Odwalla green drink make it into my shopping cart. My thinking is that a massive infusion of high quality proteins will speed my recovery. The items in my shopping cart are small and take up hardly any room, but the bill is up there. It's one price I pay for my longevity. I love feeling great, even with messed up tendons.

It's a lazy day with no worries. I don't even get out to the truck to unload my gear yet. Inside the house I go, feet up on the recliner, with hot and cold packs under the Achilles, and Motrin inside my mouth.

80

What a sight! Large screen television entertains me for long stretches. The MetRX protein packet and nut trail mix make a great lunch, bombarding my emaciated system with so much protein and ultra healthy monounsaturated fat that something good must surely come of it. I will get more of these pricey MetRX packets, for they are the fastest way to get the most protein to the injuries in short order. After my mom's heart surgery ten years ago, I fed her one of these every day in a blended drink. Her doctor said he had never seen anyone heal up as fast as she did. Yes indeed, proteins are certainly the building blocks of life!

DAY 13 - *Death Valley*
Tuesday, October 13, 2009
Gardnerville, Nevada - zero miles (running total: 394 miles)

The Achilles tendons are very slowly showing a decrease in swelling, with emphasis on the word very. Who knows, it could just be wishful thinking, but I believe improvement is occurring. Well, I know improvement is occurring because I am off the daily pedaling regimen, now pumping my body full of protein, and downing the pharmaceutical industry's latest weapons against swelling, so things have to be looking up. The big question is whether enough progress will be made that I can maintain it once I'm back out on the open road on the Q.

The rains have finally begun! Melor is at our doorstep. The Carson City news channels show visuals of where the storm will hit hardest. Even the Weather Channel is covering the unusual autumn event. Increasing winds, rain, and low visibility are the order of the day here in western Nevada. There is no letup, only hourly amplification.

Immediately west of the Freer Ranch are the Sierra Nevada Mountains, huge stony cliffs of impressive size, visible from everywhere. This day, we cannot even see them, for Melor has the range covered in its grip. So far, the winds are 15-20 miles per hour, with gusts up to 35. This is predicted to also increase. The high daytime temperature is 58 degrees Fahrenheit. Safe inside, it is exciting to witness this drama!

For dinner, Jack fixes a completely gourmet meal of halibut, further saturating my emaciated carcass with high amounts of first-class protein. My Superman feeling is beginning to return by the hour. It's like when Popeye eats his spinach. My mind sends positive growth thoughts to my body. I'm hopelessly addicted to three wheels, and desperately desire to get back out there on my trike! Well, maybe not today, but after Melor passes for sure. Of course, this pampering is mighty nice.

After a filling meal and dessert, the three of us gather in the living room for some news updates. I sit in my usual recliner, feet up, ice

81

and hot packs as needed, and Jack sits to my right in a second recliner. Stephanie sits on the couch to my left. Their two dogs have now accepted my presence. The big screen television continues to blare out the latest urgent information about taking cover and staying home.

According to their maps, a colossal mega weather cell is now centered squarely over the Gerlach, Nevada and Pyramid Lake area of the state. It shows high winds, heavy rains, and flooding for the region. This is precisely the area where I was formerly scheduled to be on the Q this evening as we are watching the news!! Reporters are hailing this as a "rare event" and make the most of their coverage by revealing all the worst that can be found. TV ratings must be high. Everyone is glued to their televisions because no one wants to go outside. Looks like Jack saved my bacon! I would have perished in the Black Rock Desert!

DAY 14 - *Death Valley*
Wednesday, October 14, 2009
Gardnerville, Nevada - zero miles (running total: 394 miles)

Back to Scolari's Market Jack and I go. I need more healing foods, and he needs more gourmet supplies. I get additional soymilk, trail mix, MetRX packets, and organic granolas. My plan is to regain some healthy weight while I'm here. This is my third day at the ranch. Life is becoming very predictable. I want to give my body all the rest it can get, so I balance recuperation needs with my impending departure. It has become apparent to me that over doing caloric intake while here is a good idea, as I now know the toll that daily tricycle pedaling takes.

Dave Wright, one of my three Badwater blog correspondents and chief cartographer, emails his proposals for where and how my journey should resume. Dave is an exceptionally thorough fellow, knows the countryside between here and Death Valley like the back of his hand, and always offers great advice. It must have taken him quite a while to type his email, for the details are impeccable and quite lengthy. I swear, if I were to go missing out there, this guy could locate me in short order. His knowledge is unmatched. A good fellow to have in one's corner.

I keep his print-out handy, and Jack and I spend time each day assessing the options with the maps in front of us. We calculate things like distance to my objective, speed of the trike, type of terrain (which definitely affects speed), and my chances of going the distance without rupturing or tearing a lower leg tendon. I feel good about the latter though, for even with the swelling, I don't think the Achilles will tear. They may experience further inflammation, but I believe that will be the only consequence. Still, I clearly don't want this journey to cripple me for life, which Desert Dune is fearful of, so I work on pedaling solutions.

This is obviously a repetitive stress injury in each tendon. That much is certain. It is odd though, for throughout a lifetime of long distance walks, marathon runs, hikes, and backpacking, no such thing has ever happened to me! Why on this trip? What's different?

Well, for one thing, my toes are curling over the tops of the pedals, and essentially pushing on nothing but the soles of my hiking boots, which are themselves in thin air. It's not like waking or running, where the toes are pushing against terra firma each stroke of the leg. Still, I'm not sure if this is the reason for my injury. It could be that I need to get the axis of the pedal farther back towards the center of my foot. Maybe I'm pushing so hard each pedal stroke that the flexure of the muscles and tendons is being exaggerated. Right now, I can only speculate, but I am sure that after this trip is over, and I have had more time to assess things, I will get it all straightened out.

Another day of heavier storm activity keeps everyone pinned down. Stephanie left on her own to visit her daughter and son up north in the Reno area. She was worried about the weather, but wanted to go. Jack and I are batching it for a couple of days. When he's at work, I feel like a trapped rat in a cage. Not that the house isn't nice, it is great, but still, my heart longs for the wide open spaces once again. Severe rain and winds don't even allow me to take a stroll through this rural neighborhood of homes on acreage. I amuse myself with the television mostly, as I can keep my feet elevated. Occasionally, I use the computer to study my injury or read the blog. It's a life of Riley.

I have to remember to feed, water, and provide outdoor breaks for the two dogs. They have a small covered area outside the garage for expelling their food excesses and enjoying the very wet and flooded outdoors. Once or twice I forget about them, and when something like seeing their dog dishes jars my memory, I rush over to let the poor forgotten creatures reenter nirvana. They are, of course, soaked totally.

DAY 15 - *Death Valley*
Thursday, October 15, 2009
Gardnerville, Nevada - zero miles (running total: 394 miles)

Rich Colley is an old friend of mine, who still lives in the greater Los Angeles area. He wants to move to a rural setting as I did in the early 80s, but as yet remains with his wife, trapped in the land of mega wattage and over population. He is a semi-retired doctor, who now prefers IT work, and has been advising me about rehab for the Achilles. Rich is one of those genius guys who always loves the challenge of something new. Whatever he does, he does it well.

His advice has been four cycles of hot and cold packs during leg elevation. Forty-five minutes of ice, followed by 45 of heat pad, with that being done twice. Essentially, it's cold, hot, cold, hot. He also advises increasing NSAID ingestion to 800 mg daily, a bit in excess of what's recommended on the bottle, considering the short time I'll remain on it. Lastly, Dr. Colley thinks that when I pedal, it should be with more pressure originating from the heel area of the foot, to reduce the stress to the Achilles tendons. Guess it's worth a try.

During a telephone conversation with him today, I learn that he just found out he has leukemia, a cancer of the blood. I am devastated! He is only two years older than I am, at sixty. He has spent his life exercising and staying fit. For years, we used to go exploring the wild Mojave Desert and Death Valley in our CJ-5 Jeeps when we were in our twenties. I can't imagine what he and his wife must be thinking.

It's another lazy day at the Freer Ranch. The dogs are my company most of the day, yet even they go sack out several times in their master's bedroom. If the slightest noise happens outside, the younger dog is up and yipping, usually with a trip to the large front room picture window over the couch to see what's going on. Every time, nothing is going on out there. What's all the fuss about? Only when Jack or Stephanie drive up is their rambunctious reaction justified.

The day has been filled with frantic national news about a boy supposedly trapped in a weather balloon that is floating out of control high above the state of Colorado. It started yesterday. Authorities are figuring out how to get him safely down, when at long last, the winds decide it and dump the balloon in a farmer's field. No one is inside. Did he fall out? Nope, he was in the rafters of the home garage all the time, fearful of a spanking. Perception among the news media is that this was a huge publicity stunt by a father and mother known for other oddball things. I'll take the trike! I like the ground.

My dinner meals since being here at the ranch look like this (a far cry from my trike cuisine): Sunday: Pizza and wine. Monday: Noodles, shrimp, and wine. Tuesday: Halibut steak in white sauce, asparagus spears, V8 juice. Wednesday: Halibut steak, asparagus, peas, and V8 juice. Thursday: Artichokes in egg noodles, white sauce, and V8 juice. I finally decided that substituting the V8 juice for the river of red wine was in my best interests seeing as how I needed all the nutrition I could get. I can't stay here forever, after all. Death Valley and Badwater Basin quietly call my name.

In life's adventure, all things eventually must pass.

DAY 16 - *Death Valley*
Friday, October 16, 2009
Gardnerville, Nevada - zero miles (running total: 394 miles)

Okay, this has gone on long enough! This is my fifth day here, waylaid off course to save my sorry soul. My feral spirit demands action, so I opt to not spend another day in a recliner with my feet up, but rather go outside and extract the trike and my gear from Jack's Silverado to make sure all is well with the components of my rig.

The day is full of glorious blue sky and a few fluffy white clouds. Typhoon Melor has left us dry at long last, and is who knows where, out over eastern Nevada or points farther east by now. Of course, perhaps the storm has lost its punch altogether and just vanished. I don't care anymore. It's time to get back into the action. I wasn't killed in the Black Rock Desert at least. I'm still alive in Nevada.

Getting the gear out of and into Jack's pickup, especially with the Leer camper shell, is like a jigsaw puzzle. I spend my morning cleaning the chain, cranks, and cassette. I lubricate the chain once it is clean, and make sure all tires are aired to capacity, which allows me to roll faster with less effort. The left trailer tire is down again after five days of sitting, in the range of 34 PSI, so I know at least one of the Canby nutlets has worked its way through the cheap bicycle tire, and into the light duty tube inside. Fortunately, it's a very slow leak, so I'm not too worried. The trike tires are all fine, as usual.

The day is so beautiful that I take the Q out for a spin in the rural countryside, no panniers or weight to slow me down. It's pure delight! This is my first ride without the load since I began, and the difference is absolutely amazing. Perhaps I should consider going without a trailer on all future trips. It would require some thought, but I like the feeling of freedom, of being only six feet long with three wheels instead of ten feet long with five. My mind puts the thought on the back burner for the time being. I still have hundreds of miles to go with the trailer, so I resign myself to the yoke of slow motion. Even with the trailer and extra weight in tow, this journey is so incredible that I am happy to be on it. Death Valley, here I come – alive!

Jack works on his Jeep's communication system while I do all my trike preparation. He has a CB radio installed above the window, between the two front seats, along with a new satellite telephone. Over to the left of his steering wheel is a mounted GPS unit. He is truly prepared. He makes a science of it. This fellow is my backup. Good to have him in my corner, just like Dave the cartographer.

We look at the trike and Jeep, and envision ways that I could be transported in the event of a physical failure on my part. The Jeep doesn't have cavernous room like his huge pickup truck, and behind the front seats is a storage area for his gear. He has a roof rack, and we experiment with placing the trike up there. It would work in a pinch, but I am not too worried. I am feeling strong as an ox after several days of full meals, of taking in far more calories than I was burning off, the complete opposite of my first eleven days.

For my final dinner with Jack and Stephanie, we again have pizza and wine, a sort of celebration before I find myself back out on the trail tomorrow. I pay these accommodating folks $50 to cover my portion of any gourmet food I ate, and for using their Advil when my Motrin ran out. Today is my final day of doing drugs! Healed or not, I refuse to subject my body to any more toxic substances, which, while perhaps speeding the healing process, definitely have known hazards.

The trike is back in the truck. My route has been decided. Tomorrow before sunup, Jack and I set out to my drop off point. Death Valley, here I come!

DAY 17 - *Death Valley*
Saturday, October 17, 2009
Scotty's Junction, Nevada to Mesquite Springs DVNP – 32 miles
(running total: 426 miles)

Tap, tap, tap is the sound that quietly brings me to consciousness from a deep sleep. There is no sunlight coming in my eastern-facing guest bedroom window. Nights are for sleeping, and that's exactly what I wish to continue doing, but I immediately acknowledge Jack's knock as the start of a busy day. No more lounging!

We have some driving to do. Stephanie is still in bed, where all rational folks are at this hour, as Jack and I chow down on some breakfast to power us up for the day. All I have to do now is brush my teeth and carry my panniers out to the truck. I have been using them in the house during my stay as suitcases, since they have handles and full length zippers. We both have on polar fleece jackets in this nippy pre-dawn air as we slide into the truck cab and prepare to head south on Highway 395. At least Melor is no more.

After today's drive, Jack and I won't be seeing each other for a week or so. He is going to drop me, the Q, and my gear off in the desert to resume my tricycle expedition. Determining the best location, considering the circumstances, has been an ongoing discussion during my stay at the ranch. I have already ridden in his truck for a few hours getting to Gardnerville, and now I am in the truck again, heading south from Gardnerville. My goal of a 100% gasoline-free round trip from and back to Oregon will not be attained on this journey, but I wish to remain as close to it as possible. My strong preference was to resume pedaling right from Jack's house, but I could not risk the consequences.

First and foremost, this specific trip at this specific time was determined by my speaking engagement at Stovepipe Wells in Death Valley National Park. I am to be the speaker at the Author's Breakfast on November 6th. Since I am attempting to generate much-needed income for retirement by the sales of my books, this is a significant career opportunity for a guy who just broke into the world of book writing in 2007. Therefore, I must be physically able to ride my trike into Death Valley on my own, and ride it to key locations while I am there. Unfortunately, this tendon predicament is crowding my plans.

This has to be my main priority. I cannot allow any male egocentric thoughts about achieving the secondary goal of pedaling an entire fuel-free trek compromise the most important objective. Death Valley is the core directive. Death Valley will guide my decisions. If my tendons do worsen, I want to at least accomplish my Death Valley goals. Thus, these factors have determined my point of human-powered departure today. It's all a matter of professional priority.

What is unsettling to me though is that my lifetime physical conditioning makes this entire 2,000+ mile trek an easily achievable end. That is why this unexpected Achilles tendon inflammation is wearing heavily on my spirit. Except for this unforeseen turn of events, the sky is my limit. I do not like it that such a seemingly minor thing can thwart my endeavor. I am in fact inclined to ignore the tendon swelling altogether, since it doesn't hamper my daily pedaling, but urging of my support crew, along with my own thoughts, keep me on the side of caution.

Enough of this negative thought, lest I continue to swirl downwards in an internal intellectual battle. The circumstances are what they are today, and being an optimistic realist, I will adjust accordingly. Physical and mental survival depends upon one's ability to adapt as necessary, and those who can do this experience the greatest successes in life, further rewarded by increased years of energetic vitality. Spending my finite time here in this life lamenting is unproductive, so I simply rework my schedule now, and prepare my feet for my next cross-country adventure. There will be other trike journeys after this one, and I will most assuredly be here to take them!

Jack is a technician when it comes to route configuration. He has our drive today mapped out to minimize mileage and maximize the hours of this day. We take Highway 395 south to the town of Lee Vining, where we stop in for Jack to have a full breakfast at Nicely's

Restaurant and Lounge. Back when I was eating a big bowl of granola and nuts at his house this morning, he only had some coffee and a light snack, so now he's hungry. While he's consuming his eggs, hash browns, toast, and coffee, I have a glass of water and we talk about the trip.

Breakfast complete, we upload a highly explosive petroleum liquid into Jack's supersonic transport, and then head south again. At Highway 120, we hang a left and drive east in the Inyo National Forest 46 more miles to the remote town of Benton. Then it's Highway 6 east to Tonopah, Nevada, and Highway 95 south to Scotty's Junction, my point of tricycle departure! Would have been several days on a trike.

Shortly after noon, we pull off the road at the intersection of Nevada Highway 267. This is where I will unload all my gear out of the truck and head west under my own power into Death Valley National Park, the boundary of which is 21 miles distant. Scotty's Junction is named after Walter Scott, a well-known conman of last century who has a castle named after him in the park. It wasn't his, but most of the public thinks it was. Anyway, Scotty's Castle, a major Death Valley landmark, is only 26 miles distant from where Jack and I are now standing.

This is a bittersweet time. I am very happy to get back to doing what I set out to do, ride a tricycle to Death Valley, yet I have become accustomed to Jack's hospitality and friendship, and will likely have to fend off loneliness for a while until back into the swing of things. The first 11 days, I had adapted well to solo travel. Having this 5-day interlude with people and normal living brought me back to luxury. Now, I had to readjust again. This time should be easier though, what with my experiences so far on the trip. From opulence to hobo living!

I have found that whenever I first start out on a solo trip, like what I used to do in my old Jeep or other 4wd vehicles for many years, it was always initially difficult for me emotionally. But after a few hours out in the vast wilds, a wonderful feeling of wilderness peace would overtake me, and I would be fine. This same phenomenon is with me on this expedition. Once out here pedaling through the secluded places, I am at one with my surroundings.

This is the stepping off point. I reassemble all my gear onto the trike and trailer. I fully hydrate myself with several bottles of water, and consume a couple of energy bars. Jack takes photos all the while, and I have him take a picture also of my miniature teddy bear Tumbleweed, who rides with me on this trek, and who also accompanied me to the top of Telescope Peak a few years ago. Tumbleweed is a rather plump little bear who needs exercise, but never gets it because he rides in either a pocket or pannier, enjoying the journey without any work on his part. It's okay though, because if I do find myself in a bout of loneliness, being able to chat with him is worth his weight, what little there is of it.

My ride this afternoon is going to take me across the northern end of Sarcobatus Flat, and past Bonnie Claire flat, into the Grapevine Mountains, which are a northern portion of the larger Amargosa Range. It is a gradual incline to the pass that will drop me down into Death Valley, gradual enough that I maintain a decent speed and make good time in my higher gears.

The elevation of Scotty's Junction, according to Jack's GPS system, is 4,050 feet above sea level. I will be climbing for roughly twenty miles, and then descending towards North America's lowest land. This countryside is wide open desert, with mountains immediately to my west. Traffic so far is zero, just the way I prefer things.

Not only that, but by the gods, I have a slight tailwind! The trike gods are sending me a good omen today. My boyhood hero from Greek mythology, Hercules, always used to say "by the gods" when he invoked their assistance with an epic task, so I now decree, by the gods, I shall use the powers bestowed upon me to pedal the length and breadth of Death Valley!

There's a strong likelihood that I'll be camping at Mesquite Springs Campground, the northernmost formal campground in the main valley. It is southwest of Scotty's Castle a few miles, and offers far more solitude than will be experienced farther south near the crowds of Furnace Creek. Of course, I prefer to camp free, but once inside a national park, options are limited for a traveler like myself. They have rules that require primitive camping to be a certain distance from many main paved roads, like around two miles up a dirt road, and that may not be practical on my low clearance British trike.

As I pedal along enjoying the remote scenery, I also consider camping just outside the national park boundary line, perhaps by a matter of yards, so that I will have the freedom to camp alone and spend no money. Mesquite Springs will cost me $12.00 per night. Well, since my business takes me into the national park, it will eventually be a fact of temporary life. All the years that I visited here in my 4wd vehicles, I would always camp primitively up some lonely dirt road, which is easily within reach when in a high clearance rig powered by fossil fuels.

The last time I stayed in a regular Death Valley campground that charged money was with my parents and sister as a child. I have camped many times at Mahogany Flat on the crest of the Panamint Range, which is a dedicated campground, but due to its extreme isolation and primitive facilities, is not a fee-based site. Mahogany Flat offers amazing views of Badwater Basin from 8,415 feet above, and it is set in the pines. I have been snowed on at this campground while gazing down into a hot day at Badwater. There can be more than 30 degrees temperature difference from the camp to the lowly and desiccated salt!

Speaking of temperature, today's ride is perfect. I have no idea how many degrees are surrounding me, but my lightweight long sleeve cotton shirt offers just the right feel. This is totally comfortable as I continue climbing to the pass. Once I reach that low portion of the Amargosa Range, it will be a fast ride down to the castle in Grapevine Canyon. The sky is clear blue. What a difference between this and my days crossing the Cascade Range! No snow anywhere in sight.

This road is long and mostly straight, and as my travel takes me from the northern end of Sarcobatus Flat and west into Bonnie Claire Flat, I notice a small group of Harleys coming the other direction. There are four, and the sight is something that would probably strike fear into the conservative collective of our refined society. If there is any basis to this fear of bikers, then my immediate future may be in question. After all, I'm all alone on a vehicle that can't exactly outrun a fire-breathing Harley. And the height of my eyes from ground level makes the thunderous two-wheeled machines appear gigantic as they approach.

I'd be willing to lay odds that these guys have never seen an old man with a gray beard pedaling a tricycle pulling a trailer before. They have beards too, but they also have black leathers, and a few other expected decorations that I do not. All eyes are on me during the final few yards before our passing, and I notice their engines are slowing so they can figure out what the heck they are seeing. These guys really get a kick out of me and my bizarre rig, which I cleverly deduce by the ear-to-ear grins on their faces, along with thumbs-up, waves, and nodding of the heads. One fellow even calls out "Way to travel."

My passage is silent. Theirs is not. It's a happy few moments when two different species of travelers connect in the wild desert hinterlands. Anyone traveling out this far on anything other than a car is surely not your run-of-the-mill citizen. A mutual respect is the result.

A couple of cars with normal people pass during the next few miles, and I wave and smile as they do. One older couple in a sedan stare at me as they speed past in the other direction, but do not return my visual greetings. Perhaps they are in such shock at beholding an unidentifiable pedaling object (UPO), that their brains don't reach the point of even thinking that I am waving to them. While on the topic of UPOs, I don't think I'm too far removed from where all the UFOs are supposed to be out in western Nevada, some weird otherworldly site called Area 51. Maybe that couple thought I was a real alien rolling along on my five wheels exploring their planet. I have to admit, with my flag poles and flagging my appearance is totally out of the ordinary.

Most folks so far on this trip just don't know what to make of me!

About 15 miles from where I left Jack this afternoon, a second group of motorcycles now heads my way. There must be at least a dozen of them, but this group consists of what is commonly referred to as "full dressers", the ultra long distance cruising motorcycles with saddlebags, trailers, and gear for extended cross-country camping. In stereotypical America, these guys are supposed to be safe to normal folks, probably a bunch of doctors, lawyers, cops, and respectable citizens.

They also slow down a bit to gawk at me, and so I wave and smile. There is no obvious reception like with the first group of Harleys. A few smile, and one even waves, but most just look somberly towards me and ride on by. Of course, since these are high-class bikers, they also have expensive two-way radio communications between them, and since their engines and wind speed distort noise, they have the volumes on their radios turned up, far enough that I am privy to their conversations chatting about me. It's gratifying to know that I am earning some "air time" on their radio waves today. They weren't all friendly like the "bad" bikers were, but at least they noticed.

Considerable amounts of water entered my mouth prior to my 1:00 PM departure today. Jack and I knew there were twenty-some miles of uphill to the crest of the Grapevines this sunny Saturday, so he kept providing me small bottles of Arrowhead water from his surplus supply in the truck. I kept taking it because doing so would maintain my limited on-board water supply longer if I super-hydrated before pedaling away from Scotty's Junction. So, as I got ready, I kept drinking water.

There aren't any bathrooms out here on this road, no big deal to anyone in an automobile, who can speed along to the next human habitation in the time it takes me to progress only a few miles. But for me, and for any cyclist or long distance walker, bathrooms need to be where you make them. Nature is my bathroom, just like for the animals. I have to drink because the high levels of physical activity require it. And so, I have to also eliminate the processed liquid on a regular basis.

Have you ever watched a documentary about space travel, climbers on Everest, or any other activity that places humans far away from modern conveniences? I have viewed plenty of these presentations, and it is very rare that any manner of excretory functions is discussed. It's apparently not the thing to do among those interested in ratings or etiquette. Propriety demands that certain aspects of living be confined to personal experience, and not openly discussed. As a result, how many thousands of citizens really don't have a clue what astronauts or Everest climbers do? Most never give it a second thought.

Of course, I do, because I find myself regularly out in the wilds, drinking lots of water, and eating as much food as I can carry or find. Since I have camped primitively my entire life, and spent much time walking through primordial woods, these things are as natural to me as being home (actually, the natural world is my home). This entire trip has been and will be revolving around outdoor bathroom breaks, some of which are taken in vegetated and treed areas that provide plenty of cover from passing motorists. The 26 miles from Scotty's Junction to Scotty's Castle offer up not much in the way of eye concealment.

The only thing out here on this flat expanse of high desert taller than me are creosote bushes, which, fortunately, seem to cluster in groups of three quite regularly for some botanical reason unknown to me. The road is on an elevated grade, so if I see a trio of creosote, I end up walking down a couple feet to the natural desert floor. The best creosote assemblages are those with one tree to the east, one to the west, and one on the road side, as they provide a semi hidden alcove. My clothing is a desert stone color anyway, so considering the sparse car traffic out this far, these stops are generally not at all problematic.

Murphy's Law often works really well for me. It's one of those deals where there won't be a car for a long period of time, but then as soon as I stop for a water offload break, guess what! Yep, along comes one from each direction. This is why I engineer my stops, the ones that have only one creosote bush instead of my preferred three, to occur where there is at least a half mile visibility in each direction. In this instance, I can see a car far enough away that I can usually finish the task at hand prior to them being able to identify what's happening. Nervousness is the only factor that can mess things up. Humans can't pee when they're overly anxious. That's enough of that. Moving on.

Yes, it's funny the things you think about out here pedaling across the Nevada desert. I've been triking for about twenty-one miles when a couple of things happen in short order. First, I reach a summit of this road, which has become progressively steeper in the last few miles as it climbs into the gradual slope of the Grapevine Mountains, thereby necessitating the use of my midrange gearing (the thirty tooth). Now, it's easy cycling time for me because it's all downhill from here, at least to tonight's camp. I upshift onto my 50 tooth ring for maximum speed.

Then, no sooner am I picking up higher speeds pedaling and coasting down the western slope of these mountains, than I see the familiar Death Valley National Park sign up ahead. The afternoon is getting on, and I have to yet find a camp, but I must stop and photograph the ICE Q in front of this entry marker. Having never ridden a tricycle into Death Valley before, the photo opportunity is simply impossible for me to ignore. I'm like a tourist here for the first time,

92

taking pictures of paved highway entry placards, something I have never done before, having passed them countless times during the past 30+ years that I've been coming here on my own. One would never think I first came here in 1955. I'm an old timer!

Photographs taken, I settle in to the Q's recumbent cockpit for a thrilling mountain spin through the tight Grapevine Canyon. This road is truly constricted, and it requires that I regularly use my dual braking system to keep the speed down. The sun is low enough now that half my time is spent in deep shade during my descent. This trike is engineered so well, and so stable, that I simply cannot disregard the overwhelming temptation to attain the maximum safe speeds possible. Miles of uphill seem to psychologically breed a deep seated need for speed. Race time!

I'm a kid once again. The two outrigger front wheels provide a stability that is difficult to describe. This, in union with my extremely low center of gravity (eight inches off the deck), allows for swift travel through the spine-tingling turns. It feels like piloting a Lamborghini through a race course. But some of these turns are so tight and narrow that additional measures are needed, like my drum brakes.

On open highways where I can reach speeds between 40 to 50 miles per hour, there is plenty of lateral room for maneuvering, and the turns are gradual enough that leaning is not necessary. This evening in snakelike Grapevine Canyon however, I must add a touch of body English to my repertoire in order to negotiate the curves successfully at speed. Trikes can tip over. It just takes an awful lot of lateral force to make it happen. This road could make it happen because it is steep, which consequently leads to faster motion!

Oncoming traffic is a slight concern, as the road is uncommonly narrow, but since I have my ears exposed to the open air and have no engine noise to muffle sounds, I can hear if a car is coming. As it turns out, I am the only vehicle in the canyon at this time today.

Even with my Burley trailer in tow, the trike handles superbly as I rocket towards Scotty's Castle, properly known as the Death Valley Ranch (DVR appears on the dinner plates). I lean into each turn, brake as necessary, and forget entirely that a heavily-loaded trailer is behind me. A faster speed could be attained if I had the standard Q model with a 31 inch front wheel track, but that's okay because I prefer my narrow track version of 27 inches due to its ability to maneuver better in really tight places, like roads with little or no safety shoulders. The Qnt does admirably well, and I am exceedingly pleased with its performance!

In short order, the five miles from the summit to the entrance to the castle are over, and I coast into the driveway of Scotty's Castle. There is a large palm tree grove to my left, shading a generous lawn area on which visitors can eat lunch in the midday heat. The late afternoon sun is filtering through the palms as I ride by and up the hill to the castle, where I snap a couple more photographs of the worthy Q in front of the striking buildings of grandeur. A castle it is!

Accurately known as the Death Valley Ranch, the name of Scotty's Castle took hold because long ago a charismatic and extremely egocentric con man named Walter Scott led most people to believe that the desert mansion was his own. In the northern portion of the park in the Grapevine Mountains, this splendid structure began its existence in 1924 and had more than two million dollars pumped into it before construction finally came to a halt. The massive swimming pool was never finished. The Great Depression even affected the wealthy.

The impressive hacienda encloses antiques from Italy and Mexico, a Gothic styled music room, and an ambiance that is pure enchantment. It was built and owned by insurance multi-millionaire Albert Johnson and his wife Bessie of Chicago, who visited during the winters. But Scotty generally remained in the area most of the time, telling tall tales of his gold mine underneath the castle. Scotty's grave is on the hillside overlooking the mansion. Today, Scotty's Castle is one of the park's main attractions. It also has a grand pipe organ worth hearing.

My trike is in an area forbidden to vehicles, with the swimming pool separating it from the castle walls, but since I am not motorized, I take my chances that I won't get a ticket. Hardly anyone is here this late in the day. Next, I ride all the way up to the National Park Service interpretation center, and park at their door. You'd never get by with this in a car. No one confronts me about my actions. Maybe they can see that I'm harmless and the trike won't hurt anything.

Inside the visitor center, I notice that the clock indicates 4:00 PM, exactly three hours since I left Jack. He's almost certainly still driving back to Gardnerville, but my daily travel is nearing an end. My progress and time was 26 miles in 3 hours, which works out to an average speed of 8.7 miles per hour, and that includes stopping for all my water offload breaks! Not too shabby for a guy with disfigured Achilles tendons, huh? I am pleased with this rate of travel. Now, if I could only maintain that number everywhere, I'd get places a lot quicker. Oops, better stop that talk, else I'll fall into the same questionable hurry-up mindset of society! Don't want that to happen.

Now I will attempt a little verbal finagling with the park service officials. Tomorrow, I want to ride the Q to Ubehebe Crater, several miles northwest of here on another road. If I stay at Mesquite Springs Campground tonight, which is at the bottom of a steep two-mile downgrade into the wash area, then tomorrow morning I would have to

94

ride back up that grade on my way to the crater. It's getting late now, and I'd prefer not to deal with that tomorrow, so I ask the NPS desk ranger if it would be at all possible for me to simply pitch my tent behind the employee quarters in the rear of the facility, an area totally invisible to tourists. It would cause no one any distress at all.

He cannot authorize this unusual request, so he gets Abby, the northern region supervisor for the park on the telephone, and then hands it to me. Abby is a very cordial lady, and patiently allows me to explain my situation, namely that I was invited here to talk about the new book, which is being sold in the park bookstores, I am tired, and my presence out behind the employee buildings would be unknown to anyone. Well, my finest whining, cajoling, and sweet talk repeatedly come up dry, as the United States government has its rules, which don't include allowing human-powered recumbent trike hobos to sleep on the ground in a little tent in the bushes at Scotty's Castle. I kind of figured this would be the outcome, but I enjoy the challenge of attempting to persuade the machine to bend its rules. There is no bending to be had. It's a machine!

I thank everyone, take a bathroom break in a real bathroom, and slide into my cockpit once again for an easy ride down, down, down into Mesquite Springs Campground. On the way, some car had collided with a boulder or something, as law enforcement rangers and an ambulance were parked along my path, but I sail on by to get my tent pitched. I pass the road I will take north in the morning to Ubehebe Crater, and then soon turn off onto the old rutted pavement of the two mile road downhill to the springs. The temperature is pleasant.

This road is steep, and allows for really quick speeds to the camp area, but it is so darn rough from untold years of use that it is shaking my trike and trailer to bits. Out of necessity for the preservation of my intact brain, I use the brakes every few yards when the speed gets too high for the gouges and ruts in the asphalt.

The campground has scattered trailers and motorhomes. Nearly all are down by the springs, so I take spot number one near the entrance and the upper restrooms. It's quiet here. The low sun casts nice lighting on the mesquite trees, creosote bushes, and surrounding hills. This is a very pleasant place to pitch for the night. I have to use my credit card at the automated fee station because it doesn't accept fifty dollar bills. I am now twelve dollars poorer financially, but much richer mentally as I soak in this grand arena. I feel safe here, having returned yet again.

It is 82 wonderful degrees here at Mesquite Springs. It is 101 degrees Fahrenheit 51 miles south at Furnace Creek. I'm happy to be at this higher elevation, which is just over 2,000 feet above sea level. Furnace Creek is 200 feet below! The warm days make for unbeatable evenings and nights. I won't need my rain fly here, nor will I need a down mummy bag, but since I only have one sleeping bag, I'll just lie on top of it until I get cold enough sometime in the night to crawl inside.

There is also no cell phone service here, even when I climb to the tops of surrounding hills. I find this odd, as I have experienced good service at some very remote Death Valley locales simply by finding high ground on foot. Oh well, guess I won't be calling my correspondents tonight, but there is a pay phone two miles away at the park entrance station that I can use tomorrow on my way to or from the crater.

The huge mesquite trees here (at least that's what I think they are called), provide a picturesque desert ambiance that I utterly adore. Everything is so relaxing, and I feel wonderful now that I am safely inside the park at long last. Seventeen days ago, I left the Pacific Ocean, and now I am closing in on North America's lowest, hottest, and driest countryside. There is no rush about anything at this point, as I am an easy day's ride to where my talk will be at Stovepipe Wells, and that doesn't occur until November 6th. So, I have plenty of time to ride to a few park attractions, take some photographs, and just marvel in this world-class desert environment.

The crickets are starting to sing their songs, and frogs by the springs are also heard. A light breeze drifts through the trees and across my campsite. After eating my packet of rice and vegetables for dinner, a fellow named Mike Cole from San Luis Obispo, California walks up to my aluminum picnic table. He is a private investigator who saw my strange and ragged form wander in to camp a little while ago. Mike offers me two ice cold V8 juices, says it looks like I could use them. He is right! We chat for a while, and then darkness calls Mike back to his tent. I take a walk around the perimeter of the campground, being careful to watch for sidewinders, which are nocturnal, then into the tent I crawl for a great end to a fantastic day.

Oh, by the way, I forgot to say that midway on my ride this afternoon, I passed a rattlesnake on the centerline of Highway 267. I stayed way over on the shoulder as I passed. Needless to say, I chose not to extend my hand in my usual friendly wave.

DAY 18 - *Death Valley*
Sunday, October 18, 2009
Ubehebe Crater trip – 15 miles (running total: 441 miles)

What a great night's sleep! It is so incredibly quiet and peaceful here in these wild northlands of Death Valley. One guy was running his generator a little late last night, and someone else finally politely yelled out very loudly in desperation for him to turn it off, which the generator man didn't do for about another half hour, but other than that, the night was perfect. Ideal sleeping temperatures here make for first-rate desert camping this time of year. I recommend this campground for folks with conventional autos that can't make it to the primitive ones.

As I'm fixing my Nutty Nuggets, Mike Cole drives up in his Subaru all-wheel drive car. He shuts the engine and strides over with two small cans of ice-cold pineapple juice, which he also donates to my cause. What a guy! I must look like I need assistance in my endeavor. Well, in any event, I admit that the canned juices from last night and this morning really hit the spot. We chat for a few minutes while I'm munching, and then he bids me farewell, never to be seen again.

I am going to ride the trike up north to Ubehebe Crater today. Nature did the impossible with a massive steam explosion that resulted from magma super heating water trapped underground. This extreme heat under pressure sent unimaginable amounts of rocky ground flying skyward at nearly 100 miles per hour, leaving a debris field up to 150 feet deep immediately surrounding the crater. This happened sometime between two to three thousand years ago, according to some theories. The crater is about 770 feet deep and over a half-mile across. Just south of it, on a trail, is a smaller crater, shaped like a football field.

Every time I have visited here over the years, the wind howls so severely that to talk to someone standing next to you requires yelling. The powerful invisible force also causes folks not to venture too close to the edge, which, while not vertical, is steep enough to result in a devastating fall far down into the massive depression. My other visits have always been in the afternoon. Today I will arrive there in the morning. We'll see if that makes a difference.

The thought crosses my mind that I could ride on south to Furnace Creek after visiting Ubehebe, but then I think, why hurry? To do so would require about 65 miles of riding, and necessarily shorten my time at the crater. Tonight will be spent here again, for I truly get pleasure from the relaxing desert atmosphere, and I want this day to be used purely for exploration. I have been an explorer from the time I could walk, so today I will explore – at my leisure!

It will be a laid-back Sunday, with only about 15 miles of triking, so I can happily meld with all that surrounds me. First order of business is to walk over to the automated fee collection machine and feed it my credit card again. I do so, but it gets stuck in an endless loop techno glitch, and refuses to produce my paid receipt. The digital display just robotically beeps and flashes: Printing Ticket. Fortunately, my credit card came back out before it malfunctioned. Guess I'll check back later.

Since I have no proof that I paid, I write a note and stick it to my tent in case an enforcer comes around while I'm away today.

Time to prepare for my ride! Having pedaled many miles thus far, today I think I'd like to travel light for a change. I will leave my Arkel GT-54 panniers in the tent to keep it in one place if the wind starts to howl later on. The ground here where I pitched is hard, so I have not used any tent stakes. I'll also leave my air mattress and sleeping bag inside. On the trike, I place my Radical side-pod panniers, and place minimal gear inside, like a coat, rain clothes, and a bunch of food bars. Rain's not likely, of course, but I'm one of those guys who prefers to be ready. This is one reason why my rig is as heavy as it is!

My helmet will also remain with the tent. I've been a good boy and worn it all the way so far, but today I'm going to don my Sequel foreign legion styled survival cap. Made in Durango, Colorado (where I used to live years ago), this hat is ingeniously designed for extended stays in hot sun, with foil over the head to reflect the heat, a large bill, and cotton flaps that cover my head, neck, and face as necessary to keep from getting sunburned. I've worn this hat for the past twenty-some years now, and it's worth its weight in gold if spending days in the sun.

The helmet is not necessary today. Traffic is virtually non-existent, and any rare car I do pass on my way to Ubehebe Crater will only be going 25 miles per hour on these old rutted paved roads, and visibility extends several miles out here. Simply put, there is no danger that requires the wearing of a helmet. My Specialized helmet is comfortable, but the Sequel hat is even better. Besides, the hat makes me look way cooler out on my trike, like some epic desert trekker traversing the arid landscape – ahh, I can hear the symphony music already. Time for the big screen!

Also not necessary on today's trike ride up north is my Burley trailer. Yep, for the first day of the trip, I will not be pulling it behind me! Oh the joy! Unencumbered miles at long last! So, I unhook it from the tricycle, and leave it between the tent and the aluminum picnic table. Trust of my fellow humans out here is high in my mind, so I shall not give it a second thought. If, in the very unlikely event, someone messes with or takes my stuff, well, that's just the way the story goes. If they want my clothes, shelter, and food, I can get more. My experience has shown that most folks are honest. And out here in Death Valley, you just don't find many, if any, campground thieves. I'm good to go!

With only 15 round-trip miles to pedal, and plenty of daylight to do it, there is no rush at all. As I pedal up to the automated money inhaler, a foreign couple is standing there reading the instructions prior to purchasing a camp site for tonight. The steel and plastic machine is still beeping as it attempts to produce the receipt that I purchased 30 minutes ago, so I figure I had better let the folks know so they don't insert money just to lose it.

As I come to a stop, I am immediately aggressed upon by their very hostile mini-dog. Now, this probably sounds funny, but when you are sitting this low to the ground, all of a sudden a little animal like this takes on larger proportions. It goes for my right hand, which is on the handlebar, so I quickly pull my arm across my body to remove my fingers from the reach of his bared teeth, then another rapid response has me in a little trike loop maneuver of dog avoidance.

From a few feet away, I tell them I have something to say, and ask if they would please restrain their animal, which they do. After enlightening them as to the machine's woes, I hightail it up the old entrance road towards the Scotty's Castle road. Gee, I was trying to help the folks so they wouldn't toss in money needlessly, and their dog tries to bite me! Sometimes, good Samaritans get the raw end of the deal. Being at mini-dog level, my ears also took a beating from the annoying barking. I came here for the peace, quiet, and serenity.

An interesting thought crosses my mind as I am pedaling up the two miles to the main road. I have spent a lifetime in the wilds, hiking, backpacking, camping, and have never once been aggressed upon or attacked by a wild animal. Even though I have been in the midst of many, the animals of the natural world have thus far shown no desire to harm me. I even sat with a wild bobcat once a few years back while alone at Mahogany Flat Campground 8,415 feet above Badwater Basin. That was an incredible experience I shall never forget!

The only animals that have ever demonstrated intent to harm have been "pet" dogs, those supposedly domesticated animals trained to live harmoniously with humans. Dogs have exhibited this hostility consistently throughout my life, not only towards me, but towards my friends and family. These are not isolated incidents at all. This dangerous behavior is such a societal scourge that I truly appreciate the rare person who has a friendly dog and keeps the dog fully under control. I have seen a little girl get a chunk of her thigh ripped open, as well as an elder lady once who was just walking along the beach when attacked by a hostile pack of three large roaming dogs. Dog owners just don't get it!

What I find most amusing is that the owner response is almost always the same, so much so that when they say it, I find it annoying now. "Oh, he's friendly. He won't bite." Well, if that's how the dog displays friendliness, then I'd hate to see it when it gets angry. The good news so far on my trike is that no dog has attacked me while riding, as they appear very confused with my three-wheeled form. I've had large, loud, and mean dogs stop eight feet away, still barking, but not sure if it's okay for them to attack me directly.

It's a great (and now quiet) day here in the northern reaches of Death Valley, a 140 mile long depression that draws tourists from around the world. Since the trike is unburdened by all my touring weight, I am able to maintain midrange gears to the top of this steep two mile grade that rises out of the Mesquite Springs wash. At the Scotty's Castle road, I pass the entrance station, which I have only seen manned once, and then turn off northwest on the world's most dreadful paved road. Word is that funding will be released in 2010 to repave the five miles to the crater, so I am one of the final cyclists to have this much fun. Some areas are so bad in my lane I have to ride in the oncoming lane. Since there is no traffic, and the road is wide open visibly, this is not a problem. It's uphill too, so coming back down, I'll not be able to coast quickly as I normally would, else I'd be hitting all the holes.

Ubehebe Crate is quite a sight, especially since it is not at all visible until you are literally at its precipitous edge! It is the highest point on the hill where it exists, so the ride to the small paved parking lot just looks like I am about to park on a hill. In fact, on this low trike, I have to stand up to see the massive crater's full glory.

There is a curb here, with a little paved walkway between the lot and the cliff edge. I want a photo of the Q on the precipice as close as I can get, so I lift it up over the curb to position it just right. While snapping some shots, a few visitors gather around to ask if I rode this trike here. I enjoy talking with these folks.

A few minutes later, I meet a couple from England, Paul and Britt-Marie Beard. They are here on a 17 day vacation to the United States. They took a couple of photos of my British trike, me, and Britt standing next to me. Then, she decides she wants to walk down to the bottom of the crater. I notice she only has a half-full plastic bottle of water, perhaps a half-liter at most, and inform her that she will need much more, as the climb back out is a real bear. Britt tells me that she will take a more gradual trail down, and it should be fine.

Paul and I are talking a while during her absence. Sometime later, up walks Britt, all flushed and overheating, with an empty water bottle. She says to me: "You were right!" Is it just me, or do these Brits seem more refined and intelligent than us Yanks with their grand accent?

The wind is light this morning. Perhaps it always is in the morning. This is my first-ever time here this early in the day. Conversations are actually pleasant because we can all hear one another. I'm just kind of hanging out enjoying this area, having all the time I need. The wind does seem to be picking up though, but I won't be here this afternoon to get hammered by it. I take one more photo of the trike with the Last Chance Range in the background to the west.

I actually hate to leave, but I should be calling my blog correspondents, so I push the Q over to the curb. My mind lapses momentarily, and instead of picking up the rear wheel of the trike to let the front two over the edge, which is a stable maneuver, I lift the front two slightly up from the right side. Well, this is a highly unstable mistake, as the trike is balancing only on one wheel, but before I can rectify it, the trike tips slightly and the bottom of the frame scrapes along the rough cement. Ugh, I hate that sound, but comfort myself in knowing that I can just think of the scratched paint as a memento of my Death Valley trip. It is underneath and will never be seen by anyone.

It is also during this little triker's boo-boo that my front chainrings contact my cotton khaki pants, leaving a nice blackened impression of chain teeth and chain on my formerly clean pants. At first I am bummed, as these are the pants I'll wear to give my presentation at Stovepipe Wells, but then it dawns on me that this might well be a good thing, as it will add to the character of my intrepid journey for all the retired folks who see this trip as a great and daring adventure. Without mishaps, where would be the challenge, after all?

Out of the crater parking lot the road steeply descends into a short curvy canyon. Unfortunately, I cannot take full advantage of this otherwise-thrilling downhill due to the pavement's exceptionally deteriorated condition. Nope, I must use the brakes frequently for several miles, swerving here and there to stay out of the worst holes and ruts. It's okay! What would Death Valley be if it were all civilized and smooth? One thing is certain. It would not be my kind of place.

Back on the Scotty's Castle road, I pull into the Grapevine Ranger Station parking lot to use the pay phone. The station is closed, as it often is, so I have the place to myself. I have heard that budget shortfalls have forced the National Park Service to cut back on staffing certain locales, and I wonder if this is one of them. An elevation sign here indicates 2,242 feet above sea level, which is about 2,442 feet higher than where I'll probably be staying tomorrow night.

Jack and I chat on the telephone for a while. I used my prepaid calling card here, but the downside is that the company charges a hefty fee just for the use of a public pay telephone. The cellular telephone does not work, so I have no choice. As always, Jack takes notes as I talk so that he can update the blog today or tomorrow. I also call Desert Dune, but only get an answering machine, so I leave a message that Jack has the latest news of the trip.

There is shade here, along with a few places to sit, so I go ahead and have a couple of bars as I gaze out over the long valley to the south, contemplating what tomorrow's ride will be like. It will be a descent of nearly 2,500 feet in 51 miles, so I am thinking it will not be a challenging traverse. I forgot to take in one major factor however during my lunch today. Tomorrow will bring my revelation!

As I pull back into the campground, having been jostled and bumped all around on the two mile entrance road, I notice the money monster is still beeping and blinking that it is processing my ticket! It has been several hours, now early afternoon. At least if a campground inspector questions me, I can just point to the machine. I did tell one Park Service employee at the ranger station, but he said he was with the water department and couldn't do anything about it.

With the afternoon progressing into evening, I take a few hikes in the hills. It's hard to describe the serenity felt here, but a state of utter peace completely envelopes me. I am happy to be alive and in this national park! I also keep an eye out for rattlesnakes in the twilight.

DAY 19 - *Death Valley*
Monday, October 19, 2009
Mesquite Springs to Furnace Creek – 53 miles
(running total: 494 miles)

At first light, a while before the sun actually saturates the landscape with direct energy, I awaken. This is generally the case when I'm out in the wilds camping. Usually a solo traveler over the years, there is nothing to keep me up much past sundown each day, so I am in the sack early by conventional standards. I don't need a lantern. I often take a late evening walk in the waning light, sometimes hiking to the top of a nearby hill to observe the vistas of a beautiful day coming to a close. It's a great way to wrap up another wilderness experience.

It's easy to awaken prior to sunrise when one goes to bed so early. And on wilderness time, a generous ten hours of sleep are effortlessly attainable without the stress of wondering when an alarm clock will chime. Thus, one of the most magnificent times of day is mine to behold each crack of dawn. I love mornings in the backcountry. It's quiet, except for the mysterious sounds of nature, and the increasing light slowly brings forth new perspective that was not available last night. How can one not have optimistic thoughts as the dawn slowly spreads its magic? This land is indeed enchanted.

I don't feel at all rushed this Monday. Sure, I have 53 miles separating me from my next camp, but they are all downhill, over two-thousand vertical feet down! My mind tells me that it should be a leisurely ride. In a national park, you cannot just camp where it suits your fancy. They have very strict rules about where tents can be pitched. This is no big deal in a car or truck, as the enormous distances of Death Valley National Park are shortened by high speed petroleum-based travel. But on a tricycle, the world is vastly different, and much larger.

Legally, my next camping option is relatively far away via trike. Between here and there, trees are nonexistent, and shade is a scant luxury. The land is wide, open, and essentially flat much of the way. After leaving Mesquite Springs, bathrooms are a thing of the past until I reach the junction of Scotty's Castle road and the Beatty, Nevada road. A block outhouse exists for motorists. It provides a parking area, eating tables, and a little shade behind the toilet structure. Obviously, I'll need to offload prior to that. Good thing a car comes only once in a rare while this far out. Governments rarely consider human powered cyclists.

Quickly, on the topic of bathrooms, so far this trip I have found that the need for solid waste disposal has been comfortably met by what pops up along the journey, except for that one morning at the California Agricultural Inspection Station, where I was not allowed to use their bathroom. Other than that one instance, there is always a market, outhouse, library, or some such building that has toilet facilities. I brought a foldable toilet just in case, but so far have not used it.

On my long overland 4x4 treks in times of yore, I have used this lightweight portable seat, and it affords the most grand views one could ever hope for while lightening the body's load. Prior to my departure, Matt Jensen, an experienced ultra long-distance cyclist, told me not to bring it, but of course, I didn't listen. I had the room to carry it, so I brought it. Old habits die hard. The difference between my Jeep travels and trike trek is that in the Jeep, I would not often come across a toilet facility on old dirt roads in the middle of nowhere for days on end. On the trike however, which is basically restricted to normal paved roads most of the time, there is almost always something during a day's travels, and usually more options than necessary. It's all a matter of timing. I'm no longer worried about it. Experience is the best teacher.

All this considered, I always eat an early breakfast to give myself time to use the outhouse at a campground. Another aspect of active trike travel that varies from passive motorized travel is that the body is continually in a state of aerobic exercise, so it burns ingested food at a tremendous rate compared to just sitting in a driver's seat in a car doing nothing more physical than turning a power steering wheel and maintaining pressure on the accelerator pedal to go really fast.

On the trike, calories are being burned more quickly than I can put them into the furnace, thereby placing me in a daily caloric deficit.

103

Under these conditions, the body extracts absolutely everything it can from each particle of food, leaving little if anything to be expelled later. This, I believe, was the reason I made it to Canby, California that morning when California didn't let me sit. My body simply processed all it could and thus the urge dissipated. Anyway, that's my take on things. I offer these thoughts for other greenhorn cyclists who may wonder. After all, who else is going to talk about it? I live outside culture's prim and proper box, so it doesn't bother me whether you like it or not.

I lie awake in the tent for a while, just relaxing, then it's up to start the day. Breakfast is pleasurable on an aluminum picnic table, with the sun just starting to warm my back. The northern end of the Panamint Range is gorgeous off to my west as the sun strikes it, producing shades of reddish purple for a short period. The smell of the creosote bushes is always my welcomed companion. These bushes smell best after a rain, but there will be none today.

Larrea tridentate emits the smoky odor of creosote, thus the name. Many folks interchangeably term this bush the greasewood, but the plants are different, with the creosote being larger and darker green. The creosote is usually found on bajadas (alluvial fan convergences) in arid desert areas, such as the Mojave and Death Valley regions. The leaves have a waxy coating that helps retain moisture in the plant, which allows it to survive in extreme heat and drought. Kangaroo rats, millipedes, and beetles apparently enjoy living under the canopies of these bushes. The creosote has small dark green leaves and can grow as tall as 13 feet.

In Death Valley National Park's lowlands, they may provide shade in an emergency situation when nothing else is around for miles. This plant is an example of a bush that propagates by sending up new offspring from its underground root system. If we view this extension of life as continual, then amazingly some creosote bushes have perpetuated themselves this way for periods far exceeding the oldest bristlecone pine trees. This logic flows from the fact that the oldest interior portions of the trunk of the bristlecones are dead matter. The living cells exist in the thin cambium layer (just under the dead outer bark layer), in the needles, and cones. The oldest living cells are about 30 years. In other words, if we do not include dead cells as criteria for age recognition, then the lowly creosote reigns supreme over the mighty bristlecone. It is an interesting matter to ponder, and the debate continues as to the oldest living thing on Earth. What do you think?

In years past, I have hiked to the bristlecone pine forest on Telescope Peak, and gazed down over 11,000 feet to the creosote forests far below on the desert floor. Whichever is the oldest in anyone's viewpoint, there are plenty of each out here!

Once the trailer is rejoined to the trike's rear axle, the tent struck, and the panniers loaded and placed on the trike, one final use of the outhouse places me in the "good to go" category. I could stay here another night, but at $12.00 a shot, it's not something I want to spend my limited finances on any more than I have to. I'm spoiled by free primitive camping! Once at Furnace Creek, I may be able to access a less expensive option, courtesy of the Death Valley 49ers organization. Production Chairman Jim Graves said something about me camping behind the fiddler's stage, which suits my pocket book just fine.

Sliding into the seat of a recumbent trike is always fun for me. It's like getting into a race car, low and reclined, ready for speed. As I pedal past the fee collection station, guess what's happening! Yep, the little beeper is still beeping, and the digital readout still says it's processing my ticket, 24 hours after I inserted my credit card for the second night. Well, I'm sure that doesn't hurt the feelings of newly arriving campers, who are precluded from paying for their stay since the machine cannot process another pay until mine is finished. Guess it's the company's problem, so I'll leave it here and be on my way!

The two uphill miles on the campground access road go by slowly this morning compared to yesterday morning, now that I have an extra 150 pounds attached. I am learning a valuable lesson every day. As Matt advised, go light! At the top, I turn right onto the rural Scotty's Castle road and head straight for that big valley before me, way off in the distance. I am actually in the northern reaches of the valley here, between the Amargosa Range to my east and the Panamint Range to my west, but it's so long, the other end is far out of my sight.

Technically, this is not a valley at all, at least that's what the scientific types among us say. Graben is a German word that means ditch. According to geologists, Death Valley is actually a graben, not a valley. A graben is a lower portion of land with parallel fault block mountains bordering either side. In the case of Death Valley, those fault block mountains are the Panamint Range and the Amargosa Range. The raised mountains on either side of this graben are called horsts, which are formed by extensions of the Earth's crust. Should this really be called Death Graben National Park? Scientific jargon aside, it appears that the valley designation will remain firmly affixed, as that is what the historic Bennett-Arcan wagon train party called it in 1849. This is all human-imposed nomenclature of course, and since nature naturally has no names at all, we realize that enjoyment does not depend upon names.

Amargosa is a Spanish word meaning bitter water. These are suitable words to describe the final flow of the liquid from the Amargosa

River, as it finds its terminal resting place in the arid southern end of Death Valley. The history out here is fascinating, so I wrote a book.

Right away the riding is a snap today. I'm going downhill from the get go! Can't argue with that. At this rate, these fifty miles will be achieved by lunchtime. If that happens, it will be the first day on this trip, and will set a personal record for me. We'll see what develops.

A very slight south wind keeps me cool. My cotton long sleeve shirt is just right for temperature control. For those not familiar with wind terminology, a south wind comes from the south, not blowing towards the south. This means that I am pedaling against the wind, but at the low current speed, it has no discernible affect on my forward motion. The great thing about a trike, well, one of many great things, is its extremely aerodynamic shape. I am nearly on the ground, and present little mass for the wind to affect, like a regular bicyclist does. My two flagpoles, one on the trike and one on the trailer, cause a slight drag due to the surface area of the flag material, but other than that, I slice through wind pretty well. If I removed the flagging, I could pick up maybe a mile per hour, but it's not worth losing my visibility.

I have been making good time so far, yet as the clock ticks and the day heats up, the wind increases its push against me. My polycarbonate sunglasses, perfect for preventing rocks thrown up by automobile tires from damaging my eyes, provide a waterless vision experience even with the growing wind. There is no doubt about it though, as the miles roll by, the air stream is becoming a force with which I must reckon. I had not thought about this before.

Wind strength increases with speed of my trike. The faster I go, the higher the perceived wind that strikes me, even on a calm day. Add to that the ever increasing south wind here on Scotty's road, and you can bet I don't have to worry about getting hot or sweating today, regardless of the temperature, which might top 100 degrees later.

In the Amargosa Range to my east are several notable canyons, like Red Wall and Fall Canyons. But the most well-known of them all is Titus Canyon, which I will soon be able to see from this road as I pass. There is a three mile dirt road that comes down from its mouth across the alluvial fan. You can drive up to a parking area there, but must stop, as the canyon is so narrow in places that they only allow traffic to drive westbound the 26 miles from the Nevada side. Canyon walls can be 500 feet high, on either side of the dirt road that is but 10-15 feet wide. It is quite an impressive slot through which to drive a car, or hike. Words cannot describe its colossal magnificence!

Edgar Titus was 29 years old when he and his younger brother-in-law, Earle Weller, left Telluride, Colorado in 1905 to seek their fortunes in Rhyolite, Nevada instead. This decision, it would turn out, was not in their best interests! They joined a third man, purchased numerous burros and a couple of horses, and set out for the Panamint Mountains on the western side of Death Valley in search of gold and silver. Their route took them from Rhyolite over Red Pass and into a huge deep canyon in the Grapevine Mountains of the Amargosa Range.

Searching for a spring to water, all they found was a tiny trickle that was insufficient to handle three men, a bunch of burros and two horses. Edgar had Earle and the other fellow wait by this tiny water supply while he took some burros farther down the canyon seeking water – he did not return. Earle set out to find him next morning. Earle told the third man, John Mullan, to stay with the supplies at the little trickle until he returned with Edgar. Earle did not return either.

As the days passed, John sat tight as instructed, but hopelessly began his slow and agonizing journey towards death in the summer heat. Two weeks later, searchers found John near death, but he recovered in Rhyolite. A note was found in the canyon that read: "Hurry on! I'm going down to investigate the spring. – Titus." Edgar and Earle died from lack of water and the extreme heat of mid summer. Word has it they were buried, but grave sites were not found. Thus the name.

Fortunately today, I shall not suffer such a fate, for I still have over seven liters of water on-board, out of my original load of nearly nine. Riding downhill, this heavy water supply does not slow me. If anything, it might speed me up. Now and then, I pull onto the shoulder or turnout for a stretch of the legs and a few morsels of a Clif Bar.

Up ahead, there is a road repaving operation. It is short, and today there appears no one working here yet. But since there are crewmen who labor out here in this remote landscape, there is also an outhouse from Joe's Sanitation. Hey, I take every opportunity I can get in the wilds. Yet, somehow, a malodorous plastic container isn't quite as nice as the natural outdoors. It's convenient, I have to pee, so my visit inside is very quick. The great thing about Death Valley outhouses is that the ultra low humidity dries everything out very quickly, so smell doesn't hang around too long.

Past Titus Canyon, I am really beginning to notice the wind. My progress has definitely slowed, even though I am still going down. On stretches of road that I would be expecting to coast, I am instead still driving power to the cranks. It's now early afternoon and my water intake is becoming more constant than ever so far on this journey. The arid wind dries my throat, thereby increasing my perception that I want water. I am not sweating, but I am sure drinking. Typical for this region.

More dangerous than other perceived dangers like wild

animals, lack of sufficient water has always been one of the prime reasons for deaths in the region. Since the humidity is so very low, human body moisture evaporates at a dangerously high rate. Mid summer in Death valley, can see the loss of a couple of gallons of water in a day just sitting in the shade! This is very serious business.

As many of the 1849ers seeking a shortcut through Death Valley to the California gold fields learned, water can be far more precious than gold and silver. Symptoms to be watchful for include: headache, visual illusion of snow, lowered blood pressure, dizziness, fainting, delirium, tongue swelling, unconsciousness, and death. Once two percent of our water volume has been lost, these effects begin to manifest themselves, first with thirst, then with loss of appetite and the feeling of dry skin. Our heart rate may increase and fatigue may come very quickly. If we cry, there may well be no tears.

This all leads to an increase in body temperature due to lack of sweating. At five percent water loss, our arms and legs may begin tingling and we may feel queasy. When we pass the ten-percent mark, our muscles will become convulsive and uncontrollable, which could lead to falling down. Our skin will wither and our eyesight will begin going dim. If we hit the fifteen percent water loss mark, we are about to become the next victim of the infamous Death Valley legends of death. Once this process of dehydration starts, it becomes increasingly difficult to even realize that we are being consumed by it, and without a second person to see this dangerous dynamic, we are unable to help ourselves.

The good news for me on this Death Valley Tricycle Expedition is that my time here this year is in October and November, months that typically present the most human-friendly thermal and moisture conditions. I am not going to dry up and die like others have throughout history. I have plenty of food and water, and I have a fast trike to get me to my destination much quicker than a prospector walking with his burros. Compared to a car though, I bet motorists think that I am probably on the brink of death as I attempt to pedal this long valley south in the glaring relentless sun. I like living on the edge, at least a well-thought and controlled edge! Thinkers rarely perish.

At one point, the road increases in its angle of decline, so I quickly upshift onto the largest chainring. I must have been a little too aggressive in my delight to maintain higher speeds, as the chain doesn't stop once it engages the metal ring, but just keeps right on going, over the top and off the outside, into an area between the large chainring and the right crank pedal. At first, I don't realize this, as I do not see it happen. I have upshifted thousands of times on this trip, so I pay little attention to it now. What gets my attention is that I immediately have no tension in my pedals anymore. A quick glance reveals my woes.

So, I coast off to the wide shoulder to get things back on track. I don't want to use my bare hands to return the chain to its rightful place, as I have no way to wash them, or get chain lube and grime out from under my fingernails. Nor do I wish to keep my leather riding gloves on when I do it, but those are my only two options right now. With gloves on, I go ahead and replace the chain on the ring, and then it dawns on my dehydrated brain that I can easily clean the gloves with something that is everywhere as far as the eye can see. Dirt! Sure enough, after rubbing them in the dirt, all the lube is gone, and they are dry. Then, just dusting them off makes them as good as before.

Once nearly at the Beatty road cutoff, which becomes Nevada Highway 374 after is passes through Mud Canyon and crosses the state line, I pull across into the block outhouse I spoke of earlier, which is also an information kiosk for tourists. It is on the east side of this roadbed. The shade of the building allows me to have another energy bar and water out of the sun's rays. I see cars up ahead on the road between Beatty and Stovepipe Wells (which is also visible off to the southwest). That is where my talk will be November sixth.

A stiff wind is now my reality, and being a former windsurfer for many years, I estimate that it is averaging about 30 miles per hour at the present. Having my rest, food, and rehydration, I'm back on the road south. At the junction of Highway 190, I pull up to the stop sign and actually have to wait for traffic before turning left towards Furnace Creek. As luck would have it, there is also a car behind me. All day I am nearly alone out on the road (a great feeling for a cyclist, by the way), but now I have cars again. This highway is the major thoroughfare that most motorists use when crossing or visiting Death Valley. Traffic is not heavy by city definition, but at least it's now back on my radar screen.

Ten miles north of Furnace Creek, my rearview mirror reveals bicyclists approaching. Thus far this trip, I have not had any overtake me, but out here in Death Valley, I suddenly have a small assemblage coming up rapidly behind me. I have been pedaling for roughly 43 miles so far today, and maintaining a decent pace considering the increasing south wind, but these pedal pushers are easily gaining on me. The reasons become apparent soon enough.

There are four of them, and not one has any panniers on his bike. Other than their helmets, lycra riding clothes, and a couple of small water bottles, these guys are speeding along like they are on a neighborhood ride. At first, my mind doesn't process this incongruous sight. Here, out in the remote expanses of Death Valley, I have a supply of gear to get me the distance for weeks, and these cyclists have nothing

109

to get them more than a few miles. If they run out of water here, they've had it! Yet, as they pass me with the usual congenial greetings, three of them don't even seem at all tired. The fourth fellow, farther behind, does seem winded as he passes. He is also carrying a bit too much bodyfat for a long distance cyclist (well, a lot more). I can't believe he's out here.

I am clearly in superior physical shape compared to the last rider, yet he passes me anyway. If I could only shed this trailer, it would be a different story, but that's just my male ego and pride talking. If he were lugging along an additional 150 pounds, I think he'd be in a world of hurt. Another mile ahead, the overweight cyclist has finally stopped and is chugging water as his breathing is labored. He appears wiped out. I am regaining ground on him, and figure to catch him shortly, which will allow me to chat and ask where they are all going.

But then, the reason behind their presence makes itself known to me! A large 15-passenger Ford van, coming north from Furnace Creek, makes a quick U-turn and pulls in ahead of the rider. There are race bikes on top of the van on a rack. Two men quickly get out of the van, load the tired cyclist's wheels on top, put him in a passenger seat, and speed off south again, only about 60 seconds before I reach the location. On the side of the van, are the large letters and logo of "Backroads" tour company, which specializes in assisted cycling tours. So that's how they do it! These guys were having fun, with no work.

Of course, those men are paying a pretty penny for the luxury of cycling through Death Valley without a care in the world. If they break down or need food, the van just pulls up and fixes everything for them. What a life! Well, that's not living on the edge at all, but I guess it's a close second for city folk who want to say they've ridden Death Valley on a bicycle. Personally, I prefer the challenge of doing it all myself, kind of like a pioneer. Perhaps someday, if I sell a lot of my books and have money to burn, I'll give it a try to see what it's like.

There are supported cycle tours from coast to coast in America, which might be fun. The one advantage I see of a supported tour is the camaraderie to be had. Cyclist touring companies perform a valuable service for cyclists who wish to journey long distances, yet prefer the added security of assistance whenever needed. These companies certainly earn their money, as the logistics of successfully pulling off a cross-country tour must be extensive, not to mention costly insurance.

I considered the idea of an automobile backup for this trip of mine, and by no small measure, Jack Freer has come to my rescue with his truck, so I am not without support. If I need help, he will come. Yet, to have a car always at the ready, within a few minutes of my location, somehow changes things for me. This is especially true considering my environmental beliefs. To have a car shadow an entire trip is clearly not preserving a sound natural world by any means. If the number of riders per car is high, then it makes more sense, like the numbers that may engage in a coast to coast tour. But to have one car for one or two cyclists, to me that is clearly not ecologically sound.

Soon, I must pull over and take a photograph. It is the one photo that every visitor wants when they see it. The place is so popular that a small sign says to please park off the pavement, because the National Park Service knows tourists often park in precarious places. I pull off the pavement with plenty of room to spare, and I am the only one here right now. With my next pedal strokes, I will be triking down deeper than the level of the Earth's ocean. This is the point of sea level, marked clearly by a large sign. I began this trip at sea level days ago.

The wind has further increased now. I am closing in on Cow Creek, which is just north of Furnace Creek about three miles. I want to stop and visit with David Blacker, the Executive Director of the Death Valley Natural History Association (DVNHA), yet I am getting tired fighting this powerful headwind, and finding a campsite would sure be nice. It is probably blowing about 40 miles per hour at this point, still out of the south. David's office is uphill to the east, and off the main road about a half mile. I don't feel like riding up that hill, but since it's at right angles to the wind, I decide to pedal on up to his office.

As Cow Creek approaches on my left, which now primarily consists of park employee housing, I am reminded of its interesting present and past history. This former Civilian Conservation Corps camp houses, among other things, the offices of the Death Valley Natural History Association, including a huge warehouse that stores numerous books and gift items that eventually go on sale to the public in the park gift shops. Many of the original Cow Creek structures were destroyed by a large fire back in 1936.

A civilian agency called the War Relocation Authority, run by the federal government during world war two, relocated American citizens who were stripped of their freedom due to their ancestry, during a time when the American president and many officials were worried that they might aid their country of original ancestry in the war effort. American citizens who had Japanese, German, and Italian lineage in their family history were imprisoned in various locales, two of which were Manzanar near Death Valley, and Cow Creek in Death Valley.

President Franklin Roosevelt issued the executive order 9102, forming the WRA on March 18, 1942. Roosevelt said, "The successful prosecution of the war requires every possible protection against espionage and sabotage." It was further felt by a fair number of governmental authorities in this country of America that "although a large proportion of the Japanese group might be found loyal to the United States, military considerations cannot permit the risk of putting unassimilated or partly assimilated people to an unpredictable test during an invasion by an army of their own people." Milton Eisenhower, the original director of the WRA, later said: "When the war is over and we consider calmly this unprecedented migration of 120,000 people, we as Americans are going to regret the unavoidable injustices that we may have done." Cow Creek was a prison compound for American citizens.

Sixty-five American citizens were imprisoned at Cow Creek to live for a very short period of time. The camp had barracks, infirmary, latrine, shower, laundry, and a mess hall. For the three months these unfortunate captives remained at here, they performed volunteer work for the National Park Service, and found themselves much better off than when at the Manzanar prison facility on the slope of the Sierras.

I park on the sloping dirt hill in front of the DVNHA offices and warehouse. The wind is really howling now, the weather is hot, and it feels good to walk inside to calm and cooled air. David and I have met before, and he welcomes my tired and sorry body into his office. I look a frightful mess, having pedaled 50 miles to get here today in the wind. I might even smell bad too, but to me, I just smell like an arid desert, which is acceptable. Who knows what he thinks of me.

David was initially responsible for getting my book accepted for sale in the visitor center just down the road, and it was he who mentioned to Jim Graves of the Death Valley 49ers that I might make an interesting speaker for this year's week-long encampment celebration. Accordingly, I owe him thanks. During the course of our conversation, he offers me water, and more water, and yet more. Not only is it wet, but it is cold for a change. All my water on the trike is air temperature, sometimes warmer if it's from the two gray bottles that sit exposed to the sun all day long. The water in my hydration pack behind my seat stays cooler, as it's usually shaded.

Dave knows I'll be in the area for a while until my talk, so we part company after about 20 minutes. He comes out to see just how I got here from Oregon, and is quite curious about this weird thing called a tricycle. The driveway down to the highway is all fast coasting, and at Highway 190 once again, I turn south for the final three miles into Furnace Creek for this night's camp. I am ready to relax!

There is a large and steep downhill near the old site of the Harmony Borax Works, a hill that I would normally reach a speed of about 30 miles per hour on just by coasting. Today is very much different however. The wind is sufficiently intense that coasting is not even possible! In fact, I must pedal for all I'm worth just to get down the steep hill. This is a new one on me. I cannot even believe it even though I am personally experiencing it. Yes, I am definitely ready for some rest and relaxation now!

There is a wide bicycle path that I pick up about a half mile north of the visitor's mecca, but it is so littered with rocks, branches, and debris that I would have been better off remaining on the highway. Part way along the path, I cut across the dirt and rejoin the highway. Up on the right is the entrance to the Furnace Creek Campground, so I turn in. There are many mesquite and tamarisk trees here, so the wind is cut considerably, allowing me to slowly trike through the loops to locate a camping site for tonight. I see no other tricycles anywhere. I am it!

Back in the late 1800s, the borax miners planted many rows of tamarisk trees to break the heavy Death Valley winds. In today's world however, these trees, or very large plants, are considered an invasive species by the National Park Service, which is on a campaign to eliminate them from key park locations. I doubt they'll do it here though, as hundreds of thousands of yearly visitors find relief from the sun under their branches. Personally, I like them. Does it really matter?

As if cued by Murphy's Law, the wind actually starts to die out once I am in the campground. The trike gods must all be laughing! After 53 miles of riding into an increasingly powerful head wind, I'm too tired to think about it, and just am happy for the calm. I meet Sharon, the campground host, and find a site in the shade of a large mesquite tree. It has a picnic table and a fire pit. I won't be doing a fire, but it will be nice to sit for dinner tonight. Yep, now it's time to relax at long last.

The fee puts a real dent in my wallet though, at $18.00! There is no relief even for people on foot or cycles. It's eighteen bucks across the board. The mega sized motorhomes pay the same fee I do, and they use waste facilities and increased water that I do not. Doesn't seem fair, but again, at least I have a home for the next 18 hours, so I find peace as I enter a mentally relaxed state. Motorhomes and tricycles – same fee!

I am a couple hundred feet below sea level now, lower than where I live at the ocean. The air temperature reflects this change, but in the evening, it feels great. As I begin to prepare setting the tent, those mischievous trike gods start their antics yet another time, as if to say: "Steve, you haven't had enough challenge yet today. Let us help you."

Their "help" comes by way of stirring up the south wind once more, and even though I am near a large tree, the invisible force comes straight across the picnic table. I will set the tent just north of the table for a little relief should the wind pick up further, but now, gusts are hitting the 40 MPH mark again, and for one fatigued man to pitch a tent

113

alone in these conditions is truly an experience in frustration! Argh!

Just getting the tent's footprint on the ground proves nearly impossible. I have to hold it in place with my feet and whatever I can pull off the trike. I am using my feet and both hands to keep my gear from sailing off. The best that can be said is that the wind is now gusty, meaning that very brief lulls come along every half minute or so, allowing me a time to rapidly do the next order of setup. During the gusts, I simply stop, hold it all in place, and take a breather. Finally, the tent is up, and now I must get my panniers inside to keep it from blowing away across the endless expanse of desert floor.

The wind ravages my REI tent, and then with a lull, I quickly detach my right Arkel pannier and toss it in the opening before the next huge gust hits. Next lull, I swiftly grab the other pannier and toss it in. And so it goes, gust to gust, item by item, until I have enough ballast in the tent that it stabilizes sufficiently so I no longer worry about losing it to the sky. Now, I am truly a worn out trike hobo in Death Valley!

And of course, you're not going to believe what happens next. I swear that trike gods must really be out there, or Murphy is watching me, because no sooner is my tent pitched than, yes, the wind dies again. This time though, it completely stops! Not even a whisper of a breeze. Well, I am an opportunist, and out in the wilds, one learns not to waste precious time, so I figure it's a good time to eat dinner, as I'd rather eat outside than in the tent. Will the gods react again once my food is out?

I do eat dinner, and even brush my teeth, with no wind. I get every last detail ready for the night, and it is still calm, so I take a walk around the beautiful desert campground. Night finally falls, and with it, the south wind gradually returns. I attempt to call Jack and Desert Dune for blog updates, but for whatever reason this pay telephone is malfunctioning. Just as well, for the wind is now back up enough that talking on the largely unsheltered phone would have proven problematic.

Once back inside the tent, I put on my sleep clothes and lie atop my down bag. It is far too warm yet to even think about wiggling inside. I have all the vents on the tent wide open, which allows a nice airflow so I don't overheat. Nights are warm here, even this time of year. Oh man, does it ever feel good to just lie down and relax! Oh yes!

Somewhere in the neighborhood of 8 PM, the 40 mile per hour south winds stop all of a sudden. Hmm, I wonder what causes such things. Just as I begin to think that it may turn out to be a calm night after all, about ten minutes later there is a dramatic shift, and I mean dramatic. Two things happen. First, the wind direction shifts 180 degrees, and now begins an assault from the north. This north wind is nothing like the south wind that has been wreaking havoc on me this afternoon. Nope. What I thought was strong wind earlier was just a gentle breeze in comparison to what quickly develops now. It's like someone flipped the switch on a colossal fan (perhaps the trike gods?).

The folks in their motorhomes may get rocked, but at least that's the extent of it for them. For someone living on the ground every night in a lightweight tent, it's a far different story. Ballast is no issue, because now I am inside too, so the tent will remain stationary. Yet whether I'll get any undisturbed sleep remains in question. This wind raises to levels between 65-70 miles per hour! It is fierce and constant, no gusts or relief. From living on the coast, I have a good feel for wind speeds of this nature, and later tomorrow my beliefs will be confirmed. The tent buffets back and forth, slapping me on the left side of my face, which is only inches from the tent wall. With my panniers spread out on the right side, I cannot slide into the center.

At some point, after about 30 minutes of these extreme winds, my right hand touches the tent floor and reveals a problem. My tent is filling up with sand. Since the tent is very small, I sit up and quickly close all the air vents. No more sand will enter, but in the morning, I'll have to empty this all out, assuming the wind is gone by then. As I write in my journal by the light of my battery-free flashlight (the wind-up kind), I feel like a real pioneer, roughing the fury of nature, even considering that I am in a campground with other people nearby.

This brutal wind continues until around 1:00 AM Tuesday morning, at which time I meekly unzip the tent door and look outside to make sure my trike and trailer are all still in one piece where I left them. They are, so I finally am able to fall into a normal and deep sleep.

DAY 20 - *Death Valley*
Tuesday, October 20, 2009
Furnace Creek – 2 miles (running total: 496 miles)

I was wiped out last night when I finally drifted off to dreamland, having ridden over 50 miles through an increasing headwind, and then battered by yet more strong air setting up camp. So, this morning, I am in no hurry to rustle my bones out of this tent. Morning temperatures are very pleasant since I am now close to 200 feet below sea level. There is not a wisp of breeze. It makes for a lazy mental state.

The sun is not yet up, but it is getting light outside. I call this time of day first light, and I really enjoy it as much or more than any other. This is especially true in the desert, where the smells of the land and bushes are like an old friend to me, having been coming out here since childhood. Most folks are still asleep. Only the rare individual who wants to get an early start on the road is getting up yet.

Like an apparition, a shadow appears on the side of my tent, and since I have already zipped open the front door a smidgen for some fresh air, my eyes capture a fleeting glimpse of the furry phantom on a rapid trot past the tent entrance. Only inches away is a coyote, likely snooping for a left-over morsel of camp food, something that he has learned is best taken before all the humans arise. I like close encounters with animals. This one doesn't even know I saw him stride by.

It can get truly hot here at Furnace Creek, and just the two days that I was up at Mesquite Springs, which was in the mid to high 80s, it was 101 degrees at Furnace Creek. Today, and for the foreseeable future, temperatures are supposed to remain more in the high 80s to low 90s. I certainly will not have any worries of freezing to death here!

Furnace Creek is the heart of Death Valley tourism, with the vast majority of park visitors coming to see the facilities at least once during their stay. There is a wonderful museum, with information about such things as the area mining, early people, and famous explorers. At the visitor center, which is open all year, are impressive interpretive displays, the centerpiece of which is a huge physical topographical map that is a three-dimensional diorama. Also here, people get their park entrance passes and hiking trail information, while browsing their comprehensive collection of Death Valley National Park gifts. The bookstore is run by the Death Valley Natural History Association. Inside a small theater runs a continual Death Valley presentation for tourists to get acquainted with the region. During the cooler months of November through April, rangers lead walks and talks.

Andrew Laswell first settled here back in 1874. He is thought to be the first white homesteader in the Death Valley territory. Together with Cal Mowrey, they grew alfalfa and other crops so that they could supply food to the hungry silver miners in the Panamint Mountains to the west, which are readily visible from my camp. The two men are credited with utilizing the innovative idea of irrigation ditches at Furnace Creek. History reveals that Andrew and Cal became significantly challenged in their business, to the point that their partnership suffered. It was not the growing of the crops however, that was the root of their problems, but rather that they were at odds on how to manage the finances. This led to a shooting of Cal by Andrew, and while not fatal to Cal's body, it was to the joint business venture. By 1875, Andrew moved on to other pursuits, taking his hot temper with him, and apparently becoming involved yet again in another shooting elsewhere.

This region is full of incredibly fascinating tales of the old west, and the museums here give folks a good background. There is an outdoor borax museum that has old wagons and even a train locomotive. During most of my former trips to Death Valley over the years, I explored the secluded backroads in my 4x4 vehicles, staying away from tourist centers like Furnace Creek, but this year on the tricycle, I will have plenty of time to take in all the delights here that I have missed before. Since I have just over two weeks before I give my talk at Stovepipe Wells, I'll have plenty of time to walk around and visit all the attractions. Guess I am truly a tourist this time around.

And once Jack arrives in his Jeep, scheduled for this coming weekend, we will be traveling a few of the immediate area's old dirt roads. This is an arrangement that we concocted. Jack would be my failsafe backup guy for the trike expedition, and I would be his personal guide into the backcountry. This works well for both of us, and we'll likely have a blast as we explore what's around that next bend in the canyon road. He has a small Jeep similar to the one I bought in 1975. Mine was called a CJ-5 and his is called a Wrangler.

Once up, a slight breeze begins to keep things cool and pleasant as I break down the tent. So many places on Earth breezes are nice to keep evening mosquitoes away, but here in Death Valley, those unwanted creatures with no known socially redeeming value, are unable to survive due to the extreme aridity and heat. Mosquitoes like moisture, and there just isn't enough here to get their attention. I cannot recall one time in all my 54 years of coming here when I have ever been bitten by one, or even seen one for that matter. Hate mosquitoes? Vacation here!

After breakfast, I take a morning stroll around the large campground, as people are just starting to emerge from their motorhomes and tents. I find two other campsites that are much better than the one I am in, numbers 29 and 30, and perhaps I'll see about reserving one for tonight. I like them better because they are tucked away in little mesquite and tamarisk tree alcoves, totally protected from the sun and wind. They are also extremely private, and privacy is the one aspect of camping that I really value more than others.

I am supposed to meet up with Jim Graves, the Production Chairman for the Death Valley 49ers organization, because he told me this past summer that he would try to get me a campsite over by the fiddler's stage. This stage is a place where music is freely shared by old west musicians each year during the five-day encampment. It is located between the date groves and the NPS visitor center, just to the west of the Chevron gasoline station. So, I load up the trike and trailer and pedal on over to the office of the Furnace Creek Ranch to see if they might know of his whereabouts.

Sure enough, Patrick the clerk knows who I am talking about, and provides directions through the village to RV site number 33, where Jim and his wife Nancy are supposed to be parked. Before I go though, I ask Patrick what a room would cost. It's more than what I spent up at Diamond Lake to be sure, but maybe it would be nice to take a shower, put my feet up, watch some television, and just do nothing for a day. After all, if that old wind comes up again, it might blow me away!

This office is like Grand Central Station, with guests checking out by the droves as they prepare to depart from their visit. Most of them appear to be from foreign countries, as they are either speaking a foreign language (like German), or have strong accents. Finally, having patiently waited on a bench while Patrick helps all these people, I decide to go ahead and luxuriate one more time. Out comes the credit card, which makes this spur of the moment decision way too easy, and before I know it, I have a room key and no camping worries for tonight!

Next, I get in the trike and pedal back through the huge stone gate structure of the Furnace Creek Ranch towards Jim's place. I refer to getting "in" the trike rather than on it because it really does give the impression that you're getting into a little race car. It's nothing at all like getting on a bicycle for instance, where you are straddling a skinny seat that pokes the body in an uncomfortable location. Riding a trike is just flat fun. There are no two ways about it! You're sitting in a recliner chair.

In fact, it's even more fun now that I am nearing the entrance into my seventh decade of life, than it was back when I was only three years into my first decade. This new trike is a whole lot more comfortable than my old 1954 version. That was what they call a delta trike, with two wheels in the rear and one in the front. The front wheel of that '54 was a direct drive, with no chain or sprockets at all, great for cruising my flat driveway as a tiny kid, but lousy on hills! My current trike is a tadpole version, with two wheels in the front and one in the rear. It's not so simple as the first one I had, as it requires more than 12 feet of chain and 12 geared sprockets to make it go. But go it does, and up any paved incline too! This trike is for serious traveling.

Riding the trike through this popular visitor area at the ranch is also fun, because it draws plenty of stares as I go by. Everyone just looks at me and wonders what they are seeing. Most people have never seen anything like this before, but when they do see it, smiles are a common reaction. Before I pedal to Jim's, I first park in front of the old Twenty Mule Team wagons for a photograph, and then do likewise in front of the Old Dinah steam tractor, which was a failed attempt to replace the mule-driven wagons. Mules worked – the engine didn't.

The giant wagons of the Twenty Mule Team hauled borax

through Wingate Wash in the 1880s, and are now legend. Choosing to do his own hauling from the Harmony Borax Works when borax prices dropped, borax entrepreneur William Coleman initiated this new method to get his borax to Mojave. Each team was comprised of 18 mules and 2 draft horses, the horses' heavier weight being used at the lead wagon for making turns easier.

The two wooden borax wagons each carried over 10 tons of the powder in a volume of 4 by 6 by 16 feet. The rear wheels were 7 feet high, and the front were 5 feet. They had iron tires 8 inches wide and 1 inch thick. The third wagon was a metal cylinder carrying 1,050 gallons of precious water for crew and animals to survive the arduous 20 day round trip desert journey (there are some accounts that state the water capacity of this cylinder was 500 gallons). The team moved along at an average speed of two miles per hour. The fully loaded rig weighed in excess of 30 tons. One twenty mule team left the Harmony Borax Works every 4 days, but the runs from this location ceased during the scorching summer months, with production continuing at the cooler Amargosa Borax Works until the fall of each year.

As a more efficient method of hauling borax out of Death Valley, a mechanical device was conceived to replace the mules and horses that pulled the huge and heavy wagons of the twenty mule teams. Francis "Borax" Smith, the kingpin of the business, had a massive oil-burning steam tractor built in 1896 to do the job, and it was eventually dubbed Old Dinah. This attempted improvement proved to be a big mistake when Old Dinah quickly encountered problems such as digging into the ground and rearing up on its large rear wheels. Not only that, but it had to have nightly maintenance to remain viable. Old Dinah was soon just another relic of the times, and can be seen today at Furnace Creek Ranch, in the southern dirt parking area.

When I was a wee lad of three, my dad took a photograph of mom and me standing here in front of Old Dinah, so it is a special thing today to take another all these years later. The boiler cylinder is now on the ground for some reason, but other than that, it's still sitting here, slowly weathering away. Back in the 1950s, the huge iron wheels dwarfed me. Now, they are still taller, but I stand about three-quarters of their height instead of one-quarter.

Once inside the Furnace Creek Ranch compound, I pedal the miniature streets on my miniature vehicle and trailer, past the gift shops and restaurants, past the borax museum, and through the employee housing area to a limited number of RV spots where Jim is supposed to be parked. A lady is sitting out front of a large structure that is commonly know as a fifth-wheel, relaxing with her dog in the shade. I ask if she is Mrs. Graves, to which she replies affirmatively and asks if I am Steve Greene. Imagine that! All this distance from home, and a gal I've never met before in my entire life knows my name!

Of course, how many people are going to ride up on a tricycle out in Death Valley? And undoubtedly, her husband had told her about the crazy guy on a trike riding here from Oregon! So, Nancy and I make our acquaintances, and then Jim drives up in his big silver Dodge pickup. This is also the first time I have met Jim in person. Prior to this, it was all emails and telephone conversation.

There must be something about my appearance that spurs people to deliver assistance to me. Mike Cole up north at Mesquite Springs campground kept ice cold juice coming my way, and now Nancy and Jim want to know if I'd like a sandwich, some Fritos, and something to drink. Well, I'm the kind of fellow who has a hard time saying no to food, especially since I've been eating rationed minimalistic provisions that most folks wouldn't even consider food, so I eagerly agree to be showered with their hospitality and chow.

I go through my first sandwich so quickly that Nancy asks if I want one more. Naturally, I say yes. Before I know it, another sandwich sits on my plate, and Jim opens a new bag of dip-sized Fritos. As I am making apologies for my appetite, they say not to worry, and continue to be entertained by my story of the trip and my ravenous hunger. I tell them I got a room for tonight, but will go back to camping tomorrow. Jim says he'll get me a spot just west of the stage area for my tent. He is spending his days getting the fiddler's stage and parking area ready for the crowds of thousands that will descend upon Death Valley for this 60th annual Death Valley 49ers five-day encampment.

Nancy asks if I'm a 49er member yet, and I say no. She gets me to front the $35 membership fee, which will also cover my mom and sister who will be arriving here November 5th, and goes to get my membership package from the booth out by the highway. A little later, she returns with my DV 49er membership packet, and also informs me that she was able to get me the special 49er rate for my motel room! Wow, so now I won't be billed as heavily for my luxurious splurge of a room. Can't beat that as an unexpected perk!

I thank them for the nice lunch, tell them I'm going to go take a shower in my motel room and do a laundry, and then pedal over to the motel building and do just that. The upstairs room is nice, with cable television, a small deck, and a great view of the world's lowest golf course, rimmed by the 11,000 foot Panamint Range to the west.

After getting squared away with these chores, I ride the trike on over to the National Park Service visitor center to see if my latest

Death Valley book is being sold in the bookstore run by the Death Valley Natural History Association, a non-profit organization dedicated to helping the park. Sure enough, multiple copies are there in three locations, the most prominent of which is right by the check-out counter, next to Richard Lingenfelter's epic book, Death Valley & The Amargosa. In each location, there is a small sign under my book that reads: *"Recommended By Staff."* As a new author since 2007, this is incredibly satisfying to me. Looks like my year and a half of writing has finally sent some financial dividends in my direction.

There is so much to see and do here, and new people to meet. By evening, I'm in the room, feet up on pillows as I lie on the bed watching television. I call mom on the phone, and we have a nice conversation. She wants me to go ahead and stay in the motel a second night to further rehab my Achilles. She says I deserve a break from my travels, and lovingly offers to cover the tab. What a gal! The old Desert Gypsy never lets me down.

FURNACE CREEK - *Death Valley*
Days 21-27 spent enjoying the area, with little trike riding

For seven days, I settled in at Furnace Creek, my old stomping ground since childhood with my parents and sister, and later in my Jeep as a backroad explorer of the most wild and remote regions. I will relate the story of one particular person I met during these seven days:

Late in the afternoon of October 26th, as I am walking out of the Furnace Creek visitor center, I see a well-used bicycle with an attached trailer, about twenty feet from the entrance doors. It is abundantly clear that this vehicle has seen a lot of mileage. Someone is touring a long distance, and has already come farther than I have ridden on my trip. On the pavement, near the front tire, is a bottle of beer with a note underneath. I cannot read the note.

Of course, being a fellow cyclist, I just stand here, studying and admiring what I am seeing. Being that cargo arrangement is always a consideration with cyclists, whether on three wheels or two, I find it valuable to see how others are carrying their gear, and what kind of gear they have. So, I am really checking this rig out thoroughly, and hoping its owner comes out so we can meet. Of course, I am sure that by simply going inside, I will be able to spot this person without any trouble. Cyclists don't look like regular tourists by any means! They stick out like a sore thumb. We are a weird lot by normal standards.

It isn't long before a young man with a bandanna wrapped around his head steps up, clad in a lightweight shirt, short pants, and cycling shoes. His face, like mine, is bearded, for who really wants to shave each morning when living on the ground in the wilds? His beard is still all brown. Mine now has some noticeable streaks of silver throughout the black. He introduces himself as Paul Gareau, and he has indeed been involved in some unbelievable mileages. Five Thousand.

Paul will hit the 5,000 mile mark about the time he reaches Badwater down the road. He began his cycling journey in Fairbanks, Alaska, and is heading for Tierra del Fuego at the southern tip of Argentina! When he tells me this, I laugh inside, for my friend Matt Jensen told me before the trip that I might meet up with someone cycling that far south, and maybe I should tag along. Of course I won't, because I have business here in Death Valley, but the thought is there.

He picks up the beer and reads the note. Some unknown road angel has left it here while he was inside the visitor center, so he slips the brew under a bungee cord on his trailer, although he says he does not drink alcohol. I ask Paul if he has a camp for tonight yet. He says he does not, that he just rode in from a day that included the traverse of Towne Pass, a 4,956-foot skybound summit that drains tremendous energy even from automobiles. Clearly, he must be tired by now!

Since there is only the one motorhome yet in my huge dirt area by the fiddler's stage, I invite Paul to pitch his tent at my camp if he wishes. The price is right, at $0.00 versus $18.00 at the campground. It is decided, and he follows me on over. Since I already paid for Jack and myself, and Jack isn't here yet, all is square with the powers that be, and Paul has a safe place to sack out tonight. It is good to have company.

Paul is from Mansfield, Massachusetts, and obviously likes a challenging adventure. He has an REI brand tent, like mine, but his is a different model. He is on his second tent so far, and this one has seen better days. His model has a high percentage of mesh instead of regular tent cloth, which is good for cooling and viewing the night sky, but poor for sand control if the wind howls out here, something I have already learned well. I also notice that he has Schwalbe Marathon tires, one step down from what I'm running. He has experienced two flats so far on his plain Marathons. This is a true testament to the Schwalbe company. Obviously, they know how to build extreme quality tires!

I have a tendency to talk a lot to folks I find of interest, and I catch myself doing this with my new friend. Realizing that he has chores to attend to, I walk him around the facilities so he will have a good idea of where everything is. Showers, store, post office, etcetera. Then I bug off so that he can settle in. Paul plans to stay here tonight and then resume his journey in the morning. All 15,000 miles of it! Oh, in case you are interested, his website for this trip is located at:

Editor's Note: Paul finished his ride on December 30, 2011, more than two years after this meeting at Furnace Creek in Death Valley.

The weather has cooled into the 50s at night, and predictions say low 70s to mid 80s for the next few days. The heat has broken. I awaken to a cloudy sky. Paul is still asleep in his tent. No sooner do I get my Nutty Nuggets into the bowl with the raisins and water, and eat the first couple of bites, the wind begins to blow from the north. I have an iron-clad windbreak to my south with the tamarisk trees, but the north is far less protected. Wonder how this will progress.

Within three minutes, the wind grows enough to make dirt swirls in the air and blow away anything not held down. This forces me to quickly finish my cereal because the bowl is filling with dirt particles, and I prefer my usual diet. I like taking my time eating, and enjoying nature while I chew, but this is not going to happen this morning. Grit is getting in my eyes, and makes brushing my teeth something I cannot do now. Quickly, I dive back into the security of my tent, making sure all my vents are zipped shut. Paul can't zip his viewing ports shut. I am sure his tent must now be filling with sand.

Once the wind reaches the 50-60 mile per hour range, it remains constant for a long time. There is no way I'm going outside! Fortunately, I have a copy of Gene Elmore's suspense thriller, The Return of D.B. Cooper, a fictional story of what happened to the infamous airline hijacker that got away years ago and was never heard from again. Well, this is the perfect time to read the book. Unfortunately however, Paul and I won't get to visit much unless the wind dies.

Sometime before noon, with Gene's book now finished, things calm down, so I walk on over to the store to grab some lunch. As I'm standing on the old western boardwalk in front of the quaint Wrangler Steakhouse, leaning on the old wooden railing, an Asian man speaking broken English indicates he wants a photograph. I know this because he is pointing to his digital camera, the old building, and smiling. So I move out of the way for him to get his picture unobstructed. The ambiance of this construction styling is just like out of the 1800s, so I understand why folks from foreign countries want pictures of it.

This man then says: "No no no ... you ... picture of you!" This seems like an odd request, especially since my trike is no where near, and he has no idea that I rode a trike here. But then it dawns on my wind-battered brain that my appearance is somewhat like an old cowboy, with my dusty tan-colored clothes, my faded and sweat-stained Aussie hat, and my scraggly beard. He wants a photo of an "authentic" cowboy in front of the old west building on the boardwalk. I am happy to oblige!

He bestows heaping appreciation upon me afterwards, and then moves on in his touristy pursuits.

The wind is still blowing hard down the main part of Death Valley, even though it is fairly calm here in the village right now. The huge Panamint Range, with Telescope Peak topping out at 11,049 feet above sea level, is literally just a few miles west, but these mountains are nearly totally obscured right now by the excessive level of dirt in the air. Believe me, it takes a whopping lot of dirt to hide the Panamints! Furnace Creek is about 200 feet below sea level, so the mountains appear even taller than most. In fact, the distance from the top of Telescope Peak to Badwater Basin's lowest point is over twice the depth of the Grand Canyon! These are seriously large mountains.

The Morning Report, a daily online bulletin produced by the National Park Service, is calling for high winds all night tonight and tomorrow, somewhere around 40 MPH. The air temperature is certainly not hot anymore, although heat may be preferable to living in perpetual dust and dirt, as I only have my tent, visitor center, or stores in which I can seek refuge. The tent is staying put well in its tamarisk shelter. I have six stakes holding it down, and my panniers and sleeping gear are inside for ballast. Paul tells me that his tent is full of sand.

I think that my next trike trip will be one without any agenda, no place in particular as a destination, and no time constraints like this trip. There is an old saying that the best traveler is one without these things, and I can see the merit in such travel. Stop when you want, go when you want, and enjoy the natural world for as long as you want.

Nearly all automobile drivers are fiercely intent on getting from Point A to Point B in the least amount of time possible. This is so incredibly important to them that they will lose their tempers and honk their horns if anyone or anything dares to slow them down the slightest amount. Touring cyclists, on the other hand, as they slowly pedal along the countryside, usually find the time between A and B to be the reward. As another saying goes, it's the journey rather than the destination this is the most fulfilling. Cyclists understand this concept. Car drivers do not.

On a trike, living in the raw untamed elements of the natural world, one learns to leave behind the "Hurry Sickness" that consumes the masses of society. One also learns the value of living simply with what can be carried along, and it becomes glaringly apparent that people are habitual materialistic consumers, totally out of touch with the natural world. As John Muir once said so eloquently: *"Most people are on the world, not in it – have no conscious sympathy or relationship to anything about them – undiffused, separate, and rigidly alone like marbles of polished stone, touching but separate."*

It's 5:30 PM on the 27th of October, and the winds have reached extreme levels once more. I am again hunkered down in my tent, and only eat a couple energy bars for dinner. Brushing teeth will not happen because my bathroom bag is out in the trailer. Churning airborne dirt and grit is everywhere. Winds are gusting in excess of 60 miles per hour. Paul is over in his tent. Conditions are far too harsh for us to visit or even communicate in any level of comfort. Even though yesterday morning he elected to stay a second day, we have hardly visited at all. Bummer. Tent is being heavily buffeted now!

DAY 28 - *Death Valley*
Wednesday, October 28, 2009
Furnace Creek to Zabriskie Point and back – 11 miles
(running total: 507 miles)

No longer! The time has come! The venerable Q just sits outside my tent day after dusty day, collecting a good share of dust in the winds. Each night, the Q, which is only inches from the north side of the tent, whispers to my right ear that it's time to go for another ride – time to get back out on the road of adventure!

Every day, I have been faithful in wiping the dust from the trike's frame, keeping it ready to go at a moment's notice. From time to time, I sit in the seat, either to write in my journal, eat a snack, or just pretend that we're out flying down some long mountain pass in sheer exhilaration. The Q was built for the long haul, built for speed, built for taking the pilot to exotic locales too far away for a reasonable walk or hike. The Q got me here without problem. It never faltered. I may have come up short, but not the trike. It is always ready. Today, we ride!

My Achilles tendons are no longer stiff in the mornings, and inflammation has substantially subsided. Paul will be heading out to Argentina this morning, and I'll be darned if I'm going to simply hang around this camp as he pedals away. I have a trike, so I will ride!

He will be heading south on Highway 178, which is commonly called the Badwater Road. The road passes a turnout where hundreds of thousands of tourists stop every year to get their picture taken next to the sign that proclaims 282 feet below sea level, with the blinding white salt flats and Telescope Peak behind. Today is not my day for going there, for I will wait until Jack arrives for that, but I will ride instead to Zabriskie Point, which is a little more than 5 miles southeast of here. The Badwater Road cuts off about a mile out. I will ask Paul when he gets up if he wants to go see Zabriskie Point and the badlands before heading south to Badwater. Speaking of Jack, where is he anyway?

One reason I arose before dawn this morning is so that I can eat breakfast before the winds come up and add dirt to my cereal again. Another reason is that I want to get up to the point for photographs in the morning, which is the best time to capture Zabriskie on camera. Paul arises shortly after I finish eating, and am brushing my teeth.

I explain my plan to him, and invite him to come along if he doesn't mind adding a few more miles to his 15,000. I figure a guy looking at those kinds of mileages and months on the road might prefer to pass on my side trip offer, but no. He agrees that it will be a worthwhile jaunt and great view of the valley, having never seen photogenic Zabriskie Point before. Paul has a really nice digital camera, which will get it all for his memory book.

Like I have grown to be, Paul is very adept at the camp breakdown procedure, and after he eats, the time is short before we leave. On the way out, we pass by where Gene, Wanda, and Bill are camping in their motorhomes, and tell them where we're going. I also say to come on up if they wish. Gene says they might just do that.

Out on Highway 190, I am riding the Q without panniers or trailer, stripped down to the point that pedaling is a snap. There is no weight to speak of, just the trike and myself. Paul, on the other hand, is slowed with his trailer in tow, so I keep my speed consistent with his. After all, the weather conspired to keep our visiting time to a minimum during his brief stay, so this is the final time we can chat. The time is shortly after 8:00 AM. I am going to miss Paul.

The weather is just cool enough to make riding up the moderate hill a pleasant affair. We both have light polar fleece jackets on, which are plenty to keep us warm. This overlook to which we are pedaling looks down into Death Valley, so we must gain elevation because Furnace Creek is a couple hundred feet below sea level. At the paved parking lot, we turn off the road and head for the point.

At the western end of the parking area, a paved walkway snakes up the steep and narrow ridge line to the overlook point. It is meant for pedestrian traffic, but is wide enough that I fully intend on riding up on the trike, while attempting to miss all the tourists. About half way up, there is a ridiculously steep section that challenges even foot bound people, and when Paul gets to it, he must step off and push. His load is too much for this little stretch, and had I had my fully loaded trailer, it may have likewise been an obstacle for me. I keep pedaling in my ultra low gear, and make it over to the final section where it levels out slightly. Trikes are good at slow and consistent progress on hills!

Tricycles have a definitive advantage over bicycles when it comes to terrain like this, because trikes can crawl to any slow speed

126

and still move forward with stability. Bicycles begin wobbling at really slow speeds, giving the impression that the rider may be intoxicated. We've all seen slow moving bicyclists weaving back and forth on super steep grades. Still, that little section really worked my quadriceps muscles to the max. As a bodybuilder, I love the pump.

At the top, the reward is clear to see. To the immediate south, and lower in elevation, are what most folks call the badlands, wrinkled hills with absolutely no vegetation. I call them the Wrinkles of Zabriskie. Straight ahead to the west are the upper reaches of Golden Canyon, and in the distance Death Valley and the Panamint Range, although today, the Panamints are difficult to see due to dense airborne dirt and high winds down there. Also to the west is Manly Beacon, named after William Lewis Manly, the young man who rescued the Bennett-Arcan gold seekers back in 1849. To the northwest are the impressive 400-foot cliffs of Red Cathedral. The red hues of the cathedral result from iron oxide weathering, what some would term rust. The conglomerate material of Red Cathedral is thought to be deposited debris from primal alluvial fans. Across the badlands straight in front of us are striated bands that stand out in stark relief.

This is one of the most photographed locales in all of Death Valley National Park, and I am happy that Paul is getting to see it. Our chance meeting brought to his camera a vision he would not have otherwise seen. We both immediately get out our cameras and take some photographs of each other, our mounts, and the scenery. As we are doing this, quite a few people approach us to inquire about our journeys. It is a rewarding time for us both. We share a lot with folks here.

Another ten minutes or so later, Gene and Wanda Elmore, along with their friend Bill Whitfield, arrive at the top. Of course, Gene also has a camera, and he wants to get plenty of photographs of everyone together, to commemorate their meeting with two passionate cyclists who use human power to do what the three of them do with petroleum power in a bus. A slight wind is picking up, but we are all having such a good time that it's hardly noticed.

Pictures done, Wanda tells me that she wants to watch me come down the hill on the trike. I tell her to get a head start, and then when there are few or no people on the path, I'll come on down. The steepness means I'll have to be using my brakes all the way because the turns are meant for slow moving pedestrians, not fast moving trikes. Not only that, but the old pavement has chunks missing here and there, so it is extremely rough in surface texture. As I begin the descent, I call forward to Wanda in my booming voice, and she turns to watch. I feel like a little kid saying: "Watch me!" Paul is more conservative in his

127

descent with his heavy load behind. He has a Beast Of Burden trailer.

Back down at the parking lot, Gene snaps a few more photos of Paul and me on our cycles, and then we pull out and head down the hill of Highway 190 from whence we came. I am so deprived of the thrill of speeding down roads on the trike that I go ahead and really pick up a head of steam. For several miles, aggressive pedaling in my highest gear keeps me flying along with a huge grin on my impish face. Paul is fading in my rearview mirrors, and part of me feels bad that I'm not waiting, but that's what happens to a guy who has been off the trike for so long.

This hill allows my lightened rig to maintain probably around 25-30 miles per hour, which is pure fun on a low-slung trike like this. Partway down, Gene, Wanda, and Bill pass me in their minivan and wave. When I arrive at the parking lot for the luxurious Furnace Creek Inn on the hill overlooking the Furnace Creek Ranch (where I'm staying), I pull off to wait for Paul. He may like to see the Inn, which has quite spectacular gardens and a swimming pool.

A few minutes later, he pulls up to a stop next to me, but would rather get on with his journey since the morning is getting later. I don't blame him, but I hate to see him go. It's fun to have a cycling companion, and I think that for my next cross-country trip it would be a good idea. Time is indeed short for our companionship.

We pedal another quarter mile together to the junction of the Badwater Road, where we say our final goodbyes. Paul is going to ride past Badwater, on past the Ashford Mill ruins, and then turn south on the thirty-some miles of dirt called the Harry Wade Road. This will drop him out southbound on Highway 127 towards the southern Mojave Desert. I have driven the Harry Wade several times, and have even seen a lone bicyclist on the road. It is a challenge on two wheels, for it is sandy in many spots, which tends to cause bicycles to wander back and forth as the rider attempts to maintain balance. Since many portions of Paul's journey include dirt, he is prepared for this type of terrain, and welcomes the change from pavement.

As he pedals alone yet farther down in elevation, I watch his form shrink in size. This is a good vantage point, and I can see him for a couple of miles before he finally disappears around the last curve of sight. I am so impressed with what he is doing. I cannot imagine what it must take to set out on a 15,000 mile trek alone. He told me the first day he arrived here that it's no different than what I'm doing. He said that you just take one day at a time, and do exactly what I have been doing, just camping and living in the wilds. He said that it is simply more of the same thing. Of course, it's a LOT more of the same thing!

Paul plans on camping at the old Ashford Mine tonight, which is off the highway a couple miles, up an old dirt mining road across from the mill. He'll hit the Harry Wade Road tomorrow, on his way to Baker, California. Once he gets deep into Mexico, he will hold up for a couple months or so because it will be winter in the southern reaches of South America, and he prefers not to ride through snow, ice, and sub-freezing cold. I told him that based on my experience on the Cascade traverse, his decision is a wise one! Good luck my friend!

The total riding time this morning is about one hour, so that indicates an 11 MPH average speed, not a bad way to get back into the swing of things on this trike after having been off it for several days.

Back at camp, there no sight of a tan over green Jeep anywhere. Jack may be waiting out the high winds before he ventures down into this abyss. Or maybe his Jeep hemorrhaged oil so heavily it died. Or perhaps after meeting me, he figured I'm so crazy that he will visit Death Valley some other time, when I'm not here. I cannot say.

Since the winds are very gentle today, it's time to take a much desired shower. Actually, it was time a day or two ago, but I figured why do it with all this dirt and dust in the air. I gather up all my dirty laundry, some clean clothes, and my bathroom bag and head on over to the shower facility, which is part of the pool complex, and not far from the laundry. The next couple hours I devote to chores, which is easy since I had so much fun this morning.

I have been walking about two miles per day ever since my arrival at Furnace Creek. Even prior to here, I've put in a fair amount of mileage at each primitive camp, as I enjoy walking and hiking. At Furnace Creek, I make multiple daily walks to the visitor center, bathrooms, trash cans, market, laundry, showers, and through the campgrounds. It all adds up, and could be more than I think.

Once Jack arrives, we'll be spending a few fun days exploring the old dirt mining roads from yesteryear in his little Jeep, seeing places he has never been, and upholding my end of the bargain where I act as his personal tour guide in exchange for all he has done to help me on this trike trip. With each passing day, his likelihood of arrival increases, and I am ready to go exploring the isolated backroads and ghost towns.

For lunch today, I eat more than usual since I finally expended some more calories on the trike ride up to Zabriskie Point and back. I have five bananas, one pound of red seedless grapes, and a high calorie Bear Valley Pemmican bar with water. Dinner is a real treat too! I am invited to eat in the Elmore's motorhome with them and Bill. Boy, do they ever treat me right! I am fed salad, wine, enchiladas, and pecan pie. Well, don't that beat all, from roughing it on roadsides in a severe daily caloric deficit, to luxuriating in pure comfort with more calories than my body can handle at one time. They let me sit in the ultra-plush captain's chair too. This is a great ending to a great day!

With each passing day, more large motorhomes and RVs pull into every campground out here. The place is really becoming packed now as the official commencement of the 60th annual encampment is about to begin. In Sunset Campground, where all the western music has been each night, the monstrous motorhomes are stacked in like rows of soldiers in formation. The huge dirt area where I am camping is reserved only for presenters at the encampment, people who are artists, musicians, or authors like myself. That is why Josh and Janet Pickering keep watch at the gate, to make sure who gets in is supposed to be here. The really sad thing though is that Josh is hospitalized in Pahrump, Nevada with his cancer, and Janet is having to do the job herself, in between getting rides to the hospital an hour away to see her husband. She cannot drive herself because of her inability to see straight ahead. They don't know if Josh will live. My heart sincerely goes out to her!

Editor's Note: Josh died a few days later. Janet came here with him, but returned home without him. He passed in the land he loved.

My view to the eastern sunrise is now obstructed from my modest little tent camp. The mammoth motorhomes do an effective job at that. The upside is that the folks who I meet from these large homes on wheels are very cordial to me, and I have fun visiting with them. Plus, this organization helps worthy fund raising events of the area. Furnace Creek Campground, a portion of which I can see to the west of my camp, and the one I stayed in on my first night here, is also now being dominated by gargantuan motorhomes rather than tents. This is a seriously attended affair, I am beginning to learn.

The Death Valley '49er's annual five-day encampment in Death Valley fills the local campgrounds like Sunset, Texas, and Furnace Creek. These get-togethers are held in Death Valley National Park during the month of November each year, and these 2009 festivities mark 60 years of wild fun for members. Some of their activities include: art show, costume contest, cowboy poetry, coyote howl, gospel sing, photography contest, wood carving contest, needle work contest, parade, hootenanny breakfast, horseshoe contest, wagon train enactment, pampered pet show, wheelbarrow race, golf tournament, numerous talented entertainers, quilt raffle, and vehicle tours.

Membership is open to anyone, and includes two membership buttons, window decal, yearly keepsake publication, encampment guide, and a subscription to the semi-annual Death Valley News. Membership cost for a couple is currently $35 per year, or a lifelong membership can be obtained for a one-time fee of $500. Donations can also be made to the student scholarship fund. The worthy group is based out of Amargosa Valley, Nevada, not far east of here.

From their website, deathvalley49ers.org, comes this knowledge: "The Death Valley '49ers was organized in 1949 as part of the Centennial Celebration of the State of California. It is an all-volunteer non-profit organization that seeks to expand public awareness of Death Valley and its natural resources. The mission of the '49ers is to foster appreciation of Death Valley, preserve its history, with special recognition to the wagon train of 1849, and to provide scholarships for students in the Death Valley region."

DAY 29 - *Death Valley*
Thursday, October 29, 2009
Furnace Creek – zero miles (running total: 507 miles)

On my pre-dawn jaunt to the men's room at the visitor center, a time when no one else is up, I get a surprise when I walk into the restroom. Just inside the doorway to the left is a little exhausted and frightened bird sleeping. My supposition is that it took refuge from the severe valley winds last night. This poor little bird is just trying to survive. Its head is somewhat buried in its side, like birds seem to sleep, and its breathing appears labored, as though it is recovering from extreme physical activity. I dare not disturb it, lest it panic and hurt itself in this bathroom. When I leave, the little bird is still asleep. About 40 minutes later, still long before the visitor center opens, and prior to anyone using these facilities, I discover that my miniature friend has taken flight. Fortunately, all is probably well for the bird now.

My owl friend is also carrying on this morning in the trees near my tent. He is very loud, which I love. The sounds of nature always delight my senses. The dark specter of dust that has filled the valley is now gone this morning, and the Panamint Range is again fully visible as the sun begins to paint the mountain in shades of purple and red.

My sunrise view is now completely obscured by a new motorhome about 35 feet to my east. Since my tent and trike are on the ground level, it doesn't take much to cut off the huge mountain range from my sight. Well, things are certainly changing in this parking lot.

Mom and my wild sister will be attending my presentation at the Author's Breakfast on November 6th. Mom has been requesting that I come south to her home in Apple Valley to be with her on her 82nd birthday, and also remain over the Thanksgiving holiday. Her place is about 185 miles south of Furnace Creek. Our telephone talks about this bring up the future of my expedition.

The Achilles tendon damage, which kicked in on the risky Cascade traverse, has been on my mind. They are much better now, but medical websites I have been reading indicate that such injury as this can require weeks and maybe months to fully return to a healthy state. I believe it, as I can still see how they are swollen, especially if viewed from the side. This, along with the fact that I encountered snow, ice, and sub-freezing temperatures the first week of October on the Cascade Range, are causing me to doubt returning to Oregon on a tricycle so late in the season, on the very cusp of winter itself. I was almost done-in the first time, so what might a second trip nearly two months later bring to pass? Here in Death Valley, it's hard to imagine such frigid triking conditions, but I remember them well. Something like that really burns into one's psyche forever. Cold one day, hot the next.

All things considered, I am entering a shift in my thinking. I want to be with mom for her birthday and Thanksgiving. I wish to visit with my sister also. This is important to me, more important that riding the Q back home after I told folks I would. I want to ride this incredible trike the rest of my life, and to do so, it seems prudent to let this unexpected tendon injury heal properly, so I don't re-injure it again later. Riding back to prove I can do it may thwart my future ability to physically ride, and I do not wish to risk that potential eventuality. Nor do I wish to be caught way up there in those high mountains again during such adverse weather. Sure, it was an adventure worth reliving in my mind, but not the sort of thing I would want to knowingly take on a second time. Once in a lifetime is all I need.

Thus, the plan is now a modified one, all part of the adventure. I was going to leave out of Death Valley to the north, the way I came in, on the 7th of November. Now though, my mom will rent a Ford F-150 pickup truck, and she and my sister will drive it out to hear me talk. Afterwards, we will load the trike into the bed of the truck for the trip south to their home. A new plan is alive. I have adapted.

The only question that still remains in my mind though is where the loading will occur. Mom is content with that happening right at Stovepipe Wells on the morning of the 6th. I am not. I have made compromises on this journey, but one I am not willing to make is forfeiting my chance to ride out of Death Valley National Park under my own power! I came into the park with my own sweat and effort, and I fully intend on leaving it the same way. I will risk the Achilles for the distance it takes me to leave the boundary of the park. This is important to me. I will make it so!

I have been contemplating a ride south through Badwater, over Jubilee and Salsberry Passes, and exiting at Shoshone, California. Also an option is a ride over Towne Pass and down into the Panamint Valley. Towne Pass has an elevation gain of 4,956 feet in the 17 miles from Stovepipe Wells, which is at sea level. It is a pass that is notorious for overheating cars. That works out to an average vertical gain of 292 feet per mile, which is quite severe from a triker's standpoint. Extreme grades like that are why I put the 24-tooth chainring on the front so that I could pull my load no matter what.

My inclination is the Towne Pass exit for three reasons: First, I wish to have that feather in my cap, which is purely male ego of course, but nonetheless, I covet the experience and mental rewards. Second, the twelve miles down the south face of the pass will be the ultimate thrill ride on a tricycle, surpassing any downhill pass thus far. The south face is even steeper than the north face I would be ascending, and it has many curves. To ride it on a trike would be the definitive experience for a triker, as speeds of more than 50 miles per hour are guaranteed. Third, I have spent many years of my life exploring the Panamint Valley, and am well versed in its terrain and history, and to ride my Q into it would be pleasing to my spirit. I have a few days yet to ponder this choice.

Today, my lunch is delayed, and by the time I buy bananas, grapes, mixed nuts, and a V8 juice at the little market, it is about a quarter after two in the afternoon. I am sitting on a bench in front of the Wrangler Steakhouse on the old wooden boardwalk, leisurely eating and enjoying each bite as I always try to do. I am watching the goings-on in the parking lot, the borax museum, and the post office when I hear someone verbally hail me off to my right side. As I turn, I darn near fall out of my seat! Wonder of wonders! If it isn't my long lost buddy Jack Freer standing on the same boards! Maybe it's only a mirage. Nope.

It's great to see him again. I had actually been wondering if he had changed his mind about coming, or work had demanded that he remain up north in the Nevada territory. Well, he's here now, so it's time for some more fun. He has his laptop, so after I eat, I back up my digital images on it and a small flash drive. This is a good thing to do just in case my aging digital camera were to give up the ghost. If it had, many photographs would have been lost for good. Now, all is safely backed up on two devices. That was easy.

The next few hours, I show Jack all around Furnace Creek to bring him up to speed on where things like the shower and laundry are. He sets up his tent about twelve feet west of mine, with just enough room to park his Jeep in between. Well, as soon as my friends see all the activity at my usually quiet campsite, they come on over. I introduce Jack to Jim, Gene, Wanda, and Bill. Jim Graves tells me that Jack and I are cordially invited to attend the special pizza feed sponsored by

133

Xanterra Resorts for all the 49er VIPs (guess I'm really coming up in the world). We happily accept! Free food is always a good thing.

A little later this evening, Jack and I walk on over to Jim and Nancy Graves' motorhome where the celebration is taking place. People are everywhere. There is more pizza, wine, and snacks than even this group can eat, and everyone is having a grand time. I waste no time stuffing myself, as tomorrow I will make my bid for Badwater at long last! Time to tricycle to North America's lowest, hottest, and driest land.

DAY 30 - *Death Valley*
Friday, October 30, 2009
Badwater, Artist's Palette, Mushroom Rock – 43 miles
(running total: 550 miles)

Badwater or Bust is the name of the blog that people are following to learn of my progress. It's high time I take care of the Badwater part! Today is the day. There will be no "bust" about it if I have anything to say on the matter, and I do. It's just down the road.

I feel fine. The trike feels fine. The day feels fine, full of sunshine. Jack feels fine. I guess there's not two ways about it – this is just one fine time to ride a tricycle to Badwater Basin in Death Valley. I've heard it said that a person must suffer from some anomalous psychological eccentricity to spend time in Death Valley. Well, it wasn't stated in those precise words. It was something more along the line that a person must be nuts. I wonder what those with such an opinion would say about a guy pedaling a tricycle to North America's low point?

At 282 feet below sea level, this area is the place to be for those who prefer considerable heat in summer. The highway turnout at Badwater Basin itself is not that low, but the surrounding area dips to those numbers, making it the lowest walkable land in America (when it is dry). It is possible that nowhere on the planet gets hotter than this place, with old unofficial claims as high as 150 degrees Fahrenheit, but the official governmental number is 134. Although, folks with digital temperature readouts in their modern cars have recorded a legitimate 136 degrees. Good thing it's now the end of October!

We will not always find it, because it is not always here, but depending on the weather circumstances of the particular year, we may well find a shallow lake at Badwater Basin in the central valley. Heavy rains, especially in August, can cause the basin to fill with water runoff from the surrounding mountain ranges, since they are so dry and have little vegetation to restrain the flow. Had we been here 150,000 years ago, we would have witnessed a massive lake that was approximately

600 feet deep, covering the entire valley floor. Early people may have camped along the shores of smaller subsequent lakes that grew and receded here through the years. Today, if one visits at the right time, kayaking in the shadow of Telescope Peak 11,331 feet above to the west is possible. Death Valley is truly a fascinating place with many surprises. It is a grand land of mystery and unique beauty.

Today, I am going to see more of that unique beauty. I have been here at Furnace Creek for the past week. Wednesday's ride to Zabriskie Point confirms in my mind that I should not have any problems on today's ride, for going to Badwater and back does not require any steep or grueling hills. But if I decide to take a side trip to Artist's Palette, there will be some uphill pedaling there. Either way, I'm no longer worried about my feet or Achilles stopping me.

As is my usual practice, I arise prior to the sun's appearance. The weather is calm and the sky is overcast, yet I seriously doubt there will be any precipitation today. Wouldn't that be something? The day I ride to Badwater is the day the clouds open up. Rain is so rare here that I don't even give it a second thought. There have been years when no rain has occurred. If you like things dry, this is your place!

Jack is also an early riser. This is his first sunrise here, and he is already pressed into action by the trike guy. Jack has to follow me down there and get some photographs. He says he will head out a little later, thereby giving me a head start. Considering my speed versus his, I guess that makes sense, otherwise he would just be doing a lot of waiting.

Breakfast is taken with no dirt in my cereal. I am glad the wind has departed. Although, if a north wind does come up on my way down, I will make record time. But of course, it would have to reverse to a south wind to get me back to camp. Hopefully, there will be only gentle breezes today, with no central valley dust storms to interfere with the photography. A dust event today would make this passage rough.

The mileage from my camp to the Badwater turnout on Highway 178 is 18 miles. It is mostly downhill, of course, since I will be pedaling to North America's lowest land. Gene Elmore and Bill Whitfield will run chase, as they want to photograph me on the way. Wanda has some duties with the Death Valley 49ers she has to attend to, so she will not be along today.

With the clouds in the sky, it appears darker this morning. My only jacket is the lightweight polar fleece one that I wore to Zabriskie Point on Wednesday. Leaving camp, I have it zipped all the way up, which feels just right. On a trike, I have learned that it's best to be a little bit on the chilly side when starting out on a ride, for once pedaling, the body's heat takes the chill away in short order, often within the first mile or two. Today is no exception to that general rule.

For nearly this entire journey thus far, I have worn my Specialized cycling helmet. It is very lightweight, comfortable, and gives little clue it's on my head. I have worn it to protect my head in the event that I make a steering error and ride off a steep embankment, which, surprisingly, almost happened on a couple of occasions. On a tricycle, if traffic exists, I tend to remain close to the road's edge, usually on the shoulder if there is one, so my right front tire is generally only two or three inches from the embankment. Not much separates me from riding off the road. Just one millisecond of altered focus and down I go.

This is not just a concern for mountains either. Just about all roads are above land grade to some extent, and if I were to pitch the front right tire off the pavement by just an inch, the result could well be a rollover, and bingo, where's my head? So, the helmet makes sound sense to me. If a car did ever strike me, who knows how effective it would be, but then again, that depends on the nature of the collision. I've seen enough in my career to know that sometimes accidents that look bad result in no injury, while others that seem minor have fatalities.

On my ride to Zabriskie Point, I deviated from this helmet practice. I have a Sequel foreign legion styled cap with a large bill and side flaps that offer me more sun protection than my helmet setup, while also being a bit more comfortable, so I wore it Wednesday. With the helmet, I have to arrange a dishtowel on my head first to keep the sun off, and then don the helmet. With the hat, all I do is put it on. I also like the looks of the hat compared to the helmet, as it matches my khaki clothing and the landscape. My concerns about traffic out here in Death Valley are virtually non-existent, as motorists can see me well in advance. On the road to and from Zabriskie, Paul and I rode fully in the lane, only occasionally having to move over, but even then, the car always passed just like we were an auto, with plenty of room.

Today, on this ride to Badwater, I am also wearing my Sequel cap. The helmet is again in my tent. Traffic here is so light, and drop-offs so rare, that I don't even feel a need for a helmet. I did wear it from Mesquite Springs down to Furnace Creek last week, but it wasn't necessary. The thought didn't even occur for me not to wear it on that stretch, otherwise I would have probably just worn my cap.

About a mile south of camp, Gene and Bill are parked at the turnoff of the Badwater Road, where Highway 178 comes in to Highway 190. They take my picture as I am about to turn right and head south. The clouds are still up there, casting a wonderful aura about the landscape as I make the turn. Seventeen miles to go, and nothing can stop me now! It's all downhill from here.

It's easy to maintain a good clip on this first leg to Badwater. Never does this stretch require any low gearing at all. Often, I am in my highest gear, easily maintaining a six-minute mile rate, which is roughly a ten miles per hour average. There are steeper stretches where I speed up, and an occasional mild incline where I slow down, but I feel no noticeable physical exertion increases that get my attention. Essentially, this is like the proverbial walk in the park. And since it's not summer, it's no sweat either. I'm having fun.

Every so often, I see a little brown minivan parked up ahead, and I know it's time for another photo opportunity. My artifacts of younger years full of machismo push forward when that camera is out, my feet automatically seem to pick up the pace, and I find myself cranking out every ounce of speed I can to impress these guys how fast a trike can really go. I may be hopelessly shackled by this psychological response for all my days, but hey, it's fun every once and a while! After all, I'm like a kid riding a tricycle. Look at me! Wee ...

Unless a person has actually been out in the midst of Death Valley personally, a true idea of its enormous size is probably not possible. We can look at photographs, and say yes, that's a big valley, but it's only when we are actually here in person that it hits home. I have been here many times over many years, and do have this knowledge, but even I was unprepared for really how large it is, for I have always traveled its countryside by automobile. True enough, I have done a lot of hiking too, but I have never hiked the length of the valley like Helen Thayer has. So, on this trike, Death Valley takes on a new proportion. Yep, it's big, REALLY very big indeed!

Death Valley lies between the Panamint and Amargosa Ranges. It is roughly 140 miles long by an average 8 miles in width. The length measurement begins in the south where the Amargosa River makes it swing past Saratoga Springs towards the valley, to the north at the head of Last Chance Canyon. The valley is 282 feet below sea level at its lowest point in the southern half, and rises to about 4,000 feet above sea level in the northern reaches. For hundreds of millions of years, long before Death Valley morphed into its current configuration and location, this region was an ancient seabed. The area of the entire national park is approximately 5,219 square miles.

With regards to the valley's total length, my humble tricycle expedition will cover only about half the distance! And yet, from Mesquite Springs south to Furnace Creek, and then on south to Badwater, it gives me the feeling that I've pedaled the whole distance. Out here, distances are terribly deceptive, to the point that sometimes a person's perception has gotten them killed when they think they can make it to a certain place. This is one reason visitors are advised to remain with their car if it breaks down. You don't want your mind or body to break down too! You gotta' play things safe here.

Nearing the nine mile mark, the clouds are parting at last, and sunshine is hitting the Panamint Range about ten miles west (but it looks like you could easily just walk on over to them without a care). Before I know it, I arrive at the large paved parking area for Badwater. There is a railing and boardwalk that allows physically challenged folks to also make it down to the salt. A prominent sign here describing the place and its elevation is so popular for photographs that it gets worn out at an unnatural rate. This is everyone's big photo opportunity!

I ride down to the sign, and, like everyone else who comes here, park my trike in front of it, and then take the Q's picture to show that my trusty steed made the trek in one piece, to the lowest, hottest, and driest place in North America. Of course, I'm not in the photo, so when Gene and Bill walk up, they snap some shots also. Jack isn't here yet. I am wondering if he got lost. Just joking, it's pretty hard to get lost out here! I am patient, with time on my hands.

Across the valley, I can clearly see the pinnacle of Telescope Peak, a place 11,331 feet higher than this sink, where I once stood and sat for a couple of hours a few years back. It's a fantastic hike, with awesome views from the tiny summit. Any time I have summited a mountain, I always hang out there for a while because the feeling is so uplifting. In one weekend, an athletic person could conceivably stand atop Telescope Peak and at Badwater. Time management is essential for such an attempt, but it's doable for those athletes pressed for time.

From the Badwater vista here, I can see Galena, Johnson, Hanaupah, and Trail Canyons cutting their paths up the eastern flank of the Panamints. I have driven and hiked these canyons in years past. They are very rocky, and high-clearance 4wd is clearly recommended. I won't be driving up them anymore – nearly impossible with a tricycle. Good thing I saw them before I traded my backcountry rig for a trike.

This salt is as hard as concrete where thousands of people walk out onto the valley's floor every year. On either side of the wide swath of beaten down salt is very rough salt crystallization that is formed only by nature. Farther north, it becomes so rough that white pioneers gave it the name Devil's Golf Course. A pedestrian out there can really get cut up if they slip and contact the jagged sharp spires of salt.

Air temperature is still pleasant. It was 58 degrees when I left camp this morning. I no longer need my jacket here. It will get hotter later this day, but now it's perfect for humans. The parking area is still in the shade of the mighty Amargosa Range, which literally comes right up to the salt flat. The earthquake activity of the fault zones here have caused this western edge of the Amargosa Range to be unbelievably steep. There is no transition area between salt playa and mountains.

Right up above where I am standing is breathtaking Dante's View. At 5,475 feet above sea level in the Black Mountains of the Amargosa Range (5,757 feet above Badwater), this is the view that everyone wants to see, for it is spectacular. The borax and railroad men, eager to be the recipients of the new flow of tourist dollars, developed a road to this summit in 1929. This enviable tourist spot is what prompted rival promoter Bob Eichbaum, of Stovepipe Wells fame, to build his famous road in the Panamint Range on the western side of Death Valley, known as Aguereberry Point today. It is even higher!

Up on the side of this precipitous mountain, the National Park Service has placed a huge sign at the sea level height, just to give travelers the idea of how far under the ocean's surface they would be if this were filled with salt water. Interestingly, the ocean may one day be right here. Nearly five and a half million years ago, what we today call Baja California used to be part of the Mexican mainland, and then it began pulling away as tectonic forces underneath split the land apart. Now, Baja California is slowly moving northwest.

Some geology experts say that the northernmost extension of this rift, or tear, is the area we call Death Valley, while others claim it to be in the Salton Sea. There is even some plausible scientific evidence to support the idea that this tearing of the land could extend as far north as southern Oregon. There are those who refer to this phenomenon as the Baja Rift, and one will be standing right in the midst of its lowest portions during a visit to the Badwater Basin area. This area of the western United States is part of the basin and range topography, where the pulling apart of the land is common, creating successive mountain ranges and valleys in north-south directions.

The Pacific Plate moves northerly in relation to the North American Plate. This Baja Rift is just the lowest such example of Earth crust movement. Imagine salt water someday covering the lowered land from the Sea of Cortez all the way to Oregon – about as hard to grasp as the idea that a huge lake once filled the entirety of Death Valley. Things change! It is just that we as individuals are not around long enough to see it happen. Our life spans only witness one little snapshot on the geologic scale, giving us the impression that the Earth's crust is fixed and immovable. It is far from being so.

As I stand here, I contemplate all these things, and realize how spectacular the natural world truly is. What humans do here is nothing by comparison. We can mess it up with our selfish "progress" but the planet will never be in danger. The planet can handle what we dish out. We think we are tough and can control everything, but in reality, we are so very fragile, and can be quickly terminated walking across this valley in late July. The wild plants, animals, and earthen materials survive.

After about a half hour, Gene and Bill need to get back to Furnace Creek, so they take their leave of me. While I wait for Jack to arrive, I walk around the area, and my mind ponders the millions of little creatures who live on and under this cracked salt bed. Extremophiles are tiny microscopic organisms that thrive in the extreme heat on the floor of Death Valley, existing under and within salt fissures in ground heat exceeding 200 degrees Fahrenheit. They are organisms well adapted to surviving in extremely salty and/or acidic regions. Space scientists come here to study them for clues to life on Mars. This is because extremophiles produce evaporites when the water around them evaporates, and these same evaporites have reportedly been discovered on the Red Planet, leading top researchers of the field to postulate that large amounts of water once existed on our neighboring planet. Where there is water, there is usually life. Therefore, extremophiles of Death Valley are playing a very important role, even though they may be invisible to most area visitors.

There is also the Badwater snail. These endangered creatures live in Badwater Basin under the salt crust, and can easily and unwittingly be killed by visitors who step on the moist ground under the water. The snails feed on algae in the salt. Stepping carefully in this landscape is a recommended practice.

Next to the boardwalk on the north side is a large pool of saltwater. The common photographs we see on postcards of Telescope Peak reflected in water are shot from the road side of this pool looking west. After a year of heavy rains, these pools expand, and can sometimes cover much of the valley floor. Some years, people actually kayak out here after unusually heavy rain runoff. There was a PBS television show of Huell Howser in 2004 where he was filmed as he paddled about in his kayak for his surprised viewers – water is not something that the general public associates with the sink of Death Valley. Where I walk today, Huell paddled before.

About ten minutes after ten, a tan over green Jeep pulls up in the parking area. I am out on the salt, but see it park. It's probably Jack, and I'm sure he sees me, for no one can stand out here and not be highly visible. And of course, my tricycle makes it pretty obvious too. He comes on down with his expensive digital camera, and we shoot some photos of the area, the trike, and me.

Well, it's finally time to move on down the road, or I suppose I should say on UP the road, considering that I can't go down any farther from here! Jack and I agree to the plan. I am going to ride north, and then turn right about six miles or so north of here, onto the Artist's Drive road. I would like to get some photographs of the Q and me at beautiful Artist's Palette, which is on a nine mile loop road off this main highway. He says he'll meet me somewhere on that road.

The loop road is narrow, with pavement that was poured right on the old graveled roadbed. Unlike most roadways that are raised, this road is essentially right at ground level. If I were to ride off of the pavement, it would be no big deal here, as I'd go right onto the dirt. This Artist's Drive road is so narrow that it feels like it was specially made for a trike pilot like myself. It is barely wide enough for one large car. It is also one-way, so any cars will come from behind my trike.

I have never ridden a trike or any cycle up to Artist's Palette before. I have always driven a petroleum vehicle on this loop. The road doesn't impress a motorist with any visions of excessive steepness. I have never thought of it that way myself, until today of course!

Although it does appear to be just a gradual incline as I proceed up the alluvial fan towards the canyons of the Black Mountains, I must quickly gear down to my lowest chainring. I can't believe it. It looks so easy, but I am beginning to really put some muscle behind each pedal stroke now. Not only that, but as midday approaches, the formerly cool weather affects me as increasingly hot. My body is now beginning to perspire freely, having put a little over one mile behind me. I keep attempting to pick up the speed enough to upshift to the middle chainring, but there is no way I can maintain it no matter how hard I try. This is a land of illusion, as author Richard Lingenfelter has written. This road is the grandest illusion on my trip so far!

Jack passes me like I'm standing still, even though he is only going 25 miles per hour. I feel like I'm not even moving. I keep waiting for the ground to level out. It never does, or at least not yet. At two miles, Jack takes my picture as I creep by, my shirt soaked. I am drinking heavily from my Camelbak water bladder behind my seat on a regular basis. This bladder has a tube running over my left shoulder so that I can drink on the go, even when my go is slow.

Just after three miles, about the time I know I have died and gone to triker's hell, the old rough road curves to the left and tops out, before it descends steeply, yes, down! All that work to earn three miles of distance, and now I'm going to go down, even though Artist's Palette is still a ways up in elevation from here. I am beholding a roller coaster situation ahead of me. Steep down, followed by steep up, and then again by a steep down, and so forth.

141

Using his telephoto lens, Jack gets a foreshortened picture of me on the first rise at three miles, which shows just how high I have ridden from the valley floor far far below. I take a rest up here to guzzle some water out of my bottle, and am amazed at the spectacular vistas all around. Jack gets out his waterproof Tom Harrison map (the best Death Valley map there is), and we study the elevation lines. Now it becomes clear why I am so wiped out.

The Artist's Drive road begins at 163 feet below sea level, and rises to 960 feet above where Jack just took my photograph. That is in the first three miles. This works out to a 1,123 vertical feet elevation gain in the three miles, or about 374 feet per mile! By comparison, the Cascade Range ascent I traveled early in this expedition (seems like a world away now) was a 4,000 vertical feet elevation gain in about 31 miles, or roughly 129 feet per mile. This ride today is approximately equivalent to 4,000 vertical feet in 10 miles, or one-third the distance of the Cascade ascent. Never would I have guessed!

The uphill is not over yet though, and another three miles still separates me from the prize of gorgeous hillside colors. Fortunately, while challenging, these next three are nowhere nearly as tough as the first three. And there area some brief areas of really fun downgrades mixed into the second set of three, where I can coast quickly into the next hill. With a human-powered tricycle though, I have found that even coasting fast into an oncoming hill doesn't translate into much free progress once the hill is hit. I have learned to downshift early.

At long last, I pull into the cul-de-sac parking area overlooking Artist's Palette. Jack snaps some more photographs as I pull out a few much needed energy bars! This place is gorgeous, and worth the ride.

A lovely rainbow of colors in the earth, the result of various minerals that have been oxidized from protracted exposure to the elements, greets the eyes at this location. Later in the day when the sun is lower, the colors are even more vivid. Visible are reds, yellows, greens, pinks, and purples. For those with computer expertise, digital photos of this palette can be enhanced through saturation techniques to bring out these colors even more. Apparently, scientific evidence exists here that tells of a extremely fierce period of time where violent volcanic activity was the norm. That seems to be over now (at least for the foreseeable future of probably many generations). Artist's Palette today is so peaceful and photogenic, and the average person would never guess what went on here so many thousands of millennia ago to form it. It is worth the ride to get the pictures here.

Guess what! Now I must ride back down to the valley from whence I just ascended. Wow, that makes a lot of sense, huh? The reality of it is that my body is receiving incredible longevity benefits from labors such as this. I do not mind. I like the challenge, even though at times I may sound like I'm griping. The strong survive. That which does not kill you makes you strong! I am still alive, so I must be getting stronger.

Yes, it is just as steep going back down the northern part of the loop, and we all know what that translates into: fast forward motion. I am now screaming down through the old canyons at speeds that require me to brake now and then when approaching the tighter curves. Even trikes have a point of no return on rollover physics, and I don't want to reach it going this fast. A tourist car is behind me, but I am not slowing it down. What a great feeling that is. I wonder what the driver is thinking as he follows me down the mountain.

But my fun doesn't last. As I round one particularly tight curve, which actually does a 180 degree directional change, I am faced with another killer uphill. That's funny, I never recall this the last time I drove through here with an engine in front of me. Trikes present a whole new universe. Up another mile I go, and then the road finally heads down for the duration, all the way to Highway 178. The final mile or so is straight, and I can easily see Jack's tiny green Jeep way down below, sitting at the intersection. I am rolling along so quickly now that I must be aware and apply the brakes early enough so that I don't blow through the stop sign at the bottom. If I do, I'll end up sailing into a rocky desert expanse on the other side, and quickly coming to a halt the hard way. I am not wearing my helmet. Time to work those Sturmey-Archer drum brakes.

At the bottom, Jack and I confer. He knows I must get a photograph at Mushroom Rock, a location where my dad took a photo of me sitting on my mom's lap in 1954 as a little tyke. It is a special place for me. It is also a sacred place for the Timbisha Shoshone Tribe. On the way down to Badwater this morning, I looked and looked for it, but never found the oddly shaped piece of stone.

There used to be a parking area for it many long years back, but the National Park Service removed it, allegedly at the request of the Timbisha. Jack found it while I was laboring up the final hill on Artist's Drive. That's the nice thing about having a petroleum-powered scout working with me. He can reconnoiter and have all the information I need by the time I arrive. Jack tells me it's just up the road. I thought it was south of this intersection. Shows how off I can be.

Sure enough, there it is. It is no wonder I missed it. With no parking area, and since the massive rock has weathered and been destroyed by the elements and tourists, it is now smaller and hard to see unless you're really looking for it. Perhaps I missed it because this is where Gene and Bill were watching my macho burst of speed. Maybe I was distracted. Then again, anytime I'm riding a trike, I'm having so darn much fun that my mind is always absorbed in the fun factor.

Located about 7 miles south of Furnace Creek, this oddly shaped rock stands alongside the road, appearing to nearly defy gravity. The shape is that of a mushroom, with a larger base, a slim center, and a bulbous top. It is basalt rock that has been artfully sculpted by the unrelenting forces of nature, called Aeolian Processes, and it will obviously meet an unceremonious end at some point in time since nothing can withstand such forces forever. A large portion of Mushroom Rock broke off a few decades back, partly due to people climbing on it, or, as the saying goes: "loving it to death."

Jack takes a photograph of me sitting in the precise depression of the rock where my mom held me. Mom will enjoy this photo. I have to lift the trike at the rear to get it back on the road, pulling it with the two front wheels trailing on the ground, as it is too sandy here to ride it over to the pavement.

Then, it's back to camp, or heading in that direction. Jack says he'll meet me back there, and takes off up the road, soon out of my sight. Even though it is uphill, and the afternoon sun is yet shining upon my back, this is a breeze compared to what I just went through. In fact, the slight breeze is keeping me cool now.

Before I reach the Furnace Creek Ranch, I hang a left into the long driveway of the Timbisha Shoshone Tribal village. I want t see Barbara Durham again and show her my trike. Last time we visited, I was on foot. She comes out of the office, and I get a picture of her standing next to the Q. I think it is the first time she has ever seen one of these things before. I tell her I'll be back for some Indian tacos in a couple of days, and then head back to camp to scrounge up some grub!

One fellow coming the other way in a car during the final half mile, stops, gets out, and takes my photograph as I pass and wave. He doesn't talk any, just gets the picture, gets back in, and takes off south again. Quick and easy. I may as well be an alien out here.

Back at camp, I park the trike and notice that a new motorhome is parked even closer to me now. I am starting to get a hemmed in feeling. It's only a matter of feet. Hopefully one won't park between that one and my tent. That would be unbearable.

Jack drives up and says he wants a slice of dead cow muscle for dinner. Well, he doesn't exactly put it that way. He uses the same euphemistic phraseology that everyone does who wants to mask what they are really putting into their mouths. Jack tells me he wants a nice big rib eye steak, and he wants me to have one too. I tell him it will be a cold day in hell when I eat one of those, but I'd sure like to have dinner with him nonetheless. So, we amble on over to the deluxe Wrangler Steakhouse, a place I've been sitting in front of for days, but will now go inside to partake of its delicacies.

Our waitress is Sharon Funck, the best darned waitress anyone could ask for, and the best one either Jack or I have ever had. She is happy, funny, and takes care of our smallest wishes and details. Of course, Jack is never without his impressive camera, so he tells Sharon to sit by me after dinner and gets our photograph. I'm a little soused due to Jack's insistence that I join him in two bottles (yes, bottles, not glasses) of red wine with dinner, but since I'm still sitting down and happy to have accomplished my 43 trike miles today, it's kind of fun. One thing for sure, I'm certainly laughing things up!

While Jack carved into his cow, I had a Badwater salad, or some such appropriately named vegetarian entrée. It was excellent, but didn't really fill me up. When I get back to my tent, I may have another energy bar. Food bars always hit the spot.

Sunday morning is clear and calm, except for the exhaust and noise coming from the pre-dawn lawn mowers. As usual, some crow is yakking away in the distance. Don't come to Death Valley if you don't care for the sounds of crows, as they are everywhere out here. And these crows are king sized compared to the typical city crow, black as night and twice as noisy. I like them however, and always greet them by name when walking past. "Hello crow!"

Tuesday finds my tent getting lost in a sea of motorhomes and trailers. The eastern side of our tent site has been increasingly filling up with every day that passes, and now that the festivities are well underway, most of the presenters are here. Most, but not all. The closest trailer to me is currently only one trailer's width away, but at least I am content that some space still exists between me and it. I certainly hope it stops there. Not enough room for another one!

For the past couple of weeks, my pre-dawn morning visits to the NPS visitor center restroom facilities has been a lone affair, but now, the place is getting downright crowded before the sun comes up. Every day, many people from all around the motorhome camps walk their dogs to the western end of this field, only a few yards from my tent, and their canines leave little brown presents behind for me to smell. A few folks are courteous and use a plastic sack to take their dog's excrement away for proper disposal, but most just stand around looking innocent, as if they don't know what their dog is doing, and then stroll casually away, hoping no one noticed.

It is as if there is a sign here that says: "Doggie Bathroom" or some such thing. This routine is so ubiquitous, and is done by so many different people throughout each day, that it is not even worth my time to have an intelligent conversation with the uncaring offenders. I have always wondered why they just don't let their dogs squat and defecate at their own camp (or house, if in town), rather than bringing them over to where I camp or live. Oh well, it's just another of life's sure things, along the line of taxes. The world will always have inconsiderate people. I have learned to watch for fecal matter when I walk around here.

Large owls can be heard in the trees overhead some nights. I love this sound. The past two mornings, a full moon has set over the Panamint Range to my west, just after sunrise. It is a very impressive sight. The positive aspects of this region far outweigh the negative. For years I have camped and explored far away from this tourist mecca. It is the best way to see nature and be alone. Motorhomes don't go there!

Editor's note: Days 31-34 were used to explore the Death Valley region with Jack Freer in his Jeep – no trike travel, but a foot hike of many hot miles through the full length of spectacular Titus Canyon – never hiked it before – few folks ever do, unless they are nuts.

DAY 35 - *Death Valley*
Wednesday, November 04, 2009
Furnace Creek to Stovepipe Wells – 24 miles
(running total: 574 miles)

Last night, I fell asleep to the sound of western fiddle music and singing. This morning, I awake to a less desirable resonance of air molecules. The precise time I cannot say for sure, as I opted out of the societal practice of watch-wearing over twenty years ago, but since my body's sleep cycle has been operating on the setting and rising of the sun for about five weeks now, my reckoning estimates it is about 1:00 AM. This will be confirmed later as the night turns to light, and by the ensuing activities I perform during that time.

Jack likes to eat, so on the evenings we have dined together, I tend to overindulge on my caloric intake. The pizza dinner I consumed six hours ago was no exception. It turned out Jack wasn't all that hungry for some reason, so yours truly ended up eating a lion's share of the huge pizza. It was either that or it would have been tossed out, and seeing as how my dad persistently taught me as a child never to waste food, my duty was to see every last crumb disappear from that pizza pan, which it most assuredly did. I walked out stuffed.

So here's the scene: At one o'clock in the morning, a time when I should be in deep REM sleep, my mind comes to consciousness.

146

I am receiving pressing physiological signals from my body that an immediate trip to the restroom over at the visitor center would be a wise investment of my time. Additionally, due to the warm temperatures in these parts, many people in trailers and motorhomes have their windows slightly or fully open. The bedroom window of the trailer that is only five feet from my tent is open. The man inside is involuntarily exhibiting a prominent air inhalation impediment, to such a degree that I find myself focusing on it, and would likely not be able to return to a full sleep anytime soon. First things first, however. The snoring can wait. I have to go! Of that, there is no choice now that I am fully awake.

On go my daytime clothes and boots, and off through the moonlit night I speed north. Darn, this distance hasn't seemed such a long walk before. At this time of night, no one else is up, so I have the whole place to myself, which I definitely prefer anyway. This is a good time to think, so I contemplate my increasingly confining situation.

These trailers and motorhomes have become a steel city, tightly imprisoning my modest REI tent in what would otherwise be a tranquil setting. I have always been one to steer clear of over populated locales when in the backcountry, and this experience is further teaching this to me in spades. What happened to my lone nights out on the road, where my stealth tricycle camps were visited only be a rare wild critter now and then? That last motorhome just parked way too close!

There's no way I will get back to sleep with that man's persistent guttural gasps slicing through the thin fabric of my tent like fingernails on a chalkboard. I could try making some noises to jar him into silence, but that is not worthy of my time.

The moon has just passed the full stage by one day. It is essentially bathing the desert landscape with a full beam of white light even tonight. The spherical cratered orb sits watchfully in the eastern half of the sky, not quite overhead at this early hour. Air temperature is pleasant and balmy, only faintly chilled, but not requiring a jacket for a quick walk to the men's room. A month ago, I took a night trike ride from the tiny village of Wilbur to Glide in Oregon. It was a satisfying experience despite the colder temperatures in the mountains. This night in Death Valley is much warmer. My mind thinks. I will strike out now!

On my walk back to the tent, I realize that stealth maneuvering will be essential in this restrictive situation. Sleeping people surround me. Jack is in his tent the other side of his Jeep, only feet away. Just like out of an Arnold Schwarzenegger action movie, I must covertly break down my camp and escape unobserved. Like a black phantom.

Fully awake, I stand and assess my camp in the shade provided by the huge tamarisk trees bordering my tent's south edge. I am dark enough that I blend in, and only become obvious to the eye if I stand in the direct moonlight. On the other side of these trees is a small paved parking lot for the golf course, which has sections of moonlight on the asphalt. There is plenty of room just a few feet to the south.

Breaking down the tent where it stands is not a good idea. First, it sits in the dirt, and second, I am just too close to my neighbors to be making any noise whatsoever. I have to get all my gear over onto the little paved area. I will start with the trike and trailer, for they will make a handy place to set other gear. The paved area is only about thirty feet south, but the thickness of the trees and a downed log prohibit moving the trike directly there. I am able to step over the log, but lifting the trike over it while partially loaded will not work, and would make a lot of noise in the process. I seek a solution.

My only solution is to silently walk the trike and trailer there, which requires me to make a large arc around Jack's Jeep, his tent, and the monster motorhome on the other side of his tent, where there is an opening through which people can easily walk. I attach the trailer to the trike and begin pulling the ten-foot train by the trike's front dérailleur post. This is awkward and tedious on this sandy surface, as I must hunch over to reach the trike while walking backwards, but I creep along ever so slowly to avoid any sound that might give away my clandestine mission. The trailer makes this difficult. Silent passage indeed!

At long last, the trike and trailer are now sitting in the middle of the little parking area, but since no one will be here this early, I am not worried. The 5:00 AM lawn mowers won't be in the area for another three hours or more. All that now sits at my campsite is my tent, still loaded with my sleeping bag and gear. Time for a methodical transport.

Gently, I slip back over the log, slowly unzip the tent, and ready all my gear for transport to the trike and trailer. Quietly, I take each piece over in several trips, and set it on the trailer top and recumbent trike seat. I work the six stakes, which have held my tent securely during the high winds, out of the ground. Fortunately, there is no wind tonight! Carrying them in my hands requires care, as the short aluminum spikes make sounds if struck together unthinkingly. The snoring man, only six feet from me in the trailer, yet persists with his raucous breathing, and there is no sign of stirring from Jack's tent. So far, so good. There is still plenty of moonlight left. It's a crazy time to be up and doing this, but I can sleep when I'm dead.

Right now, I have a goal to attain my freedom. The tent is empty, so I pick it up fully assembled and inaudibly carry it over the big log and onto the pavement. The beauty of these modern tents is that they can readily be moved when necessary. Now, I break it down farther away from the sleepers, and on relatively clean pavement, which allows me to shake any dirt and twigs out of it that may have accumulated over the past weeks. I can feel my freedom in the air!

With the panniers fully loaded and now on the trike, and the trailer ready to go, I make one final stealth inspection of my former camp site to ensure that I have all the gear. Boldly, I affix a short note to Jack's tent, letting him know of my plans:

TUESDAY, MID-NIGHT
JACK: WENT TO STOVEPIPE WELLS. WILL GET A ROOM AND
CLEAN UP. SEE YOU THERE.
- STEVE

My little home for the past two weeks is now history. I am sad to see it go, but I eagerly anticipate my liberty from this stifling desert motorhome park. Crowds are not my cup of tea. I seek the wilderness ways of wandering. Even though I paid for another night, my serenity is worth more. I wonder what Gene, Wanda, and Bill will think if they notice my absence later this morning, although they are now so busy with the 49er festivities that they may not detect my tiny tent is missing from the sea of steel campers. It was almost impossible to see anyway.

Atop my head goes the foreign legion styled cap that I wore to Badwater, for there is no traffic in Death Valley at night. The helmet is in my trunk. No jacket is necessary, as my pedaling will soon keep me sufficiently warm in the cool night air. There is no evidence that my midnight madness has affected anyone here. My covert mission is nearly complete as I enter the Q's cockpit and noiselessly pedal out onto the highway. No one is any the wiser. I am a trike phantom, vanished.

I have been so mentally engaged in my covert activities that I even find myself checking my rear view mirrors as I pedal north from Furnace Creek, as if someone might actually attempt to stop and capture me. Circumstances reveal that success is now mine, as I glide silently northwest towards Stovepipe Wells, only 24 miles distant.

A trike pilot could not ask for better touring conditions. When I was visiting the visitor center after first getting up, I noticed the large outdoor thermometer the National Park Service has attached to the brick wall. It disclosed 62 degrees Fahrenheit, cool enough that vigorous pedaling feels great, but warm enough that there is no unpleasant chilling of my skin. The moon is so bright that I do not need my headlight to see the road ahead. I keep the blinking red LED lights illuminated to my rear in case a rare car happens to overtake me, as well as the retina-frying marine rescue strobe on the back of my trailer. Neither of these rear lights can I notice from my cockpit, unless I turn my head rearward to either side, in which case I can see the desert creosote bushes briefly illuminated by the strobe as it fires every second.

Deserts are magical places in the dark. I have grown up spending countless nights out in this Mojave region, and what I grew to love as a kid even now mesmerizes me as a 58 year old man. Words cannot serve justice to the feelings swirling inside my head, particularly this year when I am moving silently, only eight inches from the roadbed, in a vehicle like no other. This tricycle has proven to be a grand mode of travel, opening doors to fresh, never before known experiences that demand my continued vigorous participation. Not only is my body being well prepared for the centenarian years that lie ahead by pedaling instead of driving, but it is so completely fun to move down the road in this manner, while not contributing toxins in my wake. I'm having a blast out here, all by myself! Know one knows it but me.

Water offloading stops are not an issue at night. I can see that no car is coming for miles in these circumstances. Stretching my legs allows me to just stand motionless and totally appreciate the wild world around me. There are no sounds of internal combustion engines. There are no motorhomes and house trailers out here. This is indescribable freedom from the scourge of sprawling humanity that even finds its way into the depths of Death Valley on occasion. Death Valley at night! Yes!

My lowest gears are not needed on this ride. My net elevation gain from camp to Stovepipe Wells will be only about 200 feet over the course of 24 miles, which is nothing compared to what I've been through so far, and what is yet to come this Friday. I am easily able to maintain my midrange and highest gearing during the ride, thereby ensuring swift progress in the moonlight on Highway 190. As the night begins to wane, automobile traffic begins to appear, but I can count the total number of cars before sunrise on my two hands.

The highway is at least temporarily mine, and I ride in the middle of my lane as I did all the years I drove cars. As I round the bend where the road to Scotty's Castle intersects this road, and begin my westerly leg towards Stovepipe, the eastern sky is lightening as the Earth rotates into the first stages of yet another glorious day in eastern California. This is like magic out here for me.

Approaching the Devil's Cornfield, the sun finally is illuminating Tucki Mountain, a gigantic landmark at the southern edge of Stovepipe Wells Village that is seen for miles in many directions. Arrowweed bushes abound on this vast stretch of ground, taking on the appearance of corn shocks. Soil erosion is a factor in their growth pattern. Ancient American Indians have used this plant to make arrow shafts, hence its unique name. Much of the cornfield is across from the sand dunes, south of Highway 190, east of Stovepipe Wells.

I can now clearly see my morning destination ahead, with 21 miles behind me and only about three miles to go. Bob Eichbaum was the fellow responsible for this little desert oasis, Death Valley's first tourist resort, and built a toll road to it in 1926. The toll road was his idea of paying for the road's construction, and then having a continued income stream in addition to his resort. He was one of the first to see the promise of tourist dollars, and capitalized on the idea. The location was originally called Bungalette City (Bungalow City by some). At a mid-park location, Stovepipe Wells affords great views of the nearby sand dunes, and is just a stone's throw from Mosaic Canyon, Grotto Canyon, The Devil's Cornfield, and Burned Wagons Point. It is also the stepping-off place for Cottonwood and Marble Canyons.

To my right are the Mesquite sand dunes, now bathed in early sunlight as the full moon yet hovers to the west above the northern Panamint Mountains. Mister moon and senior sun now share the sky. There is a fleeting pinkish aura about the mountains and dunes in this new day's light, a phenomenon some folks call alpenglow. The swarms of tourists out here are missing all this majestic natural splendor, still securely asleep in their metal boxes. The Q isn't a box. I am happy to have made my Furnace Creek getaway under cover of darkness.

Mesquite Flat sand dunes are those most people see and associate with Death Valley National Park, although there are many more dunes elsewhere, some of which are quite a bit higher. These centrally located dunes are easy hiking for many visitors. Bob Eichbaum drove tourists around these dunes in the 1920s, and told them the tall tale of a lost whiskey shipment buried out in the dunes somewhere. Stashed ahead of time for the enactment, the driver would suddenly stop the tourist vehicle, jump out, and dig up a whiskey bottle, proclaiming they had found part of the lost shipment. Tourists loved the drama!

The source for all this sand is the surrounding mountains to the west and northwest. The Cottonwood Mountains are the in the northern portion of the mighty Panamint Range. The sand grains in this dune field are quartz and feldspar, and began as much larger pieces of stone before erosive Aeolian Processes had their way with them. As rain in the mountains sends flash floods down canyons, rocks tumble along and are broken into smaller pieces. Over eons of time, rocks end up as small pebbles on the alluvial fans at the mouths of the canyons. Then, once the pebbles are finally ground tiny and granular enough, prevailing northwesterly winds pick them up and blow them out onto Mesquite Flat, where the dunes formed.

In as little as ten mile per hour winds, the tiny sand grains on the surface of the dunes take to flight, erasing footprints from earlier, and swirling around to create a never ending array of fresh forms, to the delight of visiting photographers who come out here in the mornings and evenings to capture impressive images. For many years, Easter sunrise services have been held on these dunes, a practice initiated by Mr. Eichbaum to spur early visitation in the 1920s.

At about 6:45 AM, I pedal past the sign that proclaims I am entering Stovepipe Wells. The elevation here is more or less sea level, depending on which hunk of ground one stands. I just passed through a highway construction zone, where workers are laying a paved parking area to more safely handle the multitude of yearly visitors who park along this highway to photograph the dune field. I waved to the guys, who smiled and waved back, probably having never seen an old desert rat riding a tricycle here at sunrise. I'd be willing to put money on it.

I'm going to splurge tonight and pop for a motel room to clean up and relax. I've been living on the ground long enough that such luxury sounds inviting right now. Rooms at the Stovepipe Wells Resort are modest and older, but clean and well-kept nonetheless. There are no televisions or telephones in the lower priced rooms, which is just fine with me. The desk clerk tells me that I cannot book for another couple of hours, something about how the computer system works. That's all right however, as I am hungry and want some breakfast. I'll keep my $100 in the wallet for the time being.

The motel, restaurant, and swimming pool are on the south side of the highway. Across the street are the general store, campground, and picnic tables. Visual inspection reveals a campground with large motorhomes, although not nearly as many as down in Furnace Creek. I am not into setting up my tent in a flat motorhome city again, where privacy is non-existent. Today is Wednesday. Tomorrow night I will be hanging out in a room that Jack has reserved, and then on Friday I will be pedaling out of this territory after my presentation, so joyfully I will not have to camp among the metallic giants any more on this expedition.

Pedaling across the pavement to the picnic tables, I notice that the general store is not yet open for business. I find a nice wooden table in the sun, which feels perfect this early. Later in the day however, I would be seeking shade. Out come my dining supplies from my small trailer, which I spread out with total abandon on the table. Having been eating atop my trailer for so long, it is pure luxury to have such a big expanse on which to eat, and to be able to sit down while doing so.

While I eat, a couple of early risers walk past and briefly question me about the trike and my journey. I enjoy sharing my epic adventure with all who ask. It is clear that they are impressed with the whole idea of what I'm doing. They may think I'm crazy, but hey, they are talking to me all about it, so I have an audience, which is more than I can say for people who travel by conventional means. I stand out as unique in a sea of mediocrity. Yep, I guess I really am a maverick.

I am content to be eating my Nutty Nuggets outdoors with such spectacular scenery surrounding me. Who wants to eat inside a building with all this natural grandeur out here? The sky is clear. The air is calm. The temperature invites outdoor living. It doesn't get much better than this after an invigorating 24 mile trike ride across the much maligned Death Valley. Others may fear this place, but it is deeply embedded into my systems. Traveling at night here is especially fine!

After eating, I notice the stage by the swimming pool where I will be speaking the day after tomorrow. It has a sunshade on top, to keep the bright light out of the speaker's eyes, but since my talk will be at a breakfast, I suspect that I best wear my trademark Aussie hat and sunglasses. I will be facing Tucki Mountain during my talk, with the Mesquite Flat sand dunes behind and to my left. Sure beats giving a presentation in some formal business setting! How could a presenter not be inspired by such imposing countryside? The scene puts me at ease.

There is time to kill now, so I sit and write in my journal, and then walk around and look at the stores, such as there are in this tiny wide spot in the road. Mid morning, people begin to congregate for one of the Death Valley 49er events to be held here today. It is a doggie dress-up contest, where proud "parents" showcase their canines wearing distinctive western clothing and costumes. I am not a dog person, even though I had a malamute while living in the remote Colorado high country years ago, so I just watch the preparations from a distance.

Well, as fate would have it, it seems I am not destined to remain independent right now. While sitting on the comfortable mesh seat of my recumbent speed machine, a humble man walks over with a pencil and paper in hand. Unlike what I have grown accustomed to, this fellow does not ask about my wheels or why I'm here. Instead, he begs my participation as a judge for the doggie costume contest. Seems that judges are hard to come by out in these secluded desert parts, and since I am just sitting here, apparently doing nothing but relaxing, I must be the perfect candidate. I am too conspicuous at times.

How can I say no? After all, I have plenty of time on my hands between now and Friday morning, not to mention that I am also a presenter for this encampment, so it might reflect poorly upon me to opt out of this impending duty. Okay, so in keeping with the old west atmosphere ever-present during this five-day extravaganza, I've been lassoed into being one of five judges for this noble undertaking, which is officially called the "Pampered Pet" contest.

I am seated only a few feet west of the resort swimming pool, but no shade is provided to the judges, so my hat will have to do. The warm sun penetrates my dark shirt, and there is no chance for chill. My doggie responsibility requires me to assess 15 dog entries as they are paraded before my eyes by their human parents, in wild costumes that include full western paraphernalia, a scuba suit, a park ranger outfit, jewels, and whatever other crazy notion sparked the imaginative minds of the owners. After this entourage, which is accompanied by the announcer telling the audience all the numerous details of each animal and why it is dressed this way or that, I must confer with my judge peers to determine winners in several categories.

We decide to seek tamarisk tree shade for our conference, as we tally our results, place the winners' names in an envelope, and then hand it to the announcer. After an hour in the sun (it was a long contest), this shade feels good. Then it's back out to our sunny judge's table and the master of ceremonies begins to break the growing wave of anticipation that has overtaken the devoted audience and dog owners. These people really get into this! Kind of like trikes and me.

As it turns out, the thoughtful organizers of this event don't want anyone to feel that their dog and costume wasn't up to snuff, so they have prizes for every dog here, in addition to the furry friends that were obviously the most popular. My fears of tomato lobbing in my direction have been unfounded, as everyone seems at peace with how it all ended. They all go back to their motorhomes as winners.

Once my room has been obtained for the night, I wonder what I might do for the remainder of the day. It's nearing noontime, so I'll be wanting to do something rather than just sit around. There is no sign of Jack so far today, so he is probably out on some dirt backroad in his Jeep, taking in yet more sights that he has not seen. I left Furnace Creek a day earlier than expected, thereby cheating my Jeep driver out of another day of guided exploration. Maybe he's fuming about being short changed. Who knows? He'll show up eventually.

Sitting back on my trike seat again, under the shade of a tree near the front porch of the lodge at the highway's edge, I contemplate potential daily activities. A very nice elderly lady walks up and asks if she might take my photograph on the trike. Now used to such requests, I smile and say sure. Pictures taken, she shows genuine interest in the tale of my journey, and continues asking many questions. There could be no better use of my time than to be an ambassador for trikedom, enlightening the motorized humans of this planet about the joys of three human-powered wheels. I never tire of such interactions, which will

154

hopefully shed light on alternative methods of travel for a society that is hopelessly entrenched in the status quo of air-polluting fossil fuels.

Writing in my journal in the increasing hubbub of daily activity, many motorhomes and trailers pass by on their way to Furnace Creek. I am very happy to be up here at Stovepipe rather than down there, 200 feet below. Stovepipe Wells is mild in comparison to Furnace Creek, which is the headquarters for all the main events. My talk will be given here. I am a newcomer to Death Valley authorship and this encampment, even though I've been a traveler out here since 1955. Accordingly, I suspect that the new guys are placed on the agenda 24 miles away from where the tried and true entertainers will be performing. This is fine with me, as a smaller crowd in my audience is preferable for my first time out.

Having inquired about my trek, and where I will be pedaling on Friday, one fellow tells me that the Towne Pass road is a 9% grade, whatever that technically means. His thrust is that it's darn steep, and will really put me to the test with this load I'm pulling. To me, it is just one more of many mountain passes that I have crossed in the past 35 days. I'll just put the trike in granny low and go. Mind control is the key. A large crow is sitting atop a twenty foot pole on the other side of the road. These blackbirds are everywhere out here. He just flew away.

Just about the time I am pondering accessing my energy bar stash for some lunch grub, I spy two men and a woman walking across Highway 190 from the general store, seemingly intent on converging on my shady and highly desired location. Sure enough, these three folks come to rest all around my trike. They look like giants from my low vantage point. Trikes are most decidedly very low to the ground.

Wayne and Eileen Kading, along with their friend Terry Peterson make their acquaintances. These folks are so darn friendly that I am thinking that we may have already met somewhere around Furnace Creek, but no, this is the first time, verified by all their interest and questions. I've met so many people during my time here that I have a hard time remembering them all. Wayne and Eileen live in Anaheim, California, and Terry lives in Pollack Pines, California.

Terry says there are no sidewalks or street lights out in his neck of the woods, and he prefers to live out in the middle of a forest, far from the suburbs and crowds, for a life of peace and solitude. I tell him that those are exactly my own sentiments. Wayne asks more than once how I can ride this trike and trailer on the freeways. Interestingly, this is a common question that I have been asked by a number of people during my trip. People who drive cars all their lives apparently come to believe that freeways are a necessary path that all vehicles must take to go long distances, although I have come all this way on secondary backroads. It demonstrates to me the degree to which our society has been indoctrinated to automobiles and the roadways that support them.

By the third time Wayne asks the question, which I had answered before, Eileen smacks him hard on the shoulder and says: "Don't you listen? He says he doesn't ride on freeways!!"

Well anyway, these friendly folks are so spellbound by my story that they invite me to lunch at the resort's old western restaurant. They want to hear more! Being one to rarely turn down food, I graciously accept and we head the 25 yards south to the café, which is a visual feast inside, all the way to the large wooden beamed hallways that simulate an old mine tunnel. I just leave my trike and trailer parked right next to the highway, full of my gear and with no lock. My fears of theft have long since diminished in the past five weeks, and with so many people milling around this place, it would take a truly daring criminal to abscond with my belongings. So many people gather around to look at the trike that a thief would find it difficult to steal without someone noticing. Death Valley is not a place most thieves would come anyway.

At this point, if someone wants my old dirty, and perhaps odoriferous, gear, they can have it. There is always more where that came from. I am in desperate need of a modern digital camera anyway, and a theft would provide my perfect excuse to acquire one. I do take my small fanny pack containing my wallet with me though, so I can pay for my lunch. Think I'll hold on to my credit card.

Our lunch goes on for quite some time. We are all merrily eating and telling stories. This fare will cost me a few bucks, but the company is well worth the expense, and being able to forgo my usual energy bar is a exclusive treat for a hobo who lives on the road. By the time a couple of hours elapse, I swear I know everything about my new friends, and they know plenty about me. These are the kind of people who you just feel totally at home with right from the start. They could be family, and sometimes seem like it when Eileen balls out Wayne for some statement she doesn't like.

Finally, our congenial waitress, whom Terry has questioned so much that we all know about her too, presents the bill. As I bring out my wallet to ante up, they all say that this is their treat, and I am to put my wallet away! Well, doesn't that beat all? I get a great lunch with great people, am entertained for two hours, and it doesn't end up costing me a penny. Riding a trike across the countryside certainly has its perks! As we part for the day, they all assure me that they will be in my audience this Friday morning to hear my further tales of Death Valley.

My old friend Matt Jensen, whom I last saw out on the Oregon coast, mentioned to me on a number of occasions prior to this journey that there are people who eagerly help cyclists on long distance tours. He said I would meet some of these people on my trip. I told him that was unlikely because I was going to be riding on the most remote backroads I could find. Matt just smiled and reiterated that I would meet these folks one way or another. He calls them road angels. Wayne, Eileen, and Terry are three more road angels I have had the privilege to meet on this tricycle expedition to Death Valley National Park.

"What's the nature of your infirmity?" are the words I hear off to my right as I am again seated on the trike, finishing up a few journal entries after lunch. I look up (you're always looking up on a trike) to see another older woman sincerely interested that a man with some sort of handicap is still able to get himself around on his own. She moves around so she is facing me.

Matt also had told me that folks would believe me to be physically handicapped while on my trike. He said that since it resembles some odd sort of wheelchair that this thought comes to mind for many people, so much so that trikers in general are aware of this dynamic response. As this lady is standing over me, guru Matt's teachings come to light yet again. Time to have some fun!

I close my journal and stand up from my low recumbent seat. Next, I move away from my trike and jump as high into the air as I can. The lady watches all this with awe. Then, I say to her that physically I am fine, and if there is any handicap, it's only in my head! To this, we both have a good laugh, and I launch into describing what this bizarre looking contraption is, why I'm on it, and where I'm going. She wants to know how I ride it on the freeways. Life on a trike is always exciting, even when things are slow. Trikes invite fun times everywhere you go!

By glancing through the Death Valley 49ers program magazine, I notice that Ted Faye, a well known Death Valley film maker will be giving a presentation this afternoon right here in Stovepipe Wells. This is exciting for me, as I have a couple of his documentaries in my home video library. Now I will get to meet him in person. There's no way I'm going to miss this. As a group of his fans awaits by the door to the room where he will be presenting, a 49er lady walks up and says he has been delayed, but is now scheduled to arrive at 2:30 PM today.

Ted finally shows up, and we all enthusiastically find a good seat. He is an interesting speaker, and knows a lot about regional history. Part of his presentation today is showing us his latest film, a documentary investigation into the lost trunk of William Robinson, an original Death Valley 1849er. Some people believe that a trunk found out here is a genuine artifact of this man, while others claim it to be a publicity-seeking hoax by the finder. Ted's new film traces the evidence

157

with interviews of key people. The movie leaves us all wondering, while drawing our own personal conclusions. His outstanding documentary brings forth further questions while it answers many. We may never know for sure if the trunk is genuine, but that's just part of the mystique of this legendary land called Death Valley. It is indeed a land of legend.

Towards evening, I call mom on a pay phone over at the general store using my calling card. I am charged a hefty fee for calling from a pay phone, but since no telephones are in the rooms, it's either this or nothing. She picked up a rental truck from Hertz, a 2009 Ford F-150 extended cab, and will be leaving tomorrow with my sister to come to Death Valley for my talk.

The plan is that after I am all done riding the trike, we will load it in the bed of the truck and drive together down to her house, so that the three of us can celebrate her 82nd birthday, and also be a family for the Thanksgiving holiday. Thursday morning around 8:00 AM they will be hitting the road for a drive up to Stovepipe Wells of about 200 miles. I also tell her that I plan on riding the trike over Towne Pass Friday, and exiting the park on the west side. She wants me to just load it up after the Author's Breakfast. I tell her that I didn't come all this way only to miss the opportunity to pedal out of Death Valley under my own power. It's something I must do. My thoughts offer no other option.

As the sun sets, it is apparent that Jack is spending another night at Furnace Creek somewhere. I wonder if he is still tenting with all the motorhomes by the fiddler's stage, or if he high tailed it out of there to get a motel room. Time will tell the tale. He is scheduled to be here sometime tomorrow – or so I hope.

DAY 36 - *Death Valley*
Thursday, November 05, 2009
Stovepipe Wells Village – just hangin' out – zero miles
(running total: 574 miles)

Today will be a time of complete relaxation, although I suppose I've had plenty of relaxing days lately. The difference is that I won't be going anywhere at all, no riding passenger in a Jeep, no exhilarating trike rides, no hiking. All I'll be doing is just hanging around Stovepipe, waiting for mom and Willow to show up, perhaps as early as the lunch hour, and also waiting for Jack to pull in, who knows when.

I'll get in some walking, but it will be minimal. Tomorrow is going to be a very demanding and busy day. It will start with the Author's Breakfast and my presentation, and then be followed by riding the trike 17 miles to the summit of Towne Pass and down the other side into Panamint Valley, finishing up the expedition at the western park entrance in that valley. Those activities will more than make up for today's sedentary choices. What I don't do to extend my life today, I will do many times over tomorrow. A day of rest is good. An ancient fellow named God is reported to have said so.

Jim Graves of the 49ers organization suggested a talk of between 30-45 minutes at the breakfast. I can probably manage that. Like most normal people, I get somewhat nervous at the thought of such things, but this talk doesn't seem to be affecting me to any significant degree like one might suspect it would. This may be a result of three very unique things:

First, I have been visiting here since I was four years old, and consequently have quite a bit of personal knowledge of the area. It helps to know what you're talking about. Second, after living on the ground in a tent for a few weeks and pedaling a low rider trike a few hundred miles to get here, it's as though anything else at this point is easy by comparison. What can an audience do to spook me now? And third, nobody here has ever seen one of these vehicles before, and since it will be parked right in front of my podium, I'll likely have the people hooked and waiting to hear all about the ride. Based on how folks have responded to the trike thus far, I suspect that maybe my audience could be more interested in the journey here than my thoughts on Death Valley or my book. Whatever the case, it will be a memorable experience.

I am sitting up on my bed in the motel room, a pillow behind my back, and a folded pillow under my heels to keep the feet slightly elevated. Check-out time isn't for a while yet, so I figure to keep my feet up and relax, giving my battered Achilles tendons the final gift of rest before tomorrow's demanding summit attempt. In seventeen miles, give or take some yardage one way or the other, the Q, trailer, and I will ascend 4,956 vertical feet, or an average elevation gain of 292 feet per mile, which is significant for someone pedaling a tricycle with a trailer. Of course, some portions will be steeper than others. Guess it won't hurt to rest the old, but powerful, body for a wee bit longer.

Maybe that's another reason I'm not overly anxious about tomorrow's talk. With Towne Pass on my mind, my mental resolve is so focused that the presentation becomes child's play.

This motel room at Stovepipe Wells is very Spartan compared to the one I rented last month at the Diamond Lake Resort. Well, you say, I did opt for the cheapest room they have here. True enough, I did, to save a few bucks, but let's consider the differences between Diamond Lake and here. This room costs me $100, whereas the Oregon room was only $59.59. This room has no television, whereas the Oregon room did.

159

This room has no telephone, whereas the Oregon room did. This room has no clock, whereas the Oregon room did. Outside this room's door, there is no snow or subfreezing temperatures, whereas outside the Oregon room's door there were both. By comparison, this room is a very poor value, yet in reality, I do not really need a television, telephone, or clock. But I must walk to the front office to keep track of my check-out time. Interesting how business models vary.

By staying in this room, I realize how out of touch I am with the natural world. I have no views of the moon and stars, no breeze, no howl of coyotes, no sounds of birds displacing air with their wings, no sunrise cloudburst, no creosote bushes, and no feeling of freedom in the wide open spaces. Next trip, I vow to do a better job of refraining from being inside. It takes time to pry oneself away from customs that have been psychologically imprinted since birth, namely, keeping huge shelters around our bodies much of our lives, always in a box of some kind.

The Achilles tendons are doing pretty well now, and I am not worried about traversing Towne Pass tomorrow. My ankles are still swelling a bit if I sit around in shoes and do no physical activity. There is no ache or pain at all however, which is a good sign.

I take this morning's breakfast lounging on my bed, a far cry from fixing my Nutty Nuggets on the trailer top at a roadside camp with air temperature low enough to make the fingers uncomfortably cold. Perhaps that has something to do with why people have evolved into building dwellers. After breakfast, I take a welcomed shower, maybe another reason why getting a room is not such a bad idea now and then. It sure feels nice to be clean. Guess it won't hurt any to emit a natural and pleasant aura tomorrow, instead of a stinky hobo just off the road.

Lunch comes and goes, and with it, a couple more of my energy bars have now taken their leave of my trailer's food supply. Never hurts to pedal less weight up hills! Since nobody came knocking at my door inviting me to lunch, it was rather unceremonious today, hard for road angels to find me when I'm locked up and out of sight.

After checking out of the room, I decide to go have a seat out on the front deck of the resort, which is only about twenty feet from Highway 190. Might as well be out here when mom and sis arrive today. It will be easy for us all to spot each other with me out front. I am leaving my trike and gear parked back near the room. It's out of my sight, but also out of sight of everyone else. Now I look normal again.

I watch every Ford F-150 that comes by. In due course, my vigilance pays off, and as a desert stone colored pickup pulls in from the east, I recognize the two desert gals inside. The Desert Gypsy, also known as Teakettle Mama, is driving, and the wild wolf sister of mine is

160

riding shotgun. The Teakettle Mama name comes from a few years back when I drove my mom all around Death Valley National Park's dirt roads in my old Ford Bronco, and we stopped at Teakettle Junction in the Racetrack Valley to get a photograph of her at the world famous Teakettle Junction sign. She was only 78 years old then, just a youngster. We had a blast for four days in the desert backcountry.

Mom and Willow have a room for tonight at the Furnace Creek Ranch, which is 24 miles southeast of here, and over 200 feet lower in elevation. They would have been here in Stovepipe earlier, but they had to check in with the motel clerk, get their possessions squared away in the room, and say howdy to Jim Graves, the production chairman for this big event, as he was the guy who helped reserve the room for them. Therefore, after we spend time together and eat dinner, they have to drive back down there. Then tomorrow morning, they have to drive right back up here. Seems to conflict with my natural earthy tendencies.

Dinner tonight will be courtesy of my most ardent road angel. Mom insists on treating me and Jack to a feast at the cozy resort restaurant, and as always, I never argue with anyone who wants to feed me, especially when the next day brings a massive physical outlay. She wants to include Jack because of his continued help on this journey of mine. Without Jack, I might be dead right now. Well, maybe that's being a little melodramatic, but he sure has been a welcomed addition to this tough expedition. Of course, without him, I would have been forced to do things totally without gasoline power, one of those inconvenient little goals I've set for myself for the rest of my life. Life's always a trade-off.

We just hang out and talk, visit the gift stores, and generally just enjoy being together again. We don't see each other that often, although when I owned a car, I made it a point to drive to southern California at least once each year for a two week visit. This year, I rode a tricycle quite a bit of that distance, perhaps in training for future trips to see my humble family. To ride all the way on my own, without a Jack Backup, would be a tour of roughly 1,000 miles one way. Double that if I ride back. If I get my act together on how to ride this trike without injuring myself like this year, perhaps that will be doable.

Later in the afternoon, in pulls Jack. I introduce everyone, and all are thrilled to meet each other finally. Mom has conversed with Jack during my ride, but this is the first time they meet. We all accompany Jack to his room, where he offers a glass of wine to anyone willing to drink it. Willow takes him up on it. I decline, not wanting that dead-head feeling again like I had after our celebration dinner at the Wrangler Steakhouse a few days ago after I rode to Badwater. Nope, no more wine for this fellow during this lifetime! And yes, I do mean it!

161

Jack tries to do a Badwater Or Bust blog update, but there is no wireless internet here. The wireless link in the customer lounge area is out for some reason. Guess all the expedition followers will have to wait a day or two until they hear from us again, builds the suspense! What happened to Steve now? My mom and sister are listening to some evening fiddle music by an event presenter.

Near the restaurant is the Badwater Saloon, which is where Ted Faye gave his presentation yesterday. Right outside the saloon is a cute little sign that says Fresh Drinkin' Water, so folks will know that not all the water around here is bad. Up until a couple years ago, the tap water here at the resort was not recommended to drink for its bad taste, but apparently they have taken care of that issue now. Around the corner from Jack's room is an old farm implement with three wheels. In my way of thinking, anything with three wheels is a friend of mine, so I have Willow take my photograph by this old time tricycle.

Now that Jack is here, I walk back over to where my room was, get on the trusty Q yet once more, and pedal my ten foot train over to Jack's new abode, where I park next to his Jeep for the night. Before tomorrow's long day, I will have one more rest in a real bed.

All this taken care of, the four of us head over to the restaurant and pig out on the fine food. It is a grand time of friendship and camaraderie. Willow and mom are completely taken by Jack's charm and humor. Dinner is punctuated with many laughs and much discussion. The food is excellent as usual. My three companions question my decision to ride over Towne Pass tomorrow. That's tomorrow. For tonight, the motto is: eat, drink, and be merry! Tomorrow never comes.

After dinner, mom, Willow, and I walk across the street to the general store for some ice cream before they head on back to the overpopulated "city" of Furnace Creek. I get another blueberry ice cream bar, made by Blue Bunny, a company I had never heard of before Wayne, Eileen, and Terry introduced me to it yesterday after lunch. It's excellent ice cream, and my last animal indulgence for this trip.

It's dark now, and mom prefers not to drive after dark, but since it's only 24 miles of country road, she'll be fine. I tell her that she looks great in the truck. She says she actually enjoys driving it. Pickups have come a long way since the 1950s.

We bid each other adieu, and they head out. I chat with Jack at the Badwater Saloon a bit, and then hit the sack early. I have a busy day ahead of me. Jack arrives later this night, but I am sound asleep by the time he arrives. His day will be relatively easy tomorrow: just document everything with his 10 mega-pixel digital camera, drive his Jeep very slowly up Towne Pass, and make sure I don't get into any more trouble.

162

His first two duties are easy. That third one though, may be the clincher.

DAY 37 - *Death Valley*
Friday, November 06, 2009
Towne Pass – just a few rough miles, only 17
(running total: 591 miles)

My bed is next to the window, so as the earliest hints of dawn begin to break around the curtains, I begin the mental preparation for arising. Jack is still sound asleep over in his bed, having gotten in here much later than I did last night. I peak out the window. Another sunny and warm day is in the making. After slipping on my expedition clothing, I open the front door for a stretch and glance over towards the Mesquite sand dunes. This is beautiful territory indeed.

As I'm standing out here, a gal walks by with the familiar Death Valley 49ers button affixed to her tee shirt. We introduce ourselves. Her name is Dee Dee Ruhlow, and she was the 1996 president of the Death Valley 49ers organization. She recognizes my name as this morning's Stovepipe Wells presenter, and we share a little information about ourselves. Dee Dee then excuses herself, and I tell her I'll see her later after breakfast.

My breakfast will be right here in the room, or perhaps out front on the covered stone porch in the morning sun. I'll be eating Nutty Nuggets again, for that "all day" charge of calories, although I doubt they'll last all day for this particular day. As an encampment presenter, I have a complimentary breakfast waiting for me come 8:00 AM at the Author's Breakfast chuck wagon parked just to the west of the podium platform, but due to my bent for health mindset, I'll likely pass today. Eggs and bacon, washed down with cow milk and caffeine just doesn't cut it for me anymore. My apologies for all you who still indulge in such animal cuisine. I used to eat loads of this food for forty-some years, so just consider me a reformed carnivore. Brontosaurus instead of T-Rex!

I must admit though, the aroma that will soon be emanating from the chuck wagon near the stage will very likely test my resolve, especially when I see folks eating the eggs and bacon right in front of me. Regardless of my daily food choices, I still can enjoy these things on rare occasion. Yes, the Death Valley 49ers do indeed put on quite a fantastic feed! Recall I ate this stuff up at Diamond Lake earlier.

While I was outside talking with Dee Dee, Jack got up, and he is now in the shower. I readily polish off a bowl of nuggets and whatever else I think might feed my brain well so that I can speak intelligently for whomever comes to see me. I'm not really a speaker, but since I want to start building up a little retirement income (emphasis on the word little) to supplement the meager $815 I'll be getting each month beginning in a couple of years, I can't afford to pass up the opportunity to talk about my book when asked. If I'm lucky, maybe my name will become somewhat synonymous with Death Valley, and the book sale royalties will eventually allow me to live comfortably on the fringes.

My life has been one of following my passions, not of following the money. Most folks seem to follow the latter, and so end up with sizable incomes once they leave the nine-to-five grind. Had I chosen that path when I used to live in southern California back in the seventies, I could now be a retired Los Angeles County sheriff's officer or administrator like a few colleagues with whom I still keep in touch. One friend retired recently as an LASD Captain, and is now raking in around 75 grand for just staying alive and breathing. Not a bad haul, I suppose.

Am I sorry for the alternative paths I've chosen? Owning a gym? Doing digital graphic design? Driving a school bus? Teaching kids? Selling real estate? Not at all. In fact, I have had experiences that most of those I know have never had, and may never have. My only loss is more income than I could probably use, given my modest lifestyle. Not having the financial freedom is sometimes difficult, but then when I realize that my philosophies have developed in ways that see past the money mirage, I am grateful. My path does not include financial wealth.

Money, power, and greed destroy many a man and woman, bringing early death through stress and poor lifestyle choices. I am not a follower any more. I am not out to impress anyone. Nor am I a consumer, despite what my governments call me. I am a citizen of the Earth, a naturalist who strives to live in harmony with my environment, happy to help those who know me. The older I get, the more I lighten my load of materialistic possessions. I will be content with a small yurt in the forest one day, not far from a small town, where I can pedal my trike for groceries. I'll have no television, radio, and maybe even no telephone. This laptop computer will eventually go away. I will live simply and greet each new day humbly. The wild outdoors is my world.

But for now, I maintain my Death Valley blog, publicize my book, and prepare for my dreams that lie ahead. And today's Author's Breakfast is one more stepping stone in that direction, a direction of independence from the machine of societal mediocrity. I eagerly chart my own path. It is a path few of affluence would choose to follow.

I am ready to head on over to the breakfast area. Jack tells me I have about an hour before it starts, but I might as well be over there meeting folks and relaxing in their company than hanging out here in the room getting nervous about the whole thing. I have a mountain to climb today, and that is my ultimate focus.

As I pedal up into the breakfast area, which is the resort parking area that has been barricaded to allow for several rows of tables and chairs instead of cars, there is still room to pedal the trike and trailer through the narrow pedestrian entryway. There are a couple of western singers with their guitars getting ready for their presentation, which will be music while people eat their breakfasts. I park my rig right under the elevated stage, so it will be immediately in front of me during my talk. That will get everyone's attention.

During the course of the next hour, I visit with a number of Death Valley enthusiasts, including three gals I met last week at the Furnace Creek Ranch swimming pool. As I was leaving after taking a shower, they were in the pool and started chatting with me, and today they have driven up from Furnace Creek to eat and listen to my tales. Donna Marschall from Kelseyville, California, Mary Ann Herman from Sanger, California, and Sandy Bucknell from Modesto, California are a lot of fun to be around. Last week at the pool, they just started talking to me like they already knew me. They looked familiar, but I didn't know why at the time.

As they talk to me this morning, it all becomes clear in my dried out mind. The day I rode the trike up to Zabriskie Point with Paul Gareau, Donna was there and met me, but I was so scattered at the time, what with Paul and many other people gathering around us for questions, that I had forgotten. At the pool last week, Donna wanted her friends to meet me too. They were pretty amazed that I had chosen to ride a trike on this trip, even though I got a ride a portion of the way from Jack. Nobody does this sort of thing – tricycles are for kids!

These three ladies belong to the Cross Country Gypsies RV Club, and have been coming to Death Valley for 15 years, since 1994. Their group spends a couple of weeks here each year. They are eager to hear what I have to say. I am most definitely not used to people gathering to hear my thoughts. Wonder if my next "profession" should be that of an orator of some kind. Nah.

Candace Lieber, the assistant to David Blacker of the Death Valley Natural History Association, arrives and sets up a table to the side of the stage as the singers are singing and folks are beginning to eat. Then, she brings several boxes to the table and starts unloading multiple copies of my Death Valley Book Of Knowledge for the audience members to purchase, either now or after I talk. She and I have emailed during the course of the last year, but today we meet in person at last.

I am happy and humbled to see my book displayed here, and even more so when a few folks come over and start buying the books.

Once purchased, the make their way to me for an autograph! Wow, here I am just a normal sort of guy (okay, not so normal – I ride a trike after all), and I am being asked for my autograph. This new experience is one of those unique aspects of my rogue lifestyle that I was typing about a few paragraphs back. How does one put a price on such things? Even if I never amount to much as an author, at least the temporary spotlight was one heck of a thrill ride. Had I remained in the 9-5 mill, this never would have happened. This is an intriguing path.

The singers are wrapping up their final song before my introduction. They are scheduled to sing again after my lungs stop spewing out words. I walk over and gulp down a final glass of water, and then fill it up again to have at the podium. One last trip to the men's room should hold me over for a while.

Jim Graves steps on stage in his western outfit and gives his introduction of me. Like in the 49er program notes, he tells the folks to ask how I got here. This trike is my ace in the hole! People are eating this stuff up. They love the bizarre. They didn't come way out here in the middle of nowhere today to be entertained by the status quo. They want things done differently, just like anyone associated with Death Valley has felt through time. This place is as far from ordinary as you can get, and so go the people who make this place a temporary home. I will give them what they want this morning.

Now I am standing on the stage, with my Aussie hat, polarized sun glasses, and a copy of my book. Jim hands the podium over to me. The audience claps. One hundred fifty eyeballs are silently looking at my two eyeballs. I wish I could silently pass right out of here and begin pedaling, but that's not going to happen yet. They are waiting to be entertained. Problem is, I'm not an entertainer.

But I am a guy with a lot more Death Valley experiences than most of these folks will ever have, so I have an edge. I have written two Death Valley books, so I am considered by many to be a Death Valley expert. Prior to this trip, a number of people back home assumed I would have a speech all typed out on paper, to which I could refer as I spoke. Heck, that really would make me nervous. I prefer to wing it, to be myself. I have somewhat of an idea of how I want to progress with this presentation, and that's enough for me. Be real – be me – be now.

Basically, there are three parts of the talk. First, I tell a little story about a couple in the 1940s who came here on a Harley Davidson motorcycle. I tell how their son later accompanies them as a wee lad to Furnace Creek. I tell this story in the third person and really doll it up, giving no clue as to this little boy's identity. I figure that the audience will figure it out, but then when I finally wrap up part one of my talk by

166

telling that the little boy was me, I hear a collective intake of breath from the crowd. Hmm, not too bad so far. Maybe I'm getting the hang of this.

Probably no one in this audience has yet read my new 720 page book, so I figure they might like to hear a few samples from it. After all, that's why I'm here. So, for part two of my presentation, I read selected excerpts from the introductory material. This is important, because when I write a book, I take considerable time to ensure that everything is phrased in ways that flow well into the mind of a reader, ways that have a dramatic effect on one's imagination. If my off-the-cuff speaking comes up short, hopefully my finely tuned written material will do the trick. This portion of the talk is not so personal though, as I am just reading, and not so animated as I was with the little boy story, but it seems to come off well. No one has left yet.

The final third of my talk centers around the topic that everyone has been wanting to hear from me ever since my arrival a couple weeks ago: The TRIKE. Oh, the joy of my trike! Not only is it an absolute blast to ride, but it provides endless fodder for discussion anywhere I go on it. It may be my imagination, but it seems like this audience is really getting into my three wheeled story. I started out on a tricycle in the 1950s, and I have returned to a tricycle in the 2000s, albeit a machine that is light years ahead of my first trike.

I explain about the wheels being reversed from what they are used to. I tell why I abandoned my car and now ride a trike. I provide brief glimpses into the highlights of the journey here from my coastal Oregon home. No one is getting up to leave. I continue by telling how I managed to ride the trike without going on the freeways. I could keep going on and on, but it occurs to me that I still want to get up Towne Pass and down the other side while the sun is up, so I wrap things up with telling them where I'm going now. With my sincere thanks to these folks for attending my talk, a generous applause flows across the air to my ears. I exit the stage, but things are not over yet.

A line of people forms at my trike as folks purchase my book. Jack is off to the side with his 10 mega-pixel camera getting it all recorded for the blog. Now the book signings begin, and I am in no rush to hurry through it. This has never happened to me before, and may never happen again. I have one life to live, so I am going to enjoy every second of this, right here and now. Now is all I ever have!

I sign quite a few in front of the stage, but once the two singers with their guitars begin warming up for round two of their ballads, the large speakers prove too much for our ears. Being a solver of problems, I quickly get in the trike and ride it over to the other side of the stage area, and then continue. The line follows me. I feel like the Pied Piper.

After a while, things slow down finally, and I am ready to head out.

Jack tells me that my talk lasted one hour, from 8:30 to 9:30 AM, and that my signing lasted a half hour, up to the current time of 10:00 AM. Seventy-five people were in attendance, not bad considering that this is Stovepipe Wells and not Furnace Creek. Had I spoken down there, the attendees would have numbered far more. Today was perfect for me though, being more intimate and relaxing. Candace Lieber tells me that $480 in sales were taken in by the Death Valley Natural History Association since she arrived here shortly before I began talking. The pressure is now off. Time to trike. Up, up, and away!

By 10:15 AM, I'm off once again on the trike, actively participating in the final leg of this tricycle expedition to Death Valley. This is it. Once over the top of the monstrous pass that lies before me, and down the other side to the DVNP entrance in the Panamint Valley, it will be over. Things are bitter sweet. It's always rewarding to meet one's objectives, but then again, I hate to stop pedaling. I have invested so much psychological energy into this trip since back in May that the thought that it's almost over is kind of sad for me.

Seventeen miles of uphill separate me from the heady thrill ride of a lifetime. This is a steep pass on both sides. Any cyclist at the top going in either direction down will indeed learn the true meaning of very serious speed on a human-powered cycle, whether it be two wheels or three. There is no denying it, even automobile drivers find this pass intimidating. The side I will be going down is even steeper than the side I am now starting to ride up. I'll get my hide up to the top as fast as I can because I want to see the grand spectacle of the Panamint Valley as I rocket down out of the park. Paul Gareau rode down this side days ago.

I suspect it will be mid to late afternoon by the time I go down the other side. Sunsets and sunrises are the prettiest times out here, so it should time out well. Seventeen miles is nothing normally. I did the 24 miles from Furnace Creek to Stovepipe Wells in about three hours. This is a steep grade as it crests over the spine of the northern Panamint Range, but my load is lighter than it has ever been now, so I hope to make decent time. Six hours should do it, putting me at the summit around 4:30 PM, with enough daylight remaining to easily reach my destination for trip's end in the Panamint Valley.

Looking at the road ahead can be discouraging at times. It is so darn long and straight at the beginning, but I am on my middle chainring, keeping up a good pace. As long as I can stay in this gear range, for most of the way, I'll meet my expectations. At the 1,000 foot mark, Jack is taking my photograph, with Stovepipe Wells now a tiny white speck on the desert floor below.

There is no shortage of heat. The sun, although mild by summer standards, takes it performance toll when pedaling up this steep grade. I freely perspire, and freely do I also suck up new water from my water bladder tube that comes over my left shoulder, for water on the go. Behind my recumbent seat on the left side, I have mounted a Camelbak hydration system in a Fastbak pouch, which allows easy access to water anytime. The Radical Lowracer panniers keep the water supply in the shade. All of this is behind and under my left arm. I also have two BPA free water bottles mounted on the frame between my legs. Water will be no problem today though, for I have two vehicles with plenty of supply that are tracking my progress up this mega mountain. My success is practically guaranteed.

This grade is not quite as steep as my ride up to Artist's Palette on October 30th, but of course, that ride was short, with uphills totaling approximately one-fourth the distance of today's elevation gain. That ride required my lowest gears on nearly all the uphills. So far, I'm still in midrange today. I am in my best physical shape today of the entire trek.

Up ahead, there is a noticeable bend in the road, where it goes from a predominantly westerly direction to more southwesterly bearing. I spin quickly into this corner with great enthusiasm of maintaining my momentum, and it seems that I can do no wrong. Before long however, this second stretch of road ups the ante on my efforts. A shift is made down on my rear cassette. Then another, until finally I am at the lowest point that the middle chainring can handle. My next shift will require changing to the smallest front chainring. Valiantly I attempt to maintain this speed as long as I can, but eventually, despite my best efforts, it is now clear that low range gearing is necessary.

By shifting onto the small 24-tooth chainring from the 36-tooth middle ring, I can now upshift my rear cassette a few notches, into the middle of the nine sprockets. This involves my right hand directing the cable to move the rear dérailleur into a position that drops the 12-foot long chain down from the largest rear sprocket. In the rear, the largest sprocket is used for going the slowest, while in the front, the largest chainring is used for going the fastest. Here is the combo: front/small and rear/large means ultra slow going. Front/large and rear/small means ultra fast going. The former makes me stronger – the latter is just fun!

I have little names for all this gearing stuff that work well in my particular brain. Low/low and low/mid are for the uphills. Mid/low, mid/mid, and mid/high are for gradual hills. High/mid and high/high are for flats and downhills. The reason there is no low/high or high/low is because there is no need to have these extremes, which put undue stress on the chain transmission system, because the full range of nine gears in the midrange chainring overlaps these unused extremes. After a lot of riding, this concept becomes clearer.

Even though I am eating bars and drinking water like there is no tomorrow, I am still unable to remain exclusively in the low/mid gearing. The farther I go, the more often I am forced to remain in the low/low gearing. Eventually, low/low becomes my reality this early afternoon, and only on the slightest of what appears to be very brief downhills am I able to upshift towards a low/mid gearing. They look like short downhill sections of maybe twenty yards, but they are not by any means downhill. It's all one grand deception of my mind. These occasional teasers are still uphills, but due to the extent of this overall grade, they only appear to be going down. Reality is closer to something like this: instead of a grade of 6-9 percent, these sections may only be 3-5 percent. It's all relative though, as it feels better to pick up speed.

It's a strange feeling when your mind says you can really speed up for a ways, but your body says no way. Regardless, when one of these lesser grades comes along, I still eek out every last bit of speed I can. My sister Willow has opted to walk along behind me for the last mile or two, and she has no problem keeping up! Gee, is this ever a humbling ride today. A pedestrian walking as fast as I can pedal.

By 1:45 PM, I pull into Emigrant Campground, sis hot on my heels, or, I mean trailer. It's nearly two in the afternoon and I'm just over half way! I have been pedaling for three hours and a half, and only covered about nine miles of road. The math will reveal an average speed, but of course, it was significantly faster up to the first big curve.

There are shade trees here, along with a bathroom. Several tourists are chatting with mom and Jack about what I'm doing, and both of my supporters are eagerly telling them of my intrepid adventure. One fellow from Japan is here with his Japanese/American buddy, and wants his photo taken next to me (even though I'm sweating like a pig). We have to go through a translation mode with his friend, as the guy who wants the photo speaks no English. We're all smiles and having a good time. They want the address to the blog so they can read all about the trip, to learn the rest of the story.

Slight doubts are beginning to creep into my mind now as to whether I can make the top before dark. The eternal optimist, I will give it my best shot. I want that ride down the other side so bad I can taste it. If it gets dark, I have a powerful headlight. Mom implores me to stop here and load up the trike. She is getting tired and wants to get home for some supper. She made a similar request of me about three miles ago, but I forged ahead anyway. I tell her that I am only eight miles from the summit, way too close to stop now. The summit will be mine. Ego!

After eating several energy bars, a few boxes of raisins, and two V8 juices, I'm on my way yet again. The air is starting to cool a tad now and then the sun is partially blocked by the massive mountains to my west. Eventually, I will be in the shade completely, but for now, it's sporadic. My temperature regulation is still working fine – sweat.

There is no timepiece on me or my trike. The Earth is rotating and hiding the sun more and more. Now I am in the shade. My sister has chosen to keep me company for a few more miles. She says she will walk with me all the way to the summit, knowing that my high speeds going down the other side will be a different story. Not long after the 4,000 foot marker, I turn on my tail light for safety. It is getting darker. I tell Willow that she must get into the truck with mom up ahead because it is getting too dangerous for her to be walking on Highway 190 at twilight. Traffic seems unusually heavy today in both directions, and it's no place to be on foot in dark clothing with no lights or reflectors.

Willow agrees, and somewhere around 4,300 feet, I am on my own again. Around 4,400 feet, I feel it is necessary to turn on my headlight and strobe. The strobe fires right up. The headlight is dead, again. Even though the company claims 90 hours of runtime, this is the second set of batteries currently in my Cateye EL-530 headlight. Jack is about to pass me again in his Jeep. I flag him down by waving my left arm and pointing to the side of the road. He immediately stops and gives me new batteries for the 530. My Cateye LD1100 tail light is still on its first set of batteries from the start of the trip. It is living up to its claims. The strobe is on its second set, but seems strong enough tonight to make the final leg of the expedition. Don't buy this headlight!

Jack drives on. Darkness finally overtakes my slow moving tricycle. Were it not for my ultra bright lights and abundant reflective devices, I would now be invisible to traffic. Even now, in complete darkness, the cars slow and pass completely in the other lane. There is no cause for alarm. The extreme physical effort needed to make this grade now feels good as the night air is rapidly chilling. I am on the verge of considering a light jacket, but am still fine as long as I keep moving forward with all due effort.

With no daylight to provide terrain clues as to my whereabouts, I have no definitive idea where I am on the mountain. I can only guess based on my experience up here. It seems like I am getting close now. The curves are much tighter, which is what happens on this north side near the top. The two support vehicles play leapfrog with me on my climb. Sometimes when I pass mom and sis in the pickup, they stay parked with their headlights on to illuminate me for upcoming traffic. On Towne Pass, motorists generally keep the pedal to the metal to get up and over. Mom is clearly worried, but I have long since left that mindset behind on this long human powered journey.

Now it's getting windy, in addition to all of all the climbing I'm doing, and the wind is coming from over the top, meaning that I am pedaling into a headwind. Although still a light wind, it is doing me no favors as it heads north. A National Park Service law enforcement ranger has passed me twice tonight in his Chevrolet Avalanche patrol vehicle. He must surely think I've lost my mind.

Up ahead, I notice two vehicles parked off the side of the road. I wonder if this is the summit. As I near, which takes what seems like eternity at this point, I can tell they are way off to the side. I know that this summit has an ultra wide parking area on top for cars to cool and people to stretch, so I hope this is where I can begin my descent.

Yes, it's a large parking area all right, and both the F-150 and Jeep are parked here, far off towards the west side, with their engines running and headlights on so that I can see them clearly. I pull up to the first vehicle I meet, which is Jack's Jeep. He rolls down the window. I ask him if this is the top. He says yes!

I set the brakes on the Q and get up to stretch my legs. Mom's truck is about 15 feet ahead. Jack tells me that it's five minutes after six. Just in the minute I've been standing here, the wind, which is noticeably stronger at the summit, is really making me cold. After weeks of living out of my panniers, I know right where my down vest, polar fleece jacket, and rain/wind jacket are, and I waste no time putting them all on and fastening them completely. I also put on my polar fleece skullcap and heavy Shift Torrent motorcycle foul weather gloves. I can't believe how cold it has become! It will be a cold ride going down into the Panamint Valley tonight, as I'll be coasting all the way, expending little physical effort. This ought to prove exciting!

Jack, who didn't bring a jacket at all, and is only wearing short pants and a short sleeve shirt, has his heater going in the Jeep, and has the window down only about half way so we can talk. He wasn't expecting this turn of temperature. We had both figured I'd summit during daylight, and lack of heat would be the last thing on our minds.

"There are fist sized rocks ahead in the road in several turns." Jack tells me. He has done reconnaissance while I was making my slow headway tonight, and apparently enough rocks have fallen directly into the lane that he strongly feels that it would be very unsafe for me to continue. There is also a lot of traffic this Friday night, and Jack says that if I'm speeding down to the bottom and have to dodge these small rocks, I could end up crashing or hitting a car. The rocks pose no problem for automobiles, but could be disastrous for a speeding trike pilot at night. This is a new development I had not contemplated.

Mom comes back to talk briefly in the cold wind. She has already heard Jack's report. Everyone is tired. I am so bushed that I can feel the beginning stages of hypothermia coming on, even with all my heavy clothing. I'm actually shaking a little bit, but I doubt it's noticeable to them in the dark. After giving me her opinion of what I should do, she high tails it back to the warmth of her cab.

I look Jack straight in the eyes. He has his interior dome light on. I ask what he thinks. Jack is a straight shooter. He tells me it's finally time to call it a day. It's just far too risky to go any farther under these conditions. I'm so wiped out that my judgment is probably impaired. To proceed now could put a bad ending on a good trip. It's just not worth the prize of flying down this grade ahead of me. Nothing is that important, he assures me.

For a moment, I consider all this. I know he's right. My condition is deteriorating, and it wouldn't take much to plunge me into a dangerous thermal regulation problem. I make my decision, and tell him we end it here, at the summit of Towne Pass.

Jack gets out and we wheel my trike over to mom's truck. The wind is picking up even more as we begin the puzzle of getting it all in the bed for high speed transport to mom's house in Apple Valley. I get my panniers inside the truck's rear seat area, which is only a partial short seat, but enough for mom's short legs. My sister will ride up front, for she is tall. All gear stowed at long last, Jack and I congratulate each other on our achievements, thank one another for the experiences, and we say farewell. He will spend another day or two in Death Valley. He turns the Jeep around and heads back down the 17 miles to Stovepipe.

It is so cold and I am so miserable, that all I can think about is getting into the truck. I will drive us home to mom's. Willow had purchased a CD of one of the western singers she heard at the stage, and we listen to the songs on the way home. Partway down the grade into the pitch black Panamint Valley, I realize that there were no summit photographs taken. My old digital camera doesn't do too well at night (at only 1.3 mega-pixels), but we are too far down and no one, including me, wants to go back up. We all forgot at the top. It just goes to show how minds dulled by tedium (Jack, Willow, and mom), as well as a mind dulled by extreme exhaustion (me), are not the best decision makers.

What a great shot that would have made, with me and the trike under the pass sign at night. Not only didn't I get my ride down, but I didn't even get to bring the moment at the top home in pictures. Oh well, this has been an expedition of a lifetime, and I am still very satisfied with how things all transpired.

173

Down below and across the valley, we see the lights of the Panamint Springs Resort off in the distance. We turn a few miles short of that, and head south past Ballarat and over the next mountains into Trona. From there, we pass through Red Mountain, Kramer's Junction (Four Corners for all you old timers), and then south to Victorville. Once in Apple Valley, we refuel the truck so we don't have to do it tomorrow morning when mom and sis return it.

We pull into mom's driveway, and she suggests unloading the truck in the morning. I just as soon get it done tonight. It only takes about five minutes. The trike is secure in the garage, and the panniers are placed in my guest room. Around 11:45 PM, my head finally hits the pillow. It has been one very long day. I think I'll sleep in late!

THE END
* * *

ADVENTURE TWO:
EASTERN SIERRAS

**Florence, Oregon to Apple Valley, California
via an inland route over several mountain ranges
980 miles, 21 days (age 60)**

BACKGROUND INFORMATION:

Two other trikers began this journey with me, for a trio of triangular travelers headed for Apple Valley. Gary Bunting was from southern California, USA. Glen Aldridge was from British Columbia, Canada. Gary was 66 years of age, Glen 61. Gary rode a Catrike Road pulling a Burley trailer. Glen rode a Trident trike with no trailer. I rode an ICE trike, and, based on my prior experience, pulled no trailer.

DAY 1 - *Eastern Sierras*
Friday – August 26, 2011
Florence, Oregon to Scottsburg, Oregon - 38 miles
(running total: 38 miles)

I arose about 5:00 AM, allowing plenty of time for breakfast and the settling of the remaining nerves. There is always a degree of anxiety before setting out on a trip of this magnitude, although this time around, it was far less than my first solo journey, having done it before and also having a couple of other guys with me this time. You know

174

how fear goes: it's a demon that loses its grip in the presence of company. Glen showed up a little after 7:00 AM. Our scheduled departure time from the local bicycle shop, Bicycles 101, where we were to meet Gary, was about 45 minutes away. The bicycle shop was 4 blocks down the street. Plenty of time for semi relaxing preparation.

By 7:30, all three of us were in the bicycle shop parking lot, along with my friend Matt Jensen, who was going to ride the first 20 miles south on the Oregon Coast Highway with us to make sure all was well. Matt owns an immaculate Easy Racer titanium frame, long wheelbase, recumbent bicycle with fairing, quite an impressive set of touring wheels. Three local well-wishers were also there to see us off, making it a noteworthy turnout of 7 semi-crazy people.

The atmosphere was typical early morning coastal fog, a bit on the nippy side, but absolutely perfect for pedaling, especially up the hill just south of the bridge, our first little challenge less than a mile away. I shot a short introductory movie with my digital camera so folks could better visualize the occasion.

My overall traveling weight this trip was roughly 270 pounds, which included my body, all the gear in the cargo bags, and the trike. Two years ago, with the trailer along, my gross traveling weight was about 100 pounds greater, as I packed everything but the kitchen sink to make sure I'd have plenty of supplies and back-up supplies. This trip, I felt elated to be so light and maneuverable, and wondered how Gary would fare with his trailer, which was smaller than the one I had pulled. He had less weight in his trailer, but with his bodyweight being about 70 pounds more than mine, his total triking weight was closing in on what I had pedaled in 2009 to Death Valley National Park.

There were many variables we would experience during this ride, one of which was how long the trip would take. Glen had to be back home by mid to late October, but I figured we would make that time line. My mind was allowing about 6 weeks for our travels, considering there were three of us with varied levels of ability, although Gary was figuring maybe around 4 weeks. Glen wasn't expressing any prediction. Gary was actively trying to shed excess pounds, hoping to get down to the 200 mark during this journey, and a concern he had was that he would end up slowing down the expedition due to his physical conditioning. It was all for one, and one for all, so it did not matter.

My position was that we would take as much time as necessary, while having a wonderful time as three trikers out in the freedom of the natural world. Time we would cast to the wind, replacing it with joy and grand camaraderie. This was to be the first such trek for Gary and Glen, and they were relying on my expertise to a large extent, even though I

175

only had a couple thousand miles under my own belt thus far. We would work as a team, and by late September or early October sometime, arrive as a well seasoned triker crew in Apple Valley, California.

At 7:57 AM, with no further legitimate reasons for hanging around the parking lot, and fear well under everyone's control with four of us supporting each other psychologically, we all began pedaling out onto Highway 101: 13 aluminum wheels (3 trikes, 1 trailer, and 1 bike) were now underway. Traffic was happily very light, as the summer vacationers were just getting up from bed and had not yet hit the road for their next motorized motel or campground.

In seven blocks our foursome arrived at the Siuslaw River bridge, which takes about 7 seconds to drive across in a car, but seeing as how it's slightly uphill on the south side, and we were pedaling south, our time varied. I had told Gary and Glen that my strategy for this slight incline, which requires riding in the single narrow southbound traffic lane (zero shoulder) is to upshift to maximum speed possible before reaching it. We entered the drawbridge in high gear at around 12 miles per hour, but on a trike with this minimal grade, we really began feeling the quadriceps burning and the lungs aching about two-thirds of the way across. Fortunately, it was foggy and cool, and there was nominal auto traffic. Early morning has its perks.

The few cars that were affected by our crossing were all courteous and curious, and none demonstrated any negative feelings whatsoever. I took photos of Gary, Glen, and Matt as they came across, fog visible around the bridge. Matt is a veteran cross country cyclist, and proved very valuable on this first morning, providing sage riding advice to Gary and Glen, and also making a crucial field adjustment to Glen's new trike along the way. Matt is the man to have along when anything breaks! He had greased and adjusted my rear hub a couple weeks prior to the trip (I watched and took photos for the Trike Asylum website). He knows his stuff as well as anyone could.

Our pedaling foursome was passed by two women about two miles south of town. Paula and Beth Brown, senior cycling sisters seeing the state on their two wheeled uprights, stopped to chat for a few moments as our group reassembled after the first noteworthy hill. They were on an Oregon tour, loaded for tent camping, and clearly experienced. The fragile male egos of our group were bolstered, knowing that these easy going female minds were zooming by us with all their cargo gear strapped to the sides of their bikes. One of them pulled a Beast Of Burden (BOB) trailer. The other had no trailer. We were all doing the same thing, but they were doing it much faster.

The morning route took us through 20 miles of wooded coastal landscape, full of huge evergreen trees, with glimpses of the ocean here and there. The morning cloud cover was holding, keeping our hill climbing pleasant. There was a custom car show this Friday through Sunday just south of the small town of Reedsport (where we would be turning inland), so while triking along, we were passed by a number of cool old cars and hot rods. Then, we came to Gardiner Hill!

This hill is quite noticeable on a human powered tricycle. Riding south, it takes longer to reach the summit, as it is more gradual, with a series of ascents and level portions. The south side of the hill drops off fairly steeply, reaching the bottom in one near straightaway. Well, as our luck would have it, Mr. Sun decided to make his appearance just as we began our ascent on the north side of Gardiner Hill. It felt hot compared to the weather so far this morning, but of course, it was nothing when held against what we would encounter later in the trip out in the vast dessicated deserts!

Once Glen and Gary reached the summit, where Matt and I were hanging out enjoying the scenery and chatting, we began the descent. It's not too long, perhaps just over a mile, but it's fast and a real thrill. According to Matt's computerized speedometer, we reached speeds of 43 miles per hour. Gary's rig pulled out in front, a time when a trailer delivers a slight advantage. Gary and my rigs have very low seating positions and steep rakes to the seat backs, with our rear ends just over 7 inches off the asphalt, making the trikes very stable at speed and in corners. Glen's rig sits considerably higher, making it much easier to get in and out of, but compromising handling and lateral stability. He made it just fine on his new trike however.

After we had descended the hill and crossed the Smith River just south of the tiny town of Gardiner, Matt and I pulled into a dirt turnout to wait for Gary and Glen. The drawbridge into Reedsport was immediately ahead, and Matt figured it would be best to cross as a group of four cyclists for everyone's safety (traffic was still very light though). As Glen slowly steered into the off camber turnout, his trike tipped over as he came to rest at an angle. Matt quickly dismounted and helped him up, unscathed, but somewhat embarrassed. Gary then pulled in, worried that Glen had suffered a heart attack when he saw Glen's flag topple over behind the bushes.

The four of us had lunch at a little Mexican fast food restaurant just south of the bridge about a half mile. The morning had been fun, and everyone was now warmed up by the food, sun, and relaxed fellowship. We also became an unsolicited audience of an older woman who was extolling the virtues of her chosen God and religion. Matt had successfully gotten Gary and Glen the first 20 miles, that initial mental

177

hump where typical fears are most resistant to taking an overland tricycle journey. They now had a taste of open highway, hills, and light traffic. We were truly on our way to southern California!

Matt turned his shiny titanium bicycle northward and began pedaling solo back to Florence. Glen, Gary, and I left Highway 101, heading east on Highway 38 along the Umpqua River, beginning our ride into the Coast Range of Oregon. Glen had placed a Canadian flag on a horizontal pole, protruding a few inches to the traffic side of his trike. Passing motorists knew he was touring from Canada, and it helped his visibility. His Trident Stowaway trike was blue, as were his panniers, so the flag stood out well since it was red and white. Glen also had a high visibility yellow flag mounted high from his rear rack.

Gary's Catrike Road was bright yellow in color, with matching panniers, and his Burley trailer was also a high visibility yellow. He had orange flags mounted to the trike and trailer. My ICE Qnt trike was red, with matching red panniers, although I was running my bright yellow rain covers on the bags to keep me high in the eye of motorists. Two flags flew from my pole, one yellow with a happy face, and one day-glow orange. We three overland trikers presented an unmistakable entourage moving along the side of the road.

Custom cars and hot rods continued to pass going the other way as they headed to the show. We passed a house trailer that had turned over and was torn to pieces on the shoulder, with orange emergency cones keeping traffic away. A few miles east of Reedsport, in a huge open field of many acres, we stopped to view a large herd of elk, lazily basking in the warm early afternoon sun. This is a serene ride, with the beautiful river to the left, elk to the right, and forest in all directions. The increasing size of the mountains shielded us from the sun, helpful on uphill grades.

As the afternoon wore on, it was easy to remain warm while pedaling, with the temperature probably around 70. The many shaded areas felt good. The first day was coming along just fine, with no negative incidents to dampen our spirits. Morale was high.

Prior to departure on this trip, Gary had asked for a general idea of our itinerary for the ride. He wanted to plan our overnight stops along the way. Based on my past experience, this was not really a doable exercise, as the daily variables on an overland trike journey are too many for sticking to a predefined schedule. You never really know how each day, indeed, each hour, is going to play out. This is one reason I recommend not making any overnight reservations ahead of time for trike treks. It just causes too much stress about making the next stop.

I did however attempt an itinerary for the first few days that I emailed to Gary and Glen, tossing out some potential daily mileages we might accomplish, along with where we could spend those nights. I made up this tentative schedule all the way to Crater Lake National Park, hoping to provide them with a mental construct of what we had in store. For the first day, I listed the first potential overnight at Bunch Bar river landing, a large turnout with block outhouse right next to the river. It would have made for a 52 mile first day, and is where I camped on my first night two years prior when I pulled a trailer.

This did not come to pass. By the time we pedaled into the tiny mountain village of Scottsburg, 38 miles from Florence, Glen and Gary were ready for calling it a day. It didn't matter to me one way or the other, as my prime motivation was to make for a pleasurable experience for the two men, traveling only as far each day as they felt comfortable. The camaraderie is what it's all about, not the mileage. Scottsburg is a picturesque locale on the Umpqua River, with the sounds of water rushing to the sea, and evergreen trees all around. This was a fine place to pitch our tents.

Gary and I followed Glen along the tiny main street of old little houses, until Glen stopped to ask a local woman in her yard about a place we could camp. Her miniature dog kept up a yipping streak as we all talked. There were no camping areas in the mile-long village, but she said there was a nice lawn at the Scottsburg Historical Society building a couple blocks east, so we headed on over.

The lawn was on the east side of the building, right next to the highway (just a single lane in each direction), and the last vestige of town before the road re-entered the woods. By this time of day, there was minimal traffic, but still the custom cars and hot rods were occasionally rolling down the road to the coastal car show. Since the evening was yet early, there was no pressing rush. Gary and Glen began pitching their tents while I sat on my recumbent seat and wrote in my daily log journal about the trip. This was my lot each night.

From the east, a lone man on a Giant brand bicycle, loaded with cargo bags, rode over to our cozy camp. He introduced himself to me as Rex Harrison, just released from the state mental hospital. Seeing two tents going up, along with the three tricycles, Rex felt this might be a suitable place for him to also camp tonight. Heck, this was becoming a cyclist's retreat real fast, it seemed. With this many people and tents, I hoped the local sheriff or residents would be receptive to our peaceful need to simply sleep, perhaps thinking this was all pre-arranged.

Rex had acquired his bicycle from a pawnshop in Eugene, Oregon a couple weeks prior. Since he was receiving $674 per month from Social Security and $200 per month for food stamps, he wanted to ride a bicycle around the state of Oregon to celebrate his new freedom from the hospital. Eventually, he was going to return to Sweet Home, Oregon, a place he calls home, to panhandle. Rex planned on riding to Florence the next morning. I immediately like the man – very calm.

I had a nice talk with Rex, who was very friendly, and who innocently shared any information asked of him. He had a certain childlike naivety about him, very trusting, and didn't seem the least bit embarrassed concerning his situation. As it was beginning to finally get darker, I excused myself from the conversation to set up my tent while I could still see to do so. Glen and Gary were already set. Rex pitched his tent about 30 feet east of our trio of tents, which were closely spaced, kind of like circling the wagons of old-west pioneers.

Whenever I tent camp along side a roadway where most conservative folks might become alarmed, I usually wait until just before dark to erect my portable house, maximizing my chances of not being told to leave the area. A Douglas County Sheriff squad car drove by, heading inland. The officer did not stop, even though we were just a few yards from the pavement. Guess we all looked innocent enough. During the darkness, headlights pierced the thin nylon tents now and then as a car or truck rolled by, but the night was quiet, and we all survived without incident.

DAY 2 - *Eastern Sierras*
Saturday – August 27, 2011
Scottsburg, Oregon to Elkton, Oregon - 19 miles
(running total: 57 miles)

I arose before sunup to cool morning air, and began taking a few photographs. Gary and Glen still were asleep. Rex was just up also, breaking down his tent with the expertise and speed of a well seasoned cyclist. As I began striking my tent, Glen and Gary finally poked their heads out of their tents, happy that they had made it to their second day on the road, likely feeling as though their overland triker seasoning was well underway. Rex pedaled off for the coast, as we waved to each other, and I knew I'd probably never see this gentle giant again. We were all hungry. Good thing a market was only two miles ahead.

That very tentative itinerary I had tossed out to the boys earlier had us arriving at Mazama campground in Crater Lake National Park by the afternoon of day six, which would have worked out to about 196 miles by that time, or a 33 mile average per day. Now, that seems doable on the surface, but to those familiar with the terrain that exists between our departure point at the sea and the extinct Mazama volcano, it is an

180

extraordinary feat, especially for any triker still on the learning curve of pedaling overland, as Glen and Gary were.

We were now in the Coast Range on day two, which gets more challenging as the miles roll by and the mountains get steeper. Then, there is a region of lesser hills, still a workout, but easier at least. After this comes the mighty Cascade Range, a huge mound of elevated ancient volcanic ground that demands the most from any cyclist regardless of athletic prowess or experience. Not only that, but the final ultra challenging miles up the caldera of Mount Mazama, an extinct super volcano, to over 7,000 feet elevation in the national park are real killers, steep ascents that fan the flames of fatigue in all human powered bodies. Better have some energy bars ready.

So, the three of us were now, not surprisingly, creating our own itinerary right on the spot, in real time. That's one aspect that makes triking overland so exciting – you never know what's around the next bend or what the next day holds in store. Each hour is written as you live it, with no editing or detached review possible. Our days spread out before us like a riveting mystery novel. Where will we be tonight? What will happen to us in between now and then?

Two miles of relaxed pedaling brought us to Bob's Market at Well's Creek, a well stocked food store for the local rural residents and road-bound tourists. We shopped for our anticipated breakfasts, and then relaxed at one of the two small wooden picnic tables in front of the store. We met Bob's son, and learned that Bob's family had finally sold the market to new owners recently. Then, guess who pulled in during our dining. How did this happen?

Yep, sure enough, Paula and Beth pedaled up to say hello again. How did we get ahead of them? Well, they had ridden 7 miles off the highway yesterday afternoon on a little rural side road to camp at a cool spot called Loon Lake, and then this morning, ridden the 7 miles back to Highway 38 before heading east again. The two sisters had taken a steep 14 mile extra ride, and were now about to pass us again after a few words of greeting and well wishing, as we continued to fuel our bodies with calories for the morning's push. Paula was from Bellingham, Washington and Beth was from Corvallis, Oregon.

Today is sunny and warm. It felt good to sit in the shade while eating breakfast. Glen's arthritis was flaring up at times, causing him observable pain during certain movements, but being the trooper he is, it never slowed him down. In fact, Glen is a strong rider, capable of making good time on a tricycle. Gary's knees have been talking to him on occasions of hill climbing, nothing really serious, but a concern I wonder about. There are many grueling vertical miles yet between us and southern California. Gary is likewise a warrior with iron resolve, and keeps on trikin' hour by hour.

I told Gary and Glen that with each new day, their bodies will be stronger than the day prior, and by the end of the first week, they would be finding this overland triking business much easier than when we started. That which does not kill us makes us stronger, I reasoned, yet I wondered if they bought into the ideology on this warm day with the sun's rays easily keeping cold at bay.

Twelve miles past the market, on mostly level terrain, and 14 miles since Scottsburg, I turned my trike into the Bunch Bar river landing, where I had camped on my prior ride through here. The huge shady trees made for a cooling rest until my two teammates caught up. We all chatted under the overhanging limbs, listening to the Umpqua River, and I informed them that in 5 more miles we'd arrive in Elkton, Oregon, a small town with library internet access, a butterfly pavilion, and an ice cream shoppe. Ahh, that last one got their attention!

With Labor Day a few days off, families were still vacationing in this northwest paradise, so as the day progressed, cars increased. There are adequate shoulders on this portion of the expedition for the most part, so we rode without any significant fears of being struck by motorists. This journey of ours was indeed progressing without a hitch. Spirits were high as we pedaled on.

Arriving on the western outskirts of rural Elkton, we pulled our three tadpole tricycles into the parking lot of the Elkton Community Education Center. Immediately we spotted two tour laden bicycles, one with a trailer, parked in front of the ice cream shoppe and library, and needed no prompting to realize who their owners were. The Brown sisters had been here for quite a while, patiently hanging out while one of their husbands drove from Corvallis, Oregon to pick them up, as this was the final destination of their journey.

Being the helpful gals they were, Beth and Paula offered all their remaining rations for our own food supplies if we wanted them. I wasted no time accepting walnuts, energy bars, and anything else with calories they wanted to send my way. It wasn't that I was selfish, not allowing Gary and Glen any of these goodies, but rather that those two trikers had so quickly disappeared into the air conditioned ice cream shoppe for food of a different kind that they weren't here to get any.

After bidding the ladies adieu, I finally entered the building. While my buddies were scarfing the cold stuff, I used the computer in the attached library to update the Trike Asylum website/blog about the expedition's progress thus far. Glen had brought along a tiny netbook computer, and was busily catching up on his emails. Gary was inhaling another ice cream cone treat. All our cares were temporarily dispatched as we unwound from warm pedaling. Gary then went next door and toured the amazing butterfly pavilion, where you can walk among plants inside a large enclosure and have many unique and beautiful butterflies flitting about you, while listening to a personal guide explain to you what you're seeing. These volunteers absolutely love to do this work!

Gary and Glen then came to me and requested a meeting, and asked if we could hang out here until later in the afternoon, perhaps after 4:00 PM, knowing that a huge uphill existed just past this town, and if we waited until later, the thick forests would have it all in the shade. It was still 14 miles to the Tyee campground where we had been considering pitching the tents this second night. I agreed this was a good plan, so our minds stepped down into yet a deeper level of relaxation. Shortly after 4 however, they decided it would be best to camp here at the Elkton RV Park on the river. Fine with me. We were having a blast on our grand adventure, so time was cast to the wind!

We pedaled the Catrike, Trident, and ICE another half mile down to the riverside campground, and went inside to pay our fees, which totaled $18 for the site, or $6 apiece (with tricycles and tents, you can all get into an area where only one RV or car can fit – oh the joy). When we came out of the office to ride the trikes to the campsite, we got our first unwelcomed surprise of the journey. Glen discovered his left front tire was flat. It was only flat on the bottom, but my keen mind rightly deduced there would always be a bottom, so it's flat period. Gary and I rode our trikes the 50 yards to the grassy camp site, while Glen pushed his along the gravel driveway – at least we had a nice place here.

The roaring Umpqua cascaded through the rocky river bed nearby, making for wonderful sounds as we got on to the business of helping Glen with his rubber misfortune. We had been triking only on paved roads, so had he picked up a goathead or nail in the last few miles today? Glen had Schwalbe tires on his Trident, a brand known for their superior durability, but they were not the Marathon Plus model of tire that Gary and I had strongly encouraged him to use (the kind that Gary and I use). Glen's tires had just recently been introduced by the company, so the jury was still out on their pros and cons. A Schwalbe rep had encouraged Glen to give them a try. Wrong time to try new.

I have run Schwalbe Marathon Plus ever since I got my trike, and have never experienced a flat tire with them! They are hands-down an incredible tire, one that inspires true confidence in a world full of tire assassins. My arsenal also includes EarthGuard tire liners inside each Marathon Plus, along with Kenda Thorn-Resistant Q-tubes, which offer a significant advantage in tube durability and flat resistance. This

183

unbeatable combination works every time for me.

Back to Glen's dilemma: Gary is a helpful fellow, and with his analytical mind and career engineering background, he went right to work getting to the bottom of Glen's bizarre flat. After removing the quick-release wheel and dismounting the tire and tube, Glen took the tube over to a campground sink and searched for the breach, as nothing noticeable appeared at our initial inspection. Upon his return, we saw the tiny pinhole leak. Trouble was, we could find no intruding object in the tire, nor was one found in the tube at the hole. Neither were any spoke ends out of place, nor any anomalous condition of the wheel liner that could have caused a pinch. This wasn't a tear. If something had punctured this tube, no evidence now existed.

Glen prepared and affixed a tube patch, and as Gary was reassembling the tube and tire on the rim at the picnic table, which was not going well, we all heard a very powerful and brief hissing of air. Gary asked what it was, thinking it had come from another campsite. I responded that Glen's right front tire had just gone flat, which was met with incredulity from Glen and Gary. "You've got to be kidding!" Glen said. The trike was on its right side. Glen got up and pinched the tire in his hand. Totally flat in seconds!

Okay, this was getting too weird. Both front tires flat? What were the chances? With the left front repaired, we remounted it on the trike, and then dismounted the right front. Repeating the procedure, Glen returned from the sink with the other tube, and sure enough, it had an identical tiny pinhole leak. And, just like the left side tube, the minuscule hole was in a place where no road debris puncture could have possibly done it, being in a protected location near where the tire meets the aluminum rim. We had two tubes with tiny holes in the same general region. This seemed far beyond any chance happenings.

As before, Glen prepared and affixed a tube patch for the second tube. After Gary reassembled the tube and tire on the wheel, we placed it back on the trike. Two flats had been fixed within minutes, both tires having gone flat in the campground while not riding anywhere. No sooner had the right front wheel been remounted, then we were treated to another sickening symphonic sound. Yep, sure enough, another flat just occurred, again on the left front tire. We wondered if Glen's first patch had let loose, but it had not. We were faced with a third tiny pinhole in a similar location to the other two, away from the road bearing surface of the tire. Glen's patch was holding fine. Three flats? Is this guy jinxed or what? And these are Schwalbe tires no less, the gold standard of cycling tires protecting the tubes!

Humorously, Glen had been relating all the things that had been going wrong prior to coming down from Canada for this trike trip. The Trident trike was not his initial choice for this overland journey. He had sold his TerraTrike a few months earlier, and opted for a German HP Velotechnik Gekko trike to replace it. Circumstances didn't favorably work out for him to acquire the Gekko, so he next consulted with and ordered an Azub T-Tris from the boys in Czechoslovakia. All looked to be a go, all the way down to the panniers, but that deal was nixed when it became apparent to Glen that Canadian import duties would have added more than 30% to the delivered price, putting it way beyond budget. Okay, that's rather stiff governmental assessment!

So he finally settled on the Trident Stowaway from an American based company, and brought it down to Florence the day before our departure on this journey. I had strongly advised him to have Schwalbe Marathon Plus tires, EarthGuard tire liners, and Kenda Thorn-Resistant Q-tubes installed before leaving. Thursday afternoon, on the eve of our journey, the local bicycle shop in Florence was installing Schwalbe tires that the company rep had recommended to him, saying that the Marathon Plus tires were overkill for our trip. Overkill?

This is where the story gets truly fascinating! The owner of the bike shop, along with his mechanic, told us Thursday around 4:30 PM that they had to inflate the tubes to 180 pounds per square inch (PSI) in order to get the tires to seat on the Trident rims. This clearly was far beyond any engineered limits for those tubes, but by blowing the tubes up that much, it forced the Schwalbe tires to meet the rim all the way around the circumference. They did this for all three wheels.

Fast forward to the Elkton RV Park on this second day's afternoon. Gary noticed that when we spun the tires and watched the white stripe on the tires, the stripe was not equidistant from the rim all the way around. It looked like the tire was wobbling, like some drunken sailor trying to walk back to the ship after shore leave. We were successful at mounting the tires at the picnic table using a small hand pump and normal pressures – at least that much worked in our favor. But we wondered about the precision of the tire to rim match.

Taking all evidence we had at the time into account, we three overland trikers kind of figured that these tiny, nearly invisible pinhole leaks that kept cropping up were likely the result of tube failures from the severe over inflation of the tubes the day before yesterday in Florence. Gary was skeptical of the new model of Schwalbe tire, wondering if they had not matched the sizing up properly to 20 inch rims. Glen was skeptical of the Trident rims. Something was clearly amiss. This should not have been happening! No tube should have to be severely over inflated to get a tire to seat.

185

I then informed Glen that I could call Hostel Shoppe and have 3 Marathon Plus tires and Q-tubes delivered here to Elkton so that we could get him back on the road. It would mean hanging tight at this camp for an extra day or two, but Glen was not willing to let his misfortune hold up the expedition. He was also very concerned that if this problem continued to manifest itself, even with new tires and tubes, and if it happened while we were out in the very remote mountains somewhere, we would really have an even bigger mess to deal with than we did now. If this was a rim sizing issue, he was right. We were now only 57 miles from where he had stored his car, and options existed here that we'd lose farther along if something went wrong.

Thus, Glen finally decided to get a ride back to Florence with campground host Marv Fredrickson in the morning, have the bicycle shop make things right, and then somehow hopefully meet up with us again farther along. I never was quite clear on his indeterminate plan, but he figured not to tempt his seemingly cursed fate any further with the current setup. With his British accent, he instructed Gary and me to head out tomorrow morning without him, and he'd be in touch via cell phone with updates about his wayward situation.

It was getting dark, we hadn't eaten, and our temperaments were shorter because of this exasperating tube, tire, and rim mess. There were restaurants in town close by, but we decided to eat out of our panniers due to the late hour. It morphed into a fun evening of camaraderie by camp light, especially since we all realized that our trio would become a duo tomorrow, and we forgot about the troubles.

We hit the sack, with a big change in the air.

DAY 3 - *Eastern Sierras*
Sunday – August 28, 2011
Elkton, Oregon to Tyee BLM Campground, Oregon - 14 miles
(running total: 71 miles)

The three of us awoke to sunny and clear weather once again. The morning was crisp, but not enough to need jackets. Our tents were damp from morning dew. Despite the beautiful day unfolding, a sad ambiance hung heavily over our little tricycle hobo camp. Glen would be departing from us today, and it might be the final time we see him. Glen is a great fellow to be around, with a funny sense of humor, and always an interesting take on the reality of the moment. Neither Gary nor I wished to see him go, especially so darn early in the journey. We had just begun! We had only ridden together for two days! It's funny how much bonding can occur during that short time. Glen was part of our tricycle

186

crew, but now he had to go.

Around a quarter to ten, Marv pulled up in his big red Dodge dual wheeled pickup, and we loaded Glen's disabled trike into the bed. Short good-byes and hand shakes changed the dynamic of this trip within minutes. Glen got into the passenger seat, and then he was gone. Gary and I were kind of quiet for a while with our loss. About 10:30 AM, we finally had reloaded our trikes and headed out onto Highway 38. We didn't know if Glen would rejoin us, but I personally figured it was a very long shot even under the best of circumstances.

Today was shaping up to be the hottest thus far, and we both could feel it. Just past the town of Elkton, we turned south on Highway 138 and began our push for the Coast Range summit, which starts with a mile-long uphill that's straight as an arrow. We could see the entire challenge out in front of us for a half mile as we neared the bottom. This was one of those "spin and grin" affairs where you just put the trike in the lowest gear and keep on cranking those pedals around and round. Since we got such a late start seeing Glen off, the sun was now warmly shining right on the roadway between the towering evergreen forest. We weren't going to get cold, that much was certain!

At the top, I waited for Gary, getting some photos along the way. From here on for a while, until we reach the summit, the road would be a series of ups and downs, mostly ups, interspersed with a few level sections. The downhills that occurred between the ever increasing uphills allowed momentary exhilaration of high speed coasting, a good rest after a long hard climb. When riding trikes in the mountains, you work your tail off for what seems like forever to get to the crest of a hill, and then in short order, you're down the other side. Then, it's another uphill. Rest, work, rest, work. The downhills usually seem way too short of duration, but then you realize if you were going the other direction, they'd be very long killer uphills.

Gary's left knee was beginning to talk to him again, more frequently and emphatically with each successive uphill in the very warm sun. At times, I would drop in behind him so we could talk. As his knee would complain with pain, he would take a short break, and in a trike it's easy because you are already reclined on a comfortable seat, which is even further reclined due to the hill's incline. Then we would pedal a little farther up the hill, always under total control regardless of speed since we have three wheels, and balance is not an issue like it is on a bicycle. Our pace was measured and slow, but it was a very good diversion being able to talk about the trip and life in general. The mileage didn't matter, after all, but rather that we had a good time being together on this adventure.

Sometimes Gary would voice an apology for holding me up, but I insisted I didn't see things that way. He surmised that since I was capable of faster speeds and higher daily mileages that I must be reluctantly giving in to his pace. This was not the case. What I lost in distance, I gained in friendship and fun that I would not have had if riding solo. An overland trike journey is far and away more than just how fast you get to the other end! In fact, it's precisely what happens in between the departure and destination that determines the quality of the memories. The middle of the story is what counts.

Highway 138 is listed by the State of Oregon as a bicycle friendly road, and most of the way it has nice wide shoulders. Occasionally, where the side drops off to the river below, the shoulder just disappears altogether, but since visibility is good, and our trikes really stand out from the surroundings well, cars and eighteen wheelers have no problem passing us just like they would any other car. We were extended full courtesies.

During my first trip on this road two years prior, I sometimes cringed at the really narrow portions, checking my mirrors like a madman, but this trip, I never gave them a second thought, as I have come to realize that the fears instilled by well meaning friends about cars hitting me and knocking me off the road are almost entirely unfounded, being groundless thoughts that those non-trikers illogically accept and perpetuate. The drivers of those big logging trucks are very courteous, and I have come to see them as my friends, not as frightening metal monsters about to devour me. In fact, Gary and I spoke with one driver on Day Four at a Taco Bell restaurant, a guy who had extended every courtesy for us, and he voiced that he found our trikes really cool, and he enjoyed watching us.

As the day wore on, the lengthening shadows of the forest kept us in the welcomed shade. Our constant companion was the sound of the rushing river. We were tiny travelers in a forest of giants. Now and then huge stately oak trees graced our path, along with old scenic barns of bygone eras. Throughout the day, we shared our abbreviated times about Glen, and how we missed him. Both of us hoped he would return, but knew this was probably now an expedition of two.

The sun was still fairly high in the sky as we approached the turnoff for the Tyee Bureau of Land Management campground up ahead. It was on the west side of the river, so we had to trike across a long concrete bridge. This campground was about a half mile off our course, but it was such a nice one that it was well worth pedaling an extra mile to have the amenities, like well manicured campsites, picnic tables, river front, odorless pit toilets, and responsible campground hosts. Heck, they even kept the gravel at each campsite raked like you see in Japanese gardens! Can't beat that, right?

But wait, it gets even better! Yep, for only $10 per site, that worked out to $5 each, since there are two tent pads per site. Sure beats pitching a tent on a road turnout with no amenities and traffic whizzing by only yards away! What a serene forested setting. This is what trike touring is all about! I love Oregon's wild places.

As Gary and I were pedaling around the campground upon first arriving, trying to determine which site we liked best, he came to a short and small rise in the roadway at the end of one loop. Being in higher gears, his left knee intensely shouted to gear down, and as he did so, the chain came to rest between two cogs on the rear cassette. Now stopped, Gary figured, as most of us would, to just let gravity allow the trike to slowly back up ten feet to the level ground, but since the chain was stuck between cogs, it put massive stress on the rear dérailleur arm once going backwards. This bent the arm noticeably inwards towards the spokes of the wheel.

Well, that was the end of shifting to the rear for Gary! Needless to say, he was not a happy camper, and we weren't even camping yet. He became glum, and wondered if this spelled disaster for him only one day after Glen's calamity. I went ahead and got the site, as he began setting camp. After pitching the tents, we hoisted his Catrike onto the picnic table to see if the arm could be fixed. This was to be no high tech solution out here in the boonies, but rather a calculated reshaping by hand and screwdriver. I could see the anguish on Gary's face as he tweaked his high end gear. Would it work?

He would bend and tweak, and we would visually assess the arm. Once we got it pretty darn straight, he held up the rear wheel as I hand pedaled and shifted the gears. It was working. After taking it for a spin around the campground path, he felt it could be better, so back up on the table it went.

About this time, a homeless fellow named Mark Goss from the next campsite walked over smoking his cigarette. He was a bicycle mechanic in Medford, Oregon before he got laid off from Marty's Cycle. Mark and Gary continued working on it, and I spoke to Mark's wife who had joined us at our table. Finally, after a couple more trial runs under Mark's keen eye, Gary exclaimed that it was shifting even better than it had before the little accident on the hill. Happy day! Gary would remain to trike another day. It would have indeed been traumatic for me to lose two trikers in two days. Gary's mood improved dramatically, and Mark made a beer run down to a little store about a mile south. We all ate and shared stories into the night.

189

I hit the sack first, as Gary stayed up and talked with the couple at their roaring campfire. Feeling sorry for their temporarily homeless condition, he administered a little financial boost. It was a moonless night, so dark that without a flashlight, you could not even see the slightest form to get up and take a pee in the bushes; it was all totally by feeling the tent, the darkest I had ever not seen. My level of sound sleeping was so deep that I never heard Gary come back from next door and get in his tent.

Gary kept his Catrike right next to his tent each night, covered with a dark gray TerraTrike cover, so it virtually disappears once the sun goes down. He detached his trailer at each camp for ease of maneuvering. At one point in the middle of the night, I became aware of a bright light and talking. Mark was at Gary's tent, and then walked past my tent on his way out. He said he had walked over to see if Gary was all right. Gary wondered if he was coming over to score some bike parts to later fence for cash. We'll never know, but I was so sleepy that night, I didn't really get what was going on.

DAY 4 - *Eastern Sierras*
Monday – August 29, 2011
Tyee BLM Campground, Oregon to Glide, Oregon - 36 miles
(running total: 107 miles)

Last night's visit from Mark was the topic of hushed conversation as we packed up to leave. We got an early start and silently pedaled back out to the little country road that would lead us the half mile over the bridge and back onto Highway 138, which is mostly just one lane in each direction. Gary and I were both well rested and fresh. His knees were feeling fine this morning. Next town would be Sutherlin on the Interstate 5 freeway, where we planned to grab a late breakfast.

Today we would ride the steepest portions of this Coast Range traverse, which meant slow going to keep Gary's knee in check as it would hopefully toughen up to the rigors of mountain triking. Gary's stamina was definitely improving a little each day. It was overcast thus far, which translated into an easier ride on the challenging ascents. No sweating like a pig for a while. At times, it got downright dark and pleasantly cool in the densely forested mountains, even though it was daytime. Light just barely filters through the tree canopy.

Traffic was light, as it usually is every morning before the tourists begin hitting the road. Mostly we were passed by eighteen wheelers, who always extended maximum courtesy to our tiny little tricycles in front of their colossal towering trucks. Trikers really do wield a lot of power, slowing down even the biggest of adversaries! Trikes offer a significant safety advantage over standard bicycles.

After finally reaching the top, with several rests along the way for peeing and eating, the final ultra long descent was pure joy. We got to rocket along at high speed, coasting many miles to Gary's delighted knee. First stop was Taco Bell, where Gary bought a broiled chicken burrito, kind of a brunch for him. I had my usual bowl of Kashi Seven Grain Nuggets (think Grape-Nuts, only healthier). Under the bridge at Interstate-5 we rode, stopping for a moment at the Sutherlin visitor center to use their cleaner toilet facilities, and then down the service road that paralleled the interstate on the east side.

Five miles farther south, we came to the small town of Wilbur, and stopped in at a tiny market to get some bananas and mixed nuts. The sky was still predominantly cloudy, but patches of blue were beginning to show through. Both of us tried to eat at least one banana per day for the potassium, and I kept the nuts in my panniers for later on when I was starving on the road. They make for a super caloric infusion with lots of healthy fat for triker staying power. A number of local residents found our trikes and journey of interest.

A half mile south of the little store, we turned off this road onto a shortcut to the town of Glide. It's called the North Bank Road, technically known as County Road 200, and this rural route cuts off about 20 unnecessary miles that would have taken us south through Medford, a pretty big city best avoided on trikes. These particular 19 miles on CR 200 to our next overnight wind their way through the mostly dry grass foothills of the Cascade Range. There are sparse oak trees, along with occasional evergreens, and it is a road that is best ridden at night or on a cloudy day, for if the heat is on, this stretch will melt even the best cyclist. There is scant shade to be found anywhere!

Well, as luck would have it, those wonderful clouds that had graced our ride to Wilbur began disappearing faster than one could imagine, and as we began pedaling up the first long steep grade out of town, Mr. Sun made a full and spectacular appearance, as if on cue. It's still August – temperatures can still cook! Sure enough, the steep grade combined with the rapidly increasing heat really had a way of slowing down our forward progress. Of course, at the top of this first killer hill, there is a welcomed respite in the form of a cooling downhill, so that was our prize for the effort and sweat.

Now, downhills are nice, there's no doubt about that, but considering that we are heading east up into the foothills of the Cascades, in the back of my mind I can't help but think that every yard we laboriously earn pumping the pedals going up is a yard I'd like to keep! For every downhill, precious yards are lost, requiring that we again labor to regain them on the next uphill. The only consolation of course is that over the miles, we have a gradual net gain in elevation, so the roller coaster effect does lead to higher ground eventually.

Downhills are fun adrenaline pumping times, and all cyclists love them, but the uphills are what force us to evolve into capable overland trikers. Uphills make us much stronger. They improve our cardiovascular conditioning. Our hearts get stronger. Our blood pressure is improved. In the long run, uphills turn us into super pedal pushers, fit humans able to ride over any terrain. Thus, we must thank the uphills on each occasion we meet them, for they are truly our friends for life, literally! Uphills extend our life, whether we like it or not. Downhills only give us a thrill and fast miles.

The North Bank Road took its toll on my riding partner Gary. Still coming up to speed on long haul triking, and improving every day, the steeper than normal grades and very warm sun made for a real test of will. He commented that these 19 miles were much more demanding than traversing the entire Coast Range had been, and we both thought that the gradients were noticeably steeper. Of course, the sunny heat also was a significant factor today.

Our progress kept us on the shortcut for a long time, and eventually, it began to get cooler as the sun moved lower towards the horizon. At one point, three curious llamas gave us their undivided attention, having never seen tadpole tricycles before. The last time I had silently pedaled past here it was night, so they were asleep. This traverse between Wilbur and Glide kept us using the full range of our gears. Those dérailleurs really got a workout. As we reached the Umpqua River crossing near the end of this county road, the sun was just setting, making for beautiful photos from the bridge. By now, our copious water supplies were running fairly low.

We ended the day's journey in Glide, Oregon, a relatively small town, but having many services compared to others like Elkton. We had now traveled 107 miles from our trip's commencement point on the coast. To demonstrate how these trike treks are never predictable, that original tentative itinerary I had made of the first week for our group was showing us at Clearwater Falls Campground this evening, which is 52 miles farther along than we were now. That's the fun and adventure of overland triking! You never know what each day or week will bring until you are actually there. Surprises always keep you alert as you assess and reassess your situation.

We rolled into the town of Glide at dusk, stopped at a local convenience store for some food, and inquired about motels. Gary was wiped out, and insisted that we luxuriate this night. Being one who goes with the moment, I was willing to exchange my tent and sleeping bag for a room and real bed. The clerk told us of a motel about a mile east on Highway 138, so Gary decided that would be our stop for today. A man in the parking lot, seeing our rigs, and apparently feeling sorry for us, offered his front yard to pitch our tents, and access to his bathroom and water supply. It was a tempting offer I would have taken if solo (a bird in the hand is worth two in the bush), but Gary politely thanked him anyway, and he drove home.

By the time we arrived at the motel, it was dark and we were using our headlights and taillights. One nice thing about this small town is that they have a wide cycling path parallel to the highway, so it was an easy pedal to the motel. Gary and I both have Cateye lights front and rear, and boy do they ever illuminate everything well.

Things then took a turn for the unexpected, or worse depending on one's frame of mind. I wasn't thrilled, but could readily adapt having done one of these overlanders before. Gary wasn't happy, but seeing no other options, and feeling his back was against the wall, realized our situation was not as he had hoped it would be (his description was not quite so docile).

The motel's office was housed in an adjacent restaurant, which had closed 30 minutes prior to our arrival. We saw people in the rooms, but the hotel staff had left the premises and were tucked into their homes somewhere unknown to us. There was no way to acquire a room this late. Our luck had run out! Now, our minds quickly searched for options, as it was really starting to cool off and the air was damp.

Assessing several alternative choices that we could see, we opted not to pitch our tents at the school yard, figuring we might be evicted mid night. Not far from the motel was a motorcycle shop called Mike's Trikes (go figure), so we rode around behind the concrete block building and erected our tents out of sight of the highway. A storage unit facility was up a short hill to our south, and kept our camp bathed in light all night, but we were tired, so we slept anyway. I slept atop my bag with my clothes and warm jackets on, only removing my shoes so if the local law might find our habitation contrary to their way of seeing things, I could relatively easily strike my tent and move on.

Gary smelled motor oil. Sure enough, Mike's Trikes had been dumping used oil from the Harley-Davidson and Honda motorcycles on the grass next to the back of the building. We were too exhausted to call the EPA, which was all well and good because Mike would have likely pressed trespassing charges against us in retaliation. Gary pitched his tent farther from the oil pit than I did. Needless to say, this was clearly not an ideal sleeping arrangement, but it was getting late and we were bushed. It had to do. One thing that is quickly learned as a trike hobo is that you do not always have the most preferable overnight solutions as options while out on the road. You sleep where and when you can!

DAY 5 - *Eastern Sierras*
Tuesday – August 30, 2011
Glide, Oregon to Susan Creek Bureau of Land Management
Campground - 12 miles (running total: 119 miles)

I saw light outside my tent, and not from the storage facility either. The way I could tell the difference was that the storage night lights cast a shadow of my trike upon the tent wall, whereas the coming daylight did not. The first dim light of day was upon us. The sky appeared overcast again. We had survived the night without incident, other than the disgusting smell of dirty oil. Our tents were quite damp. It had not rained, so it must have been our proximity to the river, along with local humidity dynamics of pitching on thick grass. Our camp at Tyee Campground the other night left our tents bone dry, and we were even closer to the river, so who knows how it all works. One thing I did know was that I needed a shower. Gary was thinking the same thing.

Neither of us had any desire to remain behind this building to eat breakfast, so we began pedaling eastbound on Highway 138 again, as I knew of a little convenience store and gas station in Idleyld, a tiny wide spot in the road not far away. By the way, if you're wondering how to pronounce Idleyld, which causes everyone fits when they attempt to decode it, here is what the locals will tell you: it's idle, and then you just pronounce the sound of the letter Y, and simply add the "ld" ending, which produces the name IdleYld, like Idle Wild.

The little store at Idleyld sits just off the two lane highway, with mountains and forests all about. By now, the sun had just come over the mountain and into this narrow river valley. There is a small picnic table out front, so this was perfect for the two of us to chow down on some grub. I fixed up some of my Kashi seven grain nuggets and raisins, supplemented with a banana, V8 Juice, and some Frito-Lay fruit and nut mix that I bought inside. Gary got his banana and something else.

Today was going to be a short and easy ride to the Susan Creek BLM campground, which was only about 9 miles farther up the road from this picnic table. Susan Creek has hot showers and other amenities that we decided we'd like to indulge in while relaxing for a day. While eating breakfast, with the Catrike and ICE parked next to the table, anyone who happened by stopped to inquire about what we were doing,

194

obviously loaded down with our baggage. One Forest Service official spent some extra time learning all about our trip. The gasoline pumps were only a few feet away from our table, but the fumes did not reach our noses because the wind was in our favor.

The ride to the campground was leisurely and comfortable, consisting mostly of flat terrain and mild hills, causing no strain to knees or joints. We were able to keep a decent pace without even trying. This was welcomed news for Gary's knee. Shower and luxury, here I come! My shirt was very sweat stained from the North Bank Road.

Two years ago, on days 4 and 5 of my expedition to Death Valley, I was riding from Susan Creek Campground to Diamond Lake, only the weather and conditions were just about the opposite of today. It was the fifth day of October, an early blizzard had hit these mountains, and I was pedaling over this daunting range at night in subfreezing temperatures. Thinking back as I triked along today, with plenty of warmth and sunshine, I marveled at the difference. Gary and I were going to make a measured and gradual traverse of the Cascade Range on this journey, taking multiple days to cross it, and being 5 weeks earlier in the year than my previous traverse, death by hypothermia wouldn't be a possibility this time around.

Also by day 5 on that prior Cascade traverse, my Achilles tendons were both significantly swollen, a result of using standard platform pedals, regular hiking shoes, and foot straps to keep my feet on the pedals (I didn't realize the reason at the time however). Having learned a hard lesson on that trip, my current pedals were the SPD binding type, where my cycling specific shoes attach to the pedals, similar in concept to ski bindings. Triking long distance without a binding mechanism like this is, in my opinion, asking for a whole lot of avoidable trouble, and I unconditionally recommend not using pedal foot straps of any kind on a tricycle (where your feet are behind the pedals, rather than on top like a bicycle). The human foot does not work well over long distances with straps and regular shoes – low blood volume!

Approaching Susan Creek Recreation Area, the road is a long straightaway in huge trees, with a single passing lane. The shoulder is plenty wide for recumbent trikes, and the riding is easy. Up a hiking trail to the left are the Susan Creek waterfalls, a beautiful cascade of water, and one of many such striking falls that has caused this road from Medford to Diamond Lake to be dubbed the waterfall route, placing it as one of Oregon's top tourist byways. We snapped a photo at the campground sign and then coasted down into the campsite area.

Since it was very early afternoon, we had our pick of campsites, except for those right on the river. Gary happily accepted my choice of site 14, the same one I camped in on my prior trike trek through here, only that time it was raining. Today was sunny and very pleasant. The cost was $14, and since they allow two trikes for the price of one car, we spit it for $7 each. This is one great perk for touring tricyclists. There isn't an extra fee for a second vehicle!

Essentially, for seven bucks, I had a nicely manicured gravel pad upon which I could pitch my tent, a huge picnic table, fire pit, and complete toilet facilities with normal running water, not to mention immaculate and private hot showers! What a deal. Oh, and I almost forgot: All this is cozily nestled at the base of colossally sized evergreen and deciduous trees, with the roaring sound of the ever-present Umpqua River just yards away. Yep, the life of a trike hobo is very good most of the time. This was living!

Campsite #14 is also next to the shower facility. In my panniers, I have a small 3x3x1 inch nylon bag that stuffs into itself, and when unstuffed, it becomes a bag large enough to carry clothing, bathroom bag, towel, you name it. After loading it with what I needed, a quick walk and I was only seconds from warm water cascading upon me in a private shower, a much needed interlude from days of pedaling up hills in the hot sun. My shirt appeared to have permanently discolored regions where the sweat had altered the dye. Most of that occurred on the 19 mile North Bank Road to Glide, a hot and steep day Gary and I will not soon forget.

On an overland trike journey, one does not carry enough clothing to change into fresh everything everyday. Space is at a premium on a tricycle, and weight is always a concern. Lots of clothing also means a lot of extra and unnecessary weight. For everyday wear, I had two pairs of pants on board, along with four lightweight cotton shirts, and eight pairs of socks. Next time, I will bring only three shirts. Even though they are very lightweight, they take up precious cargo space and add just that much more to the weight needed to be pedaled up the mountain passes. Being fashion conscious falls to the wayside when pedaling cross country. I don't care what anyone else thinks on the road.

The shower, my first since departure on this trip, felt great, and upon my return to the campsite, Gary left for his time in nirvana. Well, that night we both were fresh as daisies for a change! My buddy pardoned himself for a while, and ended up taking a long afternoon snooze in his sun drenched tent. He was indeed bushed, and needed some extra shuteye.

Later, Gary made two of his Mountain House brand freeze dried meals because he wanted me to try one. What a treat! Not only was I clean, but I got to eat spaghetti as good as any from an Italian restaurant. Of course, it might not have been quite up to that standard, but from a trike hobo's standpoint, it was the best on Earth.

We had so much time at the campground, having arrived here so early from Glide, that we even got some firewood and had our first campfire. Often on a trike trip, you arrive later in the day, have ridden many miles, and are dead tired. Under those circumstances, one of the last things you want to do is deal with building a campfire. Just lying down and getting to sleep are usually the priorities. But tonight was different. We would have all the luxuries for a change! Warm, sunny, dry, clean, well fed – it doesn't get much better than that.

DAY 6 - *Eastern Sierras*
Wednesday – August 31, 2011
Susan Creek Campground to Boulder Flat Forest Service Campground - 24 miles (running total: 143 miles)

At first light, I got up, roused Gary, and we ate breakfast. Today we would begin our Cascade summit push in earnest. Sure, there had been plenty of hills thus far since leaving Sutherlin at Interstate 5, and plenty of challenge too, but now, past Susan Creek, things were about to change dramatically. This is where the mountain truly begins to make its presence felt. The grades become more serious, and they seem to go on forever when pedaling a tricycle.

Last night, I had a dream that while riding the trike, both brake cables and both shifter cables snapped within seconds. As dreams often go, things got weird. There were four other people on my trike with me during this trip (must have had huge thighs to pedal all that weight), so I had them all start pushing up the mountain as I pedaled in only one gear and steered. I was happy to see the Q in perfect working order this morning when I got up to reality.

On the tentative itinerary I had given Glen and Gary before the trip, I suggested that we might push from Susan Creek Campground to Clearwater Falls Campground during this day, a distance of 40 miles. This seems easy based on mileage alone, but the terrain makes them a tough forty. Gary's stamina had been improving gradually each day, but I wasn't sure if he would feel like reaching Clearwater Falls by this evening. Time would tell the tale. I was open to whatever his needs or desires would turn out to be, as I was happy to have company and someone to talk to on this expedition.

Seven miles up the road, we stopped and chatted with Roy Hewson, a 66 year old fly fisherman from Cave Junction, Oregon, who comes to these parts every year to catch fish. Like myself, he was living

197

a vegan lifestyle, and as we preached to each others choir about the health and longevity benefits, Gary was thinking "Where's the beef?" Roy certainly didn't look like a traditional 66 year old American male, a tribute to his health regimen. He began this dietary alteration a few years ago after suffering some typical issues associated with an unhealthy and sedentary lifestyle. Way to go Roy!

The day was becoming increasingly warm, so it was a welcomed afternoon lunch break when we stopped at the Dry Creek Store, 18 miles east of Susan Creek. Past this store, the grades become even more serious, so we took our time, bought some sandwiches and ice cream bars, and ate like kings out on the front boardwalk porch on a hand hewn log bench. At this store two years ago, recreational hunters advised me to turn my trike around because of deep snow a few miles ahead. After eating my bananas and V8 Juice, I ignored their warnings. And I ended up pedaling through the night.

But today was different. Warmth was here in abundance, and mostly what Gary and I sought was shade. We talked with the gals running the store, discussed our journey so far, and gave little thought to adversity. There were campgrounds coming up along the way, so we could take our pick short of Clearwater Falls, which was yet 22 miles distant. Gary's Catrike Road and my ICE Qnt were both in fine operational order, so our carefree minds enjoyed the moment.

Six miles beyond the Dry Creek Store, we pulled in to Boulder Flat Forest Service Campground, which was on the other side of the highway, right on the river. This road crosses the Umpqua River numerous times in its ascent, so in places the river is on our right, as with Susan Creek, and now it was on our left. The day was still mid afternoon, so there was no rush in setting camp. We picked an inviting campsite on the water, chose where to put our tents, and once again set about establishing another trike hobo camp. Gary fixed yet another Mountain House dinner for us both, and I chopped some garlic I had brought along, but forgotten about at last night's spaghetti dinner.

Not far past this campground, we would be running into major construction tomorrow morning, good timing as there is less tourist traffic earlier in the day. Today we had ridden for about 8 hours, so Boulder Flat was a good choice. Gary was getting stronger every day, evidenced by shorter waiting periods along the way while he caught up.

This campground was much smaller than Susan Creek, with no host, and not quite as fancy. There were no showers, running water, or flush toilets. Outhouses with minimal ventilation were our lot for the night. The only water supply was either what we brought along on the trikes, or what we might choose to extract from the river. Of course, since I have been known to camp on roadside pullouts, by comparison, this was pure luxury! There was no fear of eviction. So you see, with the commonly perceived negative aspects also come a few welcomed ones.

DAY 7 - *Eastern Sierras*
Thursday – September 01, 2011
Boulder Flat Campground to Diamond Lake Lodge - 27 miles
(running total: 170 miles)

August 2011 was history. We were starting the day only 27 miles from Diamond Lake, where we could take showers again and even have the luxury of a laundry, not to mention some of the most gorgeous lake views around. Twenty-seven miles sounded like an easy ride, but those 27 were unrelenting with their vertical elevation gain. We got another early start, not doing breakfast at the campground.

A practice I had fallen into at times was pedaling 3 miles at my own pace, and then pulling over in some picturesque spot while I waited for Gary. This kept us in very close proximity to one another, and with his ever improving cardiovascular condition, made for a predictable plan. Other times, I would ride along behind Gary so we could talk and enjoy each others company. Just shy of 5 miles, after having experienced the first indications of road construction, I pulled over, ate breakfast, and brushed my teeth. Gary pulled in as I was putting my gear back in my panniers, and we chatted for a bit as he ate an energy bar or two.

After 6 miles of riding from Boulder Flat, we beheld the full blown road construction zone, where the State of Oregon was in the process of widening the road, installing huge shoulders, and building heavy concrete retaining walls to keep falling boulders from the cliffs above from landing on automobiles. This would eventually be a triker's heaven. Today however, it was causing concern with Gary because his Catrike was still in pristine condition. I like keeping my ICE in great shape too, but with a few nicks from previous treks on it, I figured that I acquired it to use, and if use meant a scratch now and then, so be it.

Heavy equipment was everywhere, the road was rough dirt and mud, and on little one-wheel drive tricycles, it might prove the ultimate challenge. Gary was somewhere behind me, perhaps a mile or so, as I pulled up to a lady with a stop sign in her hands. She informed me that all cyclists, whether two wheels or three, were prohibited from riding the next 8 miles of Highway 138, and that they would have to load my trike into the back of a truck to shuttle me through. I told her one more triker was yet on his way, and to watch for him.

Then the pilot truck arrived, followed by a long line of cars and trucks heading west down the mountain. It turned around, and the lady driver lowered the tailgate for me to load my trike in the back. By now, a long line of motorized vehicles was now behind me. One thing about human powered trikes is that you always go to the front of the line!

I noticed that the pilot truck bed had a bunch of metal and wood debris in it that would really mess up my Q, so I jumped up and cleared it all to one side first, cognizant that many motorists were waiting for me to get the job done. Having done that, the truck driver immediately behind me assisted me in getting the trike into the truck. Normally, this would be a one-man job on a day ride, but with fully loaded panniers for an overland journey, it took two of us to successfully raise the trike without damaging it. A heavily loaded trike is so totally unstable if lifted that it should never be attempted alone!

For the next 8 miles, I sat in the bed of the truck to make sure my rig didn't shift around and get dinged up. I watched the miles fly by, realizing the free ride I was getting, and all the pedaling I would not have to do as a result. I also knew that Gary would be happy for this lift, once he got past the thought of putting his flawless Catrike in the back of a truck. These would be 8 otherwise grueling miles that Gary's knee would thank him for!

I was dropped off at the eastern end of the zone, at a small lake called Stump, and an elevation of 3,875 feet. The sun was getting hot again, so I rode over to the shade and waited for Gary to come through. The elevation was increasing, but we were still far below the more than 7,000 feet of our summit in Crater Lake National Park. An energy bar somehow found its way into me, along with a few guzzles of water now and then, as I watched all the traffic coming and going.

At one point while I was waiting, a supported bicycle tour approached from the east, heading down the mountain. The lead rider zipped past the flagger gal, and boy was that a mistake. Her older supervisor was also there talking to her, and both ladies made themselves audible to the cyclist over the din of engines. He stopped in a hurry and turned around. They were going to have to load his bicycle, and in succession, all the bikes of the entire tour, into the pilot trucks and shuttle them to the western end of the construction zone. For cyclists riding DOWN a mountain, a task full of exhilaration and joy, riding in a truck is a bummer. For cyclists riding UP a mountain, it may be seen as a gift from heaven.

After a while, and a few cycles of pilot truck shuttles, I noticed Gary's bright yellow trike in the bed of a truck. He told me that he hadn't been that far behind me, but they had to wait until this particular pilot truck came around again (there were several due to the distance of construction), because the other ones were smaller and would not hold the trike and the trailer. Gary had ridden in the cab and chatted with the driver the whole trip. The female flagger at this end had a camouflaged cap that read: "HUNT ... like a girl."

Gary expressed his concern about the shuttle, and asked if my trike had been damaged. I told him that the very front of the crankset guard had a small scratch, but that I saw it as a souvenir to remember this trip. His trike had made it unscathed. Once again, after 8 free miles, we were pedaling on our way, up and over the Cascade Range.

But now, it was early afternoon, and the sun was not hidden by the towering evergreen trees. We were on the final grade to Diamond Lake, with Clearwater Falls Campground not far ahead. When we arrived at the campground, it was still too early to pitch our tents, so on we continued. With that free mileage, we had avoided a long pull up some of the most relentless portions of the road, so time was yet on our side. The prize this evening is well worth all this time.

As I pedaled along, admiring the stately forest both sides of the road, I recalled two years prior when I pedaled this portion after midnight, with two feet of snow on the sides of the plowed road, ice on the pavement, temperatures too cold to stop for anything longer than a few seconds, and a full moon playing hide and seek with the thunderheads. I was barely able to stay warm enough, generating just enough heat by pedaling that I kept myself from shaking, wondering how long it would take me to arrive at the lodge. One thing about that trip, traffic was nearly nonexistent in the middle of that frigid night!

By contrast, today I perspired and sought shade to cool off and empty my water supply. The conditions were taking their toll on both Gary and me. Gary's stamina and knee were being put to the test, one that, while daunting, was going to be mild compared to our final push in two days up the side of the Mazama volcano caldera in the national park. Today we had saved about 1400 vertical feet in the back of a pilot truck, so what we gained here would really be needed up higher. Despite the climb, the scenery is world class stuff.

Around 6:30 PM, a time still sunny due to daylight savings, I stopped at the turnoff for the Diamond Lake Lodge, the paradise that Gary and I longed for tonight, which sits just over 5,000 feet elevation, high in the upper reaches of the Cascade Range. The lodge was only about half a mile below on a smaller road that paralleled Highway 138. I parked in the shade, now plentiful due to the huge shadows of the roadside forest, and took a nap on my comfy mesh recumbent seat. Eventually, I heard the tinkle of Gary's handlebar bell, and got up to greet him. He got in the habit of waking me with his little bell, because trikes are so quiet otherwise that you can't hear them coming.

Down the short grade to the lake we coasted, and into the parking lot of the lodge. Diamond Lake was glimmering like billions of diamonds in the late afternoon sun. I remained outside with the trikes as Gary went in to secure lodging. He was definitely wiped out, partly due to the fact that he was not getting as much rest as I was coming up the mountain. I always waited until he felt rested to continue on, but still, I had more time than he had at each rest stop. It wasn't fair, but then again, life isn't always fair.

He got a room with a small kitchen facing the lake. It was the only room left that night, so we had to pay more for a kitchen we didn't need or use. With the two single beds inside, and our trikes and gear, things were tight, but after climbing this mountain to this point, we didn't care. All we wanted was to relax, clean up, eat, do laundry, and enjoy the wonderful vistas.

At the restaurant, Gary was a changed man. Now dressed in his normal clothes, and all spruced up, he even treated me to dinner, which included Black Butte Porter beer, made by the well known Deschutes Brewery in Bend, Oregon. I had a Cobb salad and a mouth watering chicken pot pie (yeah, I know I'm vegan, but my body needed protein, and this rugged mountain establishment only catered to carnivores).

DAY 8 - *Eastern Sierras*
Friday – September 02, 2011
Diamond Lake Lodge to Broken Arrow Forest Service Campground - 6 miles (running total: 176 miles)

A week ago this morning, Glen, Gary, and I pedaled out of Florence, now 170 miles distant. In a car, we could have traveled this distance to Diamond Lake easily in one day. Trikes are different. It had taken 7 days to arrive, but car travelers will never know the adventure we were having! They'll never know the agony of pedaling up and up and up in the hot sun. They'll never know the pain of hurting knees or numb toes and hot spots. They'll never know the uncertainty of where they will stay that night. Hmm, maybe they're better off? Nope! We're trike hobos, and we thrive on challenge and uncertainty!

We already knew that today would be the shortest of the entire journey, at only six miles. I knew why. Gary was yet to find out, beyond only my explanation. Tomorrow we would have to pedal into and through Crater Lake National Park, a distance of only 28 miles, but one that would tax any triker to the max, for the inclines were even steeper than what we had experienced so far. My intent was to position Gary as close to the national park entrance as we legally could be, thereby making tomorrow's ride to the rim as short and painless as possible.

The climb up the caldera would push Gary far beyond any trike ride he had ever taken, and I wanted him to be fresh for it. Today's ride would be only 6 miles of mostly flat ground along the eastern edge of Diamond Lake, so it would be super easy and leave us totally feeling great. We were in absolutely no hurry at all today, a first for this eastern Sierra ride, so we did our first laundry at the lodge before leaving.

We didn't even have to pedal on the road to get to our next camp at Broken Arrow Campground at the southern end of the lake. There is a beautiful bike path all the way around this magnificent body of water – talk about utterly relaxing! The lake was immediately on our right, and the woods were on our left. We met a husband and wife couple on recumbent bicycles from Eugene, Oregon, who had ridden their bikes all the way across the United States. Both of them were 75 years old, making Gary and me seem like youngsters. They had even ridden their bikes in other world countries. Adventure abounds.

Gary and I pulled into Broken Arrow mid day, chose a great campsite not far from the newly constructed modern showers, and set up our tents in the trees. We had a spectacular view of Mount Thielsen from the camp, and later as the sun set, it was aglow with captivating orange charm, often called alpenglow. We split a Mountain House dinner, the last one in Gary's panniers, but we could resupply these freeze dried delights at Mazama Campground tomorrow.

The night finished off with Gary checking maintenance on his trike, and an inviting campfire using wood a neighboring camper had left. Gary had another shower and was now very well rested. His spirits were up, his knee was happy, and we were about as ready as could be expected for tomorrow's ride to the top, the final significant vertical gain in the state. Day 8 was a breeze. Day 9 would be a different story!

DAY 9 - *Eastern Sierras*
Saturday – September 03, 2011
Broken Arrow Campground to Mazama Campground at Crater Lake - 28 miles (running total: 204 miles)

Judgment Day was upon us. Even though it was yet dark outside my tent, I could barely detect the first hints of a lightening eastern sky. Gary's tent was a few trees over, but sound travels well in the nocturnal forest, so I proceeded quietly to begin the day. It's not that I wanted to get out of my cozy warm sleeping bag into the thin crisp mountain air (I'm not that crazy), but I realized the two of us would need all the daylight we could possibly get to accomplish today's demanding ride, so I toughened up my spirit and opened the air release valve of my inflatable NeoAir ThermaRest mattress.

Hoping the brief hissing noise did not awaken my sleeping tricycular companion, once my body weight had evacuated most of the air, I sat up, put on my shirt, a down vest, a polar fleece jacket, and a polar fleece cap. On cold mornings, I dress from the top down, maintaining core body temperature. Once my upper body quickly warms to what it was inside the down sleeping bag, I then slip my lower body out to slide on my pants, socks, and shoes.

Oh, another trick I employ is to place my clothing in the bag with me about 15 minutes before I begin my dressing, thereby taking the invigorating and unwelcomed chill off the clothing before it touches my skin. Putting on freezing clothing tends to speed up one's morning-time need to immediately pee, so warmth is a good thing! At least my Lake cycling shoes have Velcro attachments instead of laces.

I was very deliberate and slow with stuffing my bag while inside the tent, and then rolling up the air mattress, thereby keeping noise to an absolute minimum. Gary enjoys his sleep, so I wanted him to have a little more before I rustled his bones. His body and mind would be pushed far past their limits today, much farther than he has ever known on a tricycle, so getting up to a frigid dark sky would be just one more demand. By the time I became aware of his moving around in his tent, the sky was definitely brightening up quite a bit. There wouldn't be sun for sometime yet, but at least I could see what I was doing now.

Mornings can be tough for some folks, and this one clearly did not set well with my triker friend. I came to find out later that his tent was atop a mound in the ground, so he didn't get to sleep until well after midnight. Add to that my early start, and you have a warhead seeking a target. Okay, so I can't be everyone's friend all the time, but hey, I saw my job as getting my fellow trike hobo safely up and over this massive super volcano, so now I took on the role of commander, one that necessarily brings with it occasional less than happy teammates.

Gary expressed his objections to arising so early on such a cold day, saying he did not understand at all why we had to do this. My reply was that I realized he did not understand, but that he would very well understand later this evening. I reiterated the extreme difficulty of the next 19 miles to the top, at over 7,000 feet, and how it would require every minute of daylight, and every ounce of physical and psychological strength we could muster. The final 9 miles from the rim of the caldera were all downhill to the campground, so at least we would get some rest coasting to the end, but the first 19 would likely eat up all of our sun-filled hours today at our current rate of progress. Enter the gauntlet.

It was cold. Constant movement felt the best. When we finally had the panniers loaded and got settled into our frosty trikes, the sun was just barely peeking over the mountain ridges and through the trees. The expedition got under way again around 7:00 AM for the trek into the one of the nation's most pristine and spectacular national parks. From the campground to the northern entrance of Crater Lake National Park, it was about 5 miles, mostly uphill of course, which felt great as our bodies warmed and jackets came off. That's one good thing about trike trekking: it doesn't take much ascent time at all to turn up the temperature. We were committed, and the first leg was going well.

When we arrived at the turnoff from Highway 138, our path for the last several days now, we could see the long uphill straightaway to the entrance gatehouse. If we had remained on 138, we would only have had another mile before reaching that road's summit, and then a 10 mile straight downhill to central Oregon's Highway 97, which was the route I had taken two years prior on my ride to Death Valley, because Crater Lake was buried in snow and not hospitable for tricycles. If we had chosen that route today, Gary's day would have been very easy, one of about 50 miles, all downhill but for the first 6 miles, except that we would have missed Crater Lake. Later, he may have wished we had.

At the park entrance, I showed my National Parks Pass and rode on through. When Gary arrived, he purchased a senior citizen Federal Recreation Pass, a one-time fee of $10, and good for life. The inclined pavement stretched out before us, disappearing into the forest at the horizon line. We were in! We began pedaling up a mountain that blew its top in a very big way roughly 7,700 years ago, give or take a few minutes, wiping out all life for many miles in all directions. This national park is one where you have no clue about what you are going to see until you literally get to the edge of the caldera, where the stunning blue magnificence of the massive lake blows you away. The volcano blew its top, and the views blow your mind!

We had about 14 more miles to go before we would have this view, 14 more miles of very steep ascent through most of the day, 14 more miles that would put Gary's knees to the ultimate test. This ride I highly recommend for any triker who finds the opportunity to take it. In fact, I would like to someday ride my trike around the entire circumference of the caldera's knife edge rim, an extra 35 miles of absolutely breathtaking vistas in all directions. I have driven it in a car several times, and there are few locales that surpass the stunning scenery. On this trek however, we would not be taking this additional little jaunt, which would require an entire day, as there are some very daunting hills, not to mention many photo opportunities.

After a few miles of pedaling, we crossed the miniature Pumice Desert, and traffic was stopped at the other side for a helicopter operation. National Park fire crews were monitoring a forest fire outside the park's western boundary, and this was their helipad, necessitating the delay of tourist traffic every once in a while as the scouting helicopter would land or take off. Current forest management strategies include allowing lightning strike fires to burn naturally if no human lives or structures are in imminent danger of destruction from the flames, so this was a wait and see affair. The fire burned and the smoke rose.

Air temperature was now in the mid 70s, darn near perfect for comfortable triking. Shadows still crossed the roadway, so shade was easy to park in when a rest was needed. For quite a while, I rode behind Gary, as we kept a slow but steady low-gear pace. Eventually, as the ascent began extracting its toll in knee and stamina demands, we would rest every 100 yards or so, remaining in our recumbent seats, and then begin pedaling on towards the top once again. Numerous short rest stops like these kept Gary in the game. Our pace didn't matter however, as the scenery was worth it every step of the way. The prize at the top was worthy of the effort necessary to reach it.

Roughly 12 miles from last night's camp, Gary requested that I pull on ahead and proceed at my own pace, feeling that he was holding me up. It wasn't an issue for me either way, as I was super pleased to be here today, but I went ahead to remove any undue influence that my presence behind him might have been placing on his mind. This is a hard ride for anyone, and we all conquer it in our own personal ways. I would ride for a while until I felt a need to get up, walk around, and take photographs, and then hang out in this gorgeous corner of nature until Gary arrived and we had a chance to visit for a while.

I felt sorry that my friend may not be enjoying the experience to the fullest due to his physical conditions that seemed to be increasing by the hour. Gary's knees were really speaking to him once again, and not in ways a triker would wish to hear. Needless to say, this continual climb is a true challenge for even fit cyclists, and since Gary was still on the curve of fitness, it was much more difficult for him. At one point, he informed me that it felt like his heart was really pounding. I told him to take his time and as much rest as he needed. Time was not important to me. Gary's well being was!

Sometime around 4:00 PM, he informed me at one of our rest stops that he had decided to rent a U-Haul truck once we got to Klamath Falls in a day or two, and truck his trike and trailer back to Florence. By now, seeing the increasing agony he was suffering, I

206

supported any decision he might wish to make. I would get him safely to Klamath Falls and bid him a fond farewell if that is what he needed.

As the rim was in my sight at long last, I pulled over into a huge turnout, and made a cell phone call to my mom and sister in Apple Valley, the expedition's intended terminus. I informed them of Gary's condition, and that I might be riding solo from Klamath Falls south. The reception was excellent up on this high mountainside, where you'd swear you could see all of western Oregon and even the Pacific Ocean (you cannot). About 45 minutes after I had pulled off here, Gary pulled in. I pointed to the rim, and told him that we were almost there. Enthusiasm for the views was far from his current mindset, unfortunately. Even though we could see the cars parked at the first rim overlook, and could even make out people walking up to see the lake below the horizon, we both realized that it would take Gary quite some time to make it there at his current pace.

I attempted to raise his spirits by saying that once at the uppermost reaches of the caldera rim, we would then be coasting at high speed the final 9 miles down to the national park's main campground, Mazama. The sun was getting low in the western sky, so after sufficient rest, we headed on up for the final push to the visible summit. He was eagerly looking forward to those final miles downhill, having pedaled uphill since sunrise. This morning's early start was now making sense.

I pedaled my loaded trike on up to the caldera's rim, right up to the edge of the ancient deep blue abyss. Below me was a colossal lake with the deepest blue water anywhere on the planet we call home. This volcano used to be over 12,000 feet in elevation, but after its massive eruption, it collapsed into itself. During the ensuing 7,700 years to the present, it has been filling up with rain water and snow melt. This lake is a closed ecosystem because no streams or other water sources feed it. Until humans dumped fish into it in 1888, there were none.

Below me was Wizard Island, a relatively small mountain rising out of the lake. It resembles a wizard's hat, and resulted from later smaller eruptions. There is a boat ride you can take to this island. The huge Mazama caldera is about 4,000 feet deep, and is roughly half full of water, so it is a couple thousand feet to the water in front of my tiny trike. If you ever want some incredible photographs of your trike in a stunning pristine setting, this is most definitely the place!

Across the lake on the eastern side rises Mount Scott, visible to me as I walked around on the rim. I have climbed this 8,932 foot peak in the past, the highest place in the park, and the views from its summit of Crater Lake below are unsurpassed. The distances one can see from up there are vast, all over Oregon. Put your trike in your car, drive on up there, and have a great ride around the perimeter road.

About 6:00 PM or so, judging by the sun's position, because I never wear a timepiece, I reached a pullout where a number of National Park Service vehicles were parked. There were a couple of fire crew trucks and a law enforcement SUV. The personnel were standing at the little stone wall that overlooked the western side of the park, observing the smoke from the forest fire down below in the distance. I pulled in on my bizarre little tricycle, right up to the group of NPS officials, who promptly looked at me and wondered who I was and what I wanted.

Arising from my trike, I removed my black helmet, introduced myself, and asked the law enforcement woman if she knew whether Mazama Campground was full this late in the day. She made a call and confirmed that the massive camping area was filled to capacity, and informed me that the next place to camp was located about 10 miles south of Mazama, outside the national park boundary. This wasn't looking good for Gary, because in national parks, you cannot just pitch a tent anywhere you want, like you can normally on an overland journey.

I advised her of Gary's deteriorating condition, and asked if there were any options, for I did not know how much farther he could go today. It was more than 20 miles to that next campground outside the park from this turnout, and even though all but the next mile was downhill, that distance would place us on the highway outside the park after dark, and with us both being tired, it seemed out of the question and unsafe after a day this rough. As I was talking to some of the fire crew, Gary rounded the corner and pulled up to us, looking wiped out.

The law enforcement lady asked him to sit on the stone wall, and evaluated his physical condition, as she was also an emergency medical technician. After some questioning and his answers, she walked aside and privately consulted with the fire crew boss. They then both approached Gary and me, and indicated that we could pitch our tents at Mazama Campground in campsite E-18, which the fire crew was only using to park one of their large fire trucks. This news really brightened our outlooks, and we realized that now it was just a matter of riding another mile up to the turn to the main lodge, and then heading down the caldera to the park campground on the southern side.

After we finished answering many questions by the fire crew about our tricycles and the journey we were on, we headed out once again. It was nearly sunset as we finally began our coasting down to camp, a real thrill ride with tight turns at the top, necessitating braking for the first mile or so. Then, the road opens up, so we were traveling along at speeds in the 40 miles per hour range. What a difference from the trek up the mountain. The miles were flying by at breakneck speed instead of creeping by at the pace of a very relaxed hiker.

Of course, now we were no longer in sunshine, and the deep forest made it appear even darker, so on went our headlights and taillights. I was actually beginning to get a little bit chilled, but figured I could make it without having to access my jackets in the panniers. On the way down, we observed one lone bicyclist lying supine on a huge boulder, arms outstretched to the sides, with his loaded bike looking like a war casualty in the bushes nearby. He appeared as exhausted as we felt, as he still had one mile of torturous ascent to reach where we just left. Our trikes were so quiet, he didn't even hear us go sailing by.

Twelve and a half unbelievably demanding hours after leaving Broken Arrow Campground at Diamond Lake this morning, we arrived at the Annie Creek Lodge and Restaurant, which happened to be an "all you can eat" smörgåsbord. We decided that since it was now 7:30 PM, it would be best to eat first (we were starving, of course), and since I had camped at this campground many times in prior years and was familiar with the layout, we could navigate to site E-18 in the pitch black of darkness, on full stomachs. This is a huge and convoluted campground.

The restaurant was nearing closing time, so we lucked out once again! We parked our trikes right outside the window of the table where we sat so that we could keep an eye on them. Then, it was off to the smörgåsbord to get our glutinous fill of gourmet foods. We had earned it! Gary's achievement, by far exceeding any rides he had ever taken on his Catrike, was nothing short of phenomenal. He had ridden from the central Oregon coast to Crater Lake National Park, a crowning accomplishment in its own right. He was dead tired, but happy to be sitting down to a grand meal, knowing what he had done to get here. Time for a beer and recounting the day's struggles. War stories!

Gary agreed that we would have a meeting tomorrow morning at breakfast to see if he still desired to finish his ride at Klamath Falls, Oregon, with me going on alone. We had come about 203 miles so far, with nearly 800 more miles needed to reach Apple Valley, California according to the originally planned route. One thing I had learned about Gary on this trip was that he is not inclined to quit anything he starts, so that optimism would hold through the night.

Dinner done, Gary cautiously followed me as we slowly pedaled on the old worn out paved driveways through the bustling campground to E loop. Pedestrians with flashlights could not identify us. We looked like two little alien spaceships hovering along the ground with our LED lights. Once at E-18, we had to pull off, and I had to walk in with the headlight off my trike to find a way to get our rigs to the tent area. The fire crew truck was large enough that it blocked the normal

209

easy entrance. I located a path through a thick cluster of pines that was barely wide enough to pull our trikes through. Once inside, we set our tents in the dark using only our headlamps for illumination. The toilet facility was just one site away, so we were in triker's heaven once again.

DAY 10 - *Eastern Sierras*
Sunday – September 04, 2011
Mazama Campground to Rocky Point Lodge on Upper Klamath Lake - 40 miles (running total: 244 miles)

Before we two weary trikers hit the sack late last night, I had issued an executive expedition decree, and that was to sleep in late! My buddy had absolutely no problem with that one, considering that we had been up since before sunrise that long and challenging day. And we did just that. I slept in unusually late, finally getting dressed and leaving my tent because I heard the fire crew preparing to leave, and I wanted to personally thank their leader once again for allowing us to pitch our camp here. The fellow was a real life saver, and kindly accepted my thanks. Then, within minutes, they were gone for the day's fire work.

The sun had been up for a while by the time I got up. Yes, it did feel great to know this day's ride would be an easy one. From here, we would be coasting many joyous miles down off the Mount Mazama caldera to the miniature village of Fort Klamath, out on the flat of the Klamath Valley. There would be little effort needed for most of the day, and I was fine with taking my time and taking it easy!

I had finished breaking down my tent when I noticed Gary poking his head out of his yellow tent. I reiterated there was no need to rush at all. He was indeed a happy camper this AM. As he got himself going, I fixed my breakfast at the picnic table, thoroughly enjoying the incredible ambiance of camping in the woods up here on the spine of the Cascade Range. Even though this is a large camping facility, designed for thousands of people, it still felt very isolated and calm.

Next, trikes all loaded once again, we pedaled over to the Annie Creek Restaurant so Gary could get a smörgåsbord breakfast to start his day. What a day and night difference from yesterday morning! Today, we were warm, knew the miles ahead would be largely very easy, and felt no pressures to get anywhere by any time. Yep, that's the way to travel by trike. We had no cares. Gary took a shower, while I chatted with some folks at the campground general store. The Crater Lake Trolley was getting ready to take passengers down the mountain to Klamath Falls. Life was good! Our trikes would be flying today.

By 9:30 AM, we slowly pedaled out onto the road once again,

auto tourists wondering what we were. From the restaurant, it was only a matter of yards to the south entrance/exit of Crater Lake National Park, as Mazama Campground sits right on the park's southern border here. We were now on Highway 62, a mountain road that crosses the Cascades and drops out onto Highway 97 north of Klamath Falls. We would only be taking it to Fort Klamath however. This portion of 62 is all downhill for many miles, and we were coasting at fast speeds in the 30s and 40s. Cars that passed us got quite a show. A couple of young guys in a Mini Cooper gave exaggerated thumbs-up signs out the windows, and yelled: "That's the way to travel! Cool!" Love that stuff!

Once off the volcano altogether, the final few miles into Fort Klamath were flat, so we remained in high gears and kept up a good head of steam. Out here in this sunny wide open valley, it's all agricultural and ranch land, with cows and crops everywhere. Behind us, we could see the huge mountains that we had just descended. A powerful sense of serenity washed over us both as the reality of this extended breather became apparent to our well worn bodies.

At the tiny town, there is only one quaint general store and market, with old wood plank creaky floors. It had a fair selection of basic groceries, along with some fresh nectarines, which we bought. A touring motorcycle group that had passed us coming down the mountain was still there, and found our trikes fascinating. Gary, being a Honda Gold Wing rider himself, chatted up quite a storm while we ate on the quaint front covered boardwalk. Another man who was authoring his first book quizzed me about the ins and outs of the publishing business.

Following our totally relaxed meal, we prepared to depart this comfortable little wide spot. The temperature was already up to 79 degrees Fahrenheit, and it was not yet noon. It was shaping up to be a warm one – good thing we had many flat miles of pasture land ahead of us. With his trailer, Gary asked my help pushing his rig backwards off the porch area. It reminded me of when I pulled a trailer two years prior, and the difficulties I had in maneuvering out of one-way tight spots. I was extremely happy to be trailer free this time around.

About a quarter mile south of the store, our route now took us onto Highway 34, a narrow two lane road with unlimited visibility due to its flatness. Across the valley, we could clearly see the mountains that we would be paralleling as the road makes a kind of zig-zag line over to them, first on Weed Road and then on Seven Mile road, apparently staying between ranch acreage. Gary told me that his knees were feeling fine today and that he was well rested. He also indicated that he wished to continue on this trike trek to its finish in southern California. Great!

The Catrike and ICE made fast time across the valley, with

211

their identical gearing, heading first south, then west, and sometimes southwest as the road angled. Both trikes had large chainrings of 52 teeth, and small cassette cogs of 11 teeth, so a fast pace was fairly easy to maintain, even in the heat that gradually grew into the mid 80s by mid afternoon. Gary's knee must have been feeling better today, as he and I were evenly matched on this portion of the trip. This was loads of fun.

Out here on an overland trike journey, there is a lot of time to think, especially when the road is really long, flat, and not physically demanding. So, as I contemplated my sidekick's knee dilemma, my mind sought reasons and solutions. Gary's small chainring was 26 teeth, the same as mine. However, he was powering notably more weight down the road than I was, including a trailer. Riding up and over the Coast and Cascade Ranges during the past 9 days, the 26 seemed perfect for me. Now I wondered if that same 26 was too many teeth for Gary's needs considering his overall traveling weight, thereby placing considerably more stress on his knees as a result. Rolling weight makes a difference!

On my Death Valley trip a couple years before this one, I had pulled a trailer, and my overall weight, including my own body, was a little more than what Gary's was this year. On that trek, I ran a small chainring of only 24 teeth, and really felt that I needed it to make those long and steep mountain passes. Two teeth can be a life saver! My feet and tendons became problematic on that journey, and that was with a 24. If I had been running a 26, there would have been a chance that I might have injured my feet even more than I did, and possibly my knees.

Knees are funny – they can feel fine one moment, and then in an instant, be sending very painful signals to the brain once a certain threshold is reached. It's usually not a gradual transition from healthy to injured, but unexpectedly and dreadfully abrupt. If a trike is not geared down sufficiently, the stress on a triker's lower body can be extreme over the long haul, and this may have been a crucial point for Gary. My experience shows that a 24 ring can save knees when pulling a trailer.

I also wondered about how the next days would play out. His knees were not causing him pain today thus far, as we had been coasting for many miles, and then simply maintaining momentum in high gears out here on the flat. But the knees just don't hurt a lot one day, and then heal by the next. Sure, they seemed okay so far today, but what would happen when we again got into some hills? I figured we would find out between here and Klamath Falls, as the road would eventually leave this valley in places, and climb over many small, but steep, mountain hills.

As the afternoon wore on, we were riding south on Highway 34, now along the western wooded hills. Evergreen trees provided welcomed shade frequently, and the times we were in the sun, we knew today was heading to the upper 80s, into numbers that make overland trikers lose lots of liquid through perspiration. Good thing we both had ample water supplies on board, around two gallons apiece.

By mid afternoon, I was keeping an eye out for potential forested spots to pitch our tents for the night. The area was heavily treed, and many little side roads provided easy access off the pavement where we could readily hide our trikes and tents from passing motorists. Now and then, as the terrain became increasingly hilly, I would pull out into a promising area to wait for Gary, and I would walk into the trees to find open areas covered with abundant pine needles, comfy spots upon which we could sleep in blissful peace. Places like this are where I prefer my wild hobo overnights with nature.

Gary and I took an energy bar break sometime after 4:00 PM, and he wanted to see what might be available at a place the map showed as Rocky Point, on the western fringe of Upper Klamath Lake. So, we pedaled on as the mountain and evergreen shadows moved easterly, making our ascent efforts easier and cooler. The small downhills now and then on the undulating landscape proved momentarily delightful. This was easy ground compared to where we had already traveled.

An old sign for the Rocky Point Lodge appeared to us at 5:30 PM, and we pulled up together at the entrance off the roadway. It was paved, but dipped very steeply downhill on the east side of the road towards the lake's shore. I asked Gary if he wanted to coast on down there to see if there was any camping, thinking that if it was not something we liked, we would have to then pedal back up this insanely steep grade to where we now sat on our recumbent seats. In response, Gary asked me if I liked taking chances. That was the answer, of course! We immediately dropped down the impossible grade, surrounded by huge red-barked ponderosa pine trees. Down, down, down we went, using the brakes continuously and hard on the steep and tight curves.

The lady host rented us a tiny little spot right on the water, barely large enough to fit two trikes, a trailer, and two tents. Erecting the tents was slowed as people walked by and wanted to know all about our vehicles. Gary loves to chat with folks, so by the time I had my tent up, he was still in the process. It was nice to set up on the grass rather than in dirt. I was literally inches from the lake shore.

During this ritualistic camp activity, the wind unexpectedly began to build quite rapidly. The fast moving clouds began spitting water upon us. The wind upped the ante, and the tent in an adjacent site suddenly blew over. Quickly, Gary and I staked our tents into the ground using available rocks as hammers. It appeared the rain would also increase, so on went the rain flies as fast as we could manage them

213

in the now very powerful wind. No sooner were the flies secured and the ballast of our panniers tossed inside to hold the tents steady, than we found ourselves in the midst of a full blown squall from the southeast, raging across the gargantuan lake like an invisible hungry monster.

This wind required that we also make sure our trikes were secure, for it was forceful enough to move them. Anything not held down was immediately lost to the northwest woods. But as fast and surprisingly as the unseen air movement came upon us, it also stopped, leaving the trikes and tents lightly damp. I think this was a record time for getting ready for a night's camp, despite how it started out so leisurely. Within minutes, the sun was again shining, but down here at lake's edge, surrounded by tall trees, the sun only hit the water.

After showers, clean clothes, and a fine gourmet dinner in the Rocky Point Lodge, we retired for the night. The warmth had returned, so I just slept well into the night in the cotton bag liner on top of the down mummy bag. Later though, I slipped the liner and me inside to avoid early morning chill. I was aware of light sprinkles a couple times that night, but the tent held it all at bay.

DAY 11 - *Eastern Sierras*
Monday – September 05, 2011 (Labor Day)
Rocky Point Lodge to Klamath Falls, Oregon - 34 miles
(running total: 278 miles)

To the east was the grand lake, and the mountains on its eastern edge provided the foundation for a stunning sunrise. We had gotten plenty of sleep, and the day was shaping up to be another dry and warm one. We took our time this cool morning, as there was nothing extremely daunting in our path, or so we thought until we spoke with a touring bicyclist who had pedaled in during the later evening last night and pitched his tent in the site immediately adjacent to ours.

He was riding solo, and today was going to pedal up to Crater Lake, having never been there before. I filled him in on what to expect, and he filled us in on what was ahead for us today, as he had just ridden in from northern California the day before. He was obviously making higher mileages than we were capable of, largely due to his ultra light load and extreme fitness level. For example, his tent was a teeny tiny one-person container that required his panniers to be left outside under the fly. He barely had room to dress inside, a way cyclists save weight.

This young and helpfully friendly biker described one mildly challenging hill on our way to Klamath Falls today, and he showed me photos on his digital camera. He had crested this obstacle after probably

214

70 miles or more of riding yesterday in the heat, rating it as moderate. It was called Doak Mountain, and his digital photo of the summit revealed an elevation of 4,776 feet. The good news was that this climb is short.

More good news was that Gary and I would come upon this over sized mound of mountain this morning sometime, beating the afternoon heat rise. The question in both of our minds was how his knees would hold out on the ascent. He was still on for continuing with the expedition, so spirits were high. The life of a trike hobo is always one of many daily uncertainties. The only thing certain is uncertainty!

Breakfast complete, we pedaled partway back up the terribly steep driveway to the lodge, but midway up, noticed a paved rural road heading slightly downward to the south, which would make the final and most agonizing yards back up to Highway 34 unnecessary. The sign indicated that Highway 140, which connects Klamath Falls and Lake of the Woods, could be accessed on this unknown road, so we decided to chance it. We pedaled south through a rural forested neighborhood of modest cabins and opulent chalets, prefab homes and boat docks. Finally, we arrived at Highway 140, not far east of where we would have intercepted it had we returned to Highway 34. That was a lucky break!

Pointing our trikes left, we headed east into the morning sun, bound for Doak Mountain and Klamath Falls. While riding this relaxing scenic byway on nice shoulders, we occasionally noticed thick white clouds hovering at our level. They were large bug clouds, thousands of minuscule insects called midges, which had been introduced to this somewhat swampy area many years ago to decimate the thick mosquito populations. Yep, midges eat mosquitoes, so midges are my friends, even though they got into my nose, mouth, eyes, and ears each time we rode through the white herds of them buzzing only feet from the road.

After some easy riding in high gear speeds on Highway 140, I noticed what appeared to be one hell of a long ascent a couple miles ahead from my flat ground of marsh covered landscape, and assumed it to be our pathway to the Doak Mountain summit. Gary was bringing up the rear, and not yet able to see it from his location on the road. I increased my pace, which of course, is non productive realistically because momentum doesn't do squat on a grade of this magnitude and length, but it made me feel like I was at least going into battle on high alert, a wholly imagined advantage, simply psychological!

Even though this was Labor Day weekend, and today was Labor Day, traffic was light. Perhaps most families had already headed home for the summer. The road was plenty wide so there were no issues with feeling pressed by automobiles and trucks. As always, motorists of all descriptions were courteous and accommodating to our bizarre low

215

slung three wheeled contraptions – or should I say five wheeled contraption in Gary's case with his Burley trailer in tow. Between the two of us, we had eight wheels rolling down the endless highway.

As I approached the bottom of the impending hill, I noticed a cycling tour van coming down, with enough racks on top and on the trailer behind it to hold many conventional bicycles. This was the lead vehicle for a supported bicycle tour business. Gearing down as my ascent began up the slope, I met the first of numerous bicyclists speeding down the western side of exposed Doak Mountain, and we all exchanged waves. These women and men had no pannier cargo systems on their bikes, and only carried minimal water, either in bottles or in a CamelBak bladder system, so their effort to traverse the mountains was significantly less than ours was about to be. What kept Gary and me slower was the weight of cargo, necessary on self supported tours.

Some of these cyclists, more experienced than others, either that or more crazy, were racing down the hill all bent over at breakneck speeds, while others, often what appeared to be wife/husband couples, kept a slower pace using their brakes. By now, as I was about a fourth of the way up, Gary was beginning his ascent, and was also seeing these unencumbered folks ride the other direction past him. Almost makes one want to join a supported tour. Almost, but not quite – at least for me.

Doak Mountain is heavily forested, but this road is four lanes over the summit, leaving the two of us under direct assault by the warm rays of the sun, and as we progressed up the mountain, like little ants dedicated to a cause, our body temperatures began to rise from exertion. I guess we could cool off more by stripping off our clothing, but that might create more of a stir than we would want. This was one of those "spin and grin" climbs, where you just pedal along in low/low, keep a steady pace, and know that the top will be yours eventually through persistence. I had a large water supply, which was certainly necessary.

Due to the different design of our trikes, our water bladders were located differently. I had two CamelBaks, one on either side behind my recumbent seat, with a water line coming over each side. At 100 ounces each, I could sip about 6 liters, or 200 ounces before running the bladders dry. I also had two 24 ounce water bottles on the mainframe between my legs. Gary's seat and cargo design only allowed one 100 ounce bladder situated directly behind his back, behind the seat, with one water tube. This is because he was running a pair of Arkel panniers behind each seat side. He had one 24 ounce bottle on his mainframe, but carried additional water in his Burley trailer. We were good today.

With my small 26 tooth small chainring and large 34 tooth rear cog, I knew I would make the top, albeit slowly. I was in no danger of hurting my knees, as the gearing did not cause me to reach the level of force necessary to push a knee past its limits. Had I been pulling a trailer like I did on my previous trip, I would have certainly wanted a 24 tooth chainring. Not being able to gear down sufficiently for a given grade is what destroys knees and feet eventually, as repetitive stress injury.

As I existed in my own little world of temporary physical suffering, knowing that I was achieving more fitness with each pedal stroke, I could only imagine how Gary was doing. It was relatively hot, now being mid morning, and the sun was relentless. The incline was pretty steep, and even though we knew the summit was probably less than 3 miles from the western base, the ride kept us resolutely fixed upon the goal. I was really hoping his knees had recovered enough to make this grade today, but knowing the effort I was expending with no trailer and a 26/34 front/rear combination, I was cautiously optimistic about his identical gearing and significantly greater rolling weight.

At the summit is a sign announcing what to car drivers is nothing more than passing interest if even that, but to us another feather in our caps of physical achievement and endurance. Most motorists likely don't even notice or care about the top of the mountain, having sped over the pass in total sedentary delight, keeping air conditioned cool, while listening to favorite songs from a CD. Overland trikers see things differently of course, just like life in general. We take a protracted rest at the top, chowing down on a couple of energy bars and guzzling more water, eagerly anticipating the high speed easy ride down the other side. Life is different out on the edge of normal reality! Only a mile!

In the shade of the trees, I stood and ate a high calorie bar, while studying a governmental solar powered radio relay station and web cam inside a barbed wire enclosure. This compound also made for a perfect vision shield for me to offload some organically filtered water, with passing motorists unaware. As I awaited Gary's arrival, it dawned on me that he might like a shadier area, because I had to walk up a loose dirt slope to get to the shade of the trees, not to mention that this was on the opposite side of the road to our travel, which would necessitate him having to cross 4 lanes at the summit crest to get here.

So, I got back in my trike, recrossed the 4 lane road, and coasted down a little ways from the summit to a little dirt road, some huge boulders, and nice evergreen shade. Once he reached the summit, he would be able to see my trike, with its yellow pannier covers, and yellow and orange flagging. I found one cool (literally) boulder that made for a grand shaded seat, and would offer it to Gary once he pulled in. But in the meantime, I had a Clif bar, making it a two-bar summit. A pleasant breeze was blowing over the top up here, and I quickly cooled to a comfortable temperature. Gary would like it, as the cooling air was not perceptible at all coming up the western slope. It was only right near the summit that the breeze manifested itself. Oh, the simple joy of air!

Rough mental calculations, which are always subject to scrutiny, unveiled the relative difficulty factor for this short climb. It seemed to come in around 330 feet or more of elevation gain per mile, enough to make you know you had been well worked and needed calories. About the steepest ascent I've triked on an overland expedition thus far was the Artist's Palette grade that rises from the eastern side of Death Valley. It was a 1,123 foot elevation gain in 3 miles, or 374 feet per mile. The longer, but gentler, grades like the Cascade Range will wipe you out too, but these short and sweet affairs are quick and to the point! Proper gearing is absolutely essential. Miss the mark on your gearing setup, and you're in for a world of hurt. Gary was proof.

Halfway up this short pass, we got our first views of Mount Shasta in northern California (we were still in Oregon), an awesome sight of glaciated snow in late summer. Gary's small yellow Catrike at last appeared on the horizon of Doak Mountain's summit crest. He would be coasting down to my location within seconds now.

His Catrike pulled up and parked behind my ICE, and he just sat there for a while. I walked over to assess his condition, and it became apparent the climb had extracted a heavy toll. I extended a hand and helped him to a standing position, but he stood there bent over for a bit, hands on knees. I told him about the great boulder in the shade, motioning with my hand, then helped him walk over to it, which necessitated a slight decline in soft dirt. He was somewhat unstable because his knees were in a lot of pain once again, just like on Mazama.

As Gary sat there and ate a bar and drank water, the somber tone of his voice reflected a spirit that had been vanquished from its goal. I could feel his reluctance hanging heavily in the air as he stated that Klamath Falls would have to be the end of his ride. He would have to rent a U-Haul there. His knee pain was too great to bear any longer, and we were still an appreciable distance from the town, with lesser ups and downs yet to go. The torturous gauntlet had more to give us.

The distance wasn't that far as day rides go, but considering his knees, these next miles would prove excruciating for him. We sat and talked for a long time, allowing the joints to recoup what ever they could in the short term, the cooling breeze lifting his collapsed spirits. Gary is a physically and mentally strong man, and I knew this was not easy for him. He is a very driven type of guy who usually reaches his intended objectives in life. Overland trike journeys add a new dimension.

We set out again, speeding down the eastern face of Doak

Mountain, but feeling the sting of a new plan that neither of us had truly anticipated before we began this journey. Sure enough, this undulating terrain kept the pressure on his injuries, the intermittent downhills and flat straights not providing enough buffer to keep him in the game. Lower gearing could have well made the difference. Twenty-four teeth.

Gary wanted to find a nice motel for his final night on this trek, so just outside the western limits of Klamath Falls, I hailed a local police officer and asked directions to the closest area with decent motels, telling him of my battle scarred trike warrior and the need to minimize any further pedaling for him. The young cop, recently returned from a military tour in Afghanistan, expertly directed us the final 7 miles into town, which required negotiating some higher speed interchange areas.

The Olympic Inn, a Best Western motel, offered up the finest options for the night. Patterned after the lodge at Crater Lake, with its wood walls, lodge-like atmosphere, and photos of the lake on walls, we had laundry facilities, and also were treated to a full dinner and breakfast smörgåsbord as part of the price. They even allowed us to wheel our trikes into the room. Boy, did that ever get the attention of elderly couples who saw us in the hallway! Two men bringing tricycles into their room was not an expected sight. Once inside the room with two trikes and a trailer, we had scant room to navigate anywhere inside.

While I showered and did my laundry once again, Gary called around and set up for a local U-Haul dealer to deliver a small rental van to his motel room tomorrow morning at 8:00 AM, by which time I would be long gone on my way to California. We had a relaxing dinner, and then I called Jack Freer, the fellow who provided expedition security for me two years ago, and got directions for a last minute route change that would take me through Reno, Nevada. Due to the extremely hot temperatures lately, especially out in the northwestern Nevada desert near where the Burning Man civilization occurs each September, I felt it would not be wise to trike that roasting route. Time to adapt as needed.

Gary called an old high school friend in northeastern Oregon whom he hadn't visited in years, and planned on driving over to his place after he loaded his Catrike into his car once back in Florence. He also insisted I take any of the energy bars from his panniers that I might need to replenish my own supply, since he would not be needing them anymore. The plan was to meet Jack mid trip near Yerrington, Nevada and restock with food bars I had mailed to him prior to departure, so now I had more bars from Gary. I might have to go on an eating binge to make room (by the way, these bars get quite heavy, so plan wisely).

We discussed the current state of affairs, our thoughts about it all, and shared feelings on our impending separation tomorrow morning.

219

Having ridden together for 11 days now, the change would necessitate a reworking of our recent reality. Uncertainty is always certain. It's amazing how quickly and well you get to know someone on a journey.

Gary had pedaled his trike a challenging 278 miles, from the central Oregon coast to just shy of the California border, and he had done it the toughest way possible, over the crest of Mazama volcano and through Crater Lake National Park. He had truly pushed his limits, exceeded them, and left the boundaries of the imagined far behind. What he had succeeded in doing is a laudable feat, an overland tricycle journey in its own right, an accomplishment of which he can justly and forever be proud! He did not fail. He achieved something that is utterly not achievable by most, joining the elite band of trike hobos forever more.

After saying goodbye to Gary, I left Oregon and crossed the invisible northern California border. Political boundaries, such as this one, are imaginary, and are just like the other imagined boundaries in your mind that hold you captive. Break free ...

DAY 12 - *Eastern Sierras*
Tuesday – September 06, 2011
Klamath Falls, Oregon to Canby, California - 86 miles
(running total: 364 miles)

One convenient thing about staying in a motel is that a computerized wake-up call starts a triker's day. There is no sleepily attempting to determine if first light is hitting the tent walls, and then going through the temporary trauma of leaving a warm mummy bag. Nope, in a motel, you easily arise to warm air and a handy bathroom. Doesn't get any easier than that! I'm getting too pampered.

Having eaten my complimentary breakfast in the lodge dining hall, I wheeled my trike out the doors of the room and motel, a fun little solo puzzle of how to direct a fully loaded heavy vehicle through heavy doors that are designed to return shut automatically (Gary was still eating breakfast and I was itching to get going). Gary brought his chain lube out front in the parking lot so that I could lubricate my chain for the next leg of the journey, then we bid farewell and off I triked at 7:30 AM, into rush hour traffic. Cars were everywhere downtown.

Since the motel was on the north side of the east/west street I needed to ride, and since it was situated at a major intersection, I had to ride the sidewalk east one business block to reach a traffic signal so I could cross onto the road. I was in downtown Klamath Falls, and had several miles of heavy traffic riding before I could return to the rural settings past the city limits. I also had to ride through the town of

220

Altamont, a neighboring city that is only separated by a signpost.

With the sun still very low on the eastern horizon, I finally reached Oregon Highway 39, which would take me the final miles to California. It is a narrow two lane road with minimal shoulder, but as always, motorists of all descriptions extended me full courtesies. My mind was flashing back to 2009, when I was also on this same highway early in the morning on my way to Death Valley National Park. Today I was again riding solo, and having revised my route last night due to weather concerns, had just over 700 miles to go before the Q and I reached Apple Valley in southern California. I was very happy to have no trailer behind me this trip, moving along at a much faster clip with much less effort! I really have come to prefer fast and light travel.

By now, Gary's U-Haul truck was at the motel and he was loading up the Catrike Road and Burley trailer for the day's drive back to Florence on the coast. What had taken him 11 days on his tricycle, he would now retrace with petroleum power in far less than 11 hours. What a difference in our morning activities today. Life had changed for us both. Either way it's life's grand adventure. We were both still breathing.

About 10:00 AM, I reached the Oregon/California border, an invisible line dividing autonomous political governments, heralded only by a huge blue steel sign reading *Welcome to California*, and adorned with an illustration of poppies, the state's celebrated orange flower. Overland expedition triking is all about pedaling beyond boundaries of many types, mental and physical, and today I crossed the boundary into another state in the country called America. Boundaries are in the mind.

Gary had come so close, but he made the right choice because there are no towns on this route where he could have rented a truck until far south in Susanville, a ride of about 4 or 5 days when towing a trailer. I wondered how long it would take me without a trailer. There are also some grueling steep mountains between here and Susanville, and his knees probably would not have held together.

At the state border, the route changes from Highway 39 in Oregon to Highway 139 in California, and with this numerical change comes a wider road with noticeably smoother pavement and wider shoulders. Well, California may be financially bankrupt, but at least they provided a nice trike lane on their way to monetary annihilation!

Another 30 minutes along this wide open flat road through northern California agricultural and ranch land brought me to Tulelake, California, a small town with grain towers and a well stocked market. I bought a couple of bananas, a quart of V8 Juice, and a large bag of mixed nuts and raisins, which I enthusiastically devoured right out front on the sidewalk in the shade of the store. Well fueled, with nuts, fruits, and vegetables instead of petroleum, I again hit the road, shifting up into high gears, making quick work of the flatlands stretched out before me.

The miles rolled by, out in the grand landscape where cities and people do not exist. I could see for miles in all directions, watching horses in their pastures, and passing potato farms. There was one major road construction portion, but it wasn't down to dirt, the traffic was light, and they let me ride through unhampered.

After a couple hours, the terrain began getting hilly, and the boundary line for the Modoc National Forest loomed ahead. It was on this pinyon and juniper forested line that I had camped during my previous trek, which was necessitated by the added weight of the trailer I pulled. Here I was today, about mid day, at the same spot, with many hours of riding yet ahead of me. This was a dramatic illustration for me of how slow I had been pedaling two years ago. Yes, for me, fast and light are now the watchwords. No more trailers! It's not even open for discussion anymore. Give me freedom and ease. I want to fly!

Eventually, as the dry juniper forests gave way to the stately ponderosa pine forests, with elevations and road steepness increasing, I reached the California State Agricultural Inspection Station, a remote outpost staffed by Produce Inspection Officer White, who came out with her digital camera to take photographs of me pedaling into the giant portal. I was the only vehicle anywhere around, and she apparently found me fascinating. I looked like a big bright road bug.

I parked inside, shaded from the increasingly warming rays of the sun, and chatted with her for a while. She was White, and I was Greene. She drove a car, and I drove a tricycle. We had a good time as I cooled down, refilling my water bottles as I guzzled as much cold water from her tap as I could handle. I gave Officer White, who lives in Tulelake, the internet address for Trike Asylum so she could read all about trikes in her copious spare time this far out in the sticks, then, I silently disappeared farther on up into the mountains.

This is an interesting day because the annual Burning Man civilization just disbanded yesterday, and so I was being passed by hundreds of automobiles and trucks going the other direction as they returned home from the week-long desert extravaganza. All the vehicles, whether just a passenger car or a huge 18 wheeler loaded with props, were completely covered in a fine white silt from the massive dry lake of the incredibly remote Black Rock Desert.

These people are what most would term as alternative lifestyle addicts, and many of them let me know how cool they thought my alternative means of triangular locomotion was. This constant positive reinforcement helped the tens of mountainous miles roll by under my three wheels much easier, keeping my mind actively engaged, and supporting my spirit as I gradually ascended into the high reaches of the Modoc National Forest. Although rather conservative while growing up, nowadays, I feel much more at ease with these folks than those still trapped inside the uniform box of orthodox conformity. If you are unfamiliar with Burning Man, spend some time at their website for a very eye opening journey into the bizarre: http://www.burningman.com

From the website: "Once a year, tens of thousands of participants gather in Nevada's Black Rock Desert to create Black Rock City, dedicated to community, art, self-expression, and self-reliance."

In 2009, it took me two days to pedal from Altamont, Oregon to Canby, California, a distance about six miles less than my ride this year from the Klamath Falls motel. This year, as I crested the final rise of this forested section of road, and could see the valley below that contains Canby, I realized that I was easily going to arrive there in just one day, with the sun still pretty high in the western sky. Weight was the main factor. These final miles are downhill, steep and long enough to achieve speeds near 50 miles per hour, so I was now rapidly closing in on Canby. It's nice to end the day with a tricycle thrill ride out of the mountains! The final few miles are flat, but fast – a long distance day.

I knew right where to go this time around: to the Canby town park. Canby is a tiny wide spot in the road, with old run down houses here and there, an old defunct gasoline station on the main highway, and a motel that has seen better days. The city park is small, but provides concealment from the highway and a pleasant well groomed lawn. The only public restroom is a plastic outhouse that sits in front of the old gasoline station across the highway. I'll probably need it come morning.

Last trip here, I also rode through a few thousand goathead thorns at this city park, but this year, being about 5 weeks earlier in the season, they were not to be found anywhere. As I ate, it felt good to have shaved off an entire day. Today's ride was actually easier than the two days combined last trip. I wasn't in any hurry, but felt a certain egoic pride in knowing I had made 86 miles during daylight hours. This was the first time I had ridden a trike that far in one day, so I allowed myself a little personal gloating and celebration. Nobody knew it but me.

As last time, I pitched my tent on the concrete portion of the park, under a huge old oak tree, even though inviting thick grass was only a few feet to the south of me. Town parks have a nasty habit of using automatic sprinklers in the wee hours of the morning, so I dared not chance it. Last time, they never activated, but since I was here a different day of the week this year, they watered before sunrise!

DAY 13 - *Eastern Sierras*
Wednesday – September 07, 2011
Canby, California to 38 miles north of Susanville, California - 52 miles
(running total: 416 miles)

This year, I was getting no cellular telephone service in this town of Canby, but I had a strong signal two years ago. That didn't make sense to me, but it is what is, so I let it go. Also last time, I refilled my water at their facets, but for whatever reason, the water was shut off this visit, even though it was over a month earlier in the year.

My original route had this journey heading east out of Canby, but due to ultra high temperatures well in excess of 100 degrees in the northwestern Nevada desert, I made the eleventh hour choice to alter the route, which also cut down the total mileage to southern California by a bit. I would instead head southwest up into the pine mountains once again, and even find temperatures there in the mid to upper 90s.

The blue and white plastic outhouse came in mighty handy after breakfast. I parked the trike right next to it, and could hear truckers drive by on the road just a few yards south. After conducting my business, I settled into the trike's cockpit, clicked onto the pedals, and headed southwest on Highways 139/299 towards the quaint little village of Adin, on the other side of 5,173 foot Adin Pass. Yep, it was back up and into the Modoc National Forest once again for some extended uphill pedaling, about 22 miles of it, before I'd eat lunch at the general store.

By mid morning, I reached the summit, and parked to take some photographs. A benevolent lady, driving a white Ford Crown Victoria the other direction towards Canby, slowed in her lane and asked if I needed assistance. That was so nice of her, seeing me up here on this mountain all alone, on nothing more substantial than a bizarre looking bicycle and then going the extra mile to ask a total stranger if he needed help. I thanked her for her concern, said I was doing well, and waved as she drove on. Interactions like this restore my faith in the human condition, and let me know that if I truly did get into some trouble out here in the wilds on my trike, I could count on being rescued by strangers. People are out to help me, not get me. Paranoia is not needed.

Down the south side of the pass, it was high speed coasting for several miles, followed by about 8 miles of flat and rapid high gear pedaling through the Adin Valley into the little town of Adin, reminiscent of an older American ideal, the main street lined with huge old cottonwood trees. The general store and market is a grand place to spend an hour, with its old wooden plank floors and ambiance that invites lingering. So, I lingered, ate more food (2 bananas, 1 quart tomato juice, a container of plump and juicy strawberries, and a bag of Frito-Lay fruit and nut mix), and used their old fashioned bathroom. I love this place, and recommend your visit! Not much here though.

With an extra bag of fruit and nut mix stashed in my panniers for later, I departed the shady main drag and re-entered the dry farmlands of Highway 139 south. At the general store, I had refilled both my 100 ounce water bladders, having emptied them on the mountain ascent, so now I was again full of water, a necessity with temperatures seeming to increase with every passing day. Full water bladders also mean a bunch of added weight once again!

The afternoon was a mix of landforms, and I used all my gear options from L-1 to H-9 at some time as the hours rolled on. Just south of Adin I had encountered thousands of grasshoppers in 2009, but this year, not a one made its way into my face. It must have been too early in the season for them I guess. No goatheads or grasshoppers.

Eventually, the road began attaining some serious elevation again, and its short undulating hills made for low gear climbing, followed by brief coasting. I approached the roadside pullout where I had pitched my tent in 2009, but just like yesterday on my way to Canby, it was early afternoon, way too early to set camp, and I felt fine for many more hours of daylight pedaling. So again I rolled right on past a prior campsite, and compressed another day into my ride with less effort than last time with the trailer in tow. The difference on these two days really amazed me, and reinforced the lesson that had led to me adventuring with only my trike. Yes, it was worth lightening my load!

This was like a little informal scientific test, where changing the weight variable was the primary difference. This was the same road, and I was equally physically fit. This time my gearing was higher, and the weather much warmer. My traveling weight was about 100 pounds less. So I learned a valuable lesson that would have been but intellectual speculation had not I ridden this route again. It couldn't have been better designed. I knew that I had completed 4 hard days riding in only 2 easy days. To me, that is powerful evidence. Fast, light, and easy – yes!

This Modoc forest region covers a lot of ground, especially when traversing it on a tricycle. First, it's up into the mountains, and then down into a valley, and then back up again, down again, and the cycle repeats. The views are really nice for those who enjoy the wild wooded backcountry. There are hardly any Forest Service or BLM campgrounds between Canby and Susanville however, and the one perfect camp I did pass at Willow Creek came too early in the day to stay, unfortunately, as it would have been ideal for me because no one else was camping there. I almost stopped, second guessing myself.

225

I passed a lake as the day was getting on into late afternoon. The view was quite calming, with clouds filtering out the sun and its attendant heat, the sparkle of diamonds as the light was scattered to my eyes, and a group of ducks landing atop the shimmery surface. I believed this to be Eagle Lake that afternoon, perhaps wishful thinking, knowing that Eagle Lake is nearer Susanville, but tomorrow I was to learn it was not. During the 15 minutes or so it took to pedal along the eastern shore, a light rain teased me, and cooled me from all the uphill effort.

My planet's rotation was not letting up, and the star that makes life possible here kept inching towards the tops of the western mountains, still partially obscured by the scattered rain clouds. I began looking in earnest for a cozy place to pitch my tent for the night. It was truly remote out here, with no humans for miles, only a very occasional entrance to some wealthy person's ranch that sat far back in the forest, not visible from the road. I was passing many turnouts, but preferred to find something a little farther from the roadway. With typical fencing on either side of the right-of-way, options were very limited.

Out in this long lonely high country valley, where I could see miles ahead, it became obvious that if I wished to set my camp while the sun was still shining upon me, I best do so soon. About three quarters of the way across the valley, I saw the road gaining elevation on the other side, and knew that to pedal up the incline would put me in those hills after sunset, so I opted to take a large pullout just ahead, where a gigantic gravel mound made by county road crews could conceal my tent from any southbound cars or trucks. I was about 38 miles north of Susanville, according to my reckoning based on milepost markers.

This camp seemed custom ordered almost, as there was a rather large area of bark chips on the south side of the gravel mound, perfect for setting a tent over, making for a comfortable foundation. Behind me was the fence that ran along the road's borders. Captivating puffy clouds were everywhere, and the nearly full moon was already mingling with them as the sun was in setting mode. The whole thing was picture perfect, and because traffic this far out in the boonies was very light midweek, camping only a few yards from the pavement was easy.

The expansive flat valley to my east made for a surreal scene. As is often the case, here I am out in the middle of nowhere, or seemingly so, living with no schedule or demands, and enjoying all the natural world is presenting. For those who love dancing with the simple beauties of nature, it doesn't get much better. More than 400 miles were now behind me. Tomorrow I will finally reach Susanville, but for now, I am content out here on the edge – no people, no noise, no boundaries.

226

DAY 14 - *Eastern Sierras*
Thursday – September 08, 2011
38 miles north of Susanville to 30 miles east of Susanville - 68 miles
(running total: 484 miles)

I was sleeping soundly, but just prior to first light, I heard the unmistakable sound of an eighteen wheeler slowing as it pulled off the road, right in front of my little trike and tent. The rear of the trailer was just past the large gravel mound, a mound that may have kept a sleepy trucker from running over a sleeping triker. A light breeze was blowing and a light rain tapped out a rhythm on my tent walls. After 20 minutes, the trucker rolled on south. The rain had stopped. By the time it was light enough to begin my day, the tent was dry. Breaking down camp prior to sunrise kept my actions unnoticeable, but it was a moot point because no one was driving this far out on a Thursday morning.

It was a bit chilly to eat here, so I decided to trike on over the nearby forested hills to the south of my camp and find a nice breakfast spot once the sun warmed up the setting a little more. I pedaled over a final rise before the next valley, only to behold what was clearly Eagle Lake, a huge body of water far bigger than the one I had mistakenly believed yesterday's lake to be. I saw a large turnout below, with dirt roads that went to the lake's edge, so decided to pull off there and eat.

Today was going to be a hot one, not just warm, but hot! I could tell because as I fixed my roadside breakfast, the hydrogen and helium orb felt like it was burning my backside, and it was still early. I watched ducks and other wildlife as I ate, and listened to their wild sounds. After eating, I noticed that my left brake cable was loose at the wheel, so I made a quick adjustment to bring it in line with the right side. This was important because once I crested the final summit of the national forest above Susanville, there was a 4 mile descent at a 6% grade, which meant fast speeds, no place for maladjusted brakes!

But it seemed like it would be a long long while before I made it that far. At the south end of the Eagle Lake valley, Highway 139 takes a steep up-slope into yet another challenging wave of Modoc National Forest mountains. Gary would have hated what I was now seeing, and with the heat finally beginning to reach heretofore unfelt levels on this journey, what was coming would be no picnic! The mountains were not as daunting as the Cascade Range, but the temperature was exceeding anything that Gary and I had experienced anywhere in that range.

The grade was relentless, a seemingly eternal L-1 pedaling marathon, with slow speeds and plenty of perspiring. I was drinking water like there was no tomorrow. My mind wandered to what the original itinerary had planned: triking through the northwestern Nevada desert region, that was even more searing hot than here. At least I was at high elevation in a pine forest! Hot, yes, but trees nearby if I really needed them. This road left me in the sun for hours and many miles.

Ever heard of false summits? Those horizon lines that you swear are at long last the top, only to find that another, even larger and more difficult, summit lies right behind them? Well, the final miles to the overlook of Susanville is full of false summits, and in this heat, they teased my swollen mind over and over, so much so that once the real summit arrived, I could hardly believe I had made it. But sure enough, there in front of me was the welcomed yellow road sign that described the insane down grade ahead. Hallelujah!

This ride allowed speeds that were so fast I had to brake and lean into some of the tighter turns. The coasting speeds felt great, with the wind dramatically cooling my steamy body, even though this side of the mountain was composed mostly of dry grass and barren hillsides with only sparse trees here and there. Translation: no shade anywhere. The timing was perfection, as my water supply of 248 ounces was nearly exhausted. The good news was that right at the bottom of this hill, where Highway 139 ends, there is a Grocery Outlet food store, and I could buy all the water and cold drinks I wanted. Here I come!

The songs and views of eagles, frogs, and pronghorns at Eagle Lake were now long behind me as I raced down into the civilization of Susanville. Once in town, I pulled into the Grocery Outlet parking lot, and realized that a public library shared a common wall with the market to the east. Perfect, I thought, as I realized I could update the Trike Asylum website with expedition news, eat and drink to my heart's delight, and then lazily ride to a campground to call it a day. I had only come 38 miles today, but the heat had definitely sapped my reserves and I welcomed a lazy afternoon. A public temperature reading at the local bank indicated 94 degrees, and it wasn't over yet – still climbing.

My mind was in vegetable mode, feeling somewhat refreshed in the air conditioned library for the hour it took to get the text written and the photo uploaded. The ICE Qnt was outside, not secured in any way, but my experience, and that of other overland trikers, has repeatedly demonstrated that there is little fear of someone stealing a tricycle with bags full of dirty clothes and food bars. Whenever I leave it, I park right in front of a busy place, and take my wallet and digital camera with me. Everything else is replaceable. By this time in the journey, my camera held more value to me than my wallet, because I would never be able to replace the photographs I had taken of Glen, Gary, and me on our trip.

After the library, I shopped Grocery Outlet and ate the food by my trike out front. Then I refilled my empty CamelBak water bladders and water bottles. During this time, I was approached and spoken to by a variety of what some might call less than desirable people. It's just a time when you get a gut feeling that you are surrounded by folks who may not share your own values of life. Four guys got out of a Ford pickup at one point, as dirty as dirty could be, with filthy dreadlock hair. They paid no mind to me, but this got my mind to thinking again.

There are two prisons not far east of Susanville. One is federal and the other is state. What this means is that many of the inmates' friends and relatives take up temporary residence in apartments in Susanville while their object of affection is serving the criminal sentence. What I was seeing certainly was consistent with this dynamic of prison towns. As I was contemplating this, a man in his mid 80s walked by and began questioning me about the trike and what I was doing. He used to own a bicycle shop in his heyday. He was also convinced that I was handicapped and steered this contraption with my feet.

I showed him the handlebars, and dispelled any physical impairment notion. I asked him if there was a campground nearby, and he indicated there was one about a half mile away, but that I would enjoy camping down by the river primitively better, about a mile west, which was not on my route. Then he wanted to know how I was going to get to southern California. I told him I'd be riding US Highway 395 from here south, and he quickly informed me that I would meet the grim reaper out there with all the traffic: "Hamburger! They'll make hamburger out of you!" he emphatically said. I didn't stand a snowball's chance in hell of reaching my destination alive or in one piece.

Well, of course, he was thinking with bicycle brains and 395 of the old days, when there were few decent shoulders along this route. Riding a tricycle nowadays is a different story entirely, but I was not going to attempt convincing him. My time was becoming valuable again because I was now thinking that I should not camp around here at all, so I decided to head on out of this northern California prison town. I had just dwindled away 2 full hours thinking I had no farther to go, and now I decide to go. At the very least, I was now well rested, well fed, and the website had an update for those following my triangular shenanigans.

The highway ahead was mostly flat all the way into Nevada, the sun was still rather high in the sky, being just past 4:00 PM, and I was refreshed with a motivation to keep on triking for a while. I pulled out of the parking lot into the busy city street, and started booking southeast as fast as my legs and lungs would carry me. Before you knew it, I was past the city limits, and soon to pass the turnoffs to the two prisons. I was making good time, and had been told by a couple of folks in

Susanville that there was a KOA out here 15 miles, so spirits were high.

The shoulder was very wide and well paved, so it was easy to remain in high gears and crank out the miles. The trouble was though, that mile 15 came and went, as did mile 20, and mile 25, and there was no KOA campground anywhere to be found. There was one small no-name campground about a mile south of Highway 395 on a sandy dirt road, so that did me no good on a one-wheel drive tricycle. The shadow of my trike and me was stretching ever farther ahead of my eastbound figure, so I knew it was time to get serious about finding a sleeping spot. Up ahead, just past the 30 mile spot from Susanville, was a 24-hour convenience store and gasoline station. The sun was nearing its set. I would see what they had to say, throwing myself on their mercy.

I pulled in, ravenously hungry again after cranking out 30 miles in record time, so bought a couple of sandwiches and V8 juices, along with some bananas. I talked to the clerk about anywhere here I could simply pitch a tent overnight. He pointed to a large steel storage bin on a small hill just beyond the store, right off the highway, and said he would notify the owner I was going to tent there. I had permission, so I could relax even though there were people coming and going continually at the brightly lit gas station, and nonstop vehicles zooming by.

The day finished with me riding through a few goathead thorns over to the storage container, which kept me hidden from the cars and trucks on US Highway 395. The bright lights of the store were not going to be a problem for me because after such an active day of 68 hard fought miles, I would have no problem at all sleeping. I had been kept relatively cool during this final stretch as big rigs and motorhomes would speed by, creating a huge cooling air blast with each vehicle. Bring it on, I thought, the bigger and faster the vehicle the better!

DAY 15 - *Eastern Sierras*
Friday – September 09, 2011
30 miles east of Susanville to southern Reno, Nevada - 65 miles
(running total: 549 miles)

My tent was in direct line with the first light of day, so I was up like a bunny before the sun. The convenience of a mini-mart 30 yards to the west meant a warm flush toilet, a triker's friend on a cold morn. After packing away my totally dry tent, I rolled the trike over to the little wooden picnic table on the walkway of the mini-mart in the parking area. As I ate, I visually checked my tires for goathead thorns, and found three of the little buggers. Since I run Schwalbe Marathon Plus tires, there is absolutely no danger of flats from these gremlins of

230

the bicycle world, so I just pulled them out with total confidence that no air would follow through the microscopic holes. I love these tires!

The distance to the northern outskirts of Reno, Nevada from this gasoline and food outpost is about 55 miles via 395, and much of the route is flat and fast, although hills do finally show up towards the Nevada state boundary. Every once in a while, there was a descent that brought a grin to my face. The closer I pedaled to Reno, the heavier the traffic became, but since US 395 is four lanes in many spots, and since the shoulders are super wide most of the way, this increase presented no problem at all. Gary and I could have easily ridden side by side!

As I rode along, I realized that here I was, just over two weeks into this trip, and my Achilles tendons were perfectly normal, with no swelling like what happened to me a couple years ago on my first trip when I wore regular hiking shoes and used pedal straps instead of SPD bindings. So, with many miles yet before me, my head came up with a little rhyme that kept me amused with my own intellectual genius: *"Day after day, Pedaling away, Achilles tendons still okay."*

I crossed another imaginary boundary with a sign that informed me I was entering the Silver State, otherwise known as Nevada. There is a human outpost at this border, named Border Town, and it sits on a large hill overlooking a massive and foreboding dry lake, with residential homes off to the north, across the arid expanse of desert. It was a slow pedal up to Border Town, and now the highway dipped down into the dry lake drainage, and then began a daunting ascent on the other side of the valley, where the pavement looked like it went straight up in the shimmering heat induced visual distortion, just like in old west movies.

Once across the Nevada state line, Highway 395 takes on the appearance and characteristics of a full blown American freeway, with two lanes in each direction and exit signs, suggesting that this was a limited access roadway. There were no signs indicating that human powered cyclists could not ride here however, so I booked on down the long slope at a respectable clip, knowing that in a few minutes the endless sun drenched uphill on the other side would be my companion.

The day was really beginning to cook, with temperatures in the low 90s already. Traffic was heavy, with that annoying rubber tire whine of motorized vehicles a never ending drone in my ears. The shoulder was more than ample, so all I had to do was keep turning the crank until I got to Reno, or wherever my speed would take me before sundown. Pedaling up out of the dry lake sink was tough, and I was going through my water supply at break-neck speed. Jack had told me to exit the highway at North Virginia Street, because several miles past that, it really does turn into a super freeway with 5 lanes in each direction, and state law prohibits cyclists. Glad I had called Jack back in Klamath Falls.

Sure enough, as North Virginia appeared a quarter mile ahead, there was the sign telling me to get my sorry carcass off the petroleum based roadway ("BICYCLES MUST EXIT"), dumping me onto surface streets I had never ridden or driven before, and leaving me with only my faith in the state's road planning division that I could make it to where I wanted to go. This was fine with me because I was really hot, almost out of water, and in need of some shade from the sun. I pulled into an unusual business called Sierra Zoo to ask directions and get water.

In the shade of the parking lot, a friendly Mexican American family began chatting with me about my trike and trip. We had a lot of fun talking as my body temperature slowly returned to normal while I guzzled the final drops from my water bottles. Once inside the air conditioned reception area of the zoo, I purchased a pint of ice cold Arrowhead water, talked to the zoo keepers, used the restroom, refilled all my water containers, and then pedaled out into the hot hilly up and down terrain as I headed into the town of Reno. This surface street had no shoulder this far out, but as I got closer to the city, shoulders would appear every once in a while,and disappear just as frequently. Visibility is perfect out here, so cars gave me plenty of berth.

After many hot hills, I finally began dropping down into the city limits of Reno, Nevada, a bustling gambling hot spot for the state. I passed the university, where I noticed college aged people on bicycles, and then crossed some seriously busy 5-way intersections packed with bumper to bumper petroleum puffers on their hurried harried way to somewhere else. Putting on my invisible "share the road" armor, into battle I went! Well, that's a little dramatic because even though traffic was insane at this Friday afternoon rush hour time, I was, as always, granted full road rights by every motorist who was gawking at my bizarre looking rig and attempting in vain to figure out what the heck I was. My power was in my weird appearance. Trikers have an edge!

With my bright yellow pannier rain covers, and my yellow and orange flagging, I stood out as the most visible vehicle around. If you don't want attention, don't ride a trike in the city! Attention is yours whether you want it or not, which of course, is a great safety advantage trikers have over bicyclists. My route took the Q and me straight down the main drag of Reno, a street choked with massive colorful casinos, thousands of people, and a blatant "in your face" commercialization designed wholly to separate gamblers from their money. It was a jungle.

Everything about Reno is bizarre, so all the pedestrians and motorists staring at me probably just figured I was one more oddity among millions. Now on Virginia Street, driven by every gambler who ever visits this mad money mecca, the road remains two lanes in each direction, but with cars parked at the curb, and the sidewalks brimming with throngs of humans, the only place left to pedal my tiny tricycle was in one of the lanes. In my favor was the fact that signals every block kept rush hour traffic slow, so my pace matched what the cars were doing. In fact, when there were traffic backups, my trike and I moved right to the head of the line, using what little space I could find. I know it sounds horrible, and to a greenhorn triker I suppose it would have been a triker's hell, but I actually thought the experience was fun.

As time went by, the air temperature dropped into the upper 80s, and the shadows of the colossal casinos kept me well shaded, so I turned on my flashing taillight to aid visibility. Looking off into the distance, it was clear the air was not, clear that is. Air pollution is a part of life here, a far cry from where I started this journey on the pure Oregon coast. Well, diversity is one of life's spices! I like to breathe air.

At long last, having passed through several miles of the most downtown portions of downtown, the road began to widen and I again had some breathing room. This was the southern portion of Reno, and as the sun was moving closer to the horizon, I recalled a motel I stayed at once years ago with my mom and a friend of hers. So, when I reached the Meadowood Courtyard, I pulled in off the busy main street and got a room. It was a hot hard day, and I wanted to relax in style. Besides, there was no place to camp in this over sized human zoo. I got caught up on laundry, had a nice shower, updated the trike website, and then went to sleep in total quiet, trike inside the room for security. To date, I had pedaled almost 550 miles from the ocean.

DAY 16 - *Eastern Sierras*
Saturday – September 10, 2011
Reno, Nevada to Topaz Lake, Nevada - 63 miles
(running total: 612 miles)

The room's telephone rang at 5:45 AM since I had requested a wake up call from the front desk. My internal clock works pretty well however, and I had actually arisen about 15 minutes prior. I prefer the wild spaces to a gambling metropolis, so after eating a complimentary breakfast just off the motel's lobby area, I hightailed it out of there. The sun was just cresting over the eastern mountains at 6:53 AM as I pedaled my trike out of the parking lot, southbound on Highway 395.

It was now Saturday morning, so there were no work-bound commuters in cars today. Streets were mostly empty and wide open, and I kept a fast pace in high gears through all the successive green traffic lights right out of town. The air was yet crisp, so maintaining speed was a snap. The 2 bananas, 1 blueberry yogurt, and 2 Quaker instant oatmeal packets would last me for a while before I would have to delve into my cargo stash for energy bars later on.

At some small town several miles south, I had to pee, and since this was a major route through Nevada and California, and I was not yet out of residential and commercial areas, I stopped in at a custom cabinet shop that happened to be open on a Saturday morning. As their old shaggy company dog came over to sniff me, the lady owner pointed to a plastic outhouse. Works for me! A trike hobo takes what he can get.

I was now on my way to Carson City, the capitol of Nevada. This portion of highway allowed motorists to travel 70 miles per hour, but again, the shoulders were so darn wide that I actually had more room most of the time than the car lanes provided! I couldn't complain. At one point, a large white sign with black letters proclaimed: BICYCLES MUST EXIT, just like the one at North Virginia Street yesterday. I could see the "Old 395" highway about a quarter mile to my west, but since they were doing some road construction through here, they had those large concrete dividers placed along the shoulder, and on the other side where the exit had been for bicycles to leave the freeway, the off-ramp was heavily excavated, with a lot of construction machinery everywhere. It was literally impossible to exit even if I wanted to.

Like a rat, I was trapped! I was on a slight down grade here however, so I cranked along at 20 something, pretending that I could keep up with my neighbors whizzing by 50 miles per hour faster. As the miles rolled by, I watched lucky bicyclists on their Saturday morning rides on Old 395 leisurely pedaling along, but still there was no method for me getting over there, separated by several fences and expanses of farmland. At long last, as a really steep uphill approached, an exit allowed me to depart this high speed madness onto the old country road, where I discovered a shaded gully with lots of trees where I could inconspicuously offload water. Then, up the hill I went, after a food bar.

At the top, I met a couple of bicyclists, and asked directions into Carson City. This old section of highway turned into the mountains, and the lady told me about a convoluted route that I was sure not to remember. My only other option was to re-enter the cyclist-restricted freeway, ride downhill about a mile on the shoulder, and exit onto the main street of Carson City, which I opted to do. It was much faster, very direct, and harbored no chance of me getting lost in the hills and wasting needless time and calories trying to find my way.

The on-ramp displayed a sign prohibiting vehicles of my propulsion paradigm from entering the sacred realm created exclusively for oil burners. Still in possession of an aggressive attitude when necessary to deal with certain adversarial aspects of life, I let the sign be damned and proceeded full speed ahead. It was over in an instant, as my 52 tooth chainring and my 11 tooth rear cog shot me down to the next exit in nothing flat, where I continued to coast at high speed onto the main surface street of town, right into an Albertsons supermarket to resupply my cereal bin with some vanilla almond granola. In front of the market, comfortably on my recumbent seat, I scarfed down on a large box of strawberries, a banana, and a Naked brand protein drink, while a local business executive, casually observing my apparently nomadic lifestyle, wanted to know how a well educated gent like myself had the time to take a journey like this.

I told him I had rethought life, decided that money would no longer be my master, and had embarked on a multifaceted odyssey to exist in a simpler and gentler manner on my planet. Of course, he likely thought this impossible in our modern society, as he enjoyed a brief weekend respite from his demanding work commitments, yet for some strange reason, was reluctant to leave my presence. It was as if he may have ever so briefly seen the insanity of his 9 to 5 routine flash before him, and perhaps glimpsed some light on my odd path. I wondered if our conversation would have any impact on his future as I left the parking lot. One can only hope. I am happy to have evolved past the norm!

Saturday traffic through Carson City was still light, which was pleasurable in the restricted downtown area around the capitol building. Towards the southern end of town, the streets widened, and traffic thickened some as it headed south to Gardnerville. At one point, I just hopped onto the wide sidewalks, as the town had opted to turn the former road shoulder and bicycle lane into a third southbound lane for cars (we all know how important it is for commerce to keep those cars speeding along unhindered, right?). It was just easier for several blocks, but then I returned onto the roadway for the rural area to Gardnerville.

Once in Gardnerville, I noticed a growing number of emergency vehicles with blaring sirens screaming past me. I stopped at a store to cool off and get an ice cold protein drink, but they did not yet know what all the commotion was about. Local high school kids were holding a car wash in this parking lot, and wanted to wash my trike. Some of the older girls were provocatively dressed to attract their testosterone laden male counterparts. I continued in the 86 degree heat.

As it turned out, there was a lightning strike forest fire in the Pine Nut Mountains north of Topaz Lake, Nevada, and all fire fighting and emergency personnel from local, state, and federal agencies were dispatched to go fight it. You'd never know there were so many of these vehicles if this event hadn't made them all come out of the woodwork. For hours, they passed me going up into the mountains, as the sky was becoming increasingly black with thunderheads. The air temperature was cooling dramatically now, allowing for more vigorous pedaling without overheating. Up ahead, it looked like rain was drenching the terrain.

Then the road got serious in its up angle, one of those "spin and grin" grades where you throw time to the wind with the goal to simply keep making forward progress. A little sprinkle of water hit me in the face. I tried to ignore it, but another one came, and then yet another. Wouldn't you know it! I had been pedaling for days, sweating up a storm in the ever present hot sun, even through the Oregon and northern California mountain ranges, and now the weather was flip-flopping in a big way. Before I could stop and get on my rain gear, the clouds opened up above me, one of those deals where you get wet so fast that it's not worth putting rain clothing on top of already wet clothes. I like being watered by the trike gods on my most excellent hobo adventure.

Becoming wetter by the minute, I spied what looked like an abandoned building up ahead on the left, accessible by a short dirt driveway. This was the Simee Dimeh grade I was ascending, and I wondered if the rain would let up today. I pulled the trike under a wide overhang of the roof of this building, a commercial property with "for sale" signs on it. There was scattered furniture inside, but no people anywhere around, so I figured I might as well hang out here for a bit to see what develops. The building was surrounded by a stubby juniper forest, which smelled wonderful in the rain.

A breeze was blowing, and for the first few minutes, I was getting a little chilled, but as my clothes dried out, I discovered the breeze was kind of balmy, relatively speaking. Once my shirt was mostly dry, I put on my rain jacket, contemplating options in my head on what to do next. More fire fighters sped by in their big fire trucks. The rain finally let up as the blackest clouds began to migrate to the west of my location, probably now covering and raining on Gardnerville far below.

For a few moments, I contemplated pitching my tent for the night right here on the concrete covered porch, but as the roads became drier, and passing traffic was throwing up hardly any spray from the tires, I decided I should move on up the mountain, and see if I could make it to Topaz Lake before dark. Normally, it would not have been a question, but since I stayed put here for about 40 minutes, I lost a fair amount of riding time. Shortly before I got back in my trike to leave, fire vehicles began returning down the mountain. What nature had started, nature had also extinguished, beyond the ability of mere mortal humans.

The summit was slow in coming. I passed billboards with

photos of taco dinners and other culinary delights for 99 cents at the Topaz Lodge on my way to the top of more than 6,000 vertical feet above sea level. By the time I reached the summit pass, and started descending towards Topaz Lake, I needed to turn on my lights, even though the hour was not that late, because the heavy black cloud cover was totally obscuring the sun. The sprinkles started again. It was getting darker real fast. On each downhill section, I poured the coals to the furnace to make time before the sky opened up again. It was looking far more foreboding now than earlier. I was in for a real soaker it seemed.

And then, spread out before my watchful eyes, was the lake, all downhill. This would be a 40 mile per hour coast to the lodge, which I had decided to stay in tonight because it was readily apparent a huge rainstorm was imminent, and I just didn't feel like pitching my tent in those conditions tonight. My timing was a little better this time. As I rolled down the ultra steep driveway the final 50 yards to the motel on the side of the mountain just above the lake, the heavy rain began. I parked the trike under the motel overhang just in the nick of time!

It was getting so dark by this time anyway that proceeding farther to a campground and trying to set a camp was out of the question. I happily paid the clerk the hefty fee for a room, figuring that it was only money, and why not live out my adventure called life as I see fit at the time. Money, what little I have of it anyway, is my servant, not my master as it is with so many humans I know. I updated my trike website again with the motel's free computer station. More than six hundred miles were now knocked off, and I was about to sleep like a king on a king sized bed in this drenching night-long rainstorm.

DAY 17 - *Eastern Sierras*
Sunday – September 11, 2011
Topaz Lake, Nevada to Bridgeport, California - 44 miles
(running total: 656 miles)

Now past all the sprawling major metro areas, the wake-up call I postponed until 6:00 AM, but, just like in Reno, I was awake and moving before that dreaded telephone chimed in. It's absolutely amazing that my brain works when I'm off duty at night. Heck, I'm just happy that it works as well as it does during my waking hours. It's like I schedule a wake-up call in my brain, and somehow, it wakes me right on cue! Does that happen to you also? Triker brains are amazing!

The sun got the drop on me today, and was already slightly above the mountains to the east by the time I left the motel. Clouds were also present, so I wondered what the day would bring in the way of weather. Now up in the mountains with cloud cover, riding was easier than in the heat of the Modoc National Forest several days ago. My trek was moving south, into the eastern Sierra Nevada Range, known for deep snow later in the season. Hopefully, I had planned the timing of the trip well enough that I'd pass through these mountains before any early and unexpected white stuff made its way down.

About a half mile south of the Topaz Lake Lodge, I pulled into my second California Agricultural Inspection Station, and left the State of Nevada behind. The gal there did not take any photos of my trike, and just motioned me through without asking if I was carrying any fruit flies into her state. Guess she figured I didn't have room to hide any of that contraband in my cargo bags. Do fruit flies honor state boundaries?

This is a very beautiful stretch of road, called the Eastern Sierra Scenic Byway, which goes from here up to and through the small old town of Bridgeport, California,. As the elevation increases, so do the trees change from dry juniper and pinyon to larger evergreen varieties. I passed through the small villages of Coleville and Walker, and then the climb into the Sierras began in earnest, at least from the mindset of a triker who is pedaling up the grade. What takes minutes in cars requires hours with a self propelled tricycle. My estimate, based on my daily averages since Day 12, was that I should be able to make it to the Yosemite portal town of Lee Vining for my overnight camp today.

There were enough areas of mid range gearing that I made decent time, but what I was heading into made me wonder if I really wanted to get there any sooner than I had to. The sky was again darkening, and much sooner today than yesterday. Mountains tend to create their own weather patterns, and I was now getting higher than yesterday's ride. A crack of lightning, so loud that it made me jump, sounded off to my port side. Okay, that's getting a little too close for me, one of those deals where you start counting "one thousand one" but never get to the two! Moments later, it happened a second time.

For a few interesting miles, helicopters swooped right down over me to fill their hanging buckets with water from a nearby water reservoir, apparently in an attempt to extinguish yet another lightning strike fire. With my slow moving trike on this grade, I got to watch this helicopter activity for quite some time. I also got to watch numerous lightning strikes in the mountains above me, right where I was headed, a tiny unshielded triker with my lightning pole (also known as my flag pole) just asking for a mega volt zap. Wouldn't that make a great story!

The grade up to Devil's Gate Pass, at an elevation of 7,519 feet, is roughly 27 miles long, and about 7 miles from the summit, guess what happened. Yep, sure enough, a sudden and sustained rain burst forth from the thunderheads above. In nothing flat, I was soaked, far more than yesterday. By the way, I did try putting on my rain pants yesterday, but learned that the nylon webbing inside got hopelessly stuck to the exaggerated lug sole of my mountain bike shoes, so I just gave up. I had worn these pants two years prior when I used standard hiking shoes on the trike, and those shoes slipped through just fine. Lesson learned: get rain pants with no mesh lining! And, test ahead of time.

Even though I had my expensive Gore-Tex mountaineering rain jacket on, it was not enough to keep me dry. I also had on my rain and windproof motorcycling gloves, but with standard cotton pants, and no coverings on my shoes, a thorough soaking was my destiny today. Motorists attempted to swing way wide to keep their tire spray off me, but in some areas that was not possible, so I took even more soaking. I wonder if those drivers thought I was a little bit nuts. Gee whiz, even I started wondering about that myself. Normal I'm not.

But then it occurred to me that I was not locked into some cubical at the office in a mega city, shouldering the stresses of deadlines and negative human interactions. I was not stuck in rush hour traffic and listening to honking horns. This water is no big deal. Humans are waterproof. So is my tricycle. My clothes will dry. I was having the time of my life, and after crossing the summit, it was all one big thrill ride down the other side into the quaint mountain town of Bridgeport. So here I am, doing about 40 miles per hour in the pouring rain, with petroleum propelled humans in their climate controlled automobiles wondering what in the world was wrong with my brain. Either that or wishing they were having such a gloriously wonderful adventure.

You know how you really know you're soaked? When you can feel cold water running down the crack in your rear end, and exiting into the mesh of your recumbent seat, that's how! Once you reach that point, there is no longer any thought of staying dry. You can only get so wet, right? Then, you might as well have fun with your situation! It's only water. It was a free shower and laundry on the move.

So I was having fun, with my aggressive attitude of rocketing down the mountain on my ICE trike, water spraying into the air from my three wheels. I was making my own little water vapor trail. How cool is that? It was a lot of fun until the shoulder up ahead disappeared at one point on a straightaway and those miserable rumble strips, instead of stopping like they normally do, ran off at an angle into the dirt at the side of the pavement. This necessitated me coasting over them at high speed, something that is doable on dry pavement with only a little bit of shake, but on wet ground, I found myself instantly cocked partially sideways to my direction of travel, facing somewhat towards the traffic lane on my left. It was over in a split second. I turned in the direction of the skid and straightened myself out before I flipped. Once the episode was finished, I can say it was definitely thrilling in a strange sort of way.

By the time I had Bridgeport in my view, the air temperature had dropped even more, and at speed, with my wet clothing, I was getting very cold. Even wearing my heavy waterproof gloves, my fingers were cold enough that I had to keep placing my hands behind the handlebar grips to keep the wind off. Water was pouring off the bill of my cap, and my sunglasses made things look even darker. I had no clear glasses, so it was dark glass or no glass over my eyes.

My original intent this morning was to ride up and over 8,138 foot Conway Summit south of Bridgeport, and camp somewhere in the vicinity of Lee Vining, a small eastern Sierra tourist town near the otherworldly Mono Lake. That would have made for a day's ride of roughly 70 miles, a doable objective during a 10 hour trek in these early days of September. However, the deteriorating condition of my body that resulted from the colder wet weather demanded that I seek shelter in Bridgeport, cutting my day short at 44 miles. Those elusive 26 miles would just have to wait until tomorrow, and hopefully dry sky!

To attempt any more mileage today would have been foolhardy, so after rolling into historic Bridgeport, I found the Silver Maple Inn, an old motel my mom and I had stayed in many years ago. It's nothing fancy, but it offered warmth and dryness, two things I was in desperate need of at the moment. Into the office I walked, dripping water, and attempting to speak to the clerk with my wind-numbed jaw. I can only imagine what she was thinking, seeing this really strange bike drive in during a high altitude rainstorm, and so I offered up my most intelligent speech to assure her I was an educated man who happened to get caught in less than ideal circumstances.

As I removed some cash from my wallet to pay for the room, I glanced at the wall clock behind her and noticed it was only 3:30 PM. Gads, I would never have guessed it! The sky had been so dark for so long now that I would have sworn it was much later, especially with my dark sunglasses on. For the briefest of seconds, the thought occurred to me that Lee Vining was still within my reach today, but I again decided that attempting to ride over Conway Summit could be disastrous, so I semi reluctantly stayed put. No sense in pushing my luck. I was here in one piece, and would live to ride again tomorrow.

I parked my trike right outside the window of my room where it was fully visible to me. The extra deep roof overhang kept the Q totally out of the weather. There was no way it would fit in this little bedroom. Besides, I had to turn on the furnace and lay all my clothes out on chairs to dry, which took up all remaining floor space. I prefer cotton pants, shirts, and socks, which work well until they get soaked, and then they require extended drying times. I turned up the heat to get the job done, but it became too unbearable for me, so I had to open the windows and let the breeze through. Being so early in the day, this was the first time that I actually watched some television at a motel.

The historic courthouse was right across the little dirt street to the east of my room. If I recall properly, it is the oldest functioning courthouse in the State of California. Back in the 1970s when I applied for a job with Mono County, I visited the inside of this stately old building, and it is quite worth one's time to see. As it began getting dark, the sky also began to clear, and a while after nightfall, I could see the nearly full moon outside the window. It would have made for an incredible night ride! Oh well, I'm comfy, and will enjoy my lot.

DAY 18 - *Eastern Sierras*
Monday – September 12, 2011
Bridgeport, California to McGee Creek Campground - 60 miles
(running total: 716 miles)

Today I arose early, while yet dark outside. My clothes were dry. The sky seemed mostly clear. I had many long miles of mountains ahead today, the dramatic ups and downs of the magnificent eastern Sierra Nevada Range, so I wanted to get cranking as soon as possible. I could feel the deep high altitude chill in the air as walked out the door of my room and placed my loaded panniers on the trike once again, a ritual with which I was by now well accustomed. I would wear my polar fleece jacket with my rain jacket over it, along with my heavy duty water and wind proof motorcycle gloves. I would not be cold for long though.

The wheels of my tricycle hit the southbound pavement of Highway 395 again as first light was beginning to paint the eastern sky over western Nevada. This part of California was next to receive sun, but due to the relatively small mountains between the two states here, I would be riding a long time in the very nippy shade. The good news was that I had 13 miles to pedal up to the crest of Conway Summit, and that activity would keep my furnace burning, providing warmth despite my totally exposed trike. The engine of any vehicle gets warm and hot going uphill, and since I am the organic engine of this little rig, I was about to start the warming process. This engine does not poison the air however.

The gearing I had chosen for this trek was working out perfectly. The middle chainring of 39 teeth provided an ample range that got me up many gentler inclines, such as some of the ones on this grade,

241

and when need be, the small ring of 26 teeth got me up the rest with little effort. It was slow, but it was also not difficult from a physical stress or endurance standpoint. I estimated that it required a little over 3 hours to reach the top, but not being a wearer of a chronograph, there was no way to know. It didn't matter anyway, as I do what I can.

While pedaling, I always have plenty of time to take in the awesome vistas. While soaking it all in, my mind drifted to my mom's and sister's birthdays, one of the reasons I was making this trip south in the first place. Willow, my sister, has hers the middle of September, and before the journey had begun, I told her on the telephone that my arrival time would likely be the very end of September, or maybe even the first part of October. Riding with two other trikers, I could not predict how the odyssey would play out, so I left it open. Mom's birthday was in November, so I knew I'd be there for sure by then.

Reflecting on the daily mileages I had been pulling off since going solo, I began to wonder if it might be at all possible to reach Apple Valley, where my mom and sister both live, by my sister's birthday. That would be special, but up to this point, I had not seriously entertained the idea. My body was doing fine. I had no issues with Achilles tendons swelling, and my feet were holding up well, with only minor hot spots at times, which were quickly vanquished by getting off the trike and standing now and then. My knees have always been non-problematic for me, so there was nothing physical to prevent me from pushing the distance envelope if it looked realistic.

I was still too far out to know for sure at this point of the journey, as the weather can play an influential part in a day's progress, but once I got through the eastern Sierra Nevada mountain portions of this ride, the rest was wide open desert, and perhaps I could make the birthday in time. My nature has always been one of competitiveness within myself, seeing if I am up to the task of doing something new, pushing my own limits. This thought was now in my head, and it wouldn't go away. The trip had not started with a set time frame in mind, but triking by myself, I now had only my self to satisfy.

I missed the camaraderie that had developed with Glen and Gary. When the journey started, I was open to however long it would take. I was in no hurry, wishing only to have a good time together and keep everyone healthy and happy. They were no longer with me however, so any amendments to the schedule were now my choice. Actually, there had never been a schedule, other than I had to be at the Los Angeles County Fairplex by the third week of October for the Recumbent Cycle Convention. There was more than ample time left.

Low lying foggy clouds graced the summit that I was now

approaching. Huge snow banks adorned the hills to the southwest of this pinnacle of 395. Traffic was very light this early. Other than the one Mexican family that had stopped to get their photos taken with me about two miles back, I had no company on the way to the top other than the natural world that so abundantly surrounded me. I am at peace in nature, which is the determining factor behind my choice of tricycling routes. Traffic does not frighten me, but it interferes with my personal enjoyment of my planet, thus I pedal the roads far less traveled.

Having taken the practically obligatory summit photo, as if it were Everest rather than Conway, it was time to descend, and descend it would indeed be! Two signs provided dramatic clues. One read: 6% GRADE 4 MILES, and the other: STEEP GRADES SHARP CURVES AHEAD, and had an iconic depiction of an eighteen wheeler truck tipping over. I was well aware of this grade from many years of automobile travel through the area. This would be one hell of an electrifying tricycle ride to the bottom! It just doesn't get any better!

Clicked into the pedals once again, helmet secured, I easily pedaled over the top. Within seconds, I was speeding faster than I could pedal, and noticed the big overlook rapidly approaching. Well, I just had to get that photograph too, the one that would dramatically show the elevation loss I was about to experience, so I braked and rolled into the turnout. Trike against the guardrail, I snapped a few photos of massive Mono Lake at the bottom, spreading out for miles, and could determine essentially where Lee Vining sat way down there. The road coming out the bottom of this mega hill was a thin tiny ribbon, with semi tractor trailer trucks appearing like miniature toys from this high vantage point.

This was no place not to make sure my trike would not roll while I was off it, for if it ever got away from me, well, you get the picture. Speaking of pictures, my original intent was to hold my digital Kodak camera in my right hand, secured to a small tripod, so I could take a movie of the ride down, but it just wasn't worth the potential consequence of flipping the trike at 50+ miles per hour. Nope, this type of descent would have to be filmed in the future sometime after I acquired a GoPro Hero digital camera, the minuscule electronic wonders that attach to the helmet, leaving the hands free to operate the controls of the trike. I had thought about getting one for this trip, but decided it was not a wise investment of my limited funds. I'll save up!

Descending Conway Summit is a screaming adrenaline rush of the highest order on a recumbent tadpole tricycle, where one's every fiber of concentration is focused intently on controlling the trike. Very low sitting trikes like mine are extremely stable at this speed, and instill tremendous confidence in the rider, but you still have to keep both hands on the grips and a couple fingers of each hand lightly ready at the brakes. Control is simply a matter of keeping the bars straight, not looking anywhere but straight ahead, and not making any abrupt directional movements. Use only peripheral vision to notice anything to the sides, for if you turn your head to look, it could well result it severe wobbling, which at this speed then results in seriously crashing.

Even though the shoulder is very wide here, it is just too risky to ride on it at high speed. First of all, there is always junk on highway shoulders, and I don't want junk popping up in front of me at speeds where sudden swerving to miss the debris could roll the trike, and thereby really ruin my day. Secondly, if something unexpected were to happen, I wanted to be away from the guardrail to give myself some maneuvering room. It's clearly time to "take a lane", as cyclists say.

I only brake on descents if an approaching curve demands a slower speed. The more open gradual curves, as these are, allow body leaning to compensate for a trike's inability to lean, with only slight braking necessary in a couple of instances. Since there are two lanes in each direction, my position in the slow lane was not an issue for passing cars, and since the traffic was still very light anyway, the road felt like it belonged to me for my personal run at light speed.

Most drivers were cautiously doing about 55 miles per hour down this steep mountain pass, so they were not passing me at much of a speed faster than my own, which is a real head trip compared to normal triking on flat or uphill terrain. Imagine going nearly as fast as petroleum powered cars! It would have been fun to glance over and see their faces, but glancing over could have spelled disaster for me.

Reaching the apex of 8,138 foot Conway Summit, I was averaging just under 4 miles per hour, so 4 miles would take about one hour. On the way down the other side, those 4 miles at 6% grade whipped by so fast that I was wanting for more at the bottom (it took less than 5 minutes). The final miles into Lee Vining, (population 398, elevation 6,781, gasoline $4.99) where I ate an early lunch at a little store, were slightly downhill and flat, with easy uphills. The shoulder remained plenty wide. In fact, most of US Highway 395 has fantastic trike shoulders most of the way from Susanville to Victorville (I don't know who Susan and Victor were, but I rode between their two villes with no issues concerning petroleum propelled vehicles). Commenting on this highway, it was not uncommon to see that my shoulder was even wider than the automobile lanes to my left! I recommend this route.

South of Lee Vining, the road enters a more heavily forested mountainous area on the way to Mammoth Lakes snow resort area. As with my experience the prior two days, I noticed storm clouds brewing once again over the peaks, and making their way over my head as I pedaled through the woods. Would I get a drenching yet again today?

There is a beautiful loop through the June Lake area, with the northern portion intersecting US Highway 395 about 5 miles south of Lee Vining, and coming back into the main highway another 6 miles south of that. Gary has a good friend who has a cabin in there, and we were contemplating doing the loop originally, but since I was now solo, I pedaled on by the 16 mile diversion route. Another 4 miles past the southern entrance to June Lake, I crested Deadman Summit, at 8,041 feet above Earth's ocean. Happily, I was feeling very much alive and overflowing with energy as I took in all the mountain splendor of this amazing area. I find myself wondering how this summit earned its name.

I stopped mid afternoon at the Crestview Safety Rest Area, graciously supplied by the California Department of Transportation. It is a couple of miles south of Deadman Summit. This is the only formal rest area along this section, and is a wonderful place to stretch, offload solid waste, eat, take on water, and enjoy the forest. The parking area is huge, way off the road, and nestled in the towering pines.

South of Crestview, the weather finally caught up with me for a while, but not in liquid form like on Saturday and Sunday. No, today it was hail for about 15 minutes! And, because it was my lucky day, the hail was not the really big kind that hurts when it hits. The hailstorm was really pretty light, so it was kind of fun while it lasted. Even though I came through it predominantly dry, I was again motivated to get off this high region quickly, so I took advantage of the downhill segments and pedaled like hell. It can be hard to outrun a storm on a tricycle!

As it turned out, I was successful in my quest to ride out of it, and back into sunshine. I was totally dry in nothing flat. Oh the joy! The views up here are absolutely spectacular, rivaling any alpine region. It is one captivating ride, especially since the ultra wide shoulders would keep even a novice triker calm. If you enjoy miles of forests and magnificent mountains, consider a trike ride through the eastern Sierras!

Terrain was mostly downhill now into the Mammoth Lakes area, a major eastern California ski mecca. The afternoon sun was steadily moving westward, and I didn't know what I would find for camping, but I was making great time in high gears, so kept on triking south and east towards Crowley Lake. There was one more high pass to cross at the southeastern portion of this high plateau, but the ascent from this side is mild, and I doubted I would make it that far today. There were campgrounds along the way, but they were off the highway far enough (measured in miles) that I preferred to find something, primitive if necessary, right along the roadway. If I were to have any hope of making my sister's birthday in time, I could not afford the luxury of side trips and lingering for too long.

Crowley Lake was up ahead in the distance, on the left side of the highway, and there was a side road that might provide access to a hidden niche where I could pitch camp. I was now in the full shadow of the Sierras, and motivated to end this day's ride. It was my lucky day, as I next read a sign that told about McGee Creek Campground. Wow, just in the nick of time, I took the exit, rode a couple hundred yards, and rolled into the graveled entrance to McGee. How quaint! An old log cabin was the office. Immediately I loved this place! Time to relax again.

The couple who owned this cozy slice of mountain heaven were laid back and very friendly. I got a great little wooded campsite right on the bank of McGee Creek, with aspen trees all around, and the sound of rushing water. I pitched the tent, and then walked over to the office and bought an ice cream sandwich. Sixty miles moved past my three wheels today, a ribbon of pavement that would have taken a motorized vehicle about an hour to travel. I crawled into my tent, 711 miles from Florence, Oregon, and all was well.

DAY 19 - *Eastern Sierras*
Tuesday – September 13, 2011
McGee Creek Campground to Lone Pine, California - 90 miles
(running total: 806 miles)

McGee Creek provided a pleasing audible backdrop to last night's sleep, but this morning I realized the moisture dynamic was such that it may not have been the best idea. I had placed the rain fly on the tent last evening when I set it up, as the sky was clouded enough to seem like it could rain. Well, it didn't rain, but the moisture in the air from the creek had my fly very damp, as was the tent footprint. The tent itself was dry however. This necessitated draping the fly and footprint over some nearby bushes to hasten the drying process after shaking, but since the camp was in the shade of big trees early in the morning, I would have to put some items away damp, a common hobo occurrence.

Last night, my mind invented a jingle about triking that went like this: Peddle when you have the mettle; Coast when you're toast.

Sometimes I play with numbers just for the heck of it. I discovered that since leaving Klamath Falls, Oregon, I have been averaging 66 miles per day. This was encouraging to me, because back in 2009 when I pulled the trailer behind my trike, a 50 mile day was considered really moving along. Forty mile days were common if the terrain was hilly. The difference for me has been noteworthy, both from the standpoint of less wear and tear on my body, and also being able to travel significantly farther each day for the same amount of effort invested. My daily 2009 trailer mileage fell far short of what I was experiencing this trek, by about 15-25 miles each day. Amazing.

With these new numbers, I realize I can reach destinations in less time, which makes the notion of trike travel that much more inviting. Sure, it's still slow compared to high horsepower motor vehicles, but it's clearly faster than before, plus, the health benefits for my body, mind, and planet are compelling. If I am now averaging 20 more miles per day than I did with the trailer, that works out mathematically to roughly 140 additional miles per week, or about 280 more miles every two weeks. It's an interesting concept to ponder.

Riding along Highway 395 this morning, I was facing almost into the sun. The road began climbing slightly to a commercial development called Tom's Place, which is actually shown on maps and highway signs. The grade is gentle, not requiring low gears. Just past Tom's, I reached Sherwin Summit. At 7,000 feet, this summit is high, but the southbound climb was hardly noticeable compared to the climb yesterday morning up much higher Conway Summit. A sign up ahead read: TRUCKS – 8 MILES OF DOWNGRADE ¾ MILE AHEAD. Oh yes, some ultra fast triker miles are almost mine! This is addictive.

Riding down the Sherwin grade is not quite as fast or thrilling as the Conway grade, but it is nonetheless quite a heart pumping charge. What it lacked in top speed (45 instead of 50 miles per hour), it made up in sheer length. It was twice as far to the bottom as the Conway ride, which translated into a mega rest for me. This was because I was now descending into the Owens Valley region and the Mojave Desert. I was leaving the high mountains behind, yet still beside the eastern Sierras.

When going down these exhilarating descents, your legs are essentially motionless. I keep one leg extended to stretch those muscles, and one fully bent, and then after a while, I pedal forward half a stroke to extend the other one. Sometimes, if there is a right hand curve, I position the right leg back, and in a left hand curve, the left leg back. It seems to work best for my brain that way, as if I'm leaning into the curve and the inside leg has to be retracted to clear the ground. Of course, it's all psychological, but it feels right for me.

By 10:30 AM, I arrived in Bishop, California, a large town for these parts that includes a fancy Indian gambling casino and relatively cheap gas. Midway through town, I pulled into the shade of a local supermarket and purchased a bunch of grub, and then sat under the large tree and scarfed it up. It was an early lunchtime for this trike hobo.

Parked next to me was a racing styled motorcycle, same color

247

as my trike. When its owner came out to leave, we talked about our respective trips, and compared how much ground we could each cover in a day. Then, he used an electric switch to bring the fire breathing cylinders to life, put on his helmet, assumed the bent-forward motorcycle posture for this kind of bike, and took off for tonight's destination of San Francisco. How long would it take me to get to San Francisco (assuming I even would be motivated to go there)?

Today I was riding through the length of the Owens Valley, a stretch of US 395 that untold thousands of tourists drive every year, and throngs of skiers use to access Mammoth ski resort that I pedaled past yesterday. The key word to describing this part of the route is straight. Essentially, Highway 395 pretty much heads due south for miles upon miles, through the towns of Big Pine and Independence, both of which appear to be on the fringes of ghost town status compared to Bishop. Independence is the county seat, but it's drying up in more ways than one. An overland triker is able to make pretty decent time through here. It is not super exciting riding compared to other locales, but the views of the towering Sierra Nevada Range immediately to the west are always stunning. I love this eastern Sierra route, especially on a trike.

The openness of the road along here makes finding a spot to offload water a bit frustrating at times. Clearly, a triker drinks a lot of water while pedaling in the sun all day, and not all of it is utilized internally for cellular rejuvenation. So, I found myself on the lookout for places to pee now and again. I had to develop a new plan.

The highway is two lanes in each direction most of the way, with a very wide center dirt divider, so the opposing lanes are pretty distant. When I would find a perpendicular ravine, I could sometimes park past the ravine, then walk back into it, and with sufficient creosote bush concealment, do the deed. By the time southbound traffic was upon me, they were looking at my trike (just past the ravine) and they missed me altogether. The cars on the other side were far enough away that they didn't even know I was in there. The plan works!

It's a fact of life. Trikers don't always get the most desirable bathroom conditions. During the week, the traffic here is sparse enough however that you can time it to minimize any mental anxiety that may prohibit a steady stream flow. Then, before you head out again, be sure and guzzle some more water so that you can repeat this cycle several times before sunset. Trikers need a challenge – keeps the mind sharp!

I stopped at a Chevron food mart in Independence to cool off and get something really cold to drink. Back by the refrigerated section was a air conditioning vent, so I just stood there as I contemplated my choices of beverage. The air was noticeably warmer now that I had dropped elevation from the high country, so shade and cold felt good again. I asked the store clerk about campgrounds south by the town of Lone Pine, and he encouraged me to camp at Diaz Lake Recreation Area, right on the highway, with beautiful shade trees, a lake, and full service campground. Another man standing nearby seconded the motion, saying I would love it. So, after finishing my drink and refilling the water bottles, I pedaled off for Diaz Lake.

They had said the campground was about a mile and a half south of Lone Pine, and I felt confident that the final miles between there and here were an easy chunk to handle given the flat road and higher speeds attainable. What I did not count on however was the growing south wind, which quickly intensified once I left Independence. This invisible air I was riding into grew and grew, to the point that it really slowed my progress and extracted a toll from me in the form of noticeable energy depletion. This was not going easily for me.

Well folks, I didn't get to the northern outskirts of Lone Pine, heralded as the little town with lots of charm, until dusk, and I realized that by the time I rode through it, went on to Diaz Lake, got a campsite, and started pitching my tent, it would be well after dark. This still seemed doable because I have a headlamp I could use, and the air was warm enough to pull it off, but then I thought back to what I had been told in Susanville, California many days ago, about the KOA just a few miles outside town. That campground didn't even exist!

What if these guys today were incorrect on their distances? I decided not to take that chance. After fighting a very powerful headwind the final 20 miles, and having ridden 90 miles this extra warm day to reach this town, I opted to spend a wad of money for a quick and easy solution. A bird in the hand is worth two in the bush! Yep, once again I got a motel. The one upshot to this little story is that I could spread my damp rain fly and tent footprint from last night out in the room for them to dry thoroughly as I showered and ate from my panniers. Thus far, I had pedaled just over 800 miles, so my mind convinced myself that I deserved a wee bit of luxury before I died.

DAY 20 - *Eastern Sierras*
Wednesday – September 14, 2011
Lone Pine, California to Kramer's Junction, California - 122 miles
(running total: 928 miles)

Up before dawn, I ate breakfast, loaded the trike outside in my parking space, and began my daily ritual of pedaling south, becoming more confident by the mile that I could get to my destination in time for

249

my sister's 58th birthday. Making this happen was fueling my drive, along with my own inner quest for always reaching new personal bests. Before the trip began, I was roughly estimating three weeks of travel. It now appeared possible that this might have been a fairly close estimate, even in light of slower daily travel early on in Oregon. Only by pushing my own limits will I ever know how much I am capable of accomplishing. I was primed, and with the road a very familiar one to me at this point, I figured I could really knock off some serious mileage today.

The road shoulders are super wide on most of this highway, and they continue to be today. There are no traffic worries in my mind whatsoever. I couldn't be more calm if I had my own dedicated tricycle lane. In reality, I DID have my own tricycle lane, wide enough in fact that in many parts three trikes could ride abreast, but nearly always wide enough for two trikes side by side. That old man at Susanville who said I would be made into hamburger had no idea how easy this really was. You do not have to be some extraordinarily macho trike road warrior to make this ride from northern to southern California on a tricycle. There may be some spots in Reno that you'd choose to use a side street, but most of the way, it's a snap.

Many drivers of cars, trucks, and motorcycles waved to me along US 395, giving thumbs up signs and other friendly gestures with big smiles when they see me. This is so cool when it happens! No matter how hot or tired I might be, this kind of interaction always lifts my spirits and sends me emotionally soaring.

I had left my motel room about 20 minutes to six, and about 3 miles south of town, the sun finally began to peek over the tops of the Inyo Range to the east. On the other side of those mountains was Death Valley National Park, one of my destinations on the 2009 tricycle journey. As I rode south, Owens Lake was to my left, dry as a bone, and often the source for many area dust storms on windy days. Fortunately this morning, the air was calm as could be: no headwind like yesterday afternoon, and no choking dust in the air. But later could be different.

By the way, the Diaz Lake Recreation Area came up on my right about the same time the sun began to rise. It appeared to be everything those men yesterday said it was, but I realized that I had made a good choice by calling it a night in town, as it would have been around a 95 mile day had I camped here, and with that headwind, I was pretty wiped out last night, ready to bed down.

Somewhere north of Olancha, I met Claudia Wit and Christian Ewen, touring northbound on their diamond framed bicycles, fully loaded with Ortlieb panniers. Visitors to the United States from Europe, they were young and so excited to see what they could of western

America. I stopped when I saw them, and they turned and rode over to my opposing lane to chat a while. They were riding from Anchorage, Alaska, and tentatively headed to somewhere unknown in Mexico. Wow, that made my jaunt seem trivial in comparison! With their strong accents, they asked about routes in Death Valley, and having spent a lifetime visiting there, and writing a couple of books about it, I was able to help them. Their website: http://ccgoesamerica.blogspot.com/

As I approached the seemingly dying town of Olancha (not much left nowadays), I passed the Crystal Geyser natural alpine spring water factory. I had no idea this is where they bottled all that water I see in the supermarkets everywhere. Their facility was huge, and I wondered why they had chosen this location for it, seeing as how there were no large towns anywhere close, and Olancha was nearly a ghost town in a forsaken stretch of very lonely desert, with only a Chevron mini mart and gas station evidence of anything modern that might be flourishing. I did stop at the mini mart, which was a welcomed relief to get out of the increasingly hotter sun, and bought an ice cold V8 juice and banana to have with one of my Clif bars on the trike.

I passed Cactus Flat road, some boarded up buildings, a rundown trailer park, and a turnoff to Death Valley via Highway 190 (101 miles to the east). Distances are much larger than they appear out in this country, whether you are in a car or on a trike. With elevation steadily dropping, the ride was progressing at a good pace, even though I had to stop occasionally to remove my feet from the pedals to alleviate nerve compression that was my occasional companion, which resulted in pushing the speed and distance envelope. Just outside of Ridgecrest, California there was a significant up grade, but the gathering clouds made it tolerable. Highway 395 splits off at Ridgecrest, with Highway 14 continuing on in to Los Angeles, a place I did not wish to visit.

I was now out in the wide open spaces of the northern Mojave Desert, with thousands upon thousands of creosote bushes instead of pine trees. Another long uphill took me to the remote ridge (*book's cover photo*) over the final valley before I would reach Johannesburg and Red Mountain, old gold mining towns from the later 1800s. I could see Red Mountain from the top, far distance for a trike rider, and the nearly full moon was now rising above it. The day was getting late, and eventually the sun began setting behind the creosotes to my west, and finally behind the now distant mountains called the Sierra Nevada.

The good news about riding up this grade this late in the day was that I did not overheat, and was thus able to maintain a decent pace with relatively minimal water consumption. Riding up into Johannesburg would pose another challenge, but judging by the passage of time, I might be pedaling up that ascent in the dark. Above and across the valley, during that magical period of the day called twilight or dusk, I was fortunate enough to witness the longest duration meteorite I had ever seen in my entire life! It flew across the heavens, southwest to northeast, larger in size than most, and about 5 seconds in duration. That would have made an awesome photograph if my camera was ready, but I doubt the auto focus could have honed in on it quickly enough.

As I was descending into the valley north of Johannesburg, it became totally dark, and my trike's lighting kept me visible to what seemed like a lot of cars and trucks. US 395 is only two lanes here, one in each direction, and the shoulder is minimal (enough to barely contain my trike), so the anxiety level raised slightly, until it was obvious that the drivers were still giving me plenty of room, and none of them were honking or expressing any hostility. Besides that, my speed going down the grade was in the 30s. It was a much faster grade, but since it was dark, I could have easily outpaced my headlight, so I braked regularly to keep within my visibility limits. No time to get going too fast!

Pedaling up the other side, towards the old gold mining town of Randsburg, my pace dramatically slowed to low gears. It seemed like a load of eighteen wheelers were out tonight, heading south to Kramer's Junction and Highway 58. At long last, I rolled into Johannesburg a while after 8:00 PM, and pulled into a Texaco mini mart and gas station that had already closed for the night. It was quiet and peaceful.

They had a small wooden picnic table out front, so I sat on the bench and unloaded some meals from my panniers. At least I would have a regular table at which to eat. The ultra bright lights above the gasoline pumps illuminated me very well. A few neighborhood dogs barked, sensing my presence in this old run-down town. It had apparently rained here earlier, and the smell of desert sage was like magic to my senses, an aroma I had long loved since my first days visiting this region as a kid with my dad.

After eating, I used the cell phone to call my sister in Apple Valley. The connection was excellent. I was probably about 80 miles from her house, and informed her that she could plan on my arrival by her birthday. I had ridden 97 miles today, figured that was far enough, and so settled into my recumbent seat to grab a night's sleep, or at least the best I could manage considering the insanely bright lighting.

I tried napping and sleeping, but it wasn't working out for me. After a while a pack of large roaming dogs walked around the building, and I sat motionless staring at them as they were sniffing this and that. The huge German shepherd locked eyes with me, and I wondered what would develop. He seemed to be the pack leader. He may have sensed that I was in no mood to engage any aggression from him, and that if he tried, it would be his mistake, so he quickly departed with his buddies in tow. One thing about pedaling cross country is that it toughens one up mentally, and anyone with a modicum of sense, including animals, knows to allot wide berth to a seasoned overland trike hobo.

Traffic was now almost nonexistent, the moon was virtually full, and I had been wanting a night ride ever since this trip began. Not only that, but I also wanted an ice cold protein smoothie drink, the kind made by the Naked juice company, which I could see in the refrigerated section of the locked mini mart next to me, but the only place I could have one tonight was in Kramer's Junction, an all night trucker's stop about 28 miles south of my present location. So, guess what happened!

Yep, I headed back out onto old US 395 and lit out for Four Corners, now known as Kramer's Junction. The weather was pleasant, and I was able to maintain high gears nearly all the way. The shoulder was no longer as wide on this old portion of 395 as it had been for the past several days on the newer and improved portions, but at this hour, even most of the truckers had packed it in for the night, at least the ones heading south on my route. The east/west Highway 58, which I would intersect at Kramer's Junction, was always loaded with eighteen wheelers all night long, as it was a conduit from Barstow to Bakersfield, California. That would be dicey to ride at night, but wasn't on my route.

As I continued down the hill, barely aware I was riding through the Mojave Desert since everything was dark and cool, the glow of lights from Kramer's Junction grew larger. I passed the massive acreage that housed a colossal solar collection facility, pedaled past the airstrip, crossed the railroad tracks, and then came to rest at the 4-way traffic light. In the days prior to these lights, when only stop signs were regulating the traffic crossing, collisions and horrendous fatalities, especially at night, were far more common, as mesmerized sleepy drivers never even slowed for the cross traffic.

So here I was, a diminutive vehicle known as a tricycle in a sea of gargantuan big rig trucks, realizing that even as sleepy as the drivers were, they would not flatten me. The lumbering diesel engine of the eighteen wheeler a few feet behind my trike idled at the red light. The driver wanted to turn right onto Highway 58, but had to wait for an ICE Qnt tricycle that was poised to cross the intersection. That kind of power could go to a triker's head. Actually, these truck drivers are real gems in my opinion, consistently extending all courtesies to me this entire journey. I feel completely at ease in their presence at this stage of my triking life, and know that if need ever be, they would rescue me.

I pedaled into the Pilot Travel Center on the southwest corner of the intersection, another super brightly lit mega petroleum station for motorists and truckers, with an indoor facility that included an all night restaurant, grocery store, automotive supply store, gift shop, restrooms, and showers. You name it, and it could likely be found in this place. This was one of three gasoline stations on the four corners, and it was always hopping 24 hours every day. I could have whatever I wanted.

Okay, so where did I park? Right on the front sidewalk to the left of the front doors, with my ICE trike facing an ICE machine. How apropos, I thought, as my ICE trike was showcased by the large ICE letters on the white solid water dispenser. Well anyway, I was hungry again, having booked down here in record time from Johannesburg, so I got my money, hurried inside, and purchased my protein smoothie, a bag of trail mix, and another drink called Muscle Milk. Time to relax!

That filled me up, so now it was time to finally catch some shuteye. It was indeed like daylight with all the lighting, but when sleep calls my name, it can overtake me just about anywhere. The recumbent seat finally served as my bed for the night. I didn't feel like pitching a tent out in the bushes behind the building because tomorrow I wanted to get an early start and surprise my sister and mom.

Nine hundred twenty eight miles were now behind me, with only 52 to go! Piece of cake, I figured. Of course, sometimes my ego has a way of presenting what turns out to be delusional, but at least I was psychologically primed for whatever might come my way. I'm really close now. The sweet smell of reaching my goal was in the air!

DAY 21 - *Eastern Sierras*
Thursday – September 15, 2011
Kramer's Junction, California to Apple Valley, California - 52 miles
(running total: 980 miles, journey complete)

The great advantage of sleeping on a tricycle seat is that you can be mobile at a moment's notice. First light brightened the eastern Mojave sky. I fixed myself a bowl of granola, ate, and then conveniently walked inside the always open travel center to use their bathroom facilities. Hey, it doesn't get much easier than that! All that was missing was a picnic table, but I didn't care because today I would finally reach my destination, and just that knowledge overshadowed any perceived personal inconveniences. I could handle it all today!

This final stretch of US 395 is the oldest section that has not been refurbished in decades. The often miserable shoulder is sometimes adequate between here and the town of Adelanto, sometimes cracked and potholed, sometimes unrideable, and sometimes nonexistent. Long stretches this morning are only one lane in each direction, and this is what the old man in Susanville was referring to when he made the hamburger comment so many days ago. Still, he was incorrect from a tricyclist's standpoint, as I was to experience fine motorist manners all the way today. Trikes just pop out at car drivers, making them counter-intuitively safe. Bicycle Brains don't work for tricycle pilots!

Mister Sun was rising as I hit the first long uphill portion just south of the travel center. The desert morning was cool, as desert mornings always are, but my experience has taught me to enjoy it while I can, for today was going to be a scorcher. The sky was perfectly clear, and I was much lower in elevation than I had been yesterday, so the heat of yesterday was a mere prelude for what was in store for me very soon.

Less than 50 miles stood between me and a nice house full of all the luxuries expected by middle class Americans, a distance I reckoned should be a snap through an essentially flat desert landscape. My daily mileages usually far exceeded this number, with yesterday almost two and a half times it, so the impending arrival at my family's house was now nearly a given. Of course, getting too cocky is not wise, so I let these thoughts go and just zoned into the task at hand.

As the town of Adelanto neared, my body began shutting down. This was really strange, and I attribute it to several factors. First, the temperature was upper 90s and I was in the full sun the entire time. Second, the highway was so old with very rough pavement that the triking experience was just one big vibrating sensation that had to be endured. No where thus far had the roadbed been so poor for so long. Imagine death by shaking. Third, I had not slept deeply or for very long last night, and consequently was pretty darn tired going into this final day. Fourth, my water supply was now nearly exhausted once again, the arid hot air sucking me dry continually. And fifth, the hot spots at the fronts of my feet had gone beyond the typical numbness and discomfort that an aggressive cyclist experiences, to a point where my feet were just flat aching severely from swelling. None of these issues were enough alone to bring me down, but combined like this, they took their toll.

I had unwittingly picked a genuinely hot day to roll into the hottest region of the trek. Bummer! But that was my lot. Eager to impress my sister with my speedy arrival, since she had thought I was spending the night in Johannesburg where I called her, I was relentless in my drive to cover the miles as rapidly as I could. Picture the wicked neighbor lady in the Wizard of Oz ferociously pedaling her bicycle near Dorothy's house. It was my inner competitive nature once again pushing me forward into my outer limits. Yes, isn't ego a wonderful thing? It's something that can get you killed if it really gets out of control, as good judgment is thrown to the wind. My goal was set, and unwaivering.

The closer I got to Adelanto, the slower I seemed to travel. I was rapidly running out of steam, and actually found myself thinking that perhaps I should place a telephone call, asking my mom to rent a pickup truck to rescue me. What? This close to the finish? My mind was slipping from lack of sleep! With twenty-some miles yet to pedal, there was no way I could even remotely consider throwing in the towel now. To do so would forever leave me wondering if I could have gone the distance. It wasn't my way. Even if I didn't get there until midnight, I would pedal my little tricycle the entire route to mom's garage come hell or high water (fortunately, there were no storm clouds today, so a desert flash flood was not likely, but it sure seemed that Satan was on my tail).

On the northern edge of town, a Chevron mini mart loomed large, so with my remaining vestiges of physical and mental strength, I rolled up onto the sidewalk in front of the building's front glass windows, sweat pouring from my carcass like a water facet at full tilt. It was air conditioned inside, and I relished the relief as I picked out some cold offerings to buy. One of the clerks, having seen my trike outside, began questioning me about my trip, but unlike my normal response where I gladly talk to folks at length if they wish, my answers were brief so that I could start guzzling some cold liquids. I was nearly in shock.

Truly, I was spent. Having bought the goods, I sauntered outside, into what seemed like a blast furnace! I set my food and drink on the trike's seat, and then bent over and wheeled it around back to the shade of the building so I could eat and rest. My shirt was drenched.

I was moving in slow motion, every effort sluggish as the shade was still plenty hot. I took my sweet time, in no hurry to leave, realizing that I must rest sufficiently to successfully finish my ride. I ate, brushed my teeth, and then just sat there on the hard concrete for the longest time, nearly dead to the world, and thinking that so few miles never have seemed so unattainably far. I felt like I was just surviving this last leg of the journey. Triking enjoyment had left me. It was now simply a matter of transporting my tired bag of bones from Adelanto to the southern portion of Apple Valley. Pushing too hard had finally overtaken me.

The vision of a quest yet stood before me however, a goal of propelling myself using my own power from my home on the central Oregon coast to my family's home in southern California. I had to prove to myself that this was possible, that I could indeed survive in life without owning a petroleum powered vehicle. I sensed the independence that would soon be mine, passing a milestone in my life on the way to a new world, a world that for me was a cherished destination. I could indeed live simply, slowly leaving all my perceived contemporary necessities far behind as I pedaled way beyond imagined boundaries.

At 2:30 PM, on the 15th day of September 2011, I attained two objectives, one of having completed the physical trip, and one of achieving a mental victory as I pedaled the final 15 feet up the driveway. My sister came out of the garage with a cold bottle of Fiji water in hand for me, followed by my mother with her camera. My sis had made a small welcome sign with a photo of me leaving for my trike trip in 2009 pasted upon it. It read: "Yay Stevie, You Made It!" Now I didn't have a concern in the world. My mom and sis would take good care of me after my 487 hour journey. On that, I could count! Time for a shower!

THE END
* * *

ADVENTURE THREE:
PACIFIC COAST

**Florence, Oregon to Atascadero, California
along coastal highways 101 and 1
875 miles 19 days (age 62)
hiker/biker campsites**

DAY 1 - *Pacific Coast*
September 03, 2013, Tuesday
Florence, Oregon to Bastendorff County Park, Charleston, Oregon.
57 miles (running total = 57 miles from Florence)

At 6:45 AM, I heard the laundry room door open, and the familiar voice of Matt Jensen say: "I'm in the garage Steve." We had arranged to leave the house at 7 AM, so things were proceeding according to the schedule. My human powered ICE Qnt recumbent tadpole tricycle was fully loaded with panniers the night before, so only my final preparation this morning stood between me and pedaling out of the driveway for the wild ride south along the Oregon Coast Highway and Pacific Coast Highway. I had eaten my bowl of granola, brushed my teeth, made my cozy bed, and mentally prepared myself to begin pedaling long hard hours on the road each day, and sleeping each night on the ground outside in a tent. The transition mentally can be a challenge, but at least with someone else sharing the experiences, thoughts were kept manageable.

Three of us had agreed to embark on this journey as a team. Matt and I would be meeting up with the third member tonight, at

257

Bastendorff County Park in Charleston, Oregon. His name is David Massey, and he drove to Coos Bay in a rental car from his home in Glendora, California. From Coos Bay, he would be pedaling his Azub TRIcon tricycle to our camp this evening at Bastendorff.

Matt used to have a Catrike 700 recumbent tadpole trike, which he sold a couple years ago, and today he is pedaling a Surly Long Haul Trucker touring bicycle loaded with his gear in Ortlieb panniers. David and I have Arkel and Radical Design panniers. Only the hours of this day and a few miles separated Matt and me from David. From the departure point in Florence to the campsite David would be securing for us mid afternoon, 57 hilly and picturesque miles paved our path.

The morning is warm already. September is typically the most pleasant month of the year when measured in terms of human comfort zones. Matt and I ride south on Highway 101, only 5 blocks from where I live, cross the Siuslaw River bridge, pedal up the hill south of town, and begin our forested coastal ride in earnest. The trike is slower on uphills, so Matt pulls ahead out of sight. I'll catch up eventually.

I see a car parked up ahead, and a man waves me to pull over. He is a close friend of mine, and wishes to say goodbye one more time, while wishing me all good things. He hands me a small piece of paper with a quotation on it, one that I had included in one of my books. Uttered by Marcel Proust many years ago, the short thought says: "The real voyage of discovery consists not in seeking new landscapes, but in having new eyes." I thank my friend for his thoughtfulness, we speak briefly, and then I return to the road to reunite with Matt.

The huge evergreen trees tower above my diminutive tricycle as I enjoy the landscapes from my reclined position, a view that traditional bicyclists do not have with such ease. Highway 101 has wide shoulders here, making the ride a breeze. Matt and I speak briefly with a man called Len from Colorado, who is also riding a tadpole trike (two wheels in front, one in rear), except that his is powered by an electric motor, allowing him to travel 160 miles per day with little physical effort on his body. Hills that I slowly labor up using human power, Len flies up with electric power. We bid him adieu, and continue on.

Crossing the Reedsport bridge, we pedal south through Winchester Bay, stopping at turnouts with ocean views for a Clif or Odwalla bar and water now and then. The day has already exceeded 70 degrees Fahrenheit, so seeking shade in which to eat and rest is the order of business, especially since we are warm from pedaling up steep hills. It feels good to cool our bodies, and get our feet off the pedals.

Today it is fully sunny and a robust 73 degrees Fahrenheit. A trucker's weigh station is up ahead. It is a huge scale used to weigh the big rigs, the tractor/trailer units everyone calls semi-trucks. In 2009, I rolled my trike and trailer onto one of these in the Cascade Range of Oregon. The displayed number was 350, which I figured was accurate because prior to leaving on that trip, my calculations revealed the rolling weigh (including the organic engine called "me") was about 375 pounds. Ugh! Wiser after a couple of overland journeys, this year's trek is easier due to less weight. I pull onto the truck scale with my ICE Q trike. The red-lit number popped up at 250 pounds. My calculations this year put my rolling weight at 265 pounds. Newbies always pack everything including the kitchen sink. Live and learn the hard way is always the name of the cycling game! Run light, fast, and easy – the only way!

Eventually, we arrive at the huge bridge that spans Coos Bay, variously called by folks the North Bend bridge, the Coos Bay bridge, or the Conde B. McCullough memorial bridge. Conde designed this bridge in the early 1930s, but failed to give any serious thought to human powered humans, especially cyclists. A major renovation was just completed prior to our crossing today, yet the state made no modern modifications to accommodate cyclists any better than Conde's short-sighted creation decades ago. Many cyclists live in sincere fear of this bridge on their Pacific Coast adventures, but there is an easy bypass that avoids the bridge and the two automobile-congested towns south of it. Today, Matt and I will cross the bridge however, because we are going to meet David in Charleston, so the bypass is not appropriate.

On the south side of the bridge, we stop and relax in a beautiful park setting, using the bathroom and refueling with a snack. A few more miles and we stop at a Safeway supermarket for additional calories in the form of mixed nuts and V8 Juice. As we coast down a hill into the small town of Charleston, west of Coos Bay, the drawbridge is in the "up" position so a fishing vessel can cross underneath it. All the cars stop. I pull forward to the head of the line on my trike to take a photograph of the tilted roadway. The fishing boats are photogenic.

At long last, the fifty-seventh mile is completed and Matt and I arrive at the Bastendorff Beach road to the campground. The uphill grade is insanely steep, not meeting any modern requirements for reasonable grade, and requires me to stop four times to rest on the way to the top. Fortunately, it is only about 50 yards long. Even in my low/low gear on the trike, which gets me over the longest and steepest highway grades on mountain ranges, I must mash on the pedals hard and slow to reach the tiny summit. This is the world's steepest paved road.

Matt and I find David already in a campsite, his tent pitched, and his electronic devices in full use as he documents his adventure thus far and calls his wife to keep her posted as to his safety. The sound of the jetty foghorn pierces the air every 30 seconds to warn ships. We pitch our tents in the same campsite, after some rest and relaxation to recover from the first day's miles, which are the most difficult of the entire trek just by virtue of being the first day. As the days roll on during a tricycle journey, they get easier because the body adapts to the expectations placed upon it. We three cycling rogues eat dinner and enjoy the camaraderie of our endeavor. It is fun to share.

On coastal overland journeys such as this, where state and county campgrounds are common, the order of the evening camp is as follows: 1) find a level place to pitch the tent, 2) pitch the tent, 3) toss your gear in the tent, 4) take a shower, 5) fix and eat your dinner at the picnic table while sharing your experiences with fellow cyclists, 6) write in your journal, 7) use the bathroom one more time, and 8) hit the sleeping bag to rest your weary body and drift off into dreamland. I have found that there is little to no desire to do anything more. The days of pedaling are long and challenging, so the essentials of survival rise to the forefront of one's needs. Imagine taking a 57 mile day-ride at home, but then getting up before sunrise the next morning to do it again, and imagine doing this yet again every day for the next 18 days.

The body needs as much rest and recuperation time as possible. The scant hours of the night are really not enough initially for the body to be ready for the next day. It does get easier day by day, but the process can be rough for the uninitiated cyclist who does not know what to expect. On a recumbent trike, the legs grow noticeably in strength and muscular size over the weeks, while the upper body is reduced to a lean and gaunt appearing presence. The evening's procedure becomes well understood, and you become very efficient at setting and breaking your camps. Within the first week, you know where all your little items are stashed in the panniers. The procedure outlined above is typically all a cyclist has time for each evening if covering the maximum amount of ground possible during the daylight hours. It's a trike hobo life out here.

I drift off to sleep, occasionally hearing the distant sea lions at Cape Arago, a few miles south. Bastendorff campground is on the Cape Arago Highway, a road that dead-ends at the cape where the sea lions bask on the rocks. Sea-faring ships enter Coos Bay here.

DAY 2 - *Pacific Coast*
September 04, 2013, Wednesday
Bastendorff County Park to Humbug Mountain State Park, Oregon
60 miles (running total: 117 miles)

Cycling teams typically arise prior to sunup, beginning the

striking of camp when there is barely enough natural light to see what one is doing. This is the normal order of life for a trike hobo. This morning, I become aware of noises emanating from my team members' tents, and as I peer out of my tent door, realize it is yet dark. I am an early riser, but today, David and Matt are up, and are already removing gear from their tents using the light from their headlamps, so I get up from my warm sleeping bag, dress, put on my headlamp, and begin what is to be another day of mileage similar to yesterday. My body is rested, yet I can feel the residual effects of a challenging first day on the road.

We all work in total silence, like a well oiled machine, tending to our similar shared chores as our tents silently come down and are stashed away in our cargo bags on our cycles. Silent striking of the camp is common, so as not to awaken other campers who drive petroleum powered vehicles and can afford a few more hours of slumber. Trike hobos do not have this luxury typically, and must make the most of every daylight hour, even when it means beginning prior to daylight. Trike hobos are like phantoms of the night. We arrive at our camps silently because our vehicles make no noise. We cause no pollution of the air shared by others at the campground. Only if other folks see us silently roll in do they realize we have arrived. In the mornings, while all others are still sleeping, we silently break camp and depart, our phantom-like presence keeping us virtually invisible to normal people. They get up first thing come sunrise and wonder, what happened to those guys with weird looking bicycles? We are gone, without a trace. The trike phantoms have moved on, never to be seen again.

I like to eat a bowl of granola for breakfast on my overland journeys, so I sit at the picnic table and do so once my trike is fully packed and ready to go. Matt and David have some other minimal bit of food compared to my "elaborate" fixings. Just before I sit down to my highly anticipated granola feast, Matt walks over to me and quietly informs my brain that he will be returning to Florence this morning, where he also lives, duplicating the ride we had yesterday. I nod in acceptance, yet tell him I will miss his presence. Resigned to his declaration, I eat in silent contemplation. Matt then approaches David and likewise informs him of the decision to return home this morning.

Just prior to departure, David and I line our trikes up side by side for some photos. After the picture, we all depart down the crazy campground entrance road, and ride about a mile to the junction where Matt will turn left and head north, and David and I will turn right and head south to southern California. David and I now begin our ascent of the mountain on the Seven Devils road, infamous in its ability to reduce any cyclist to a struggling bioform attempting to make it to Bandon,

Oregon, only 24 miles distant. I had given David the option, at his sole discretion, of riding to Bullards Beach State Park, just two miles north of Bandon today, for our second night's camp, or riding to Humbug Mountain State Park, another 36 miles distant, as he has a schedule.

David is a high school teacher of computers and art, soon to retire, but for this year, his district has allowed him three weeks to take this tricycle trip so the students can follow along online in the adventure of it all. He must be back at work on Monday, September 23, and must arrive in Morro Bay, California no later than the evening of Friday, September 20, where his wife will pick him up in their truck. Thus, I leave it up to him how far he wishes to ride each day to maintain his needs. David chooses to ride to Humbug Mountain State Park today, 60 miles distant from Bastendorff County Park. I wonder if this 60 will be easier than yesterday's 57, but from prior experience, I suspect so.

So, we begin today's ride over the summits of the seven devils on the Seven Devils road, appropriately named because it feels like satan is right on your heels as you pedal up the long slow grades. In our favor, the morning is overcast, so we have no bright hot sun upon our bodies as we had yesterday. At some time in the past, a cyclist took the time to paint the names of the devils in the two lane roadway, so I snap a photograph of "Devil #2" as I come to a stop to rest momentarily. There are only five devilish summits yet to conquer before we head back down the mountain on the other side towards Bandon. Matt said that this portion of the coastal route had the steepest grades of anywhere between Canada and Mexico. David and I hope he is right. With the seven devils behind us, we pass the South Slough National Estuarine Research Reserve, where visitors can hike the trails through the forest. As committed trike hobos however, and tired to boot from out-pedaling the devils, David and I simply photograph the sign and press on south.

A little farther on along the ridge line, a rural resident has placed a couple dozen tiny elf figurines in the miniature forest in front of their home. I can't resist some photographic moments. My diversions of picture-taking always put me behind David, something that will repeat itself every day. I love to document my triangular adventures for others.

At last, we approach Whiskey Run road, a tightly wound narrow road that drops in elevation quickly off the peaks of the seven devils. There is no high speed triking to be had here however, for the curves are so tight that without constant braking on the trikes, we would end up upside down in the borrow ditch and woods. This descent is a welcomed respite, despite the needed attention to curve management. What the devils took away, the trike angels return to our fatigued legs.

Once in the small coastal village of Bandon, we pull into Ray's

Food Place market and chow down for lunch. We park right in front of the main entrance by the windows on the sidewalk of the store. The deli eating area is on the other side of the window, which makes for easy monitoring of the trikes just outside. Next, we stop by Mother's Natural Grocery, a health food store I've been visiting for the past 19 years. She makes the most incredible cookie for health nuts like myself, called the "Everything cookie", which is loaded with so many life-extending goodies that I can't name them all. Lastly, we pedal through Bandon's Old Town area for some photo ops on the boardwalk. Somehow I cut my right index finger here, and blood is everywhere my hand goes. My former paramedic training stops the gusher, and I bandage it sufficiently.

We pedal on south out of Bandon, David opting not to ride the extra mileage along the scenic bypass route on the cliffs. We remain on Highway 101, which is easier, less mileage, more direct, and wide shouldered all the way (the bypass is narrow with no shoulders in many places). David and I have figured out that to arrive at Morro Bay by September 20, which is what his schedule calls for, we must average 48 miles per day. If we take all the scenic bypass routes, as someone not on a schedule would probably opt to do, we would not get him to Morro Bay on time to get back to work. Good thing retirement for David is not far off. Then, he can take overland trike journeys without the time crunch thing hanging over his head. It's okay though, because this is his first overland trike trek, which will be hard enough on him without adding more agony to the mix.

In the miniature village of Langlois, there is a sign board near a tiny grocery market that reads: "BIKERS FREE WATER STOP" so we pull in, fill our water bottles, which are near empty in the warm sunshine heat, and get some fresh fruits to eat. Folks gather around our bizarre looking "bikes" and ask all the typical questions all overland trikers hear time and again while on the road: "What is this?", "How do you steer?", "Are you handicapped?", "How far are you going?" and so on. We sit in the shade of the storefront, ambassadors for trikers everywhere.

Back on the road, we pedal through the nearly non-existent "town" of Sixes, Oregon, where a grange is one of the few things to see from the highway. On the side of the old wooden building is a sign that reads: "SIXES GRANGE – 856 MARKETPLACE BINGO HAND CRAFTS", which is painted in black. Shortly after Sixes, atop the Cape Blanco summit hill, we pull over and sit on the guardrail for a drink and energy bar. As we prepare to leave, David discovers one of his gloves is missing. It has to be here somewhere because he had it on when we stopped. This drove us nuts for quite some time. The glove was nowhere to be found! And we were overly thorough searching for it, even considering a wind that may have taken it across the highway. We never did find it. He finishes the ride today with only one gloved hand.

By the time we arrive in the town of Port Orford, the fog has rolled in again, largely obscuring the Pacific Ocean that lies immediately to our right. We pedal on, not stopping because we want to get to camp as the day is wearing on quickly now. We are tired, looking forward to hot showers at Humbug Mountain State Park campground. The boundary for the state park is a few miles prior to the camping area, and David is beginning to wonder if we'll ever make it before dark. But sure enough, it is indeed around the final bend where 101 turns inland for a while from the ocean, in a tight canyon with big trees everywhere.

We decide to splurge, and instead of paying $5.00 each for the hiker/biker camp, which is in the dirt far from the showers, we pay $17 (split two ways because we are on trikes), get the site next to the shower complex, and use paved walkways exclusively. This is just in time because the sun sets and by the time we hit the sack, it is mostly dark once again. This is why a trike hobo's routine is as it is.

Well, actually, the $17.00 was not split tonight. I paid the whole enchilada because David had no money with him. Why is this? Was he unprepared? Nope. He learned a hard lesson today. On recumbent trikes, it's like you are sitting in a recliner chair, as opposed to a conventional bicycle where you are sitting upright. David had been keeping his cash, more than $500.00, in a money clip, which he had placed in his pants pocket. First rule of triking: *Never carry anything you can't afford to lose in your pants pockets*! Sure enough, somewhere after the Langlois market and here, that money clip and its contents left David. Needless to say, David is somewhat bummed tonight, but we are tired, so decide to figure it out tomorrow. When he called his wife this evening, he did not mention this little hiccup to her, so as not to worry her.

DAY 3 - *Pacific Coast*
September 05, 2013, Thursday
Humbug Mountain State Park to Harris Beach State Park, Brookings, Oregon - 49 miles (running total: 166 miles)

David is still quiet and reserved this morning as the fog surrounds our little camp. The sting of losing five hundred smackers is still there. I mention that the next town of Gold Beach will have several banks, and he can access his money at home from there, and be back in business. We decide to hit a bank in Gold Beach, break camp after breakfast, and pedal onto the fog enshrouded Highway 101 again, in the tight little canyon. It's early, and petroleum powered vehicles are far and few between. The air is cool, so we make good time, that is until I see something that forces me to stop immediately!

David didn't stop. I last saw him cranking on ahead around the next curve. I pulled into the large dirt parking lot to the right. It was too early for anything to be open, but what was staring at me from above didn't care about business hours. Two creatures from the Jurassic period of time dared me to visit them, so I did. I parked the trike, yanked out my camera, which I always carry around my torso for quick access, and stepped way back to capture the moment. Have you ever photographed your trike about to be stepped upon by a tyrannosaur? Only in Oregon! David surely wonders what happened to me again.

David uses all the latest and greatest electronic gadgets, gizmos, and gear on this trip: a portable solar array that he places atop his panniers to charge his devices, an iPad, an iPhone, and who knows what else. As I pull in behind him, playing catch-up once again, he is dialing a number on his iPhone. The fog is heavy, but the signal is strong because we have gained elevation out of that little Humbug Mountain canyon. Pompous grass is growing wild alongside the highway, and the farther south we travel, the heavier it gets in places. This grass is the fancy looking stuff with puffs begging to be photographed. So, I do.

At one large turnout overlooking the vast Pacific Ocean, I meet a fellow named Tim Cassese, who is pedaling his Surly Long Haul Trucker bicycle south along the same route David and I are following. He is tall, lean, and a very happy fellow. Tim asks me if it's going to rain today, having determined that I live on the Oregon coast. Guess he figures since I live in these parts, I will have a pretty good handle on weather patterns. He had heard on the radio last night that rain was predicted today for the southern Oregon coast. I tell Tim that it will not rain today, and that these clouds and foggy conditions will dissipate come midday. He is relieved to know this. We say goodbye as he departs slightly ahead of me. Cycling the coast, you meet many others doing the same thing. Some you see again, others it's a one-time meeting.

Since the morning is foggy and cool, we make great time into Gold Beach, a southern coast community with full services. We cross the bridge on the north end of town, pedal up the steep hill into the downtown area, and stop at the Umpqua Bank so David can remedy his financial poverty situation. Next, we take a while and do a midmorning calorie refueling at McKay's Market. My nectarine looks perfect, but it has a consistency closer to an apple than a nectarine. David resupplies his Gatorade stash, I guzzle three Odwalla chocolate protein monster drinks and eat some mixed nuts, and we answer more questions from curious onlookers of our trikes in the parking lot. It's a very good thing we scarfed up on all the high calorie food here in Gold Beach, because what came next was enough to do a triker in.

After we leisurely pedaled past some gigantic rock monoliths in the ocean, called by some sea stacks, our gauntlet ramped up a few dozen notches in short order. The first visual clue of the impending challenge were some words written in chalk on the shoulder pavement: "HILLS ARE FUN!" it read. A quick look at our elevation profile maps confirmed that the mystery author was simply trying to give followers a little pep talk for a big obstacle: the longest and toughest hill on the southern Oregon coast! I call it the Bellview hill because Bellview Lane is at its summit in the woods. It was still somewhat foggy, but the air was warm and somewhat muggy. I was sweating like crazy at the top, and had to unbutton my shirt to vent the heat, until the breeze and fog started chilling me a tad. Once the wind blows, it's easy to get cold.

Just over the top, it was clear we were going to have one hell of a thrill ride going down the south side of this monstrous mountain summit. This was one of those great downhills where braking was not required, and the grade was steep enough to allow a seemingly endless increase in coasting speed. Thirty, thirty-five, forty, forty-five. Wow, this is making up for the north side agony. Half the hill we are dying and crying, and the other half we are flying. This is one of those 50 miles per hour gems that comes along now and again on the Pacific Coast route. Even though it is the uphills that build us and make us stronger trikers, it's those downhills that keep us stoked and begging for more!

I have not seen David for quite some time by now, up to my old antics of picture taking, but as I round the final curve of the humongous downhill heading into the straightaway, I see David at a pullout with tourists, waiting with his camera to get a movie or photo of me. I am having so much fun at this speed, I do not even stop to say hello to him, nor can I even take my hand off the handlebar to wave for fear of losing control, but rocket on by at break-neck speed as the road levels out and the sun comes out. Tourists are everywhere. They must think I'm crazy.

The ocean views are spectacular, some of the best on the entire Oregon coast. Oregon's coast is very different than California's coast, which is much drier and barren of the big trees. I see a beautiful floral bouquet on the guardrail, likely where someone was killed in an automobile accident. It makes me sad. Everyone is worried that I will be killed on a trike, but somehow the statistics of 50,000 annual deaths from cars in the US each year seems to put it in proper perspective.

This afternoon, we reach and cross the Thomas Creek Bridge, the highest bridge in Oregon, at 345 feet elevation above the ocean immediately below it. David crosses first in the ample shoulder lane, so that I can take another photograph, of course, as he pedals this Pacific Coast landmark. On the next hill crest, I take a water break, while David takes a cell phone break. Breaks are necessary when pedaling all day!

Around 5:30 PM, we roll into Brookings, Oregon, a full service town that is about six miles north of the California border. Harris Beach State Park is on the north end of town, and offers great camping, fantastic views, awesome hiking, hot showers, flush toilets, and even a laundry room. Now, once again loaded to the hilt with cash, David pops for the entrance fee, and gets us another regular campsite near the laundry and showers, with paved pathways to keep us pristinely clean after our showers. Our daily camp duties are slowed now and then by the curious walkers who just have to know all about our vehicles, somewhat different from their gigantic and invasive RVs. Again, we are stealthy trike phantoms who roll in and pedal out with no toxins or noise to betray our presence. We are truly a world apart, a universe apart.

Tonight, I pitch my tent, eat my dinner, take a shower, and then start a laundry. The laundry room closes at 9 PM, but it is still early enough to get one load in. What I didn't count on however was that one of the dryers was out of order ("sorry for the inconvenience" the sign read), and other users were not returning in a timely fashion to remove their laundry. Another sign read that this room is locked precisely at nine, no ifs, ands, or buts, and any laundry still in here is locked in until morning. Well, as it turns out, when the official comes to lock the laundry, my clothes are still damp, having started them later than expected. So, I gather my clothing up, walk in the dark back to the trike and tent, and set it all on my trike seat to wait out the night. The laundry opens back up at 7 AM, so I figured to be the first one in!

DAY 4 - *Pacific Coast*
September 06, 2013, Friday
Harris Beach State Park to Trees of Mystery redwood forest, California
44 miles (running total: 210 miles)

Up like a bunny at barely first light, I deflate my ThermaRest NeoAir Fast 'n Light mattress, slide into my clothes, and prepare to hit the laundry. David informs me it's not quite 7:00 yet by the time my tent is packed away, so I eat my granola, brush my teeth, and leave last night's dinner remnants in the private bathrooms. I am waiting at the door with my damp clothing when the official returns to unlock it. In no time flat, they are dry again, and my laundry miscalculation from last night doesn't even slow up our departure from Harris Beach State Park.

We fly into town, only a mile south, and drop into Fred Meyer to restock any supplies for our early morning ride into the next state south of Oregon: California, here we come! The sun has come up by now, and David poses with his trike in front of a large bear dressed in a Viking suit of armor. Then, it's simply the final flat miles to the state line, where, of course, we come to a grinding halt to capture our obligatory "Proof of Being There" photographs just in case anyone doesn't really believe we did all this crazy stuff. Of course, it also serves the purpose of stroking our egos that we have pedaled through the southern half of the Oregon coast and are about to enter another imaginary political container, one that is far more bankrupt than the one we are leaving. Why is California washed up financially? Well, one quick clue is that the pavement improves immediately at the line, from rough Oregon paving to glass-smooth California paving! There is obviously a significant difference in riding enjoyment once south of the state welcome sign.

We also enter Del Norte County, the Redwood Gate to the Golden State. This crossing into California is far removed from the crossing that I encounter on my inland trike route that enters the state in its northeastern corner, in agricultural landscapes as far as the eye can see. It's all flat land out there, with potato farms and horse pastures everywhere. Here on the Pacific Coast, it's all huge evergreen trees and even larger redwood trees. Wow, the difference is striking!

The day is warming up quickly. There is no fog this morning so far. Shade is what we seek. Up ahead! Look! Its a gigantic tree, and David decides it needs some water, being out in the relentless sun and all, so we stop and perform our good deeds for the day by keeping this giant alive and thriving. As I roll up, David looks like a little ant under the tree's spreading limbs. I capture another photo of the trikes from the front. My hat is hanging on the flagpole, a little trick I do when I am really pumping out the perspiration, as the breeze makes quick work of drying out the Outdoor Research cap I got at REI, called the Sunrunner.

This western coastal section of northern California changes continually. One hour you're in huge woods, and the next you're crossing some agricultural farms. At times, we see orchard workers on platforms pulled by tractors, doing whatever they are doing with the particular crop they are harvesting. The terrain is pretty flat, so we make incredible time flying south in our highest gears, reaching flatland sustainable speeds of 15 miles per hour at times. With only a 52 tooth big ring, holding 20 requires a lot of extra effort when fully loaded, and is not worth the caloric expenditure or potential for joint injury. Holding at 15 for a while gets us down the road well, and our spirits are high. We pass several sculptures along the road made from horseshoes. Before we know it, the northern California town of Crescent City is upon us.

This town was devastated by a major tsunami years ago, but we take a chance and stop at a Grocery Outlet discount market to eat some lunch. The speeds we sustained to get here used up our energy reserves, and the food was welcomed. We meet some town officials who are really interested in our trikes. It was a fun visit. We are now only 351 miles north of San Francisco according to the state road signs. My, how time flies when you're having fun! In Crescent City, I see the perfect delta trike for sale at a gas station: it has a huge fan that propels it forward. But today, neither David nor I need it because the road is so darn flat that we can go as fast as our legs, lungs, and gearing will take us! What a rush. We get some incredible photos of the trikes at the beach as we ride past, towards some terrain that is entirely different.

Of course, all things must pass, this we know. And so, the flat gives way to what cyclists call the Crescent City hill. This is no ordinary hill, but seems more along the lines of the Bellview hill we traversed not long ago in southern Oregon. Yep, my eyes are telling my brain that it is about time to "spin and grin" once again, a mental state where a triker puts the mind somewhere else, and the feet just keep spinning away at those pedals until the summit is reached. Maybe that fan powered delta trike would be just the ticket for this impending monster.

A sign at the bottom reads: NARROW SHOULDER NEXT 10 MILES WATCH FOR BICYCLES. Hey, what about tricycles? I'm getting a complex. Of course, there is a message carefully hidden inside those words, one not understood by petroleum powered humans, but deeply felt by human powered humans such as David and me. That message? Prepare to fry and cry for the rest of the afternoon. Well, that's not all the message. The rest is to prepare (eventually) to fly down the other side. What goes up a monster hill must also rocket down at some point. If a trike hobo survives the torturous ascent, he will be rewarded with a heart-throbbing descent, at high trike speeds.

We enter the Redwood National and State Parks somewhere along the seemingly endless ascent. We pedal up for what seems like hours. I have not worn a timepiece for more than 20 years now, so my only clue is the position of the sun. David knows the details, but we do not speak on the way up. All our life powers are concentrated in the goal of summit acquisition. I see the top. I reach the top. It is not the top! It is what is known as a false summit. Bummer. Up we go again. More of the same. Death comes slowly and in measured doses as the sun knows no mercy. After a while, I really do see the top. I reach the top. It is not the top! Another false summit. How cruel this flat Earth can be. Christopher Columbus just had to go and prove it wasn't flat, so now I pay the price. We pedal on, again, hoping for the top, but now mentally defeated, as if there really is no summit to the laughing colossus.

Time marches on. I see the top! I reach the top! It really is the top this time! Six miles, according to the roadside milepost markers, have passed since we have known flat ground. We rest. We eat energy bars. We prepare for what must be the ultimate yahoo ride, a real Mister Toad's Wild Ride is in store for two very wiped out trike hobos. Not far from the top on the descent, there is a traffic stoppage for a construction zone. I enter the line of cars and wait just like them. David went through on the last pass. The light turns green. The cars begin moving. I keep pace easily, actually having to brake because they are moving slower!

We all exit the zone together, and I am still pacing the automobiles. What a trip this is! The road is so steep, I am not holding anyone up. I am also not riding on the shoulder anymore because at high speed, trike riding on shoulders is simply foolish. I take a car lane. Car passengers and drivers are amazed to see the show of this little human powered tricycle coasting at such speed. It's two miles before the road levels out. It was an 8 mile experience over the top of this mega mound.

Our journey still has us up quite high in elevation compared to down at the beach. David and I pass the boundary to the Del Norte Redwoods State Park. Now David is taking a lot of photos also, amazed at the size of these trees, giants that even a camera with a wide angled lens cannot fully capture or do justice. Only the human eyes and our brains allow full appreciation of this amazing place.

At another high point, we see that the Mill Creek campground in the Del Norte Redwoods State Park is open. We are exhausted now, and turn in to camp, but what we see is heartbreaking. The sign indicates it is another 2.2 miles to the campground off the highway, and as we pedal forth anyway, the road plummets at a grade far steeper than what we have been climbing all afternoon. The road is so degraded from years of no maintenance that potholes and cracks are huge, and very uncomfortable on our trikes. About 50 yards down the insane hill, we stop, look at each other, and simultaneously realize that no, we clearly do not wish to descend this aberration after our hard-fought elevation gains today, and we most certainly do not wish to climb this monstrosity first thing tomorrow morning! Word is that this campground is a triker's dreamland once there, but the price is just too stiff for David and me to pay, so we return to the main highway and pedal on southward.

This option we have chosen is also not without unknowns. There are no known campgrounds now for a very long distance, much farther away than we can reasonably pedal in these waning hours of daylight. Our destination tonight is fully uncertain. The road is extremely narrow, with practically no shoulder area much of the way, and the car traffic is exceptionally heavy. We use our flashing taillights, and car drivers are courteous. It is also very dark in here because the massive redwood trees filter out much of the sunlight that remains this late in the day. We are too tired to slide into worry mode now. We just keep our forward motion, and realize we will make a spur of the moment decision at some point, perhaps a wild stealth camp in the virgin woods tonight!

We finally descend again to the level of the mighty Pacific. Sun is low. The large sea stacks are impressive in this late light. The road turns inland, and before we know it, there we are! I see Paul Bunyan and his blue ox Babe standing there on the left. Paul is waving to me. Babe keeps him company. The light is almost gone from the gigantic statues, and no matter what, I simply must have a photograph of my ICE trike at Paul's immense left foot. David pulls in shortly, and rides to get in on the action. He knows a great photo op when he sees it! While he is still shooting away, I have an idea, and ride off across Highway 101 to the Forest Cafe so I can speak with the proprietor.

We are at the world famous Trees of Mystery redwood forest. This place, while certainly a tourist attraction of the first order, is worth the admission price. I have been through it, and highly recommend it to anyone who loves monster trees. I enter the Forest Cafe, greeted by a large stuffed bear who waves at me. I am also greeted by Billy Jo, the hostess, at whom I throw myself to her mercy. I relate our sad tale of woe, with no where to pitch our tents for the night. Might it be possible to inconspicuously pitch two small tents in the deserted gravel lot east of the restaurant? She says yes, and immediately our uncertainty is totally gone. When David pedals up to me outside, I relate the good news, and we decide to eat dinner at the restaurant, and also grab breakfast the next morning. It's the least we can do for their generosity, for there is no charge to camp. I am even allowed by the other waiter, Joe, to use their private telephone with my calling card, since there is no cellular service.

David and I pitch our tents, physically wasted from today's tests of endurance, and then walk into the restaurant for dinner. I order a black bean veggie burger, which is delicious, the first "normal" food I've had for a while – and, it's hot for a change! David spends his time on their free Wi-Fi signal, updating his website and contacting his wife. We leave a generous tip and hit the sack.

The tent flies are damp – something odd about the atmospheric conditions, for the sky is crystal clear, and the night brings a sky that fully displays the edge of the Milky Way. It is so awesome here. Serendipity has played a role. We are safe and having a great time, with two killer hills now behind us – but, of course, on this coastal route, there are many more where they came from! Yes, they have scores of friends! This route is a demanding one in many ways.

A loud recording plays 24 hours across the highway, luring tourists to stop. I memorize it as I drift off to sleep.

DAY 5 - *Pacific Coast*
September 07, 2013, Saturday
Trees of Mystery to Patrick's Point State Park, California
40 miles (running total: 250 miles)

As David I arise prior to sunup, it is clear that our tent flies are heavily laden with moisture. The night was totally clear, yet this odd dynamic with water presents itself. This large gravel lot was put in recently, and partly covers a ravine just next to our tents. Perhaps a stream or other water source that we did not observe while setting up the tents is nearby, causing the wetness. In any event, it's time to do some drying. I carry a small piece of chamois cloth (9x9 inches) that I cut out of a large old chamois for my first trike trek in 2009. I wipe off the fly as best I can, wring out the chamois, and then wipe off the waterproof pannier covers on my Arkel bags. After removing the tent fly, I shake it vigorously to clear any remaining moisture, but still, it must be stowed in a less than dry condition. Such is trike hobo life.

My tent is new for this trip. It is a NEMO (New England Mountaineering) Obi one-person tent, which I am totally loving every camp. Compared to my old two-person REI tent, this is very easy to pitch and strike, and it weighs half of the other tent I had on my first two expeditions. The Obi came in a waterproof carrying bag, suitable for easy storage in a backpack. I chose to not use that bag because when I put gear away damp like this, I do not want it tightly packed. My intuition tells me that loosely packing the gear will allow it to dry more efficiently, so, I pack it, loosely folded (not rolled) in a larger REI stuff sack, but the tent and sleeping pad I put in the sack is not stuffed at all. There is much air space surrounding all the items. Then, I place it in one of my Radical Design side seat pods, which is breathable and gets good sun during the day. The ensuing evening, there may be some residual dampness on the fly, but less than had I rolled it tightly in a stuff sack.

At the Forest Cafe restaurant, we park our trikes right out front, having loaded our gear already. Immediately, folks staying at the motel start looking at them, and then stopping by our table to chat about the trip. We are the center of attention throughout our early morning eating. David orders a breakfast, and then gets right to work updating his website with all the latest tricycling news for his students at Glendora High School. Being the crazy health nut guy I am, I order hot oatmeal, to which I add my wheat bran, green veggie power, and raisins. I eat like this normally, but on a trip where diet is compromised somewhat, I find the wheat bran added to my granola each morning (3 heaping spoonfuls) keeps my pipes running clear, which is a good thing when using camp bathrooms, or facilities less than optimal from a sanitation standpoint. Quick in and out makes for a hassle-free trike hobo experience.

We take our time, eating, talking with people, and tending to electronic business, then shove off down Highway 101 again in the early morning sunshine. It isn't long at all before we have to remove light jackets as we are heating up from our pedaling. The road is pretty flat here, so we remain in high gears and knock down some miles in short order. I take a photo of David as he pedals ahead of me, with a SLOWER TRAFFIC KEEP RIGHT sign next to him, accentuating the mode of progress from the point of view of an overland triker. Highways 101 and 1 have several names, depending on which state and where in that state you are. Today, and for days to come, this section of 101 is called the Redwood Highway due to the huge redwood tree groves with which it dances. A few days farther south on the road, the name changes.

Eventually, the highway begins to climb in elevation as it proceeds farther inland, away from the ocean. We arrive at a junction where the Pacific Coast Bicycle Route shows an alternate way to go, off the main highway for several miles. This is the old highway, and it goes to Prairie Creek Redwoods State Park, a stunningly gorgeous natural preserve of colossal redwood trees. It adds miles to the trip, but is well worth the extra distance. We stop at the offramp, discuss options, and agree that this side trip will be one well taken. Off we pedal, up the hill, and into the deep big woods with very little auto traffic.

Once we arrive at the visitor center for the state park, which also includes an incredible campground facility, we chat with a couple of young gals who are on their own bicycle journey south along the Pacific Coast. They will be staying here at Prairie Creek for two nights, so this is likely the final time we shall see them. It is far too early for David and me to call it a day, especially considering his time schedule to arrive in Morro Bay by September 20, so we head on out after looking around, taking a snack break, filling our water bottles with pure redwood forest water, and chatting with some other interested onlookers. Signs warn us to stay away from the elk. This is a refreshing rest from the road. Back onto the highway towards Eureka we merrily pedal.

In the tiny town of Orick, we stop at the little market to get some fresh veggies and nuts. David buys a large pack of ice to resupply his small ice cooler trunk, and then peddles the remainder to some folks in a camper truck, who happen to be from the Bend, Oregon region. I laugh at him for all his ice, and he reluctantly poses for a photo. We are having a great time together. After Orick, the road is flat, and takes us back to the ocean through agricultural lands with cows and patchy fog.

Past some large lagoons we ride, and then the road soars back upward into the hills once again. As it crests finally, we come into view of a huge body of water, which is actually called Big Lagoon, and is part of Big Lagoon Park. On the far side of this gigantic body of water is the point where we will spend the night. It is called Patrick's Point State Park, and there is fantastic hiker/biker camping awaiting us there. Often, it is all fogged in, and the ocean is not visible in the cold foggy air, but this time of year, it is crystal clear, not a cloud in the sky, and pleasantly warm! Patrick's Point is one of the best overnights on the entire Pacific Coast if you hit the weather right, as we are doing today. September is my recommended month, but keep in mind, on overland trike journeys, the only certainty is uncertainty! There are absolutely no guarantees.

I take a photograph of David as he crests this hill, and then he is gone, flying down towards the lagoon, and around the water to the point. After several more miles on the Highway 101 freeway, open to cyclists legally, and very safe due to the ultra wide shoulders, we arrive at Patrick's Point State Park. It is still relatively early, so pitching of the camp is leisurely and easy. While setting up our night's camp, Tim Cassese, whom I met recently, silently rides in like a phantom, and asks to share our secluded bounty overlooking the ocean on this bluff. We quickly agree, and the three of us enjoy all there is to enjoy here.

There is an impressively tall rock monolith right next to our camping area, called Lookout Rock. Being a wilderness explorer of sorts, after pitching the tent and eating dinner, I walk over to it through the trees. There is a pathway to the top! It is chiseled out of the stone, with rocks placed as necessary for foot steps. The way is narrow, steep, and precarious, but I simply must reach the top and take in the views of the grand ocean before the sun sets. I am wearing my SIDI Dominator 5 mountain bike cycling shoes, not the best thing for hiking like this, but make it to the summit anyway. Awesome vistas present themselves to my eyes and brain. I am ecstatic, and take some photographs. I return to camp, and tell David and Tim that this is a "must see" before the sun settles down into the salty water to the west. They take my suggestion and hurry on up for their own pictures and memories.

The shower facility for the hiker/biker camp is brand new. I find a shower that, while supposedly requiring quarters, operates just fine by pushing the button without money. I have made it a habit to always check first. Sometimes showers just come on, so I don't argue. This particular park charges 50 cents for five minutes. Some charge 75 cents or a dollar for five minutes. Still, no matter what the charge, a warm shower each evening is surely a treat, especially for this overland trike hobo, who is used to an inland route along the eastern Sierra, where campgrounds and showers are virtually nonexistent.

Night finally falls. David's tent is aglow with soft interior light from his electronic gizmos as he records the trip's happenings and makes cell phone calls. Tim must already be bedded down. I take a couple photos of me in the tent for kicks and grins, update my logbook by headlamp, and then quickly fall fast asleep. Trike pedaling all day long does that to a person. Sleeping is easy! As with many coastal camps, sounds of fog horns and/or sea lions are heard in the still and quiet night air. It is dry and warm all night, with no moisture on the fly or gear.

DAY 6 - *Pacific Coast*
September 08, 2013, Sunday
Patrick's Point State Park to Stafford RV Park (2 miles north of Avenue of the Giants), California – 59 miles (running total: 309 miles)

We all awaken to a dry camp. No dampness is on anything, so unlike yesterday morning, we pack away our gear fully dry this time. Tim is making his peanut butter and chocolate on tortillas breakfast. I pour my granola, adding wheat bran, veggie powder, and raisins. It is a grand morning, except for one potential issue that has been developing.

David has become the victim of an infection, which began manifesting itself yesterday, but he was hoping to beat it through the night's rest. He has medication for this occasional issue at home, but did not bring it with him on this trip. This morning, he feels really bad, and it seems to be worsening rather than getting better. He informs me that he will likely be taking his leave today, having found an airport on his iPhone near Arcata, California, where they rent Hertz automobiles. His plan is to ride south to this airport with me this morning, which is about 13 miles south of our Patrick's Point camp, and then depart in a rental car back to his home in California. Of course, this immediately saddens me, as his company has proven pleasant for me. I enjoy the camaraderie of a kindred triking spirit. Challenges often seem less daunting when shared with a good friend, and so it has been on this adventure.

This Pacific Coast tricycle adventure is now reminding me of the 2011 eastern Sierra trike journey. On both expeditions, the crew consisted of three cyclists at the onset, yet two of the three faced issues that led to them leaving prematurely. This is Day Six, and it now seems that the days between now and September 20 when I reach Morro Bay will be spent solo once again. Twelve days of solo riding now are ahead of me, unless I meet up with other cyclists along the way who wish to ride with me. Chances of meeting another trike hobo though are next to zero. There are scores of bicyclists, but a triker? Not a chance.

We pedal out of Patrick's Point, heavy with the impending separation. David really wants to complete this overland journey, and so besides the infection hitting him hard, the sadness of having to stop short is also hitting him hard. At least his final night's camp was as good as they come. He relates to me that last night was his favorite of all the campgrounds so far on this short trek.

After a lot of up and down pedaling in the typical morning fog, we arrive in Trinidad, California, hit the small market, eat some snacks, and sit in front of the post office as David finalizes his plans with his wife on the iPhone. A local war veteran who plays a First American flute, tells us of a wonderful shortcut off of Highway 101 that takes us straight into Arcata, with ocean views all the way. He says all the cyclists take it, and if we can't find it, we deserve to be lost. He points to the road near the on-ramp to the highway, and says to just take that road right there for the best ride, which he insists beats the highway experience. Okay, I say. Let's give it a shot, although I have never heard of this road before. It is a chance, but the guy seemed to know.

Well, to make a short and miserable story even shorter, this road has not been maintained by any governmental agency in decades. It is loaded with potholes, has fallen away down the cliff side, is full of huge cracks where earth movement has broken the road, and is of the "chip seal" variety that simply jitters a cyclist nearly to death. Sure, the view beats having gotten back on Highway 101, of that there is no doubt, but the going is so very slow and painfully tedious that every ounce of potential enjoyment is sucked right out of our heads. We are miserable on this most horrible of all horrible roads, just creeping along most of the way to avoid crashing, and pedaling up rather steep, but fortunately short, inclines along the cliff. This route was a big mistake!

To top it off, after a couple miles of this hellish torture, we come to a DEAD END sign! The road dead-ends into nothing, meaning that all our endurance of this gauntlet was for naught, especially considering that David feels miserable to begin with due to his infection, and this agony has only magnified his suffering! Lucky for us there is a short road that leads back to the main highway here, so we turn left, get on the steep on-ramp, and are back to smooth sailing to the Arcata airport and David's rental car. Lesson learned? Never take an alternate route if in ANY doubt – the main highway is nearly always the shortest and easiest route, well maintained, with the most gentle of grades.

Back on Highway 101 and flying along, we pass a sign that

indicates 8 more miles to Arcata. Then, it happens! We arrive at the off-ramp to the airport, so I stop to wait for David. He rolls up and reiterates that he must leave the trip now due to his degrading health issue. I take some photos of his trike, and of us together one last time, and then watch solemnly as he pedals down the off-ramp named 722. Our early hours today were shared, yet what happens next will be wholly different. Our worlds have been ripped apart, and our stories are no longer similar from here on out. We enter new individual adventures.

I do not know what became of my friend. As I pedal along towards Eureka on the flat and very fast roadway, I wonder how he is feeling, and if he will get a car and be able to drive home today. I do not keep my borrowed cell phone turned on, so can receive no incoming calls from David. This phone is very old, and the battery does not last long, so I only turn it on at evening camps to notify family of my whereabouts, and then off it goes until the next night. Since there is not always cell service, and since I keep calls short, the battery lasts long enough to eventually find a suitable recharging solution, which is often a plug in a campground bathroom, trusting that no one will abscond with it during the hour recharging. If I suspect that an upcoming camp will not be in a cell service area, I will sometimes make a midday call and simply leave a short update message saying that I am still alive and well.

The highway is lined in many areas with huge eucalyptus trees, and the smell is lovely, like the oil that comes from these trees and can be purchased in stores. Growing up as a young lad, my parents' house had five eucalyptus trees in the backyard, so I grew to love the aroma always out the back door. These trees have an orange cast, and their long slender leaves are not mistaken for any other type of tree I know.

At 44 feet above sea level, I reach the limits of a town with nearly 30,000 residents. I need to pee, and there is an opening in the heavy shrubbery to the side of the shoulder here, where I notice an old and abandoned railroad track. I park my trike at the city limit sign of Eureka, walk through the opening in the bushes, into total privacy, and realize I am smack dab in the middle of an extensive blackberry patch! It's my lucky day! After watering the old trestles, I have a grand time picking and eating all the blackberries I want. I did not expect such a treat, but since it's here, I take full advantage of it. No one will be picking these berries this far out, including bears, so might as well use them before they shrivel up. I love blackberries more than the bears do!

The next stop is the Target store on the northern edge of town. It is an easy off and on to the highway, so I pedal into the shade of the store, park the trike, and shop for an ice cold protein drink and some fresh strawberries and cherry tomatoes. I also make a cell update call here, and leave a message, figuring that tonight I will likely be back up deep in the forest, with no service. Then, into the main town I head.

When I pedal through most towns, I remain on the main thoroughfare for expediency sake, but Eureka has a bike route worth taking. Yes, it does go through back areas where bums are living in the bushes around industrial sites, but it also skirts a nice marina, and then takes the cyclist past the private member Ingomar Club, which is housed in the world famous Victorian mansion that appears on post cards and other travel memorabilia. I grab a shot of the tricycle right in front, and have a good laugh imagining this as my private residence. Of course, it runs completely counter to my way of seeing life, the antithesis of my wilderness ideologies. I am a 62 year old tricycle rider. Clearly, I don't do things like everyone else. When the herd turns right, I turn left. This expression of overindulgent opulence is a tribute to someone's ego out of control years ago, shouting to look at what I have, when nearly a billion humans are starving to death on this planet.

It requires a long time to get through Eureka, as there are many stoplights along the way. I make good time however, stop in a Chevron convenience store, fill my water bottles with ice cold water, and then book on out the south side back into the wilds. One of the first things I notice is a large billboard with Sasquatch chasing some campers in their car, as they drive through a big redwood tree. This is advertising the Avenue of the Giants, a world famous series of redwood groves that are so expansive that at midday on a sunny day, it is dark inside the forest. I have been through this avenue, and highly recommend it to touring cyclists. It adds mileage to the route, of that there is no doubt, and it adds hills and time too, but the big trees are worth the effort. I was fully planning on taking this wonderful side trip with David, but since he is now but a memory, I will remain on Highway 101 to cut down on my mileage, work load, and time frame. There are many challenging uphills on the coastal route, and now my goal is to avoid any unnecessary ones.

The road it pretty flat much of the way today, and I make good time in high gears once again. The rest from uphills is welcomed. The milepost markers seem to fly by, which is fine with me, especially since I'm still bummed out that David is no longer part of the team. My mind today says to lay down as many miles as I can as I adapt to the new solo routine. Solo riding has its advantages though, the major one being that I can do what I want when I want, on the spur of the moment, without any consultation necessary. This makes for quicker progress, yet I would rather have a companion and the fun of shared decision making.

Now the day is wearing on. The sun is rapidly getting lower. There are no state campgrounds anywhere close to where I will end up today, and now I am facing the potential for a wild stealth camp again. Being solo, wild hobo camps are easy. It's easier for one guy and one trike to inconspicuously blend into the environment than two people with two trikes. One reason I chose the new NEMO Obi one person tent is due to its ultra small size and rapid setup time. Big tents may be nice in dedicated campgrounds, but they are a liability for stealth situations. Plus, the NEMO Obi tent is dark gray and black without the fly, so it virtually disappears into the darkened night forest, a hobo dream house.

The next small town, called Rio Dell, has a camping sign, so I exit the freeway, pedal over the overpass, and quickly find within about three blocks that whatever the highway sign was referring to is no longer here. It's just a bunch of old run-down homes with no further signing of anything. I turn around, stop on the overpass, make a quick cell call in case there is no later service, and return to the highway via the on-ramp. The road is still very wide and relatively flat, so I fly along towards my unknown destination as the sun continues to race towards the horizon. The little town of Scotia comes and goes, with no available camping. Things are looking dicey. Time to get wild perhaps.

I notice the big AVENUE OF THE GIANTS sign coming up ahead. On a tricycle, one sees road signs for a much longer time period than folks in high speed automobiles. On a tricycle, I can also stop anywhere along the shoulder to take photographs. The freedom of the trike is exhilarating! As I approach an off-ramp next to the big sign, I notice off to the left side of the highway, a large sign that reads STAFFORD RV PARK, and my spirits rise with thoughts of an easy camp without any hassles. I exit, pedal under the underpass, ride down the rural road of old houses, junk cars, and barking dogs. Just when I think this might be yet another dead end, there is the RV park, not the type of camp I would usually pick, but perhaps the best solution today.

Into the RV park I silently roll. I walk up the steps of the old mobile home in which the elderly couple live who own the massive acreage of towering redwood trees. Their little "yipper" dog goes nuts, being surprised by my quiet presence. The wife tells me it's $18 for a tent campsite. I think to myself that I could stay for more than 3 nights at hiker/biker camps in the state campgrounds, but suck up my logical pride and ante up the bucks. Besides, this lady and her 86 year old husband are very nice to me, and I am too tired to seek other solutions this evening. She asks me if I would like an ice cold Arrowhead water to drink, which they sell. I ask how much it costs. She takes pity on my pedal pushing body, and just hands it to me while saying, "It's free!"

I ask if there is cell service here. She says yes and no. Over there at the road, people can get it, but just these ten yards to where you are standing knock it out for some reason. I walk over and fire up the cell, dogs barking, but not aggressing. I get service, so I notify family I'm okay. Then, I pedal way back into the redwood grove to find the tent area. Gorgeous! This camp, even though pricey, is a good one, and I'll be able to take a long hot free shower tonight to boot! I find a great place to pitch my tent right at the base of a colossal redwood tree, and as I look around, what do I behold? You won't believe this! Incredible!

Yes, just a few yards to the west, next to a tent already pitched, is ... hold onto your helmets, a (I can't hardly believe it myself) human powered recumbent tadpole tricycle! Unbelievable. I know how rare it is to see these things out on the road, but here one is in the next campsite. I call out "hello" to find the rider, but no response is forthcoming. He must be taking a shower, I think. The mystery triker's ride is a blue Greenspeed Magnum, the new heavy duty trike introduced in 2011 by the Australian tricycle manufacturer. I know Ian Sims, the owner of Greenspeed, and think that I have to tell him about this when I see him at the 2013 Recumbent Cycle Convention this coming November. I will be manning a booth there, and so will he. His trikes are legendary.

Having pitched my tent, I sit down at the old picnic table among the giants to eat some precooked rice and a 3 ounce packet of salmon, protein and carbohydrates to rebuild what I destroy each day on the road. Midway through my meal, as darkness slowly encroaches, Sid Cheek walks over and introduces himself. He is 64 years old, and tells me he is on one of his "bucket list" endeavors, that being something a person really wants to do before he dies. I think to myself that he is awful young to be engaging in bucket list things, but I have no idea if there is something that might afflict him I don't know about, thereby prematurely terminating his life power. Sid is only two years older than me, and I have no thoughts whatsoever of bucket lists. Life is yet young and vital, and bucket list activities seems somewhat depressing to me.

We talk a bit, but I cut it short eventually so I can go get into the shower across the big field before it gets too dark to see in here. As I shower, I consider Sid's undertaking. He lives in the midwest portion of the United States. He has a son in Puyallup, Washington, which is where he began his trike odyssey. He is riding from his son's house, south to the Mexican border, and then east to the southern most tip of the Florida panhandle! This is his first trike ride cross country. The distance, and solo no less, makes my head spin. Sid says that 20-30 mile days are his maximum. Today he rode 40 miles and said it nearly did him in. He is in pain tonight, and taking Ibuprofen to ease his suffering. Tomorrow, he will be pedaling through the Avenue of the Giants. I hope for the best for Sid. He is a really mellow fellow. He will be on the road for a long time.

After my shower, I crawl into my tent, put on my headlamp, write in my journal, and then fall quickly into a deep sleep, content to know that the giant redwoods loom all around me. I feel at home in this awesome forest, and the pine needles below the tent make for a very comfortable sleep. The weather is dry, with no chance of rain.

DAY 7 - *Pacific Coast*
September 09, 2013, Monday
Stafford RV Park to Richardson Grove State Park, California
47 miles (running total: 356 miles)

First thing in the pre-dawn morning, I get up. Sid is already up over at his table. I take the time to snap some photographs after eating my granola, as he is about to depart for the Avenue of the Giants ride. He rolls his trike over for me to get the pictures. I tell him I will be placing him on my websites eventually after my journey. Then, I watch as he pedals out towards Highway 101, for another day on the endless highway of adventure. He got about a 30 minute head start on me, but I will probably not see him again. Sid will be turning off 101 in two miles for the side trip, but I will be remaining on 101 for the more direct route. Not only that, but our daily average mileages are vastly different.

Speaking of daily average mileages, I am noticing on this coastal journey a different daily mileage paradigm at work. On my former trike treks inland through eastern California, where campgrounds are rarely found, I usually just pedal the trike until about an hour before sunset, judging the time based on where I see the sun in the sky. This is because camps are frequently wild stealth affairs, so I make the most of the daylight hours. This translates into a higher daily average over the course of the journey, around 67 miles per day. On this coastal route, where many known state campgrounds exist, I find I am planning the days based on staying at the next reasonable state camp, so the riding day is typically terminated earlier in the day. I suspect that on this journey, my average daily mileage will be more around the 50 miles per day range. The trade-offs for a hot shower each evening are worth it.

Today seems to be warming up rather rapidly, probably because I am heading inland, farther and farther from the cooler ocean with each pedal stroke. I pass through Humboldt Redwoods State Park early in the day, and then continue on through and past the little towns of Weott, Myers Flat, and Miranda. It is now sometime approaching midday, and I am getting really hot. There are no clouds this far inland, and no breeze either. Not only that, but my two water bottles on the mainframe of my trike have finally reached an empty state – I have one liter left in my rear

281

pannier for emergencies, but hope to find some water prior to accessing it. The elderly owner of Stafford RV Park said it was 83 degrees Fahrenheit there yesterday, but it feels like 83 has come and long since left right now on the air's incessant march towards more scorching temperatures. Of course, these numbers are not so bad depending on what one is doing, but a triker pedaling up hills in full sun has less tolerance than someone sitting on their deck in the shade.

Highway 101 is gaining elevation ahead of me, wide open in the sun. There is an off-ramp coming up, showing signs for the towns of Redway and Garberville. The sign displays numerous local businesses, something that was not shown in Weott or Miranda, so I make a spur of the moment decision to exit into the shade of the trees. I pedal into the driveway of the first business I see on the right, a small motel. I have no idea what the temperature is, but I am beginning to realize that today may be a might more intolerable than any day prior on this trek. Inside the office, I ask the rotund lady if there is a water facet at which I might fill my two bottles, as perspiration is clearly visible on my shirt. She directs me to the laundry room sink. I walk over only to find my 24 ounce Hostel Shoppe bottles are too tall to fit under the facet. I return to the office, where she somewhat reluctantly agrees to fill them in the office. I ask the woman if there is a market nearby, and she tells me of a nice local market in Redway, just up the road a mile or so. I also ask her what the temperature has been here lately. She responds that yesterday's high was 101 degrees. I thank her, get back on the Q, guzzle some water, and pedal up the hill towards the heart of town.

I locate the Redway Shop Smart market, a modern and nice looking store with all expected amenities of any well stocked market. However, things are oddly bizarre here. The town is old and rundown for such a nice market. The small parking lot is absolutely packed with cars and traffic in and out is almost perilous for a triker. As I always do, I park the trike right by the front entrance, which was a challenge because of the large number of people entering and exiting. And the people, boy are there some anomalies compared to any other market I've been to thus far! This is a different universe.

In a former life, I was a cop, so I have loads of experience with alternative folks of all walks of life. It takes a lot to unnerve me, yet this place is certainly on the spectrum of mental composure. I would say that conservatively, only about 5% of the folks I see right now are what you would consider "normal" people. Now, I realize that this discussion borders on what is called profiling, a prejudgment of people based on their appearance and outward demeanors, but what I am seeing is so "out there" that my mind certainly wonders if I have entered the Twilight

Zone or something. Turns out, there is a reason for what I am seeing.

Most people I see have not apparently bathed in quite some time, a matter of many days to be more precise. Most are well endowed with numerous tattoos, earrings, piercings, and other decorative embellishments that scream anti-establishment to the maximum. Most are smoking cigarettes, many have dreadlock hair arrangements that are filthy, and everywhere I look, the "others" are sitting in the shade on the sidewalks trying to stay cool. One is playing a guitar. Many look really out of it mentally, as if they are recovering from a bad hangover, or are on some kind of an illicit drug. Some have knives in scabbards hanging from their belts. Most clothing has not been washed in probably days or even weeks. I mean, this place is so far off the normal zone that it defines a new normal called Redway.

In all my experience, I have never witnessed something this bizarre. I've seen a lot, but nothing this concentrated in such a tiny area in such a tiny backwoods town. One man, about 5 feet 7 inches tall, stares oddly at me as he enters the store. I continue to eat my foot and drink my Odwalla protein monster drinks on the newsstand next to my trike. The trike looks so oddly out of place here! That same man who stared at me going in, now exits the store. Again, he stops by me.

He is very dirty, with earrings and tattoos. He steps out of the market entrance, cool air-conditioned freshness spilling out onto me in the oppressive heat even in this shade, and stops about an arm's length from me. He faces me directly, stares directly into my eyes, and says absolutely nothing as I sip my Odwalla and pop another cherry tomato into my mouth. Finally, after a time that would indicate to a sane person that something is really weird here, he speaks. "How are you?" he asks me in a very zombie like monotone voice, staring blankly into my eyes with his unblinking and expressionless eyes. I realize my description here borders on what you may consider overreacting, but I assure you of its accuracy. I am not one to over dramatize, but rather factually report.

So here is the scene: I am hot beyond belief in this totally still, what must by now surely be triple-digit air, even though in the shade. I'd rather eat in the market, but they have no place to sit down. The ambiance is so bizarre that all I really wish to do is finish my food and drink and get out of here. I'm tired as a result from all the pedaling in the heat, and the last thing I wish to do is engage a man clearly under the influence of some substance that is not conducive to human longevity. I am indeed a rogue maverick, but this guy, and most of the others, are not of my philosophical mindset. So, staring right back into this man's eyes, I respond with one short cold sentence: "I am not in any mood to talk." There is a noticeable hesitation as his numbed brain

283

attempts to process my meaning. At long last, without another word, he does a military twist on his right foot and ambles off into the parking lot.

Moments later, a tall dark man in tattered dirty clothing, with earrings and a nose ring, dreadlocks hanging about his chest and shoulders, and with an equally bizarre woman standing behind him, asks me if I have a knife. He has an orange he needs to peel. I simply say no, finish my last sip of protein drink, and carefully maneuver my trike out to the parking lot, where I click into the pedals and begin pumping.

On my way out of the market driveway, an unkempt gal playing a guitar on the curb, with a sign asking passerby for money, tells me she likes my trike, and wants one for herself. I smile, tell her how fun they are, and quickly pedal out onto the roadway, which is slightly downhill, allowing me to reach a high speed quickly so as to distance myself from this den of weirdness. Within short order, I sail past the city limit sign, into a dead-air canyon and a heat blast that exceeds anything I've ever felt, even out in the Mojave Desert or Death Valley on the trike. The air is also heavy with humidity, making things even worse.

No sooner am I dying a million deaths in this canyon than the road climbs a steep hill into the neighboring town of Garberville. In low/low, I am out of water already, and it was only a few miles back that I refilled the bottles. Near the top of the hill, I see a gas utility building on the left. It is very modern, and looks perfectly normal compared to the Shop Smart market. I pedal up its steep driveway and park under the shade of a lone tree, although shade in this heat is marginal at best. Once inside, I walk up to the well dressed people behind the customer service desk, apologizing for my ragged looks, wondering in my mind if they think of me what I was thinking of those folks at the market.

In my best English grammar, with the utmost in politeness and articulation being put forth, I provide the reason for my situation (pedaling a tricycle for hundreds of miles and living in a tent), and provide further clues that I am a highly educated and compassionate man who does not have any association with the readily observable populace in Redway. A customer next to me, an elderly woman paying her utility bill, is interested in my journey, and begins a conversation. I ask the lady behind the desk if she might fill my water bottles. She happily agrees, and provides not just water, but ice water! The air conditioned room is a haven to me, and I hate to leave, but I still have miles to go, so I bid my farewells and thank them for their kindness.

Just as I am about to leave the building, I hesitate, turn around, and ask if they happen to know the outside temperature today. The clerk tells me they are having a freak heat wave this week. She further states to my nearly brain-dead head that the temperature outside right now is

107 degrees! How about that! The day I decide to pedal a tricycle through Garberville, California, it is 107 stagnant degrees without a cloud in the sky. Guess this makes up for all those chilly and foggy mornings up in Oregon. Okay, I've paid my dues. I'm outta' here!

As I pedal through the remainder of Garberville 107, I observe many people similar to those observed in Redway, sitting under curbside trees, sometimes in group, smoking and playing guitars, and just trying to survive the sweltering heat. This town is definitely more "upscale" appearing than Redway though. On the ensuing uphill grades out of town and farther down the highway, I stop many times for rest in whatever shade I can find. As the afternoon rolls along, the shade stretches farther across the pavement, providing more opportunity at relief. I am just poking along now, with energy reserves running low.

Forty-seven miles into the day, a day I shall never forget, I finally arrive at Richardson Grove State Park, now fully back into deep redwood forests. Some California state parks are no longer staffed on weekdays because of the state's indebtedness, so I self-register and proceed to the hiker/biker camp, which is a tiny pie-shaped wedge of ground barely big enough for 5 tents. There are two picnic tables. I need a shower, tons of water, and some food. I need to revive myself!

Here there is a French-Canadian woman named Pierrette, who is pedaling a bicycle and trailer for world peace, all over the United States and Canada. She is an admirer of the late Peace Pilgrim, a woman who walked tens of thousands of miles in tennis shoes for world peace. She never owned a car. Pierrette was cut from the same mold as Peace Pilgrim. She was writing in her journal when I arrived. There were some other hikers there. A little later, a fellow named Alan, from Arizona, rides in on his Surly Long Haul Trucker touring bicycle. Alan is packed with Ortlieb waterproof panniers, an obvious veteran of the overland cycling clan. He wears an Arizona jersey, with the state's star and sun-ray symbols emblazoned upon it. He seems to be a bicycle hobo.

It has been a very difficult day for me, not really the bizarre people in Redway at Shop Smart, but primarily the extreme humid heat of 107 degrees. Physically, I am drained, and chat only briefly with my camp companions before I go hit the showers through the woods. After cleaning up and returning to my tent and trike, Alan walks over to talk about the trike. I tell him about Redway, and he knows precisely what I'm describing, so he proceeds to fill me in on all the details.

Alan tells me that there are many marijuana growers in that region, and the people who live on the streets there are simply waiting in hopes of being hired to work the illicit farms in the forest. Alan seems to know this from some reliable source. I just want to go to bed in this cooler evening air, so I really don't care. I excuse myself and crawl into the Obi for the night. Sleep quickly overtakes me tonight.

DAY 8 - *Pacific Coast*
September 10, 2013, Tuesday
Richardson Grove State Park to Standish-Hickey State Park, California
15 miles (running total: 371 miles)

I awake refreshed, and enjoy my morning bowl of granola amid the towering redwoods. It is quiet. Only Alan is up. The others, who drank a lot of liquor last night, are still tucked away in the sleeping bags in the dark forest. Alan and I talk as I eat. I need to do a laundry again. Heat waves have a way of making this necessary. One of the fellows who was at camp last night walked over from a nearby RV park where he is staying, and told me to stop by his tent in the morning and I could do a laundry at the RV park (just tell them, if they ask, you're with me). So, it's early, and I decide to take advantage of the offer.

The laundry room is old and somewhat run down, but here it is, and I am the only one up to use it. Once started, I sit outside and wait. Large RVs are all around me. Once the folks start getting up, the men folk walk over to learn all about my trike. I answer many questions with a smile for a long time. I figure if these folks like me, I'm as good as in here, and won't be hassled by anyone for doing a laundry, which technically, I am not suppose to be doing here since I'm not a paid guest. This is a very conservative park, with conservative patrons, and there are religious sayings affixed to all the walls of the laundry room. I do my entire laundry without negative incident. One man tells me how very dangerous my mode of transportation is. I thank him, load the clothing back in my Arkel panniers, and pedal onto Highway 101 south, heading for Standish-Hickey State Park – pedaling my unsafe vehicle.

Standish-Hickey State Park is only 14 more miles down the road, but I decide to stay there tonight. Coming from my head, this sounds rather out of place because I enjoy high mileage days, but I have two reasons for a short day. First and foremost, I have eaten up a substantial amount of my morning riding time doing a laundry and talking with all the fellows who gathered around to learn about my trike. Second, beyond Standish-Hickey State Park 2 miles, I will be departing Highway 101 after all these days, and taking Highway 1 out of Leggett, California, over the 22 very steep and long mountainous miles back to the Pacific Ocean. There is no known campground (at least in my knowledge base) for quite a ways from Standish-Hickey State Park, so I would rather pitch my tent early today, really rest up a lot, and then tackle the infamous Leggett Hill first thing in the morning tomorrow, when it's foggy and cool outside. This strategy will set me up perfectly for a moderate 59 mile day the next day into Van Damme State Park.

It is an easy day for me. Fifteen total miles through the redwood forest is wonderful. Still, it's hot though, so the shade feels good. It is certainly no where near as hot as yesterday in Redway and Garberville. I take my time pedaling, realizing that I can easily arrive at Standish-Hickey long before sunset. The state park comes into view in early afternoon. I make a stop at the market across the street, and, true to form, scarf up my Odwalla protein monster drinks (all three of them), along with a couple bananas, and other good stuff.

Regarding protein, I am maintaining an intake level of 90 to 100 grams of protein per day. I am keeping it this high because cycling is continually breaking down the muscle tissue, which rebuilds itself from protein intake. Normally, when working out off season, I train every other day, with a day of rest in between to allow for muscle recuperation. Overland trike treks are not so kind on the body, as there is no rest sufficient for muscle growth, or at least one would deduce based on extrapolated logic. I like to give my body every advantage I can, and since I know that it is being stressed maximally most days on the road, I decide to "feed the machine" all I can. Interestingly, on these trips, my leg muscles do noticeably increase in volume. I can see the results as the trip goes along, and by the end, it is clear that my legs are much more defined with more muscle mass. One-hundred grams of high quality protein each day maximizes this dynamic. No junk food for me!

I also supply the machine with high fat foods, primarily mixed nuts or trail mixes. They are high in healthy mono-unsaturated fats, which give me loads of energy for these long steep uphills. The protein may rebuild the muscles each night at camp, but it requires the fat to fuel the burn that breaks the muscles down in the first place, which leads to overcompensation, thus increased size and strength. And I eat plenty of fresh fruits and veggies at the daily market stops, in addition to the green veggie power I spoon into my granola every morning.

My largest expense item on overland trike trips is food. At the Safeway supermarkets and other stores, I spare no money in fueling my living machine. Price is not a consideration when out on a trike journey. This is unbelievably difficult work pedaling cross country, and it would not demonstrate wisdom to use money as the determining factor in what I eat. At Safeway, for example, their trail mix packages are very pricey, and the Odwalla protein drinks are too. Veggies and fruits are cheap. It is not unusual for me to spend upwards of $20 at times on a tough day. It is always at least $10 in any market where I buy "eat on the spot"

287

food. I like cold drinks on hot days, and chilled strawberries. Hiker/biker camp sites are typically $5 per night, so you can see that the food bill will comprise the bulk of what this trip ends up costing.

Shortly after 2:30 PM, I pedal into Standish-Hickey State Park campground, pay my five dollars, and cruise into the hiker/biker camping area. The area is huge, well maintained, right next to multiple private showers and toilets, with an outdoor sink for washing cycle clothing, and electrical outlets for charging electrical devices like cell phones. There are already five cyclists here, so I walk around and introduce myself to them. A husband/wife couple from New Zealand, Mike and Les who live in Aukland, are the first I meet. They tell me all about their extensive two wheeled adventures. What a couple!

Next, I walk over to another picnic table and meet Bert Lensink from Victoria, British Columbia and Vic Krueger from Vancouver, British Columbia. They have been riding together on diamond frame touring bicycles since northern Washington. They too are really nice and very enjoyable to visit. They seem to have this touring business down to a fine science. Bert and Vic are slightly older than I am. And again, I see Alan from Arizona sitting at a table, smoking one of his 25 daily cigarettes. Alan is an alternative type of fellow, perhaps a bit rough around the edges for some refined folks, but I really am starting to like the guy. He is very likable if one doesn't find him frightening. I think he's a kick in the pants to talk to, a real straight shooter who is honest to a fault, even if it puts some people off. His knowledge of this Pacific Coast route is incredible, having pedaled it before. I ask him many questions, and he usually knows the answer – impressive.

For an hour or so, we all visit, with no one else arriving, but then, sometime after 4 PM, after we have all showered, they start coming in. First a trickle, then a torrent. I realize that so many bikers are arriving now that to go around and get all their names won't really work. I want to take a group shot of us all for the website when we numbered about 10, but by the time the afternoon turned into evening, and the total number swells to 17 cyclists, all working diligently at setting their camps, cleaning up, and eating, it becomes apparent that I will simply visit and behold the activities. One gal sets up an elaborate hammock, and explains how she doesn't fall out. I greet everyone who pedals up with a smile and a welcome to our camp spiel. This is fun.

With my borrowed cell phone charged, dinner eaten, shower taken, visiting accomplished, a tomato eaten that Mike and Les did not want, and darkness finally descending upon our lively hobo camp here in the grand redwoods, I slip into my tent for the night. Fabian Brook, a cordial young man from Whitehorse, Yukon, is playing a ukulele, and the music is very nice to hear. I will not forget his strumming. Tomorrow morning, all 17 of us will be arising before sunup to begin our ascent of the Leggett hill, only three miles distant from our tents by road. My easy day today will be replaced by a working day tomorrow, and only 24 miles from my sleeping bag lies the Pacific Ocean once again, replacing the oppressive heat of Redway and Garberville. I am eager to return!

DAY 9 - *Pacific Coast*
September 11, 2013, Wednesday
Standish-Hickey State Park to Van Damme State Park, California
59 miles (running total: 430 miles)

When one family in a typical large motorhome arises in the morning at a campground, begins their day, attaches their car to the motorhome's trailer hitch, and warms up their diesel engine for several minutes prior to departure, all the other campers in the vicinity quickly become fully aware that this temporary neighbor is up and preparing to leave the campsite. Noise level is high, air quality takes a dive due to petroleum particulate matter being emitted everywhere for people to breathe, and sleeping any further usually is an exercise in futility.

That's just one family, and there are many such families and motorhomes in most state campgrounds. Multiply this scenario by a fair order of magnitude, and that is what America thinks as camping in the wilderness. I've camped for decades, witnessing this year after year. Regardless our individual opinions about this, let's now compare this common behavior to a human powered cyclist camp.

It is September 11th at Standish-Hickey State Park. The sun is not yet up. Most folks would not even call it dawn. The motorhomers are still sound asleep. There really isn't enough light to easily see to break down a tent and campsite, but with each passing minute, it does get a little bit brighter. In short order, headlamps can be turned off as dawn approaches. There are 17 cyclists here, confined to a relatively small area compared to what the monstrous motorhomes require. I hear a faint rustling outside my tent, somewhere in the faintly pre-dawn air of the hiker/biker camp. Sure enough, some of us are now already up and silently beginning our morning routines prior to hitting the road.

We are all like phantoms. It's some kind of an unwritten law of the cycle touring world. We are part of a loosely confederated group of human powered humans, brought together for a few hours daily on our shared, yet individual, journeys south on the Pacific Coast. We all have our unique morning procedures, but they all lead to the same result: We wake up, get dressed in our tents, strike our tents and pack them away

289

in our panniers, wash the sleep from eyes, eat something for breakfast to fuel the machine for what lies ahead, pack the final items in the cargo bags, and depart the campground. If words are even spoken, they float on the air softly in whispers, extending no farther than the ear close by. There are no engines, no toxins, no noise pollution to awaken all the neighbors. When the folks in the motorhomes finally do wake up and begin their routines, the hiker/biker camp is totally deserted. No clue.

By the time the typical camper is groggily walking over to the bathroom, the cycle nomads are all out pedaling the highway once again, using most of the daylight hours to reach the next overnight camp, a distance that the noisy petroleum powered motorhome humans will travel in only one hour. The two worlds are dimensions apart, and the only shared ground is the pavement upon which we all travel in our vastly different vehicles. Trike and bike hobos are aliens to those people.

I start the day on Highway 101, the same road I have been pedaling since the third of September. My trike's taillight is on, flashing its 10 LED lights, as the redwood forest engulfing me keeps out the light quite well this early. By the time I reach the tiny isolated village of Leggett, California, two miles south of Standish-Hickey, it is bright enough to easily see. Here is the sign coastal touring cyclists can't afford to miss. This is where California 1 forks off of US Highway 101 at long last, and is also where the Pacific Coast Bike Route leaves the racing petroleum puffers to their high speed drive to cover as much ground in as little time as they can. I happily turn onto California 1, called PCH, or the legendary Pacific Coast Highway. Here is where the views begin!

Of course, there is a price to pay for making this right-hand turn at Leggett. That price is the abandonment of easy uphill grades and wide shoulders. The next 22 miles to the Pacific Ocean is very narrow, one lane in each direction, and often with little or no shoulder for the trike. Oh, and did I mention that much of the road is extremely curvy with a 15 mile per hour speed limit in places? And, oh yeah, one more little tidbit about this road: It is steep, very steep, for most of its miles, with two summits. So here is the picture: I pedal the ICE trike in the lowest gears for what seems like hours (probably because it is hours), reach a summit, begin rocketing down again (but I can't go too fast because the curves are very tight in places, and can flip a trike), pedal easy for a while as I pass a sign that reads SHORELINE HIGHWAY, think I am nearly at the ocean, only to realize that directly ahead of me is, yet another summit grade I must ascend, just as steep as the first, but fortunately, not quite as long. At least I am not overheating today.

This traverse, called the infamous Leggett Hill, requires much of a cyclist's morning, but it is not as bad as the picture painted by many riders. Why? Because it is overcast this morning, 55 degrees Fahrenheit, and as I near the ocean once again, the Pacific's typical weather pattern kicks in, namely fog. So, despite the effort needed to travel these 22 miles (24 from Standish-Hickey State Park), I am not dying of the heat or horribly exhausted as I was in the Redway/Garberville 107 area recently. I have plenty of water to easily get me to the calm gray sea below the cliffs where the road opens up out of the forest. It is calm.

As I reach the Pacific, I stop and have an Odwalla protein bar and a Clif Bar. The water is so quiet and still, with hardly any surf. It is almost eerie. There is hardly any traffic here. Not even three dozen cars passed me on the 22 mile ride over Leggett Hill. This is very peaceful territory. The road now flattens out by comparison, and I can see for many miles far ahead down the southern coast from where I am standing. Many pompous grass bushes grace the hillsides. They sway gently in the slightest breeze. They remind me of home, up north in Oregon, where there are also many, but the Oregon ones seem to be more yellow in tint, whereas these are more lavender colored.

Along this route, I also find more blackberries, and never miss an opportunity to gather some up to fuel my organic engine for the ride south. After riding for a while, I notice Alan from Arizona up ahead. He is stopped smoking a cigarette, but does not see or hear me pass by. I call out "Hi Alan" as I move along, which clearly startles him. Trike Phantoms are quiet. Nobody can hear us coming. Later, I pass one of the cyclists and his wife who camped at Standish-Hickey last night. She broke a spoke. He fixed it. Good thing he knows his mechanics. There are no bike shops to the rescue this far out – just big Pacific Ocean.

At times along this Route 1, the trees form what feels like tunnels with their branches. They make for interesting photographs. This is called the Medocino coast, and today it is currently cloudy and muggy. By the time I enter the city limits of Fort Bragg, a large full service town, the sky is mostly clear and sunny. It is early afternoon, time for a Safeway market break, some Odwalla protein monster drinks, fresh strawberries, trail mix nuts, and a couple of bananas. This is a welcomed pause in the pedal pushing routine, having successfully crossed the Leggett Hill, and also making it up a grade that was beyond belief in steepness, short, but a pedal mashing low/low affair.

Here's what happens continually along the Pacific Coast: I am pedaling along the bluff overlooking the ocean. Now and then, streams and rivers flow from the mountains into the ocean. Well, where these waterways enter the ocean, there is a canyon of sorts, often small, and rarely do government agencies spend money erecting long bridges over these frequent fresh water intrusions into the sea. So, I have learned that

291

when I see the road ahead take a hard 90 degree turn to the left, often with an arrow warning motorists, I know that it is because a stream or river is flowing into the ocean. The road takes a sudden drop along the small canyon face, down to the river level, where a little short bridge has been built over the waterway. Then, it just as abruptly curves right, and up the canyon face on the south side, returning to the bluff overlooking the ocean once again. These are continual all along this Pacific Coast Highway, and the uphill segments, although usually short, are extremely steep, much more so than allowed on governmental highways built today. The higher the bluff, the more extreme and long these uphills become, and a few are mind blowing hard – you have to ride it to know!

At Safeway, I come out of the store after buying my highly anticipated trail treats, ready to refresh myself and refuel the machine for more riding. Up rolls Fabian Brook from the far north country of the Yukon, the same fellow who played the ukulele last night, along with a couple of other bicyclists from our Standish-Hickey hiker/biker party camp. We relax together, share good times of the trip, and eat our freshly acquired food. We also stash some of it in our panniers for tonight's camp, which will be at Van Damme State Park if all goes as planned. Leaving Safeway, I follow Fabian up the first hill out of town, and then he out-paces my trike and is gone. He is a powerful rider.

David, my partner for the first five days of this journey, is also a very powerful rider. I was duly impressed with his ability not only to usually keep pace with me, but sometimes pull ahead when I took my time ascending a steep hill now and then. David had trained well for this trek prior to his departure from southern California to Oregon, taking fully loaded training rides to accustom himself to the demands of overland triking, which, as you might guess, are many. Lots of trike pilots dream of becoming trike hobos, but most find out soon enough that the gulf between dreaming and doing is indeed incredibly wide. The mind may want it, but the body cannot handle the challenges of the road. I have witnessed this time and again. If you plan on joining the ranks of overland trike hobos, plan on at least one full year of all-out physical conditioning ahead of time. That means frequent and fully loaded day rides of 50 miles, along with mini treks of 2-3 days to get used to the camping end of things. There is nothing easy about overland triking!

This road soon flattens out with wide shoulders again, and I make good time south to Van Damme, arriving there well before sunset. This state park lies in a tight river valley that exits to the ocean. It is fully in the tsunami zone, meaning that if a tsunami occurs while I am camping in here, things will get really exciting, and really wet, really fast in the middle of the night. Ahh, all part of the adventure of triking along the Pacific Coast Bike Route on Highway 1. You take your chances!

When I roll silently into the Van Damme hiker/biker camp area, very small indeed, with bumps and potholes all over the ground, my Canadian friends Vic Krueger and Bert Lensink are sitting at the table. They wave to me, and we are all happy to once again keep company. Good overnight road companions are an important asset to help keep one's head together if things are going roughly. But today is smooth sailing, and all is fun. A little later, Fabian rides in (must haves stopped somewhere for a bit because he was ahead of me leaving Fort Bragg). Later still, female cyclist Bronwyn Wood rejoins this rag-tag group of pedal pushers. She was with us at Standish-Hickey State Park, one of the Wild Seventeen. Bronwyn lives in Pittsburgh, Pennsylvania, but was born in Santa Barbara, California. Her family left Santa Barbara when she was an infant, so she is eager to cycle through there now as a young adult. I take a picture of her as she returns to the camp after her shower, blue towel on her head. She wonders why, so I tell her that I want to capture the true spirit of the trike hobo life for all my readers of Earth.

We all talk a while after dinner, and then, as usual, hit the sack shortly after sundown because we know that tomorrow brings another early rise and return to the asphalt. This happens every evening, and we all become precision machines without thinking. It's kind of like the popular old movie called Groundhog Day, where the guy wakes up to the same day everyday, except that each day for us is new and exciting – only the start and end routines are identical. This grows on you.

DAY 10 - *Pacific Coast*
September 12, 2013, Thursday
Van Damme State Park to Gualala Point Regional Park, California
50 miles (running total: 480 miles)

This morning I seem to be the initiator of soft noises that slowly prods the sleepy heads of the other four cyclists into conscious awareness. I begin the day by slowly opening the air valve to my NeoAir mattress so it can deflate while I am atop it – makes for more complete emptying of the air cushion. I don't open it all the way though, as the gush of air would be disturbing to the others. Then, I get out of the synthetic Glacier's Edge sleeping bag, zip it closed, and remove my sleep clothes, replacing them with my riding clothing.

On my prior trips, I have carried and used an expensive down bag, but it is not necessary on this coastal route because the weather is warm enough for the synthetic bag. This bag is also lighter weight, and stuffs slightly smaller than the down bag. More good news is that at the conclusion of this journey, this bag is easily washed and dried with no special attention needed. On prior trips, I have also used a bag liner to keep my skin's oils off the down bag. I am not a big fan of these bag liners as they bunch up when turning at night, and they are a hassle to get them into the bag. This trip, I did not bring the liner, instead opting for some long cotton sleep pants, and a long sleeve merino wool/cotton blend pullover shirt. This new paradigm is much more to my liking! Live and learn, or trike and learn in this case. Trike hobo adaptation works.

Next, I stuff the bag into its stuff sack, fold the mattress, and then put on my socks and riding shoes before exiting the tent. Then, it's just a matter of putting the gear in the panniers, breaking down the tent, stowing it on the trike, eating breakfast, brushing my teeth, going to the bathroom, and saying goodbye once again to all my cycling friends. Eventually, there will come a morning where I will never again see these wonderful people with whom I have shared so much challenge and joy, but for now, we know a few more days of sharing are ahead where we will probably rekindle the group, so we don't get too sentimental yet.

This morning the fog is heavy, and the tent fly is damp. My little chamois comes in handy once again, but still the fly goes in the lightly packed stuff sack moist. It will dry during the sunny day, and also once it's reset this afternoon at the next new campground.

Today's stretch of Highway 1 has many river inlets, thus many insanely steep uphills as I pull out of the river drainages to regain the elevation to the bluffs overlooking the ocean. There is also an extra heavy proliferation of construction sites on the roadway. This must be my lucky trip, because so far, they are all friendly for southbound trikers and bikers, being downhill on the southern direction. Many construction areas use automated traffic signals nowadays to save paying flaggers a wage, but when flaggers are present, they always like to discuss my bizarre mode of transportation. Signals don't care what my vehicle is.

At one point, Highway 1 makes a sharp 90 degree turn off to the right, over a bridge. If a cyclist were not paying attention, he would end up going straight, which looks like the right thing to do, but find himself on Highway 128 and way off track. Later, a big yellow sign appears that reads NARROW WINDING ROAD NEXT 21 MILES WATCH FOR BICYCLES. This means the government has yet again abandoned my safety, and shoulders usually go away for a while. It's no big deal in reality though, as I have never had a close call or dangerous interaction with a motor vehicle in my five years of riding a tricycle. I am always afforded the utmost courtesy by drivers. Even if one of those "one-in-ten-thousand" young white macho males in a Dodge RAM pickup (thanks to the Dodge "GUTS, GLORY, RAM commercials) honks at me to let me know this is "his" road and I have no right to be on it, I at least know he sees me, and I am safe. He may hate sharing the road in his immature and socially challenged selfish mind, but he steers clear as he cusses to himself. When this happens (VERY rarely, I might add), I just smile and wave so he can see in his rear-view mirror that I love him just the same. Someday, perhaps, he will realize that sharing is a good thing during his brief time as a human being. Heal, not wound.

This coastal route is interesting in the sights I see. There are all manner of strange twisted trees, victims I suppose of endless days of powerful winter storms with winds that mercilessly batter the growing trunks, distorting them this way and then that. There are homes with colorful ocean floats hanging all over the porch, and old buildings with grayed wood splitting from weather extremes and salt overload. On a tricycle, there is ample time to enjoy all these oddities all day long, often things that petroleum powered humans rarely if ever notice in their high speed metal boxes. While they are surrounded by stereo music in their climate controlled and environmentally isolated worlds, I feel every gentle breeze, hear every faint sound, and smell every unusual aroma as it wafts through my natural realm inches from the ground. We travel the same road, yet exist in parallel universes, my alternative reality not even within the ability of comprehension for psychologically conditioned motorists. Only a mile for them is an epic adventure for me!

At one point in today's ride, while ascending a very steep hill out of one of the many stream and river outlets that exit into the ocean, a gigantic crane lugged up the hill behind me, barely sustaining a speed slightly faster than my own. It came and came. I could hear it for the longest time while my thighs ached as they evacuated me from the lowlands towards the bluff above. Finally, it slowly passed, so slowly that I was able to photograph it at will with no hurry. And guess what! Despite what all the fear mongers tell me about being squished by such mammoth things, like a mosquito under a human's thumb, it is just another wonderful experience on the PCH.

While entering the tiny village of Manchester, California, not too far north of Gualala, a very heavy-set woman quickly rides her TerraTrike Rover recumbent tadpole tricycle out of the first side street from my left. She has the right trike, that much is certain, because the Rover has a load limit of a whopping 400 pounds. She is very friendly, and tells me she heard I was coming, likely from a motorist who had passed me north of town and knew this gal had a similar trike. Her Rover has a pinwheel flag that spins wildly as she rides, making her very visible. Anyway, she rides with me all through her little town on the PCH, and when we exit the south end, she finally bids me a happy goodbye, pedaling back to her home. I did not stop to ask her name, being rather focused on reaching the Gualala campground early, which is 20 more miles ahead. Gualala is deeply wooded and dark on sunny days.

The Point Arena lighthouse attraction is on the route, but since it's a 2 mile side trip (one way), I opt out. I am passed by a recumbent touring bicyclist near the lighthouse turnoff, and I wave, smile, and tell him he is the only other recumbent rider I have seen so far, but the man does not acknowledge my presence, even though he passes a couple feet from me – not even a quick glance, which I find so very odd. The town of Point Arena sits on an extremely steep downhill when traveling southbound, and I must use the brakes as I proceed through the town with many pedestrians. It is literally built on the side of a hill.

I roll into Gualala and spend a while at their main market, gathering up some mixed nuts, Odwalla protein drinks, fresh fruit, and sit at a table inside to eat and drink it. This town has many Mexican workers, and my companions appear as though they have spent a long day working, as they talk in Spanish, having fun and making jokes. I understand some of what they say from my years past in school, but am too tired to study it in any detail. I put the uneaten nut mix into my panniers, attempt to make a failed cell phone call, and then pedal out the south end of this busy little hamlet, across the bridge, and up the hill to enter the Gualala Point Regional Park to camp for the night.

In this campground, Sonoma County has converted one small former walk-in campsite into their entire hiker/biker area. It is only $5, so no complaint there, but the area is so unbelievably small that any more than three bikers nearly maxes it out. The campground host tells me last night they packed nine bikers in here. Tonight, we number only seven, and our tents are so ridiculously close we hope no one suffers any gastrointestinal distress during the night. A five minute shower here is a bank-busting $1.50, compared to free showers in Oregon, and 50 cent showers in many of the California state parks. Well, at least some of us are together again, just a little closer than is really comfortable for privacy. The host tells me that if any of our gear strays beyond certain bushes (and she takes the time to delineate them), we will be charged the full $35 for camping. They are very serious about this, and do not see anything unreasonable about packing so many people into such a tiny space. There are no smiles or apologies. There is no compassion.

Alex, a very quiet and peaceful woman from Germany, is at our camp again tonight. I met her at Standish-Hickey State Park. She speaks so softly that one must be fully quiet to hear her thoughts. Fabian is here again, and now he has met and is riding with a man from France, who speaks English, yet understanding him is a challenge for me. Vic and

Bert from Canada are here, always fun guys to engage in conversation, and always seeking information on the upcoming road. It is very crowded in our little temporal hiker/biker haven, but we are having fun. After the pitch and dinner, I walk over and take my expensive shower. Cell phones are worthless anywhere around Gualala, so I use the pay phone by the restrooms to update family, and then I hit the sack. With the extreme darkness caused by the heavy trees, it is easy to fall asleep.

Tonight brings a new experience for me. This is night camp number ten on the journey, and it is one to remember. I am sound asleep, and I hear my little yellow bear bell I hang atop my flag antenna, which alerts me if the tricycle is moved in any way. Even the slightest movement of the trike causes the little bell to jingle. The sound is so unique, that even in deep REM sleep, I quickly rise to a level of consciousness, grab my Black Diamond mountaineering headlamp, and shine it on my trike. Nothing there. I figure that one of the bikers perhaps brushed against my pannier while returning from a late shower in the pitch black night, so I lie back down and attempt to sleep.

It isn't long until my bell sounds again. Immediately, I hear a huge crash sound just behind my tent. I hear Alex getting out of her tent. I hear Fabian, who sleeps in his bag on a tarp with no tent, expressing some form of dissatisfaction about something. I hear someone placing items in the food stash wooden container made for cyclists to store their food. Then, all is quiet again, and I fall asleep for the night. My trike and gear are secure, and I can no longer maintain any watch for whatever may be happening, for sleep overtakes me. The bear bell never sounds again tonight, and I sleep well, as is usual for pedaling trike hobos.

DAY 11 - *Pacific Coast*
September 13, 2013, Friday
Gualala Point Regional Park to Bodega Dunes State Beach, California
48 miles (running total: 528 miles)

The morning is cool and dark with the trees keeping out the light. I begin my camp striking routine again. While at the trike packing a bag, I notice an obvious clue about last night. There are two distinct raccoon paw prints on my recumbent mesh seat. Alex is getting up. She tells me about the loud crash sound, that it was Bert's bicycle being knocked over by a raccoon, so she picked it up, leaned it against the tree again, and put his panniers in the food locker. Bert and Vic slept through it all, oblivious that the furry night thieves had tried to steal their food.

Fabian's story was interesting. He looked directly into the eyes of a raccoon at its level, being as how he sleeps on the ground without a

297

tent. The raccoon then began dragging his bicycle helmet away into the forest, which is when he began expressing his dissatisfaction with its behavior and his gear. It was a unique night, that much is certain. Raccoons can be tenacious, but after enough evidence that people are going to stop them every time, they really do finally give up. Oh, if only there were an easy way to keep them at bay during the night. My bell was successful in its intended purpose, but that is only after the raccoon is already either on the trike or messing with my gear. Nothing on my trike was damaged, and the panniers remain fully intact. The odor-proof special plastic **containers** I purchased at REI did their job. The animals could not locate the food in my Arkel pannier. Food storage strategies are the key at overnight camps. Raccoons are rare, but best be ready.

As with every morning, I'm on the road again early, but the sun is already shining over the eastern horizon. That dark deep forest at camp was deceptive about how late it was getting. I pass a sign that reads CLICK IT OR TICKET, posted by the government to tell vehicle drivers and passengers that seat belts are mandatory – I don't have a seat belt, but then of course, my speeds are not generally fast enough to kill tens of thousands of humans every year like cars. Pompous grass abounds along this coastal route, and I always love watching it sway in the breeze. The ocean panoramas are gorgeous. On challenging hilltops, I often stop to rest my feet, eat a bar, and have some water. When it's hot, I hang my cap on my flag antenna so the breeze will dry it.

I pass through the Fort Ross State Historic Park, which used to be a Russian settlement in the early history of California. The old fort buildings are still here, overlooking the ocean. Highway 1 always has surprises, but what is never a surprise is that next hill waiting just around the corner! One thing trikers and bikers can always count on is an over abundance of steep challenging uphills. My suggestion for today is: If you don't like endless daily hill climbing, don't ride the Pacific Coast Highway. Hills are one big memory that sticks in all cyclists' minds.

As I enter the small coastal town of Jenner, California, it dawns on me that midday is here, the sun has been warming me up quite a bit, and an ice cold Odwalla protein drink (or three) would hit the spot just fine, along with some other things like bananas and whatever other healthy stuff this tiny village might offer. I pull into the parking lot of the Jenner 'C' Store and gas station, park under a tree, and remove my headgear. As I am doing so, three motorcyclists with whom I've been playing leapfrog for a while out on the road, pull in and park next to me.

We have a fun talk, and I tell them of my former days of motorcycling, on Harleys, BMWs, and other mounts. Two of the guys are on Harleys, and one is on a BMW. So the BMW guy asks me if I preferred Harleys or BMWs for the open road. I liked them both for different reasons, but said if I were to pick a bike for long haul motoring today, it would be the BMW for its ultra smooth ride and dependability. He smiled, and even the Harley guys got a kick out of it as the BMW guy was rubbing it in. Harley-Davidson bikes are not as smooth.

Then, my friend Alex, the bicyclist from Germany, rolls in silently. She gets a sandwich in the store, and we sit, eat, and visit for a while before hitting the road again. The weather is perfect, and we are really enjoying the day. Back on the highway, I turn right at the big fork not far south of town, and head towards Bodega Bay and its state park, where I plan to camp tonight. It's only 10 more miles, so the afternoon should be easy, except for those never ending uphills, of course!

There is still plenty of daylight when I arrive at Bodega Dunes Campground, a Sonoma Coast State Park. When I pedal into the hiker/biker area, Bert and Vic from Canada are already here, so now we are three, but it is yet early, and others are sure to arrive later. This hiker/biker camp is clearly on a piece of ground that was not usable for any other purpose, so the park officials designated it a hiker/biker camp. It's on the side of a deep sand hill, most of which is tough to even walk up. The only really practical tenting area is at the very bottom, right next to the paved roadway, where some grass covers the dry sand. Even here however, the ground is not level, so we all pitch our tents so our heads will be on the elevated end of the tent. Government shorts the cyclists.

Some state parks do this, giving hiker/bikers the undesirable leftover landscapes that no one else wants, but others, such as Patrick's Point, Half Moon Bay, and Big Sur, really do it up nice for us human powered humans. Clearly, there must not be a statewide mandate to provide the same level of camping experience at all parks. It must be up to the individual official in charge of each park. The good news for us tired cyclists is that the showers here are free! This is because so many thieves were breaking into the money collection boxes inside the showers that the state park finally gave up and just removed the boxes, allowing unlimited hot water luxury for grungy and hot pedal pushers.

So, I am happy, but as I am coming out of the shower, all cleaned up, a little kid, who was left holding a huge dog while his dad was in the bathroom, cannot control the massive animal, and it bolts towards me growling with saliva flying as the panicked child does everything in his power to stop the fracas. I jump into the deep sand to escape my impending sullying by the large animal, and barely escape unscathed. Out comes the dad, who figures out that perhaps he might devise a better way to control his untrained animal next time.

Alan from Arizona pedals in, and pitches next to my tent. I am between the Canadians and the Arizonan. Then Alex arrives, and pitches her tube tent up the hill from Alan's two-person tent. Alan stores all his cargo in his tent each night, as well as using his stove in there to make his morning coffee. The tent Alex has is one of those that only has room to slide into from one end. She cannot sit up in it at all, and dressing in the tent is a real chore she says. She mentions that after this trip, she will find a new tent that is more reasonable for long trips. My NEMO Obi one-person tent has slightly more area than hers, but I can sit up, easily dress, and pack away my gear while inside. Choosing the best tent for one's needs is a live and learn experience. We are all on the curve.

Other cyclists also come into camp a little later. They are new folks the five of us who have been camping together on and off have never seen before. Turns out they are heading north on the PCH instead of south as we are, thus the fact we have not seen them prior to this evening. Over dinner, they ask us about the road ahead for them tomorrow. We tell them of the mother of all uphills they will face on their ride north to Gualala. For us, it was a thrill ride downhill, but for them, it will be less than desirable. The north side is more gradual, which made it easier for southbound cyclists, although it is still very steep.

I take a couple of photos inside my tent to show what it's like. One is looking out my door towards the trike, one is of the area where my head goes, and one is facing where my feet are. This tent is very well designed, and if the fly gets wet for any reason, the tent remains dry because it is suspended from the pole, so no water dampens any pole tubes because there are no pole tubes. This was one of the factors in my decision to get it, because my former REI Arete had pole tubes, which actually contacted the fly material and would retain moisture.

Tonight's sleep is, as always, well earned and easy. The first 18 miles of the ride were easy, but then the long steep cliff hills kicked in, and the work began in earnest. The foghorn tonight is a wonderful companion with which I am familiar because in my own coastal town where I live, I hear the horn from my little upstairs bedroom. For me, it is a cozy ambiance that always puts me into deep restful sleep.

DAY 12 - *Pacific Coast*
September 14, 2013, Saturday
Bodega Dunes State Beach to Golden Gate Bridge, California (north end, Sausalito) – 68 miles (running total: 596 miles)

This morning as we are all striking our tents and gear, and as we are eating our breakfasts, we all talk about each other's intended itinerary for the day. A logical overnight tonight is the ever popular camp at Samuel P. Taylor State Park, south of Olema, California, an ideal stop-over prior to pedaling into San Francisco the next day. This is a common practice for many cyclists on the Pacific Coast route. Staying at Samuel P. Taylor sets up the cyclist to travel the following day to Half Moon Bay State Park, which is a distance of 58 miles. Sounds logical.

Essentially, many cyclists want to camp as close to San Francisco's northern end as possible, thereby making it within grasp to negotiate the sea of humanity en route to Half Moon Bay. It sounds entirely doable to think of 58 miles in one day as a realistic goal. Vic and Bert have other plans. They will enter the City of San Francisco on Sunday and penetrate its heart as they wish to stay at a hostel there for a couple of days rest, over by the Fisherman's Wharf area. They invite me to accompany them, but I am not really interested in pedaling my trike into and through the downtown portions of this densely packed metropolis. Alex is only traveling as far as San Francisco, to a friend's house, so this will be her destination point on Sunday. Then, she returns to Germany after staying there a month.

I joke around with Bert and Vic, asking them if they are worried about bed bugs in the hostel. Bert answers, "We are now!" and we all have a great laugh. Hostels can be havens for these tiny creatures if the business operators don't keep things immaculately clean. I then ask if they know why the San Francisco bay is as it is, explaining about the San Andreas fault, the mother of all faults in this region. We are having much fun with this conversational thread, as I point out all the reasons, in addition to the insane automobile traffic, that they may wish to reconsider their hostel plans. It is all a good time this morn.

All the while, I am contemplating my own plans. True, we have all more or less been traveling companions for several days now, but we ride separately for the most part, only seeing each other at campgrounds and grocery stores along the way. We have grown our friendships during this time, and the thought that very soon we will likely never see each other again has a certain sadness to it. I ask Alan his plans, and he is going to follow the "tried and true" plan of camping at Samuel P. Taylor State Park tonight, and riding the 58 miles to Half Moon Bay on Sunday. So shall Vic, Bert, and Alex camp at Samuel P. Taylor tonight, before the big day on Sunday when our little ragtag crew disbands for all eternity. This may be the final morning I shall see Vic, Bert, and Alex.

I tell Bert and Vic a few minutes later, after breakfast, that I may not stay at Samuel P. Taylor State Park tonight with the rest of them, that I may pedal on by and position myself as close as possible to the northern end of the Golden Gate Bridge. I contemplate this because it is well known among cyclists that the route to access the northern end

301

of the bridge is somewhat convoluted, and can very much challenge even riders who have done it before. Even Alan, who has indeed pedaled these very miles in the past, says it's no easy task to arrive at the bridge's cycling entrance. Alan tells me that the trick is to get to Sausalito, and to do so, follow Sir Francis Drake Boulevard. He talks of little hidden bike paths that make the ride easier, but are difficult to find.

Contemplating my past trike journeys on an inland route, where campgrounds are rare, and where predetermined overnights are not the name of the game like here on the Pacific Coast, I realize that normally I would ride until sunset is about an hour away, giving me time to pitch a camp and eat. So, I wonder if that strategy might prove more beneficial to me today, to return to the habits of former trips even though everyone else is meticulously planning precisely where they are going to stay. Knowing each day's destination does indeed instill a certain confidence in one's head, removing the sting of uncertainty, but to achieve this, lower mileage days are often the consequence. It's decision time soon.

My decision is to go with what feels right at the time. I will pedal today and see how far along the sun is when I arrive at Samuel P. Taylor State Park. I will think this all over as I pedal along, and by the time I need to decide, it will all come to me, one way or the other (or so I hope). There is no right or wrong in all this, after all. There is no best answer. Life is an adventure, and so is the Pacific Coast trike ride. What is adventure without a whopping big dose of uncertainty?

Before I go, I tell Vic and Bert to be on the lookout for where Highway 1 departs the main road southeast of Bodega Bay. Just past the miniature village of Valley Ford, the PCH takes a 90 degree turn south, and it is FAR from obvious if one is not really looking for it. Heck, even if one IS looking for the turn, it can be missed. If this turn is missed, the traveler does not know about the mistake for many miles, and eventually finds himself entering the city of Petaluma, California, way inland.

Then, our crew breaks ranks and silently rolls onto the pavement. Off I pedal, up the long entrance road back to Highway 1, where one of the bicyclists from last night turns left and heads north, straight for that horribly steep cliff hill not too far distant. I happily turn right, for some long stretches of easy pedaling on flat ground. In a few miles, I reach the turnoff for Highway 1, just past Valley Ford (population: 126), and stop to photograph the sign, which is well hidden behind some overgrown bushes (a big reason people miss this turn). Since there is no sign prior to this alerting travelers to the turn, this sign in the bushes is all the warning an uninitiated cyclist, or motorist, gets. The sign reads Tomales and Pt Reyes to the right. Turn here, or else!

While I am taking this series of photographs, Bert and Vic

pedal up behind me and ask if this is the intersection I warned them about. I tell them yes. They ask if this is where they turn right, and I confirm this is our turn to stay on track for Tomales and Samuel P. Taylor State Park. They thank me, turn right, and pull ahead, eventually riding out of my sight. The country out here is beautiful and serene.

I'm starting to get a complex on this trip that has never affected me before: On my inland treks, I never even see a bicyclist on tour, so I have no gauge as to my overall speed, but on the Pacific Coast, where upwards of 10,000 cyclists tour every season, I am continually passed every single day by many touring bicyclists. I put out the same amount of effort, yet they pass me anyway. Dynamics of tricycles versus bicycles are part, but the fact that my rear wheel is only 20 inches in diameter, versus their 26, 28, or 700c wheels, makes a difference. Further, they can stand on the pedals and use bodyweight on the uphills, whereas tricyclists cannot get that strength and leverage advantage. This allows bicyclists who are not as fit as me to pass me on uphill grades. Of course, on flat ground or downhills, the tables are turned, but since this route has so many uphill sections every day, the two wheelers pull away consistently. Maybe I need a trike with a larger rear wheel?

Just north of Tomales, in the early morning fog and overcast conditions common to the coast, I pass a turkey farm, and feel sorry for these bioforms, knowing their ultimate demise is close at hand. Past the little town of Tomales, the road really levels out for many easy and fast miles along Tomales Bay, where I see huge bulls with big long horns and shaggy fir sitting in the tall brown grass, along with large white birds that have long necks and long yellow beaks. It is as if they are all good friends. Trees, sculpted by wind and the elements, are lining the road in all kinds of shapes. Overhanging trees form natural tunnels through which I ride. Eucalyptus trees share their distinctive aroma, and the bark sometimes borders on brilliant orange.

For the most part, Highway 1 is well signed along the way. At Point Reyes, a little bustling town that many San Francisco cyclists ride to and back for a long day ride, the signs are clear, leaving little doubt I am on the right path. I stop at the Palace Market for my daily Odwalla protein monster drink infusion (usually 3 bottles, for a total of 75 grams of protein), and some bananas and cherry tomatoes. Vic and Bert have just shopped and are on their way out as I arrive. Alex catches up with me here, and joins me for lunch. I watch her bicycle and possessions for her while she walks to a nearby bank to get some cash from the ATM machine. She watches my gear while I walk a block behind the store to use the town's only public bathroom facility. I even take my own self portrait as it reflects in the glass doors of the market, the produce in the store visible all around me – I love bizarre images now and then.

Chores complete, I bid Alex a fond farewell and pleasant rest of her journey, realizing that this will probably be the last I ever see of her. I am inclined at this point to pass on by Samuel P. Taylor campground today, so I may be totally on my own for a while. I pedal on south through the small town, traffic courteously giving way to my little tricycular form. Just south of town is the Point Reyes National Seashore, managed by the United States Department of the Interior, National Park Service. At the rural town of Olema, I turn the trike's handlebars left and head up the hill to begin my ride on Sir Francis Drake Boulevard, which is a key route change off of Highway 1 for trike hobos if they want to get to Sausalito and the Golden Gate Bridge.

This road goes up and down over the rolling countryside, but the hills are short and not so ridiculously steep as many on the coast route. When I pass the boundary line of Samuel P. Taylor State Park, it is still way too early to stop and pitch a tent, especially since it is getting warmer, and I feel like putting in some more miles. I keep on pedaling past the campground entrance farther up the road, thinking about all my new friends and how I'll miss them. The road becomes narrow and curvy, with large forests and redwoods. Quite a few miles after my turn at Olema, I finally see the first proof I am on track for my golden goal of the big bridge: a sign reads SIR FRANCES DRAKE BLVD.

Then, I see a white sign with green lettering, depicting a bicycle, with the number 20 underneath it. Below the 20 route designation is a straight arrow and the word FAIRFAX. Since this area of the coast is so heavily populated with an active cycling community, the government marks main cycling routes as they do for marking main auto routes. It is a fantastic idea I have never seen anywhere else! Since I know the town of Fairfax is one I wish to go through, my mind relaxes, knowing I'm where I need to be today. I think I'm slow at times, but now I pass a hiker with pack and guitar, traveling only a fraction of the speed the trike is capable of on this flat road.

The scenery here consists of rolling brown pasture lands, low hills, and scrubby bushes and trees. It is Saturday afternoon, and traffic is moderate, but the shoulder is mostly wide, so it is comfortable to pedal along in the bright sunshine. In Fairfax, bicycle lanes and routes are the order of the day, and I enjoy knowing the government here supports human powered humans to such an extent. I see many more bicycle route signs, and am amazed at the level of support for cyclists.

I had heard that the west side human powered human path over the Golden Gate Bridge was closed for repairs, so when I see a California Highway Patrolman finishing up issuing a traffic citation to a motorist up ahead, I decide to ask him if he knows about this. He is parked on the shoulder, so I pedal up to his driver's door on my little low tricycle. His window is closed, air conditioner on inside, and he is busy writing in his log. The top of my helmet is just barely at the level of his window, so I'm nearly invisible down here. The patrolman does not even know I am here, having arrived so silently as trikes always do, and continues writing, oblivious to my presence. I extend my right arm way overhead and tap gently on his closed glass window, which truly startles him, and he jumps with surprise. Then, a huge smile comes over his face, his electric window comes down, and he says I scared him. We have a great laugh, and then I inquire about the bridge passageway. He is not sure, but thinks I can get over. I bid him a good day, and pedal on.

As I get to Marin City, still on Sir Frances Drake Boulevard, traffic gets heavier. I stop at a bicycle shop to ask directions. The lady hardly knows English, and is unable to help me, other than to let me use the shop's bathroom. I pull into a large shopping mall and ask a business owner about finding my way, as I notice the Highway 101 freeway is looming a couple blocks ahead, and know I am not allowed on it. She tells me some directions, but is not sure of all the bicycle routes. Two blocks farther east, I pull into a fire station, which is right next to the 101 freeway, dismount, and talk to the firemen working on cleaning their large red trucks. These guys are very cool, give me tons of information, show me a gigantic wall map of where I need to go, and even give me a Gatorade because the afternoon is warming up as it marches on.

The fire personnel tell me of a well hidden bike path a few yards past their station, and warn me to look into the bushes to see it. I thank them, still in doubt as to my way, and slowly pedal back out onto Sir Francis Drake Boulevard, which by now is very crowed with cars since the freeway is literally right in front of me. The firemen said the bike path is just a few feet prior to getting onto the 101 on-ramp, and what do you know! Sure enough, over a little rise through the oleander bushes, I see the bike path. Never would I have found this had it not been for their coaching! The path puts me onto a private roadway just for human powered folks, and leads over a bridge and river bed, with the Highway 101 on-ramp to my left. Then, it parallels the freeway with a little yellow line just like the big automobile roads, and is separated from the surrounding territory by a chain link fence.

Cars are speeding by me on my left, and I notice the sign for Mill Valley off-ramp ahead. This is an area I know I must pass through also, so it's another clue I'm doing this correctly. Through some residential neighborhoods I ride, up a steep hill, and then down to a busy intersection where I am not sure of the best way to proceed. It's my lucky day, as a veteran local cyclist in spandex on a fancy racing bike is stopped momentarily on the sidewalk. I ask him directions, and he tells me to take this bike path for the next couple of miles into Sausalito. He says I will arrive at the northern end of the Golden Gate Bridge eventually. I thank this young man, pedaling off with due haste as the day is wearing on quite quickly now, and I have absolutely no idea of where I will be sleeping tonight.

All my cycling pals are already eating their dinners, cozy and ready to bed down in their tents at the Samuel P. Taylor State Park campground, while I'm out here in a sea of humanity that does not care about my sorry state of affairs – oh, the adventure is running high now! If nothing else, I am many miles farther down the road than any of them, and I have been successful at finding my way almost to my end goal for today, the big orange bridge. If I had stayed with them tonight at the camp, I would have had to do all this tomorrow morning on a day where I would have to ride 58 miles to boot. The way I figure it, regardless of what tonight brings, tomorrow's ride will be a much shorter and easier 35 to 40 miles instead of the nearly 60 they will have to do. And, since tomorrow is Sunday, I reckon I'll be pedaling across the bridge first thing at sunup. I like the plan, although I'm not crazy about the hours of darkness between then and now.

On this final bike path, I see I am on bike route 5 to Sausalito, so I shift up to high gears and book along as fast as my legs will pedal. The sun is close to setting now, so I must find some sort of sleeping arrangement. Fortunately, the air is still comfortably warm. The bike path crosses the 101 freeway, which is now on my right. I see a freeway sign for motorists that points to the Golden Gate Bridge and San Francisco, and an off-ramp to Marin City and Sausalito, so I know my goal is imminent. In Sausalito, I see how I need to go (up some very steep hills), and stop quickly to ask two female power cyclists about a potential place to stay. They know of no options this close to the bridge, but tell me that if I follow them, they'll show me the final mile or so to the bridge. These fit gals power up the hills and leave me in the dust, but I see the lay of the land now, and know it's only a matter of minutes.

Then, up some more hills I ride, reaching a large pullout day-use area, which is part of the Fort Baker Recreational Area on the bay waterfront. Here, I also see the full San Francisco skyline, just as the sun is shedding its final rays on the towering skyscrapers. Even though my overnight activities are dubious and few at this point, I am clearly elated to have finally reached the famous bridge, bay, and city. I cannot see the bridge from this turnout, but I know it is literally just around the next bend in this road, so I am content to stop, eat some bars, drink some water, and offload some water in the bushes on the cliff to my left, which drops precipitously into the bay below – no place for a misstep!

There are picnic tables here, and a trash can, and the surface of the turnout is well covered with a reddish brown colored gravel. They spared no expense with this day-use area. I am now out of options, so I decide to camp right here along the road. Sure, I could ride into San Francisco right now, but I want to save that joy for sunrise tomorrow! If I pitch my tent here, I will be evicted in short order by the first cop, so, as I have done in the past at times, I choose to sleep on the tricycle.

This ICE trike has a seat that is 37 degrees off the horizontal, so it is very reclined. It is also very low to the ground, my rear end being only eight inches off the deck, so I can spread my legs out straight ahead of me, lean my neck back onto the neck rest, and be surprisingly comfortable. Since I pitch no tent, if questioned, it is clear that I am resting only, being a cyclist who was out of options. There is no law against resting, and the odds are in my favor. The growing moon is very bright, and rising over the eastern bay – it should be full by the time I reach Big Sur in a few days. I know from past experience that sleeping on the trike gets cold, so I pull all my coat type clothing out of my panniers and layer it on, zipping it all up all the way, and putting the hoods over my head, already covered by my polar fleece skull cap.

As I am settling in for a long chilly night, I cannot believe my eyes: I watch as a group of racing cyclists begin pedaling by my day-use area, from south to north, from San Francisco to Sausalito. There looks to be about a dozen cyclists, as there is a fraction of a second where I see no more coming over the little rise in the road. But it doesn't stop! These bicyclists all have headlights and taillights, and soon I realize that the first dozen was just that, the first wave. Only a few yards behind them come a continual stream of bicyclists on racing machines, all knocking down the miles at a very respectable pace – in other words, fast! I am dumbfounded. The line simply does not stop! I do not see an end until more than 100 of these rugged souls fly past my little pathetic tricycle camp! Who were they? Why out so late? Wow! What a show that was! But the show is over, and I return to my hobo life on the side of the road, while they all return to their warm showers and cozy beds.

In the past, on my inland route where it does get extremely cold in the Cascade Range and the Sierra Nevada Range, I bring much heavier jacket options, but this trip along the coast, I have minimized my clothing cache, so I hope for the best. At first, I am fine, but as time passes, I can feel the cold from the wind that is whipping over the hills to my west. The hills protect me from a full-on assault of wind, but still it curls around and takes its toll on my ability to generate internal warmth. It is coming off the ocean, and is loaded with humidity, making it seem even colder. Normally in a tent, I am in an insulated sleeping bag, inside a tent with fly that keeps me fully protected from wind. Not tonight! I am out in the elements with just the clothes on my back.

Well, not quite. I do have a very thin survival type space blanket, which is obnoxiously chrome colored and crackly when manipulated. I get it out, but the wind whips it around, making it a real challenge to get it wrapped all around my torso and legs so that it will stop the chilly fast moving air. It becomes too cold to rest my head back against the neck rest, so I keep it tucked down onto my chest to preserve heat. I draw my legs up under my knees to further preserve my body heat. Occasionally, I peek out and see the position of the moon, which is my way of telling time (I have not worn a watch for more than 20 years). No cops yet. The moon at long last sets behind the western hill, darkening me even more from prying eyes, except that there are no eyes out here to see me this time of night. A couple stops for a while in the wee hours to make-out over the bay, but incredibly, they don't even see me sitting a few yards away. Finally they leave, none the wiser.

I sleep fitfully tonight, fighting cold, and hoping for the faint sight of an impending and much needed dawn. The moon is gone now, so I know hours have passed. With every hour, the cold increases, and while my body never reaches a point of constant shivering, it seems to exist right on the border at times, never crossing over though. My mind reaches some dream states, so I am getting some sleep, but I realize how sweet it will be to arrive at Half Moon Bay State Park tomorrow, pitch a tent at the beach, and crawl into a fully protected bag for the night. Indeed, Sunday night holds the promise of luxury compared to tonight!

I doubt very much that David would have been in favor of this overnight choice at the turnout, or that he would have been very happy about sleeping on his trike here. This is exactly the sort of thing where riding solo has a definitive advantage. Do what I want, how I want, even if it ends up being a miserable option. But tomorrow will pay dividends!

DAY 13 - *Pacific Coast*
September 15, 2013, Sunday
Golden Gate Bridge to Half Moon Bay State Beach, California
36 miles (running total: 632 miles)

I have peeked out of my space blanket many times during the night, not to mention when I exit the crackly piece of chrome blanket to go water the bushes. It seemed like morning would never come, but I finally arise to offload some water, and yes! Morning has broken! At

308

least the faint light of a star 8 light minutes from me is brightening the eastern horizon, while most of San Francisco will still be sleeping for several more hours this Sunday morn. Sunday morning is so perfect for riding through this huge coastal megalopolis, as most citizens here will either be sleeping in late or spending time praying in church, meaning that the roads and town will seem deserted. While I am slowly attempting to get the blood flowing again in my icy body, having sat on an ICE trike all night, my cycling companions of the past few days are soon to arise far north of me at Samuel P. Taylor campground.

Last night's frigid ordeal was one I wanted to document, so I take a picture of my trike seat moments after having stepped out of my chrome cocoon. It retains the shape of my body because the wind has finally stopped. What a funny photograph it is. Alcatraz Island, and its old federal prison, is clearly visible out in the bay. What stories it has to tell. The lights of the city still shine through the slowly growing daylight. My trike's flag is still smiling, just as happy now as last evening. That flag has been known to lift my spirits in times like these. Overland triking is not easy in the slightest, and requires a steel mind to make the journey. Happy flags can help. It flapped hard most of last night.

I do not hang out for long here. It is still too cold to eat comfortably, and the picnic tables are wet, so I decide I'll do breakfast somewhere in San Francisco. I consider waiting until the sun hits so I can eat my granola at the table, but I choose not to spend the time sitting idle. I would rather get on the bridge so I can see the rising sun. Just seconds before I get into the trike to pedal away, a county sheriff vehicle drives by. He puts on the brakes, stops, and begins to back up, presumably to investigate me. But I am standing, putting on my helmet, and there is absolutely no evidence that a trike hobo spent the night here. Then, he reverses his direction and drives on around the corner towards the bridge, which is the south end of his county jurisdiction.

Time to hit the road for one of this journey's most memorable experiences, that of pedaling a human powered recumbent tadpole tricycle across the mighty Golden Gate Bridge of San Francisco. Yes, it's a human-made bridge in a highly overpopulated location, and yes, these types of encounters run counter to my deep love of the wilderness and my desire to pedal through serene locales with few humans, but today, I'm excited to do this, just to say I did. I suppose it's one of those ego things where you just want to share with others that you had a unique experience few even can comprehend. There is so much around me right now, so much to take in, that last night fades from my mind.

Within moments of pulling out onto the road, the final yards to the big curve overlooking the bridge disappear behind my tires, and there the orange tribute to bridge builders' ingenuity stands before me, as it has for decades, looking as it did when I first crossed it in an automobile as a kid. But oh what a difference my vantage point has today! At first, as the road rounds the curve, I am slightly below the level of the bridge's roadway, but then I plummet down a steep grade to the level of the water in the bay. This is a park-like area here where people can enjoy the bridge from below, and is where all the cyclists easily avoid the busy main highway. It's somewhat bizarre down here, as the road dead-ends into a large steel and concrete barricade designed to keep out all unauthorized motor vehicles, the kind of ultra mega security one would expect to see at a top secret military headquarters or at the White House. Warning signs are posted. I watch a bridge patrol officer in his vehicle activate the militaristic barrier, which electronically flattens into the pavement so he can drive over it, like in a science fiction movie.

As I first coasted down to this dead-end, it appeared that I could proceed no farther, like I was trapped in a cul-de-sac and would have to return the way I came. Yet, while it is indeed true that no motor vehicles are allowed any farther on this road, the authorities have granted special permission to trike hobos to go on through. It's a little known secret that only presents itself to a triker or biker if he pedals on up to the impenetrable quasi-military barrier. Immediately to the left of the imposing auto barrier is a small opening, with steel and concrete posts on either side, that is only wide enough for my trike to fit through. There is a sign that states I am among the privileged to proceed where the common citizen in a car cannot. There is also one of the region's white and green bicycle route signs as I have been seeing ever since turning onto Sir Francis Drake Boulevard yesterday afternoon. It is still Route 5, and shows access to the Golden Gate Bridge. I am right on!

I pedal past the barrier in my privileged little lane, proceed under the bridge with a view that the millions of motorists on Highway 101 will never see, and am faced with one of the steepest grades I have ever witnessed, or had the thrill to pedal up. Up is the key word here, for within a short distance, I now go from waterfront level to highway level in order to access the triker's lane on the bridge. Once at the top at highway level, I can see San Francisco in the background past the bridge. I am stoked, for it is clear I am about to finally get on this metal monster. Even up here, there are little secret passageways for only cyclists, but the way is obvious now, and I am rolling south onto the massive girders I just pedaled under moments ago. My moment is here.

Wow, what a head trip this is, in addition to the trike trip. Here I am, little stevie greene, riding his little clean green tricycle at age 62 on this world famous landmark. Never at any former time in life would I have even remotely predicted that I'd still be riding a tricycle at this age, or that I'd be riding one across this bridge into San Francisco. What a trip indeed. I am on the Golden Gate, Sunday morning of September 15, 2013, at sunrise. There is hardly any traffic. The timing was perfect. Last night's miserable sleep and cold are all forgotten as the ambiance of what is happening right now overtakes my mind, almost numbing it in the process, but I want to remain aware enough so that I don't miss the full experience of it all. I take in the views, take in some photographs, and take in the crisp Pacific air as it breezes past me on my little tricycle road. I am dwarfed by the colossal orange uprights that secure this behemoth bridge to the bay's floor. I am utterly speechless!

I cross the San Francisco city and county line, reading the sign that shows the population to be 723,959 human beings. Next to it is a yellow sign that reads BICYCLISTS SLOW KEEP RIGHT PREPARE TO STOP YIELD TO PEDESTRIANS. The two signs, plus a SPEED LIMIT 45 sign for petroleum powered humans, are affixed to the northernmost of the two towers that hold the bridge up. I stop here, point my camera straight up, and capture the tower from a trike hobo's vantage point. This early on Sunday, there are a few bicyclists already riding the bridge, but their numbers are nothing like they will be in another couple of hours. How impressive it would have been to see those hundred cyclists that passed me last night as they crossed this bridge with their headlights illuminating the pathway.

The sun to my left is warming me still from last night's endurance test, and it feels very nice. I notice the orange paint on the bridge – glad I'm not a painter! I look out to my right towards the Pacific Ocean, and notice the early morning fog bank out to sea. There are numerous small boats heading out into the ocean, perhaps fishermen. To my left and slightly forward, I see the city's unique skyline, including the trademark triangular spike building, being delineated by the morning sun and clouds. At the southern end, as I exit the bridge, I speak briefly to a California Highway Patrol officer, but unlike yesterday's discussion with a CHP officer in a car, this one is riding a bicycle! He sports a full uniform, badge, gun, and all, but his assignment is to ride a human powered bike so he has access to places the car cops can't reach.

I make a cell call once off the bridge to update family as to my whereabouts and the experience I just had. I see a sign that warns me to beware of coyotes crossing the road. I pass a high tech racing bicyclist who is bummed out because a San Francisco city cop is writing him a ticket for some reason (probably exceeding the speed limit – they are strict about cycling enforcement in these parts because there are literally countless thousands of them here). Out of respect for this unlucky cyclist, I do not whip out my camera to record his embarrassing Sunday morning bummer. It is clear he is not happy right now.

Now my body has warmed, and is politely requesting a caloric infusion, so as I pedal the steep San Francisco streets towards the beach and Great Highway route, I keep an eye out for a park-like setting to have my granola. I pass a public beach day use area, but it is down a steep grade, and since I am now at some elevation, it would require a tiring return to the road, so I pedal on. Finally, I see it, on 34th Avenue, the Lincoln Park golf course, restaurant, bar, and grill. Perfect! I find a nice spot next to a green, and chow down in the sun, watching golfers hit their little white balls into the bushes. An attractive Swedish gal, who is running the bar and grill section, fills my water bottles for me, and in her thick Swedish accent is asking all about what I am doing out here on my tricycle. Before I go, I use the restroom facilities, which are probably better than anything I'll find later. This is living today! It all makes up for last night in spades! It is a restful Sunday ride on a tricycle.

Breakfast behind me now, I pedal up and up to the crest of these residential hills, and behold the ocean down in front of me. A pit bull dog is sunning himself in a second story window, so I stop and take his picture because my sister Willow loves dogs, has a small dog-sitting business, and will love to see this shot. The lazy dog looks down at me on my tricycle, then closes his eyes again to continue his siesta. Down the hill I go to San Francisco's Great Highway, a flat section of coastline for tourists and beachcombers, where I make good time, with the famous photogenic windmills on my left.

I am now on Highway 35, which takes me back to Highway 1, which I left for my tricycular route to, through, and around the congested bridge area. Through Daly City I proceed, up the long long hill they stuck in there, but the sun still feels good this early. When I arrive at the on-ramp for Highway 1, leading to Pacifica and Santa Cruz, I am greeted by an unexpected and unwanted surprise: bicyclists are prohibited, and directed inland for some unknown and convoluted route I cannot find on any of my maps. After consultation with my silent paper maps, I make the crazy guy on a trike decision to take Highway 1 regardless of what governmental authorities instruct me to do. Entering the on-ramp, I pick up speed quickly because it is downhill, and since Daly City is in the hills, the entire portion of Highway 1 that is illegal for bicyclists (and tricyclists too I presume, although it's not specifically stated) is also a healthy downhill grade. So, I shift up to my highest gear and pedal like a bat out of hell, hoping to make the town of Pacifica before the next encounter with a California Highway Patrolman. Cops write cyclists in these parts! In Pacifica, Highway 1 again becomes a multi-use roadway that allows human powered humans on tricycles.

This stretch of anxiety producing freeway, which is not worrisome as far as traffic is concerned because the shoulder is wide and cars are few, lasts about four and a half miles. The shoulder is a mess, strewn with debris and ultra rough pavement with cracks and potholes. The ICE Q is shuttering all around because I am flying along at high speed. When able, I move into the closest automobile lane to avoid the shoulder. Being all downhill, and staying in high gear the whole way, these four-plus miles are over in nothing flat, or so it seems. No cops, no hassles, no problems, and no wasted energy doing some governmentally sanctioned work-around detour like the sign instructed south of Daly City. Okay, that part of the adventure is over.

What is in store for me now? Back on a legal tricycle highway again at Pacifica, a sign lets me know that I am going to pedal for three miles up a steep hill in the woods with blind tight curves and no shoulders. Not only that, but for some reason, perhaps because church just let out, everyone, including the faithful, is now driving a car on Highway 1, which is now just one narrow lane in each direction on this hill. There is no choice but to ride in the car lane because the wise governments do not see fit to pave a little shoulder here for folks who choose not to pollute the air supply we all breathe. Yet, grim as this may sound to inexperienced trikers, there is absolutely no problem because drivers are as they almost always are: courteous and sharing. There are no horn honks, no nasty immature gestures, and no yelling out the windows by anyone. Only actual trike experience on the road serves to drive this message home. Trike treks are not some suicidal mission of no return, despite what your loved ones tell you! Only you will know.

From pre-trip study, I know there is a big tunnel at the top of this hill, and there are also yellow diamond shaped signs that tell of its arrival soon. This is the new Devil's Slide tunnel, finally financed by the government after decades of mountain slides and cave-ins kept closing Highway 1 on this stretch of the Pacific Coast. Now, it is all secure. As I round the last curve and the tunnel comes into view, a couple parked at a turnout tell me that there is danger ahead, in the form of the tunnel. I smile, say thanks, and tell them I love this tunnel. This confuses them. I am not confused. The Devil's Slide tunnel is big, wide, and the trike lane is wider than the automobile lane, with no debris whatsoever. There are several duets of gigantic fans on the ceiling, continually blowing out car exhaust because this is a long tunnel. My telephoto lens on the camera makes it look shorter than it really is. The best news about this tunnel is that the speed limit is 45 miles per hour and it is definitely downhill for southbound traffic. What this means is that I am able to maintain a high speed throughout its length in my highest gear. Yee Haa!

Devil's Slide is over before I know it, and I rocket out the south side of the tunnel, continuing a healthy clip down the mountain cliff towards the ocean below. Terrain eventually levels out at sea level, and soon I am nearing the popular town of Half Moon Bay, where the Odwalla company is headquartered. Gee, I've been keeping them in business these past 13 days, scarfing down their protein monster drinks and eating their 14 gram protein bars. They should sponsor me! Oh well, my destination camp for tonight is coming early for a change, which suits me just fine after 68 tough miles yesterday and last night's chilling conclusion. I'll be pitching my camp in sunlight for a change, legally too.

I pedal past hundreds of people arriving at the beach here after church, and for miles every parking spot along the sand is taken, or quickly snatched up if someone pulls out. It's a traffic mess here, requiring diligence and care on my trike. Fortunately, they are all going slow looking for a parking place, hundreds of drivers eager to soak up the sun and shop in Half Moon Bay. Farmer John's Pumpkin Farm is off to my right. Kids love this place. I stop at Safeway for my daily Odwalla infusion (fresh as it gets here), along with some strawberries, bananas, and trail mix. It all fills me up, as I relax at a little metal table in the shade by the market's front doors. Half Moon Bay is a real clean town, the kind that middle America just seems to really adore.

At last, I turn off Highway 1, onto the road to Half Moon Bay State Beach, passing some fresh vegetable farmer businesses, and then check in for the day's camp. This state park is a whopping $7, so I have to ante up another $2 on top of the $5 bill I just handed the clerk at the check-in station. All the other state parks are just five smackers, and when I ask why the difference here, the man acts totally unaware that his campground is any different than the rest of the entire state of California, as if I am the first person in his job history to question this. Okay, no big deal in reality, as $7 is a pittance compared to a motel or what the RV campers are paying for less space than what I get.

The hiker/biker area here is incredibly gigantic and flat, mowed brown grass, making for a comfortable base for my tent. I've not seen a larger hiker/biker area yet. The views are great. It is totally wide open for a change, instead of choked with deep dark forests. The ocean is a few yards to the west of my tent, over a small dune, past the great hot showers. What a joy it is to bask in the sun and have more ground at my disposal than I'll ever need. I highly recommend this triker camp!

Shortly after 3 PM, my tent is erected in the most perfect coastal weather anyone could ever imagine. As I am finishing the tent preparation, Alan of Arizona rolls into camp. He is the last of the remaining 17 wild bikers from Standish-Hickey State Park north of Leggett. A couple from Germany, who speak no English, pedal their bicycles into the camp and begin their evening chores. One other cyclist comes in later, a guy from Canada, who is a loner and does not talk to anyone, but I tried. Alan rides into Safeway to get some groceries, and picks me up some additional Clif Bars while he is there. Great guy.

Towards evening, gorgeous cloud formations appear, so I whip out the camera and begin capturing them for your enjoyment now. The clouds remind me of many birds flying through the air. This day is capped by a picture-perfect sunset, and then I go to bed in a real sleeping bag with all the warmth I need. No trike seat tonight! The daily life of a trike hobo on the road is totally unpredictable, thus, I suppose, the high level of adventure associated with it.

DAY 14 - *Pacific Coast*
September 16, 2013, Monday
Half Moon Bay State Beach to Sunset State Beach, California,
Monterey Bay - 67 miles (running total: 699 miles)

Another beautiful day greets me as I awaken before dawn. Last night, Alan and I agreed to ride as a team for a while, and he suggested we arise early today because we have nearly 70 miles to reach Sunset State Beach in northern Monterey Bay for tonight's camp. Alan always gets up early, as all cyclists usually do, but he even beats the early birds. He likes to ride at a slower pace, so he allows himself more time. He always arrives at the same nightly destination as everyone else, but he gets there later and leaves earlier. To awaken me, he walks over to my trike and jingles the flag antenna, which activates my little yellow bear bell. Of course, I am already awake, just savoring the final few moments in my cozy warm bag as the sky very slowly brightens, off to the east.

We take off, and after a while I pedal past a sign that says 46 miles to Santa Cruz, and 95 miles to Monterey. Alan tells me that navigating through these two cities can be problematic, and how on a former trip, he got lost several times and had to backtrack. He offers to guide me through both towns, through all the little unknown bike paths and alternate routes that make the journey much more enjoyable, and sometimes shorter. I navigated San Francisco on my own, and yes, it can be a frustrating exercise having to stop and ask everyone you see how to get where you are going. So, I graciously take Alan up on his offer.

Today the ride is relatively fast and easy. We are out of the huge cliff mountains for a while, and maintain much higher speeds with much less effort. The shoulders are mostly over sized and clean, which suits me fine, but I know that south of Carmel, the cliffs will return in a couple of days. I ask Alan about New Brighten State Beach, but he says Sunset Beach is a much better campground in his opinion. The scenery is gorgeous in many places. At one point, I look off to the left, towards the east, on a section of road that is elevated, and gaze down into a serene and idyllic valley shrouded in morning fog. I can always spot Alan up ahead in his Arizona jersey, which has seen better days.

Up in northern California, this highway was called the Redwood Highway. Here, as I head south from San Francisco, it is now called the Cabrillo Highway. Before this trip began, my sister Willow sent me a postcard with a photograph of Pigeon Point lighthouse on it, and she wanted me to stop there and see it on my journey. So I did. I took a couple photos to show her too. There is a hostel at Pigeon Point lighthouse, and the scenery is wonderful, but I pedal on towards Sunset Beach and Monterey. The pedaling is also easier today because there is a very nice tailwind to drive me forward. My smiley flag on the trike as it sits in front of Pigeon Point lighthouse is pointing south. The original big classic light is gone in this lighthouse, and only a small modern beam shines. They must have run out of money to maintain the historic locale.

Passing the Santa Cruz county line, I am greeted by Swanton's berry farm, just one of many such roadside businesses that motorists can visit to taste goodies and load up the trunk with fresh food. As a trike hobo, I do not wish more weight, so I travel on, with just photos.

Finally, Alan and I enter the city of Santa Cruz, and in good time too, as the roads have been easy. He knows his way through here. I ask him about a Safeway. He says to wait until the one on the south end of town. There are 5 Safeway supermarkets here, and, true to his admonishment, the final one is the nicest one. It allows us to eat a little later so we won't be starving for dinner tonight. There are several short but steep uphills as we progress through Santa Cruz, and the city goes on for what seems like forever. We have come over 50 miles so far, a long day in many cyclists' minds, but we have about 15 or so to go.

Santa Cruz is bike friendly for the most part, with many signs telling motorists to be kind and share the road, plus it has bike lanes here and there. Where there are no bike lanes, the city has erected bright green signs that show a bicyclist in the lane in front of a car, with the words underneath: BIKES IN LANE. Leaving the southern end of the city, the Pacific Coast Bike Route parallels the freeway, separated by a chain link fence. There is a key intersection after the PCBR crosses the freeway, where we follow the sign and turn right. Alan once turned left here, which is the intuitive thing to do based on how the terrain appears, and ended up inland in a town called Freedom. His knowledge is very valuable. Another sign reads BE COURTEOUS SHARE THE ROAD, showing a car and bicycle side by side. I am encouraged.

We are now in sprawling agricultural landscapes, with huge white mansions and long distance views near the ocean. As the day is wearing thin, we arrive at Sunset Beach road, a narrow straight road that leads about a mile or more to Sunset State Beach, through the endless fields of green crops. The ocean is dead ahead, and camp is near again. We pay our fees ($5) at the guard house, and I learn that it is about another three quarters of a mile to the hiker/biker camp, up some very steep hilly terrain. After 68 miles, I pull off the pavement and into the tiny hiker/biker camp area, next to the showers. This campground is mostly empty out on this end. It is very far off the beaten path, and few tourists probably even know about it. As a result, it is also very quiet out here in farmer land. It is on a bluff above the ocean.

Alan bought a pizza at Safeway, and he gets out his Jet Boil stove and starts heating up sections of it one at a time. It smells like a pizzeria out here, but I eat my Uncle Ben's precooked Santa Fe rice out of a packet, mixed with 3 ounces of Starkist pink salmon, wild caught, of course, not farm bred. There is a seemingly endless field of some crop just over a tiny berm past my tent. I am surrounded by an ocean of green on three sides, and an ocean of blue on one side. I write in my journal once bedded down in my tent, using my headlamp. A nearly full moon rises. Through the first half of the night, I enjoy watching it cast moon shadows on me through my tent mesh. It is magical, and I am at peace.

DAY 15 - *Pacific Coast*
September 17, 2013, Tuesday
Sunset Beach State Park to Veteran's Memorial State Park, Monterey, California – 33 miles (running total: 732 miles)

When I tent camp on my overland trike journeys, there is always an awareness floating in my mind about the passage of the night. There are not any issues with sleeping soundly, for after a day's riding, I always sleep very deeply, and even though I arise a time or two during the night to offload a little water, I always fall back into a deep sleep quickly, having multiple REM states and vivid dreams each night. So what is this awareness all about?

As a trike hobo, I enjoy the morning hours. I've always been a morning person, rarely sleeping in late even at home. The morning is a new crisp and cool time for me, whether in the desert, at the ocean, or up in the mountains. Overland trikers who get an early start on each day learn that the pedaling is easier no matter the terrain because the

317

temperatures are much cooler than later in the day. Also, the earlier one arises, the longer the period before the incessant drone of rubber petrol puffer tires begins its annoying assault of the ears. Further, if a triker plans on attaining maximum daily mileages, the nightly objective is reached sooner, allowing a tent pitch prior to the onset of darkness. Pitching a tent in the dark is doable, and I've done it, but I prefer not.

This morning, it is yet dark when I have a vague awareness of time. Since do not wear a watch to advise me of my life's seconds ticking away on a constant basis, and have not owned a timepiece for more than 20 years now, I have only the light of the moon to guide me if first light has not broken. If the sky is moonless, but it had a moon earlier, it is typically sometime after 2 AM. But still, this is not always foolproof. This morning though, I have an alarm clock, a very unusual alarm clock, one which I am not fond of having.

Sunset State Beach sits in the heart of agricultural land, and farmers are typically early rising entrepreneurs who get up earlier than practically anyone else. First light has not arrived, but the noise of a very over sized tractor awakens me, and I deduce that since the farmer's day is now starting, it's probably getting close to my day starting, although I prefer there to be just enough natural light so that I can see to begin my camp breaking routine. So, I lie and take in life right now for a while, listening to the massive tractor in the field, and noticing the multiple super brilliant headlights it has all over it. Since this field literally borders the tent area where Alan and I are pitched, the farmer is close to us.

As a slim margin of natural light begins to barely brighten things up a bit, I look outside again. This tractor has long metal arms extending horizontally from each side, perhaps 20 feet out, making this entire unit about 50 feet wide. Eventually, it dawns on my mind, as the sun is dawning on the Earth outside my tent, that the farmer is spraying his crops with toxic pesticides and herbicides. Those long arms are spewing out poisons like rain in all directions! Well, this gets my attention immediately in a big way as the reigning president of the American Health Nut Society, so I figure I best get up and get out of here before he does the row of greenery right next to the tent.

By now, I can see slightly, but I use my Black Diamond mountaineering headlamp to hasten my progress. I can hear Alan stirring over in his tent about 30 feet away, and I already know he is pretty quick about things, although he brews his morning coffee in his tent, so he may just be on that step right now. Anyway, air mattress deflated and sleeping bag stuffed in its sack, I get dressed, put my gear on the trike, and take down my tent. So far, I have no tell-tale whiff of the sickening sweet toxins. The wind is still working in my favor, so I take advantage of it.

318

Air sustains human bioforms. Whatever is taken into our lungs is rapidly absorbed into the bloodstream and circulated to all the tissue in our bodies, and to the 100 trillion cells that make us what we are. If we can smell something, whatever it is is already circulating in our blood, as the air enters the lungs, is absorbed in the minute alveoli sacks, and becomes part of us. If I can smell it, it's too late. But, I can't smell these poisons yet, which are infused with a perfume type smell.

I walk over and inform Alan that I am going to ride down the hill to the picnic area at the park's entrance to eat my breakfast, as this tractor is getting closer by the minute. He agrees that staying here any longer is not wise, even though he is a cigarette smoker. I am ready to go, so I head down the steep slope to the bottom and will meet him there. About half way down the long steep grade, I pass the main campground where all the huge RVs are camped, and guess what! Yep, sure enough, that faint sickening smell that chemical companies place in their poisons is wafting through the air as I am now straight downwind of the farmer. But I'm on the trike and this downhill grade is steep, so I upshift and really begin flying along. Within about two seconds, I have passed the downwind area, and no longer smell the air-borne poisons.

At the picnic area by the park check-in station there is no issue with smelling this anymore, so I park and do my usual bowl of granola for breakfast. Alan and I chat. He has some kind of convenience food, smokes another cigarette, and then tells me he'll meet me where this little entrance road rejoins the Pacific Coast Bike Route, itself just a small two-lane agricultural roadway. I clean up, use the restroom, and then pedal up the mile hill (gentle grade) to meet Alan.

The sun is coming up over the fields as we reunite. Our plan today is to camp at Pfeiffer Big Sur State Park tonight, in the southern-most redwood grove in California, a ride of about 68 miles or so, similar to the distance we covered yesterday. It's doable for us, but requires an early start, which we got, and a dedicated perseverance when the hills begin manifesting themselves back on Highway 1 south of Carmel, California. We are likely to arrive late afternoon, but since hiker/bikers always get a spot, are never turned away, and since Big Sur has a dynamite hiker/biker camp area, we will get the job done through motivation of the objective. Big Sur is an excellent spot for cyclists.

This morning's ride is along very rural agricultural farm roads, and we see migrant workers driving in and being dropped off to begin their harvesting work. These folks work the fields all day long every day, regardless of whether the farmer man is dispensing toxins in the air and on the food. The bike route follows San Andreas road for quite a ways on this portion of the ride. It cuts out all the Highway 1 freeway hassle, where cyclists are prohibited for many long miles. This is pleasant riding, so there is no complaint here. There is a downside however.

San Andreas road is extremely steep in a few places, grades that are not acceptable for modern roads and governments. The steep sections are relatively short, but the one I am on right now is so darn steep that even in low/low, I must mash the pedals with all my effort, turning them at roughly 35 to 40 revolutions per minute. My front crankset consists of 26-39-52 rings, and the rear cassette is an 11-34 mountain bike configuration, so I have low enough gearing to get up nearly any hill, even this insane monster, but still it's hard-fought. Fortunately, I am in complete shade from the early morning sun, which is obscured anyway by morning clouds and fog. There are big trees surrounding a huge mansion on my left, probably the home of one of these mega-wealthy crop farmers out here. We have come about 7 miles.

Just as I am about to reach the crest of the hill, while looking off to the left to see down the mansion's driveway and gaze at the fancy gates, the trike jerks suddenly and comes to an immediate stop. I hit the brakes. My first thought is that the chain derailed to the inside of the small 26 tooth chainring, so I look forward to verify my suspicion. Interestingly however, I cannot verify this because there is no chain to see derailed. The chain has disappeared! Gone, just in a heartbeat! This hill is very steep, so I set the emergency brakes and get up, which is not easy on such a low trike sitting at such a steep up-angle. My chain did not derail. It exploded, and now I have no driveline to power the trike!

I cannot simply roll the trike forward the final 20 feet to the level top of the hill, for if I do, then whatever chain is still in the chain tubes will fall to the ground, making my imminent repair that much more of a challenge. So, I lift the rear wheel off the ground using the handle I had fabricated for my 2011 journey, and walk the trike forward ahead of me, an extremely awkward and difficult movement with my panniers attached and full. My legs must straddle the bags as I walk. Once I find a level area, I set it down to survey the damage. At the crest of this hill, it goes down on the other side, so I only have a few yards in which to secure the trike and work on the chain.

I take the cargo bags off the right side of the trike so I can have full access to the drive chain. This trike has chain tubes, as do most stock trikes, to keep the chain off the frame and off the rider's clothing. I discover that one of my links failed completely, opening up at one end, and releasing the link formerly attached to it. The broken link is caught in the chain tube due to its expanded size where it broke, and must be forcefully pulled out. Of course, I realize that the chain must also be reinserted through the tube, but since the tube is angled up in front, it must be removed so I can drop the chain back through once I break out the bad link. This will require a time commitment this morning.

So, here I am, on a remote farm road, bags off the trike in the street behind me, on my knees on the asphalt as I begin my task of making the Q functional again. Alan finally comes back once he realizes that my absence has exceeded a normal slow trike guy on steep uphills. This is the first breakdown I have ever had on one of my trips, but now I know why I carry spare chain, a chain tool, and spare master links! Without these supplies, I would be reduced to thumbing a ride on the next farm pickup truck. A trike hobo must be self sufficient if he is to make the goal. Alan does not have any spare chain supplies, so this is a lesson to be ready to deal with issues on my own.

Well, to make a long, dirty, and unpleasant story short and sweet, this job takes some time, even though I am versed in doing stuff like this at home in controlled conditions. Yes, I know what to do, but feeding a 12 foot chain where it needs to go, and keeping it there while you reassemble with the links, takes time. Alan assists as needed, by picking up the rear wheel so I can spin the pedals to help things along at the right time. I remember to insert something into the chain ends as I work so they don't slip back into the tube again, which would necessitate beginning the job anew. This mess eats up somewhat more than an hour I suspect. Anyway, it becomes clear to me that making our Big Sur goal today is probably not the wisest thing to attempt at this point. Better to relax and stop short, and roll into Big Sur tomorrow evening. This touring business is supposed to be fun, after all.

Finally, the chore is complete, the new SRAM gold master link is in place, and it appears it will hold. The chain ended up two links shorter than it was before due to the particulars of the job, and even though it is now a tad short, I will go with it to see what happens. This is the original chain that came with this trike in 2007, so I suspect that if one link broke under high pressure conditions of extreme hill climbing, another link or two may be on its way to follow suit. I don't totally trust this chain at this point in time. Who knows what another killer hill might do to it. I put the bags back on the trike, put the tools away, clean up my hands as best I can with a rag Alan found alongside the road yesterday, and off we pedal, my mind just thinking that I better be babying this thing until I feel confident about it. Bad chain? New trike? Maybe.

The road levels out in short order. It is easy pedaling on mostly flat ground for many miles, through Moss Landing and past marinas on Monterey Bay. At least I am cranking out fast and easy miles for a few hours, which is a good thing. The agricultural fields seem endless out here as the bike route criss crosses the Highway 1 freeway here and there. We are heading due south towards the town of Seaside and the city of Monterey. Just prior to getting on the Fort Ord Bike Path, Alan, is hailed to pull over by an older white haired man with a big white beard, who is standing alongside an old Volkswagen van, a vintage green machine with a white top, and Kermit the Frog decals all over. He has a Kermit the Frog cap on his head. This is interesting!

As I roll up, downshifting from my high gears, and braking to slow my rapid progress, Alan calls my name and waves me over. This man is Paul Aschenbrenner, who is a self-proclaimed "Trail Angel" for all cyclists who ride the Pacific Coast Bicycle Route each season. Paul is a former long haul biker himself, having logged thousands of miles in his younger days, and simply wants to stay in touch with the scene by helping the new younger generations of people who are just like he used to be. Every Tuesday and Thursday, Paul is out here, handing out his home-made chocolate chip cookies, power bars, and water, at no charge. He finds his happiness by giving back to his community of cyclists, and willingly hands out his goodies to all who will listen and engage in a little bike talk for a while. Paul is an amazing man, and I really enjoy his company! His daughter, he tells us, is about to complete a Mexico to Canada backpacking trek on foot along the Pacific Crest Trail. Today, she is less than 100 miles from the Canadian border Paul says, in the state of Washington. Amazing family! Thanks Paul for your tireless contribution to all us cyclists out here! You set a lovely example of peace and happiness. Keep up the support my friend.

Interestingly, had my chain not broken, I would have never had the pleasure of meeting this trail angel. Trail angels are folks who help cyclists unexpectedly. Paul doesn't arrive at this location each Tuesday and Thursday until mid morning sometime, and when we pulled in, he had only arrived about 15 minutes prior he informed us. Well, had my chain remained in one piece, we would have been somewhere south of Monterey by now. Funny how fortuitous things can be. Now, I am happy to have suffered the chain ordeal just for the privilege of meeting Paul.

After saying a protracted goodbye to my new friend, I head out and get on the Fort Ord Bicycle Path into Seaside, California. These bike paths are wonderful, like little roads for cyclists. I've never seen so many. Then, Alan and I take more bike paths through Monterey, at the south end of Monterey Bay. We stop at a Jack-in-the-Box restaurant so Alan can get some food. I fill my water bottles here. He tries to get a Wi-Fi signal, but can't, so we pedal farther into town and stop at a Starbucks Coffee house, where he finally gets his signal. In fact, he is getting signals from several businesses, including an Embassy Suites motel across the street and a McDonalds burger joint next door. Traffic is heavy on these city streets, but as always, proves courteous to us.

Back on the city's bike path system again, called the Monterey Bay Coastal Trail, City of Monterey Section, we head south, having decided to camp tonight at the Veteran's Memorial State Park, way up on a steep hill overlooking Monterey Bay. It will be a very short day, and to think we could have been much of the way to Big Sur by now kind of bums me out, but then when I remember Paul, a smile returns to my face and I am content. We pedal past the famous Cannery Row of John Steinbeck fame, and then begin our laborious ascent and assault of the city streets that seem to go straight up to the highest elevations in town, up in the woods above the bay and ocean. It is called Jefferson Street, and it is a serious taskmaster! Okay, this will be the acid test for my chain repair job. This climb is long, hard, and steep! It is also a wide detour from what we would have done by going straight through to Big Sur. This campground is well off the route, and adds a lot of sweat equity in this ride, but is our lot for tonight. This is as it is, thus peace.

Parts of the beautiful bicycle path are lined with the ever present eucalyptus trees, and at one point we pass a colossal cruise ship just before we begin the big climb to camp. The first thing we see upon arriving at the self-pay station for the campground is a white sign with green letters that reads RACCOONS PRESENT PLEASE STORE YOUR FOOD, and it has a very cute drawing of a raccoon on it. Of course, these mischievous nocturnal marauders are not so cute looking when they are stealing the food from your panniers. I pay the fee for Alan along with mine, as a little gesture of gratitude for showing me the way through this maze of routing, and for hanging out with me to assist on my chain repair job. He did not have to, but he did. I am thankful.

The hiker/biker area is on a hill, making it a chore to find the best flat spot. There are many tents already here mid afternoon, all over the place in fact, but there is not one bicycle to be found. Alan knows the score. He tells me that this is mostly a community of people down and out on their luck, who have taken up residence here for as long as they can get by with it. The people seem nice enough, yet I wonder as the bikers come in if they will worry about their possessions.

This is a military type arrangement here. Every evening, the "Taps" military song is played on a huge loud speaker somewhere through the forest trees, and every morning, that morning military song is played to get everyone out of bed, just like in the US army. You know the one, very annoying I suppose if you are trying to sleep longer. They also play over this speaker system other military songs now and then. It feels like we were just inducted into a war effort. I am also told that an army man, dressed in full military uniform, comes around to check everyone's camping slip to make sure they paid. This place is ship-shape, and cuts no quarter to slackers or bums. Good thing I'm a trike hobo!

By the time night rolls around, there are eight of us cyclists here, yet we are still outnumbered two to one by the semi-permanent nomads who arrive by foot off the city streets to avoid the cops. All the cyclists have a great time sharing stories of the road. I go to bed before Taps is played on the loud speaker, about 8 PM. Taps doesn't play for about an hour. I hear Alan joking around with the other cyclists until what seems like close to midnight. It is relaxing, and whatever powers of the universe got us here with all these people, I am happy to be breathing the forest air up here on the mountain over the ocean and bay.

DAY 16 - *Pacific Coast*
September 18, 2013, Wednesday
Veteran's Memorial State Park to Big Sur State Park, California
34 miles (running total: 766 miles)

I am the first cyclist to begin the morning routine. First, the air quietly leaves my ThermaRest NeoAir Fast 'n Light mattress. This insures that I will be motivated to get up shortly thereafter. By Day 16, I am a well tuned trike hobo, knowing precisely what to do, what order to do it in, how long it will take, and what to do next. I move with great speed, in large part because I am so excited to pedal my trike the next 34 miles to one of my favorite places on the California Coast: Big Sur, the final redwood stronghold on my journey.

Up like a bunny, having broken camp, I roll the repaired trike temporarily down to the table so I don't have to carry my supplies. The table is very damp from last night, so I want to only set my bowl on the table, keeping the rest of the stuff on my seat. The sun is now breaking through the trees, and it feels pleasant upon my face. Alan tells me that leaving this park, even though it is situated atop this mountain, requires even more steep uphills exiting via Skyline Drive and 17 Mile Drive.

Sure enough, he is right again, and we begin another test of elevation endurance, which tests not only me, but also once again that chain that so unceremoniously exploded yesterday morning. When we get to the Skyline Drive intersection, the traffic is extremely heavy as the 9-5 crowd is hurriedly rushing down the hill from their expensive homes to the city below, so they can pay their inflated mortgages and maintain their self-induced need to exceed the neighbors' net worth. I have never seen so many Mercedes, BMWs, Ferraris, and other high-end cars so packed together in one place before! This is the wealthy realm of the mountain up here, and by the time 17 Mile Drive gets us down, we coast into Carmel, which is likewise loaded with even more fancy cars, suited men and women behind the wheels, impatiently waiting in the horrible gridlock this Carmel hill always sees Monday Through Friday.

On our bike and trike, Alan and I sail past even the most impatient driver as they are stuck in bumper to bumper traffic, and making no progress at all. We coast quickly on this steep downhill to the head of the line at the signal, and then fly on through to reach Safeway just before we leave town and head up into the cliff region again along the bluffs, where only animals and trees call home. As a trike hobo, I have learned that you take Safeway when you can, no matter the time of day. Today, this is the only one we shall be passing, so we stop early to stock up on what we need. I get a couple of, you guessed it: Odwalla super protein drinks to fuel the lean greene riding machine the next 30 some miles to Big Sur. I also get some more Safeway trail mix (costs a fortune, but it's cheaper than motels), and a couple of bananas. Alan gets his stuff, and then takes a few minutes to smoke. This is one of the best looking and unique Safeway stores I have ever seen, but considering the financial level of the average resident in Carmel, California, it's no surprise the company didn't spare the horses on this one.

Alan is busy doing something with his panniers, so I take off first, as he is often faster than me overall, and I figure he will catch up sooner or later. But, as I pull out, I jokingly say to him: "See you at Big Sur." and then I'm off. I expect to see him in my mirror before long.

Back on Highway 1 once again, finally departing the megalopolises for good, I take a photo of the first sign that indicates Big Sur. Another quickly follows. I am giddy with delight as I am so close to this special place again, which also means the journey is progressing quite well at this point, despite the broken chain and two short mileage days. Now the work begins in earnest, with steep cliff side hills and high winds. The day is sunny, and the ocean views are spectacular.

Hearst Castle is now only 90 miles distant, and beyond that lies San Simeon State Park. A road warning sign shows tight and curvy roadway for the next 74 miles, as it continues far south of Big Sur. I love these ocean views, and so do all the motorists touring today, as they are all pulling out every chance they get to take some awesome photographs of the rugged coastline. The road is tight, and motorists are usually sightseeing, so everyone is going pretty slow, and cars have no issues with me. Alan pulls into view at a turnout, but stops for a smoke, so I pedal on, putting some distance between us on my way to Big Sur.

After a while, I see a gigantic hill in the distance, one of those river inlets I have described, only on a very large scale this time. As I look across the churning water of a bay area, I see the road disappear inland, only to reemerge at a horrendous upward angle to a point on the side of the cliff. If this is not enough, there is a construction job going on, so the highway is clogged, and controlled by a traffic light. There is a little button for cyclists to push to let them through, since the sensor does not detect us apparently, so I push it. The signal turns green after some cars go by the other direction, but unlike the often flat or downhill constructions I've passed so far in these 700+ miles, this one is all up hill, and a very steep hill it is. This means that a tricyclist will have one heck of a time getting through before the next wave of oncoming traffic surges from the northbound lane. Well, anyway, I make it through, and continue my ascent of this long uphill. Fortunately, the views are so spectacular, and the tailwind so cooling, I don't mind the long steep hill.

At the top at long last, I photograph the ICE trike with a breathtaking view of cliffs and Pacific ocean behind it. The yellow smiley flag is whipping so hard that I am wondering if it will just rip off the pole. It has become rather ragged since 2009, when I first started using it as my main visibility strategy, and this trip will be its last, for I doubt it can withstand another. I will retire it, and hang it proudly upon the wall somewhere at home. To me, this flag holds so many memories!

I look back down the hill, attempting to steady myself in the wind, and realize what a climb it was! Then, my peripheral vision picks up movement of the trike, and I discover that the wind is actually pushing it onward, right towards the cliff – good thing there are some big boulders placed here to keep motorists from accidentally surging forward to their demise. It is even a challenge just standing here.

As I finally approach Andrew Molera State Park, the road flattens out, having come down off the cliffs for a while. Andrew Molera is not far north of Big Sur – I am almost home free for today. The air has become quite warm now, and shade feels good once again. One minute a trike hobo seeks the sun, and the next, he scrambles for the shade. Thermal regulation is always a big issue on overland trike treks.

Not far past Andrew Molera, I enter redwoods once again, my silent pals on much of this grand journey. The hot sun is cooled by the colossal trees. I stop in a little store just prior to the campground, and get more Odwalla protein drinks – this might be a record for one day, especially considering that it is a short day of only 34 miles. Then, after a relaxing sit on their wooden bench to drink my drinks, back in the cockpit I go, and off I pedal. Alan has not yet caught up.

At Pfeiffer Big Sur State Park, I stop at the park's general store to get a neck lanyard that says I survived Highway 1, which I'll wear in November for the 3 days of the Recumbent Cycle Convention at the Los Angeles County Fairplex in Pomona, California to display my presenter name tag for Trike Asylum. I knew they carried these cool neck straps here, and was lucky because this is the last one they have in stock for this season. Whew, that was close!

I pay my $5 entry fee for the hiker/biker camp (one of the nicest and most serene anywhere), and ride on into the magnificent redwood grove where this park is situated. There is a long pedestrian and cyclist bridge that crosses the Big Sur river, and it goes right into the hiker/biker camp area. To my surprise, Alan is already here, having ridden in while I was in the general store getting my lanyard. He was not too far behind me. When I told him jokingly this morning at Safeway that I'd see him at Big Sur, I sure didn't think I would be right. Cool! Maybe trikes aren't that slow after all if the driver is motived sufficiently.

I pitch my tent, enjoying the cool afforded by the big trees. It's hot today for this place. Alan is complaining about a lot of little tiny flies that are bugging the daylights out of him. They just hatched about a week ago. Normally in the summer, there are no issues with little annoying flies. Today, they are indeed everywhere, and the only relief is if you walk around and do something. If I sit a while, they find my face, my eyes, my ears, and my nose. Well, at least I am bringing happiness to others, even if they are another bioform slightly different than myself.

Alan and I are talking at my picnic table. I ask if he wishes to spend a free no-travel day here tomorrow, which is what I am currently considering. What better place to hang out? He says he wants to get on down the road, and will leave first thing at daybreak tomorrow. I thank him for guiding me through Santa Cruz and Monterey, and tell him I'd like to treat him to dinner tonight at the fancy Big Sur lodge restaurant at the park's entrance. He is appreciative, but kind of a loner, and says he doesn't want to eat at the fancy place – too uptown for his tastes, he says. Okay, so I'll again have packaged rice and salmon tonight instead.

Today is Wednesday, and despite the chain incident and that setback in progress, I am still on track to make David Massey's necessary arrival date in Morro Bay on September 20, Friday. If I went on with David tomorrow morning, we would arrive at San Simeon on Thursday after a long day's ride, and then would roll into Morro Bay Friday morning before lunch. Yes, David, we would have indeed made it in time to get you back to your high school and students! Wow, we did it, except that David is no longer with me anymore. I surely wish he were here! I think he would have loved this journey to the very end. My best wishes go out to David this afternoon as I contemplate what should have been if our plan had worked. At least we got the timeline dead-on for arriving at Morro Bay! The plan was indeed a solid one.

Well, but David is not here, so realizing that the schedule is no longer in effect, I do decide to spend a free day here to enjoy the place I love. I will call tomorrow Big Sur Appreciation Day, and soak it all up as Alan and the other cyclists battle the big hills, especially the Ragged Point challenge just down the road a long ways.

As Alan and I are sitting talking at the picnic table, a Vietnamese woman named Lien Ton-nu walks up and queries me about my recumbent trike. She is 33 years old and lives down towards San Diego. The conversation develops, and actually starts becoming quite deep philosophically, so Alan eventually walks back over to his tent, perhaps figuring the gal is interested in me and me in her. Who knows. All I know is that he disappears at some point and neither Lien nor I really notice his absence. Sorry buddy!

Her name is pronounced "Lynn" and her level of intelligence and ideological principals are really quite impressive. We seem to be kindred spirits in so many aspects of life, and our conversation is so enjoyable that it seems to carry on for such a long time. I ask her if my talking is keeping her from anything, and she tells me that she is driving up to Monterey and Carmel this afternoon to stay with some friends, so she has plenty of time. But Lien also tells me she want to stop and see Cannery Row and some other places, and it seems to me that there are not enough hours left today to do it all, so I suggest that she should not wait much longer. Yet, apparently she is enjoying our verbal engagement as much as I am, and she keeps offering up more fascinating stories and ideas. The time does arrive however when even she realizes it's getting late for her intended itinerary, so she bids a nice farewell and vanishes into the trees. Usually, when I meet special people, I take their photograph, but our talk was so intriguing that I forgot this time.

Later, one of those tandem bicycles enters our camp, where the front person sits in a recumbent chair, and the back person sits on a typically uncomfortable bicycle seat. The rear person pedals and steers, and the front person may pedal if they want to, but because the front crank freewheels, they don't have to. This female/male couple tell us they switch off positions. The other bikers and I wonder what happens if the front person sees an obstacle that the back person cannot yet see. They say you get used to it. Other bikers roll in, so there end up being 7 of us total by nightfall. It is a quiet camp compared to Standish-Hickey.

I take one final photograph of Alan in his tent through the mesh because he does not have the fly on the tent, reading a book, before I hit the sack myself. I realize I will probably never see him again, so I sincerely thank him for all his assistance these last few days. He says it's no big deal, and he was happy to help. I bid him a final adieu, and that's that, as they say. My morning will not begin at first light tomorrow, or even sunup. I'm sleeping in for the first time on this entire journey, and I suspect that by the time I arise in the morning, everyone here will be long gone, out on the road of adventure once again. That's how life on a trike and bike is. You make a bunch of new friends, and then never see them again. We live in a temporal world anyway, so even these short friendships with folks like Alan and Lien are precious.

DAY 17 - *Pacific Coast*
September 19, 2013, Thursday
No travel today – remained again at Big Sur to enjoy all it has to offer
0 miles (running total: 766 miles)

In the early morning pre-dawn hours, I still sleep soundly, and when I become aware of faint noises that typically accompany cyclists as they arise in their tents, I ponder how nice it is to not be getting up right now. Every other day of this journey, I either began my morning chores when I heard others doing likewise, or I was the first to begin the process. I am so use to this ingrained habit that when I hear a bicyclist in a nearby tent starting to rustle around, a part of me says to get moving steve, it's time to get up! Strangely, as I hear others following suit, a certain sadness washes over me, because I know I am supposed to be part of this ritualistic morning dynamic. By lying here and ignoring what is happening out there, I know that I will never see these folks again.

As the sun begins to break through the trees, I finally give in and get up. What a lazy guy I am today, but it is nice to feel no need to rush into the expected routine. It is nice to know I can take all the time in the world to do whatever it is I will be doing today. I do not deflate my air mattress today however, because I will be using it again tonight. In fact, the tent can remain as it is, making today an easy arising. Sure enough, by the time get up, the hiker/biker camp is empty. The other cyclists have long since gone. They are all out on the road, cranking up hills, staving off the chill of the morning air , and pedaling the miles.

After a leisurely granola breakfast and finishing my post-meal oral dental care, I decide to move my tent and trike to another location about 30 feet towards the river, over where cyclists ride into the camp when they arrive. I do this because several times yesterday, a lady, who was camping with her husband across the road out of their van, walked her dog directly through my tent area on her way to the bathroom. Well, the dog was not leashed as required, and on one of these trips, the animal was fixing to urinate or excrete right near my tent. I noticed just in the nick of time and told it no. So, the little yipper starts barking at me like crazy, and the lady, who is several yards ahead and paying no attention to where her dog is, turns around to see what is upsetting her animal. I tell her what was about to happen, and she seems so surprised, but it is clear she has no intent on avoiding such a thing again. So, I figure it's just easier to side-step the potential problem by moving the tent far away from the beeline between this lady's car and the bathroom.

The move is easy this morning. The lady is not yet up over there, so she will not even know I moved in all likelihood. I just pull up the three fly stakes, remove the fly, and simply carry the ultra lightweight tent, with mattress and sleeping bag still rolled out inside, over to the new location. Then, I reattach the fly, stake it down, and I'm good to go, not in line between the bathroom and any other camper. Next, I roll my trike over next to my tent, and it looks like I've been here all along.

This may seem like a nitpicking issue to some, but in my extensive camping history, I have had a fellow camper's dog actually urinate on the fly of my tent, believe it or not. And I was standing right there watching. When I shooed the dog off before any more urine ran down the tent fly, the owner becomes perturbed and asks me why I'm hassling his dog. I tell him the animal just urinated on my tent, and politely ask him to leash his dog. He becomes even more upset, and tells me there is no way he is going to tie his dog up. Being a man of logic and slightly more intellect and compassion for others than this particular dog owner, I simply break camp and leave. I don't need to spoil my day because of a dog owner who has no consideration for others. Thus, when a dog is about to do its duty on my tent, I become proactive now.

The huge redwood trees surrounding my tiny tent, trike, and me are absolutely awesome! I will spend the day today admiring them, hiking around a bit, and simply realizing how fortunate I am to have these hours to enjoy this special place. This forest dwarfs my miniature camp, yet the forest itself is dwarfed by the surrounding landscape, which is in turn dwarfed by the planet on which it all rests. This dwarfing by comparison extends right out into the space about our planet, through the solar system, galaxy, and beyond. To contemplate such things is an incredible exercise for my head. There is no need for me to make up stories about how all this occurred in order to conquer my little human fears, because simply accepting what is and appreciating my part in it, is profoundly exhilarating for me. I am in love with the natural world around me. I am a wilderness rogue, happy and care-free.

The camp area here is covered in a thick layer of bark chips, making perfect bedding for placing tents. The ground is flat. There are several nice picnic tables, full shower and toilet facilities, and even fire pits, although it has been my experience that few cyclists ever actually use them. When we all arrive at these camps each evening, we are tired, and we are motivated to pitch camp, clean up, eat food, and just get into the tent to allow our bodies the little recuperation time we have to prepare for our early morning departure. Having a camp fire necessitates staying up to enjoy it, usually after it gets dark, but cycle nomads are almost always asleep in their tents before it even gets completely dark.

The photographs for today are just taken around the Big Sur State Park campground as I walk here and there. The laundry facility, which is rare in state park campgrounds, is at the far end of the campground area, so it takes me quite a while to walk down to it. I could ride the trike, but why? I ride it miles every day. Today I wish to walk, first carrying my dirty clothes, and the returning with my clean clothes. It is far enough away, likely about three quarters of a mile or so, that I just wait as the clothes wash and dry. There is no rush. I have all day. I also grab a leisurely shower to be ready for tomorrow.

At each hiker/biker area, there is also a steel ring attached to the post that indicates which site the biker or triker has. As the sun breaks through in it full glory, some campfire smoke is wafting through the trees from distant neighbors, and it makes for a few more neat images. One of my favorite things to do is point my camera straight up into the tree tops. How magnificent the result! I notice that my yellow smiley flag is becoming quite worn after several years of riding. Even with the heavy edging I had put on it, the material is finally coming apart. This will be the flag's final journey on my trike hobo travels.

I walk over to the lodge to get a couple of stickers that read: I SURVIVED HIGHWAY CALIFORNIA 1, with the California 1 part in the typical road sign configuration. On the way over, I a wild turkey walks right past me. These birds are plentiful around this state park for some reason, and I have also seen them in other areas and other states. You may recall I passed that turkey farm on the way to Tomales, south of Bodega Bay, a few days ago. They were being farmed for death. Hopefully, these wild turkeys will live out their days in these beautiful redwoods, unencumbered and unmolested by the species that thinks it superior to all and can do what it wants without regard to life.

The Big Sur lodge, while by no means as spectacular, large, or grand as several of the national park lodges in the United States, is impressive in the small area it has. I take some photographs of the lodge to show the ambiance that is tucked away inside the redwood canopy. Back at camp, a couple of deer stroll by, but having lived so many years in remote wooded locales during my life, this is a common site for me. Still, I love to capture these gentle creatures on film, as I did that pair a few days ago out on Highway 1. The universe smiles upon me, leading me to a trio of butterflies, something I have never witnessed before. Yes, this place is a magical realm at times, an old hippie haven from yore. I am happy that I spend the day here, enjoying the big trees one last time.

I notice that my right Arkel pannier cover, the yellow cover that keeps out rain and makes me highly visible to automobile drivers, has a new hole in the bottom. I had already had a worn spot from my 2011 journey repaired, and now I have a new worn spot to fix. These holes occur when I back the trike up into a curb to park on a hill so that it will not roll. The material on the bottom is extremely fragile, and does not play well with concrete, rocks, or the wilderness when contact is made.

By mid and later afternoon, a new wave of cyclists begin to arrive in my quiet triker camp. I welcome these fellow human powered humans because I love to hear all about their journeys, their vehicles, and their experiences. After talking to everyone for a long time, trying not to monopolize their time as they go through their end-of-day routines, I eat dinner and check into the tent early, for tomorrow will be a long day. I figured it would be about 63 miles to San Simeon originally, but one of the young cyclists who checked in about two hours ago is riding northbound on Highway 1, and he told me his computer showed 70 miles. Okay, tomorrow will be a longer day, along the high magnificent cliffs south of Big Sur, with the climb up the Ragged Point grade the longest and most challenging of the day, so I need all the sleep I can get tonight. Past San Simeon, it is only another 20 miles to Morro Bay, David's proposed end point, and then another 39 to Atascadero.

After a few days of observing the moon becoming fuller and brighter each night, tonight is the grand finale called a full moon! How special is that? Here I am at Big Sur, a magical land of giant memories and giant trees that make me feel like a little elf, and tonight the moon is round as round can be. And, it is shining directly into my tent door! I capture it on my digital camera, not much to look at perhaps, but it is my remembrance that I lived for a time on the ground in a tent on the floor of Big Sur with that wonderfully magical moon illuminating the breathing sentient bioform I call me. I am now here. I am no where.

DAY 18 - *Pacific Coast*
September 20, 2013, Friday
Big Sur State Park to San Simeon State Park, California
70 miles (running total: 836 miles)

I waste no time this morning. I am eager to start knocking off the miles, knowing the day will be a long one. While still pitch black outside, except for the bath facility lighting, it occurs to me that the cellular telephone I borrowed for this trip, to call in my location information, has a timepiece in its software. Having not worn a timepiece for a couple of decades at least, I rarely care about knowing the time, but now, I decide to activate the phone for a minute because I want to get a big jump on the day. Muffling the cute musical tone it plays upon activation, so as not to disturb nearby sleepers, I see the time is a couple of minutes after 5 AM. Perfect! I begin by deflating my air mattress, first slowly because it makes a loud hissing sound if I open the valve all at once, and that would definitely awaken other cyclists who, while wanting an early start, generally don't get up this early. Like the trike phantom I am, my activities are so stealthy and practiced that there is practically no noise. This early, I have the time to take it slowly and make sure I remain silent in all I do.

I am still bundled up a bit in layered clothing this early. I eat my granola to headlamp light, being careful to keep it pointed down only at what I am doing. Most cyclists are like this, keeping their headlamps carefully focused on their stuff. A few, on rare occasion, do not think of this, and move around in a careless manner, their headlamp wildly shining into everyone's tent close by, which wakes them up. The metal spoon I have can clang on the cereal bowl, so I am careful not to allow it. Tim, the young fellow who clued me into the 70 mile distance to San Simeon, is up now also, and he has a red cover that pops down over his headlamp for times like these, dampening the light so it does not disturb anyone if it accidentally shines into their tents. We whisper a bit, and finally bid each other goodbye and good luck as I finally shove off at first light. This is the earliest departure I've had this entire trip.

I activate my flashing taillights as I pull out onto Highway 1 for some of the final miles of this magnificent journey. The light enclosure has ten flashing ultra bright LED lights, so it is quite visible from a long way off. It is still quite cool, and there is a fog bank rolling in from the ocean to my right, over the hill. I start up the long curvy tight hill immediately south of the park, with hardly any cars for a very long time. I have the highway all to myself, and am experiencing it up close and personal from eight inches off the ground, out in the elements, able to touch plants as I go by. Petroleum humans can never know this joy of being one with the wilds during travel along the coast. I may be slow, but that slowness translates into many unique delectable experiences.

The first road sign past the Big Sur village shows San Luis Obispo 105 miles distant, and the famous Hearst Castle only 60 miles away now. I break out to the first grand overlook of the Pacific Ocean south of the little town to see a common sight in mornings here: a thick dense fog blankets the sea, making it invisible to roadway travelers. Only by hiking down to the beach can one actually see the water this early in

333

the morning. It is like being in an airplane, where the sun is shining, and you look down on clouds, knowing the people underneath them see only an overcast day with no sun.

As the road begins its typical up and down roller coaster ride, I enter areas of dense fog on the trike. I love the magical ambiance the fog brings to my senses. Portions of the road near sea level are flat for a ways, so I pick up speed. The coastline along here is quite rugged.

I arrive at San Simeon State Park around 5:30 PM, having ridden about 10 hours. There is only one other cyclist here. The farther south a cyclist rides into California, the fewer cyclists are found on the coast highway. From 17 up at Standish-Hickey State Park to only 2 here, the difference is striking, but it occurs slowly over the days, fewer and fewer the farther south. San Francisco is a popular destination point for many, doing just the northern coasts. South of Morro Bay, things start getting more and more congested, and by the time the coast highway gets down into the Los Angeles region, it is a whole different world. Passing through the San Pedro coastal area, for example, with it countless unsightly mega petroleum plants, smoke stacks, and ports of commerce for international ships, the ambiance of the northern coast is totally gone. Hundreds of thousands of humans are swarming all around in every direction. Run-down parts of towns are glaringly obvious, and the citizenry of many areas are of dubious nature, not conducive to trust or serenity as the wide open spaces of the northern areas are.

The hiker/biker area at San Simeon State Park is literally only a few feet off Highway 1, so tire whine from automobiles is nearly as loud as while riding on the trike. A very heavy fog is quickly rolling in as soon as I arrive, so I make haste in setting up my tent, eating, and preparing for the night. Even before I get to bed, the fly and my pannier rain covers are becoming noticeably damp. I am sure the morning will require me to use my little chamois before packing things away.

Unknown to me, there is a raccoon den right along the highway, only a few yards from my tent. I discover this about two minutes after I get into my sleeping bag for the night. I hear my bags being rustled, along with the distinctive tinkling of my small yellow bear bell atop my flag pole antenna. Up like lightning, I snatch my headlamp and exit the tent. The masked marauder is already gone, but the three Clif Bars I had already prepared for tomorrow's midday snack, which were sealed in a normal Ziplock baggie, have been stolen. This raccoon did not harm my Radical Design side seat pod, but rather lifted the little rain flap, unzipped it about 7 inches, and neatly extracted the small bag with the three bars inside. These creatures are amazingly dexterous, as skilled as any human. I search the bushes for his location and my bars. I can hear him unwrapping my bars, but cannot see him back in the dense bush covering that protects his den. Enjoy the 210 calories per bar my friend – you will be taking in 630 calories total, along with 30 grams of protein – that should tide you over until morning!

The stealthy dark gray and black animal did not detect the food I have in my left rear Arkel pannier, as it is sealed in special military grade bags that fully stop any odor whatsoever. Animals simply cannot detect food in these bags. I was skeptical at first when I saw the product at REI, but after this trip, and two raccoon incursions, I am convinced of their value, and will be acquiring more for my next trip! The reason the three Clif Bars were in the side seat pod is because I have been making a habit of preparing for the next day ahead of time, only this time, on my last night's camp, my procedure is clearly shown to be faulty. My luck has run out. Next trip, I will prepare the day's snacks the morning of departure so this will never occur again.

Back into the tent I go, hopeful that this will be the end of the attempted thefts, but still thinking that of all nights, this last one is full of issues. The fog is ultra heavy now, and everything is getting wet. Even standing out with my headlamp on, I can see the dense mist right before my face, and I can feel it on my skin. And now, the raccoon is about its mischievous ways, so can I get any rest? Tomorrow will be a short day, but after 70 miles today, I would sure like to sleep soundly, especially since it is the final night in my tent as a trike hobo on the road.

This campground is crowded and popular, and being Friday night, many regional folks have swarmed to this place for easy beach access a few yards away, and quick assess to the famous Hearst Castle tourist attraction up on the hill six miles north. I wonder if my raccoon friend will find the messy campers of pickup trucks and cars, teenagers and kids, food everywhere, to be more inviting than my neatly kept little tricycle camp. The answer comes, probably within the hour. Off goes my bell once more, but this time, having been alerted prior, my headlamp is ready and I am out like a flash. The LED lights on my forehead illuminate the quiet little miscreant, and his eyes glow orange when the beam hits them. He is running off again, towards the cars to my south. I check my bags in the darkness. All is well. He has not taken anything else, probably because there is nothing else to smell, and the fact that I was so fast at shooing him away this time. Raccoons make no noise.

Standing here in the wet moving fog, like a vigilant knight guarding the castle, I wonder how I can put a stop to this activity that interrupts my much needed rest and sleep. My mind ponders the situation from all angles. Even though the food bag is right outside my tent door, if I'm totally zonked out, it takes a moment for me to respond to intrusion. Then an idea comes to my tired, but still functional brain! If these creatures have such a superior sense of smell, to be able to smell Clif Bars, which are wrapped in their own sealed wrapper, which are then sealed in a Ziplock baggie, maybe I can use this to my advantage!

I think like an animal. What do they do? They mark their territory. I am an animal just like they are. Since I am up anyway, might as well mark my trike camp territory, just like they do. So, in a slight arc, between the raccoon den and my panniers on the trike, and about six feet out from the trike, I offload what water I have at hand in an arcing shape on the grass. I am chuckling to myself, thinking about what I'm doing on my last night as a trike hobo, resorting to basic animal behavior to solve an animal problem. When in Rome, do as the Romans do, the saying goes. I have done so, and back to bed I go. Despite my initial worry earlier that I'd get little sleep tonight after the first incident involving the Clif Bars, I go right to sleep, my fatigue finally overtaking me. I sleep soundly the rest of the night, with no further forays from the den of thieves who are experiencing the same weather I am, living on the same ground I am, and playing this same game with me tonight.

DAY 19 - *Pacific Coast*
September 21, 2013, Saturday
San Simeon State Park to Atascadero, California
39 miles (running total: 875 miles from Florence, Oregon)
journey complete

Morning comes, the slight light that proceeds what one would actually call daytime. I don't care what time it is, for today is a short one compared to yesterday and many other long days with high mileages. I am but 39 miles from the end of the trail for this Pacific Coast tricycle adventure, which for me is a walk in the park. Atascadero is now close.

Everything is wet outside. The fly works well, as the tent is totally dry. The rain covers on my panniers work well, as the panniers themselves are totally dry. Out comes the chamois, and I diligently spend the time removing the excess water from everything. Of course, with the fog still as heavy as it was, I ponder the wisdom of my actions. But at least I can get the tent fly fairly dry before I slide it in its bag. I can dry it out later this afternoon at my destination, where I will have plenty of time for such things, and where the weather will be warm and very dry.

Marking my territory last night worked flawlessly. Mister raccoon did not enjoy the smell I left for him, and realized that this marking marked the end of his territory and the beginning of mine. This is a lesson well learned. It works, but who would talk about such things?

Most folks are embarrassed to discuss such topics. Oh well, I guess they can get their bags opened by invaders of the night then. Of course, depending on circumstances of the trike/bike camp, this countermeasure may not be a practical one. Remember the night at Gualala, north of San Francisco? Well, the government packed us bikers and trikers in such a midget area so tightly that my traveling companions surely would not have thought too highly of me had I initiated this solution there! Our tents were practically on top of one another, and avoiding tripping over each other's fly lines was a real challenge in the dark. I know I wouldn't be too happy if another cyclist marked his territory right outside my tent.

Breakfast eaten and all business taken care of, I begin pedaling away. The other cyclist has already left before me. He is fast. I am alone, no more cyclists to chat with. The trek is winding down, and there is a certain sadness wafting through my head about finally nearing the end. While I am of course elated that another successful journey is nearly complete, and look forward to allowing my body to get plenty of rest and experience the life of Riley, there is a call that motivates all trike hobos to be out here on the open road of adventure and freedom. We are free on three out here, in the best sense of the words, traveling for hundreds of miles and never once having to stop and buy gasoline. We are not prisoners of the big oil conglomerates. I like that. I cannot explain the freedom and wonder that comes with a trike journey to anyone, for it must be ridden to be known! Only a trike hobo can know.

The final miles into Morro Bay are mostly flat, and my large chainring is the one of choice as the miles move quickly under my trio of Schwalbe Marathon Plus tires, the rubber that always gets me to my destinations without a flat tire. I have never had a flat tire. I have been warned by mystics that such words should not be spoken, lest Murphy's Law kick in, but you know what? I have spoken them many times, and still, I have never had a flat out on the road, or anywhere else for that matter. The right tires do make all the difference in the world of tire eating debris. If you enjoy getting flats, don't use Marathon Plus tires!

As I ride, the fog only gets heavier. This turns out to be a little more than the traditional early morning fog along the coast, which really never leaves me damp or wet. Even the heavy fog in Oregon does not leave me wet. But today, the fronts of my pants below the knees, the parts that face forward at 15 miles per hour, are clearly becoming soaked. My shirt is getting quite damp too, and water droplets begin to fall from the bill of my cap. My sunglasses must be wiped off frequently so that I can even see the road well. The fog grows to a visible precipitant I can see ahead of me. Is it rain? Well, let's just say this: It is as close to a light rain as you can get without saying it's actually raining

337

today. Regardless of what one might call it, I am damp and wet, and this is the only day of the 19 total days that this has happened to me. It is not heavy enough to don my rain gear, and putting on rain gear would only serve to quickly overheat me, as it is not cold as I pedal along.

Halfway to Morro Bay from San Simeon State Park, I begin being passed by bicyclists going north on Highway 1. It quickly becomes evident that this must be a bike club of some sort, perhaps the SLO bicycle club (SLO is the jargon for San Luis Obispo). For miles I watch as these rough riders are flying along towards San Simeon in the light rain. I do not count them, but there are many for quite some time. We all wave as we pass, sharing the dampness this Saturday morning on the Pacific Ocean. They are out for a fun day ride, and recognize that I am out for a long haul journey of many days, apparent due to my heavily laden tricycle. A trike hobo can't disguise his activities due to the bags.

Fascinatingly, I also see, of all things, three tricycles with this group. They are not riding together, but are spread out among the bicyclists for many miles. One of the trikes, all of which are tadpoles by the way, is a velomobile, a trike fully encased in a fairing, making for higher speed potential, and protecting the rider inside from the elements in the sky. It is orange. The trikers seem to really get a kick out of seeing me heading southbound, based on their hand gestures and verbalizations. I give them all the thumbs-up sign and a big smile. They are trike pilots.

I arrive in Morro Bay slightly before 11 AM. The huge rock, as is often the case, is fully encased in dense impenetrable fog, and if one had never seen it before, one would not have any clue the massive monolith is even there in this bay called Morro. So today, I just see drizzles everywhere as I am leaving the freeway at exit 279B, which will drop me off at the intersection of Highway 41, called the E.G. Lewis Highway. This road will take me over the coastal mountains into Atascadero, where the sun will probably be shining brightly.

Into a Chevron mini-mart I pull for a drink of protein, and to make cell calls to familly regarding progress and to my hostess where the trip will end, so she knows I am about 3 hours out from her one-acre country spread, which she happily refers to as Rancho Relaxo, nestled in the rolling hills above the town of Atascadero. The mileage is not far from here, but the road climbs over the mountains, which slow me.

The female clerk in the mini-mart asks about my trip and destination. When I tell her, she becomes sick with deep fear that I will meet my doom on Highway 41. Seen from her vantage point as a motorist, she is convinced that to pedal this road is suicidal. I have been told this before, by a triker couple in the SLO area, who suggested I ride Highway 46 instead. If a triker listens to enough of this talk, it can undermine the facts and spook you out. My reality over the past 5 years does not support this fear at all. The road I have traveled for the past 18 days has countless areas far "worse" than the one mile section that grips this clerk with fear for my safety, but still, I am grateful for her kind thoughts, but I must leave before I start assimilating her fear.

My ride over into Atascadero is wholly without incident, and indeed, it is not one that induces any fear based on what I see or experience. One mile of it is tight and curvy, just prior to the Cerro Alto campground, but other than that, this road is very enjoyable and relaxing. Even the tight section was less, what some would call, "anxiety producing" than much of what I've been riding this whole coastal trip.

As I roll over the summit area of these mountains, and begin coasting down towards town, the sky morphs into a clearing phase, with just a few white cotton clouds, sun out, completely different than in Morro Bay. The weather is warming, and life is good. I pedal my bones into Rancho Relaxo just prior to 2 PM. No one is aware of my presence. Once again, the trike phantom has arrived in stealth mode. Of course, once I twist my shoes out of the pedal bindings, the two click sounds alert Bella, the resident K9, and out she flies with a roar, er, make that a bark – make that many barks. My back is to her as I remove my helmet, sunglasses, hat, and gloves, and I greet her by name: "Hello Bella" I say. Then I hear the Rancho Relaxo proprietor greet me by name. She puts Bella in a secure alternate location until the trike is no longer part of the picture, as sometimes doggies get confused by a tricycle – there is no memory data bank for most dogs as to what they are seeing. Trike? What's that? Of course, this is true for many humans as well.

This acre of country belongs to an old high school classmate of mine. Okay, she's not old, at least not any more so than I am, but it was 44 years ago that we were seniors there. I have never met this gal before. In high school, she was an ultra popular song girl, and I was an ultra ignored nobody with no friends. So, needless to say, there were no formal introductions as our two universes never crossed paths in 69. But then, 44 years after graduation, Debbie read one of my books, and what I said resonated in her brain, so she sent an email to who she learned was somewhat of a kindred spirit. And that's how it all started earlier this year. Once we realized that my 2013 Pacific Coast trike journey coincided with her country acre of relaxing real estate, she put out the invite for me to recuperate after nearly three weeks of pedaling.

It all worked out well. I had absolutely no desire to continue south of Morro Bay, as what awaits a triker down there is not that high on my list of "go to" spots. I grew up in southern California, and am very well aware of how things tend to rapidly deteriorate the farther south one travels. The crowds grow to insane levels, the traffic makes what I've seen so far look like an infant's playpen, and the industrial workings of mechanized progress have done a pretty good job of annihilating the breathable qualities of the human air supply. Morro Bay is the perfect place to bail out of this coastal ride, out where things are still laid-back and easy, out where the air is still clean, and out where people still trust one another. This is a grand finale to a challenging trek.

So, 875 miles from home, in a place I've never been before, I am pitied and taken in by a wild woman, a confused dog, and a singing guitar man named Rob. I am fed, catered to, talked to, sung to, and more or less just allowed to relax with nary a care in the world. A warm shower awaits me, and after I shave off my scraggly beard so as not to over excite Bella with thoughts of Big Foot, I settle in to life in four walls again. It seems kind of weird after living on a tricycle and tent for 19 days, kind of like I am in some altered brain-dead state of nonthinking. Heck, I am even served the bizarre plant-based foods I normally eat, but, as most who know me already know, I am clearly not nOrmAL by any stretch of the imagination.

After all, now in my sixty-fourth year of life, I still ride a tricycle! Very few normal grown-ups would even consider it. See ya' ...

THE END

* * * * *

~

Other books by Steve Greene:
Exploring Wild Death Valley (his personal journeys)
Death Valley Book Of Knowledge (extensive knowledge base)
Free On Three (all about recumbent tricycles)
The Overland Triker (how to travel cross country on a trike)
Bioform, Evolution Beyond Self (philosophy of life and beyond)

Steve Greene's Amazon portal:
http://amazon.com/author/stevegreene

Made in the USA
Charleston, SC
04 June 2014